The Strange Case of Donald J. Trump

The Strange Case of Donald J. Trump

A Psychological Reckoning

DAN P. McADAMS

OXFORD
UNIVERSITY PRESS

OXFORD

UNIVERSITY PRESS

Oxford University Press is a department of the University of Oxford. It furthers
the University's objective of excellence in research, scholarship, and education
by publishing worldwide. Oxford is a registered trade mark of Oxford University
Press in the UK and certain other countries.

Published in the United States of America by Oxford University Press
198 Madison Avenue, New York, NY 10016, United States of America.

© Oxford University Press 2020

Library of Congress Cataloging-in-Publication Data
Names: McAdams, Dan P., author.
Title: The strange case of Donald J. Trump : a psychological reckoning /
Dan P. McAdams.
Description: New York, NY : Oxford University Press, [2020] |
Includes bibliographical references.
Identifiers: LCCN 2019040653 (print) |
LCCN 2019040654 (ebook) |
ISBN 9780197507445 (hardback) | ISBN 9780197507469 (epub) |
ISBN 9780197507452 (updf) | ISBN 9780197507476 (online)
Subjects: LCSH: Trump, Donald, 1946– | Trump, Donald, 1946—Psychology. |
Presidents—United States—Biography.
Classification: LCC E913 .M43 2020 (print) | LCC E913 (ebook) |
DDC 973.933092—dc23
LC record available at https://lccn.loc.gov/2019040653
LC ebook record available at https://lccn.loc.gov/2019040654

For Everett Daniel, who will look back and know more

Contents

Acknowledgments

My largest debt of gratitude goes to my wife Rebecca, who has always supported my projects, including even one so quixotic as this book. She read all of the chapters, too, and provided expert editorial assistance. The silver medal goes to Will Dunlop, my good friend and colleague who teaches personality psychology and conducts cutting-edge research on personality and life stories at the University of California, Riverside. Will read all the chapters and provided detailed critiques and suggestions, most of which I incorporated into the final version. So did Rick Robins, whose astute critiques helped to improve the final product. Let me also express a debt of gratitude to Lynn Goldschmidt, who provided expert editing and encouragement toward the end of my writing, when I had begun to lose confidence that what I was doing was truly a worthy project.

Let me also thank Renee Engeln, Jon Adler, and Emily Neuberger, who read early chapters and provided wise feedback, as well as Gina Logan and Keith Cox who have also given suggestions for the project. Special thanks also go to my brother, Matt Lucas, who read nearly all of the manuscript and sent me helpful comments and strong support all along. And a warm shout-out and thank you to my dear friends, Grant Krafft and Patty Cain, with whom I have had innumerable conversations over the years about President Trump, politics, and the world in general.

I owe a delayed dose of gratitude to Don Peck, at *The Atlantic* magazine, who originally commissioned me to write a psychological piece on Donald Trump in the early spring of 2016, and who, along with a team of fact-checkers and other experts, helped me fashion my ideas into a coherent article. If he had never contacted me, I doubt that I would have ever considered the idea of exploring the strange case of Donald J. Trump. I believe that Jonathan Haidt may have been instrumental in convincing Don to contact me, so special thanks to Jonathan as well. Let me also thank David Doerer and Hal Bush, who both urged me to write a book on Trump a year or so before I resolved to do so. And let me offer thanks to Joseph Carroll, the editor of *Evolutionary Studies in Imaginative Culture*, who encouraged me to explore the psychology of Donald Trump within the provocative context of human evolution, which ultimately led to the ideas presented in this book's chapter, "Primate." Mike Bailey and Jon Maner both provided invaluable assistance for that effort, as well, for which I am also very grateful. Abby Gross at OUP has been supportive throughout, and I am very thankful for her encouragement and sponsorship. Let me also thank the four anonymous reviewers, enlisted by Abby, who provided both support and critique of the project.

I have had many discussions about the psychology of Donald Trump with good colleagues over the past three years, and I know that those exchanges have shaped this book in many ways. I am especially appreciative of my dear colleagues in the Society for Personology, all of whom are dedicated to the idea that psychology can and should inform the study of biography, the apprehension of full human lives in their full social, ideological, economic, cultural, and historical contexts. In this regard, I would like to thank Jim Anderson, Sunil Bhatia, Jack Bauer, Susan Bluck, Jim Clark, Alan Elms, Mark Freeman, Gary Gregg, Phil Hammack, Ravenna Helson, Jeannette Haviland Jones, Ruthellen Josselson, Jennifer Pals Lilgendahl, Jack Martin, Kate McLean, Ed de St. Aubin, Monisha Pasupathi, Mac Runyan, Brian Schiff, Todd Schultz, and Paul Wink. Let me reserve special thanks for Jefferson Singer, whose beautifully written psychobiography of Robert Louis Stevenson provided me with the central conceit for this project, drawn from *The Strange Case of Dr. Jekyll and Mr. Hyde*. Let me also acknowledge with gratitude the late Jay Einhorn, who shared ideas with me that found their way into my writing, and the late Joe Markowitz who, like Jay, offered clear-eyed and insightful observations about the life and personality of Donald Trump.

Finally I would like to thank the Dean of the School of Education and Social Policy at Northwestern University, David Figlio. David strongly urged me to seize the moment and write this book during my sabbatical year. I would like to thank my recent and current graduate students—in particular, Jen Guo, Raffi Cowan, Hollen Reischer, and Ariana Turner—who continued to do stellar work on their own research studies even as I was severely distracted during the period when I was writing this book. Let me also acknowledge the Foley Family Foundation of Milwaukee, Wisconsin, who provided funding for my students and me for over two decades, as we conducted research on adult personality and social development under the aegis of the Foley Center for the Study of Lives at Northwestern University.

Prologue

In *The Strange Case of Dr. Jekyll and Mr. Hyde*, an upstanding London physician struggles to suppress a primal force inside of him. He invents a potion that separates out his good public self (Jekyll) from his inner demon (Hyde). Drinking the elixir literally transforms Jekyll into Hyde, a younger and more energized version of himself, a new person who revels in acts of wanton violence and lust. Mr. Hyde murders a man, and he becomes more violent and vengeful over time. Eventually, he takes over as the dominant persona, and Jekyll shrinks into dissipation. In a desperate last act, Jekyll manages to regain control long enough to write a confession. And then, he commits suicide, killing them both off.

There is some irony in the title of Robert Louis Stevenson's great novel. The case is indeed *strange*, but it was also deeply familiar to the Victorian readers who adored the book. They were horrified by the prospect of a literal split in human personality. Today we might shrug off this kind of plot development—in a book or movie—as too predictable. But in 1890 many readers surely gasped out loud when they arrived at the novel's big reveal, described in a testimonial from Dr. Lanyon: "'O God!' I screamed, and 'O God!' again and again; for there before my eyes"—where Mr. Hyde had just been, "there stood Henry Jekyll!" The case was so strange because two different persons turned out to be one. But it was so weirdly familiar, as well, and just as horrifying to know deep down, to intuit back in 1890, that one person can be fundamentally *two*—even *you*, dear reader.

Today, I embark upon the *strange case* of Donald J. Trump. As I write these first words, it is May 5, 2018. The Dow is at 24,262, up 332 points since yesterday. For the first time since the year 2000, unemployment in the United States has dipped below 4.0%. President Trump touted economic progress at a roundtable in Cleveland, Ohio, today. He lashed out at critics of his plan to build a wall along the Mexican border. If Congress does not authorize money to build the wall and stem what Mr. Trump believes to be an influx of dangerous, illegal immigrants, he may "close down the country," Mr. Trump said. Meanwhile, the special counsel assigned to investigate Russian interference in the 2016 presidential election continues his work, casting a dark cloud over the administration. Robert Mueller's investigation into the possibility of collusion between Trump's campaign and the Russians is nothing more than a "witch hunt," the president says. Yesterday, the world learned that the president reimbursed his private

The Strange Case of Donald J. Trump. Dan P. McAdams, Oxford University Press (2020). © Oxford University Press.
DOI: 10.1093/oso/9780197507445.001.0001

lawyer $130,000 for the hush money paid to a pornographic film star, days before the 2016 election, when she threatened to reveal the details of a previous affair with Mr. Trump.

One reason to date the beginning is to remind myself that I need to imagine where *you* are right now as you read this, projecting myself into the future. Countless times every day I ask myself a question that is surely on the minds of millions of Americans who are also trapped, as you once were, in my current historical moment: *How will it all turn out? What will become of all this strangeness?* I believe the question runs through the minds of people on both sides of the current partisan divide. Trump detractors imagine a joyful future when they finally awake from the nightmare. Or, in their worst-case scenarios, the nightmare never ends. Maybe the world will never return to "normal." Trump loyalists look ahead to an America that will become "great" again, as the president has famously promised. Trump will prove wrong the millions who hate him, they hope. Trump will triumph.

Even as world events hurtle to an unknowable future, I want to imagine how we will someday look back. We will look back on that strange time in the world's history when Donald J. Trump loomed gargantuan at the center of global consciousness. What was *that* about? And what was *he* about? Psychologically speaking, who *was* Donald Trump? How did he come to be? What kind of a person was he? A very, very *strange* person, I want to answer. And yet a deeply familiar one.

We begin by recognizing the *strangeness.*

"Everything about Mr. Trump is strange." Those are the words of Anthony P. "Tony" Senecal, Trump's personal butler for nearly 30 years at Trump's Mar-a-Lago estate in Florida, as reported by Ronald Kessler in a highly sympathetic account of President Trump's first year in the White House.

In the mid-1980s, the author Tony Schwartz shadowed Donald Trump day in and day out in his role as the ghostwriter for Trump's famous first book, *The Art of the Deal.* Looking back on the experience in 2016, Schwartz concluded: "Trump didn't fit any model of human being I'd ever met." He remembers almost nothing from his childhood, Schwartz recalled. "There is no private Trump."

"We're dealing with a person who's psychologically and categorically different from any previous president," stated Michael D'Antonio, who interviewed his subject at great length and exhaustively researched his life for a Trump biography. "He has prevailed in the way no other spinner of tales has prevailed."

Liz Smith, a gossip columnist in New York who covered Trump for decades, admitted, "I've known him forever, and I can't figure him out."

In the late 1990s, Mark Singer, assigned to write a profile for *The New Yorker,* tried hard to figure Trump out. Desperate for a clue as to what goes on inside Trump's head, Singer asked Trump what he was typically thinking about when shaving in front of the mirror every morning. The question baffled Trump. He had no answer. Singer tried a different approach.

"O. K., I guess I'm asking, do you consider yourself ideal company?"

"You really want to know what I consider ideal company?" Trump replied. "A total piece of ass."

Trump may have gotten the best of Singer in that little exchange, by interpreting Singer's question in a humorously literal way. But maybe he never understood Singer's real meaning, or saw no point in it. *What is it like, Mr. Trump, to be with yourself?* When you look into the psychological mirror and gaze upon the inner world of Donald Trump, what do you see? Singer was forced to conclude that Trump sees nothing when he looks inside. Or else he never looks. Frustrated by his failure to reveal the real Donald Trump behind the everyday mask he wears, Singer concluded that Mr. Trump has achieved something remarkable and utterly strange in human life: "an existence unmolested by the rumblings of a soul."

What do human beings typically see when they look inside themselves? A soul? A story? A private world of consciousness and sense-making? Dr. Jekyll saw an inner beast. Like many 19th-century intellectuals, culminating in Sigmund Freud's conception of the human psyche, Jekyll peered into a vast underground of dangerous and yet alluring characters, a private world of impulse and desire. Dr. Jekyll's great insight, like Freud's, was that the private Mr. Hyde inside him was as real as the public Jekyll. Human beings are split in two, or maybe more, Dr. Jekyll observed.

But Donald Trump turns the strange case of Jekyll and Hyde on its head. Trump refuses to acknowledge the kind of duality (or multiplicity) that Dr. Jekyll, and most modern men and women, apprehend. A common view of human nature today is that people are walking around with many different selves. Modern life is complex. We play many different roles. I may feel that I am one kind of person when I am with my wife and daughters, another at an academic conference, and yet another online. The different personas I express, the different internal characters in my life story, may conflict with each other; they may reveal contradictory features of my human individuality, like Jekyll and Hyde. We all need to be strategic in choosing the right selves to reveal in just the right kinds of situations. Some selves feel more authentic than do others. Some may even feel "fake," but we still keep those selves around because they can be useful. The different selves are all held together, more or less, by my construing them all to be part of my own *life story*. When I gaze into the psychological mirror, I see the different parts of me, the different characters who star in different scenes, and I see the story that I am living, or trying to live, through the different characters who are me.

In this book, I will explore the power and meaning of a range of intriguing concepts in contemporary psychological science as they apply to the strange case of Donald J. Trump. These ideas include narcissism, extraversion, agreeableness, empathy, attachment patterns, authoritarian dynamics, leadership styles, cognitive schemas, the role of redemption in human lives, and even the psychology of chimpanzees. But the strangest thing of all in this strange case—the singular element of his personality around which all others revolve—is Trump's peculiar orientation to himself. *There is no Jekyll, only Hyde.*

The strange case of Donald J. Trump turns out to be the opposite of what Robert Louis Stevenson described in Jekyll and Hyde. Like me and probably like you, Stevenson believed that humans have inner, hidden selves. There is always more to each of us than what appears on the surface. One of the reasons that being a member of our species *Homo sapiens* turns out to be so interesting is that each of us is a mystery to ourselves. Each of us has an opportunity to embark on a journey of self-discovery. We look inside ourselves to find inner truths.

But Donald Trump is not like other members of the species. When he gazes into the psychological looking glass, Mr. Trump does not see the different selves that comprise who he is. He does not see the many different characters, each of them evolving to live out the story of Donald J. Trump. *He does not see a story,* for there is no story to see. Michael D'Antonio may be correct in describing Mr. Trump as a successful "spinner of tales." It cannot be denied that Trump projects storied images in the minds of others—the image of a successful businessman who has accumulated wealth over time, for example, or the image of a larger-than-life celebrity or a reality TV star. In campaign rallies and morning tweets, moreover, Trump can tell a very good story. For example, in promising to "Make America Great Again," he invokes a powerful narrative, shared by many of his supporters, about the perception of American decline and a promised renewal.

But Donald Trump has no psychologically compelling tale to spin *about himself.* He does not see his own life as a story extended over time—as an inner narrative that tracks a multifaceted and developing protagonist over the long course. And as such, *he does not see himself as a person,* at least not in the way that most adult humans see themselves as persons. Rather than viewing himself as a fully realized human being who lives out a coherent story extended across a landscape of time and consciousness, Donald Trump moves through life as we imagine a superhero might, and as he imagines it, too. He acts boldly to vanquish the moment, moment by moment, episode by episode—the episodic man. As frustrated biographers have learned, Trump does not look inside himself; he does not look behind; he does not look to what may lie ahead, at least not very far ahead. Trump is not introspective, retrospective, or prospective. There is no depth; there is no past; there is no future.

Modern people repeatedly project onto Donald Trump their fundamental assumptions about what human beings are like. We expect Trump to be many things, like every other adult human being we have ever met. We expect him to have different parts of himself, held together somehow within a pattern and played out through a story. We expect depth, complexity, and change—because modern human beings are deep and complex, and they change over time. But Donald Trump's strangeness lies in his repudiation of our deep expectations, the implicit expectations that Robert Louis Stevenson made explicit in the strange case he described so many years ago. Unlike Jekyll and his Hyde, Donald Trump is *not* many things. He is one primal thing. Trump may conceal facts about his life and hide the details of his finances, but he is incapable of hiding different parts of himself—and that is because, psychologically speaking, there are no different parts of himself. Wherever he is, and whenever, Trump is strangely all there in the moment. That cannot be true, you say. Trump often seems as if he is acting, putting on a face, playing a role. There must be more behind the mask, right? No! You are looking at all of him—right here now.

Like Mr. Hyde *without a Jekyll*, Donald Trump lives mainly in the vibrantly emotional current moment. This is why he seems so authentic to many people, and so strange. This is what gives him the primal charisma that continues to enthrall millions of Americans, even as it repulses millions more. This is why, in part, Trump was able to vanquish his 15 rivals in the 2016 Republican primaries. It was impossible to take our eyes off of him in the Republican debates—and the audience remained riveted through the presidential campaign and his presidency. Dynamic and primordial, Trump is like a volcano or a wild beast. A force of nature, unleashed. When Jekyll transformed himself into Hyde, he felt a "freedom of the soul" that "braced and delighted me like wine." My "love of life [was] wonderful," he recalled. He was Trump in the moment. Every moment.

***

Before I continue with the strange case, let me tell you who I am. A professor of psychology and human development at Northwestern University, I study personality and how people change over time. Over the past three decades, my students and I have conducted a great deal of research on personality development in adulthood, with an emphasis on the inner narratives that people create to make sense of their lives. I am, therefore, the kind of psychologist who does research, writes books and articles, and teaches classes. I am not a clinician. I do not diagnose people with mental illness. I do not see clients or do psychotherapy. In recent articles and books, I have applied my tools of psychological interpretation to the lives of U.S. Presidents George W. Bush and Barack Obama.

My psychological interpretation of the life and personality of Donald Trump expands on themes I introduced in a cover essay appearing in the June 2016 issue of *The Atlantic*. In "The Mind of Donald Trump," I aimed to reveal some of the important psychological dynamics in Mr. Trump's life and to predict what kind of a president he might be, should he win the 2016 election. Like most people in the summer of 2016, I did not think he would win the presidency. Therefore, making predictions felt mainly like an interesting intellectual exercise at the time, like a hypothetical case I might pose for my students in class. The results of the November 8, 2016, election, however, turned the hypothetical case into immediate reality. Since then, I have tracked carefully how President Trump's feelings, thoughts, and behaviors have followed in line with the predictions I made, and also how he has surprised me in some ways, and motivated me to probe more deeply. As such, this book goes well beyond the original essay to explore dynamics in Trump's life and in his presidency that I was simply unable to apprehend back in 2016.

I conceive of the book I am about to write as a psychological *reckoning*. To reckon something is to estimate, calculate, or analyze it. The term *reckoning* suggests a coming to terms with something, a making sense of something that has been. It takes the perspective of looking back. I cannot predict exactly what President Trump will do tomorrow. But I feel we know him well enough at this point, we know enough about him as a 73-year-old former real-estate tycoon and reality television star who became president of the United States, somebody who has been in the public eye since his early 20s, whose biographical record is spread across an array of public venues, the subject of countless essays, articles, books, and Twitter feeds—we know enough today about Donald J. Trump to undertake a full psychological reckoning. We know enough now to come to psychological terms with him, to sort out who he has been, to probe his mind and interrogate his psychological nature. And we know enough, I believe, to consider what this psychological reckoning reveals about *us*. My analysis of Donald Trump's life and personality, moreover, may help us understand the changing dynamics of political leadership in the United States today, why many people are enthralled with President Trump and many others repelled, and what to expect from other leaders, be they CEOs or heads of foreign governments, who resemble Mr. Trump in their behaviors, thoughts, and motivations.

My psychological reckoning will be evidence-based, dispassionate, analytical, and, to the extent that such a thing is possible, fair-minded. I am not foolish enough to believe that one can attain a purely objective stance when it comes to a figure as luminously controversial as Donald J. Trump. I have political views. I have a particular moral perspective. I see the world through a certain subjective lens, as do you. But I believe that people can, and often should, endeavor to see things and people in a complex, multifaceted, and more-or-less even-handed manner—even when that person to be understood is a figure who, because people either hate him or adore him, seems to defy reasoned analysis. I believe that there are facts in the world. I believe in the power of reason and science to sway human opinion. I believe that science aims to get at truths and that truths can indeed be found, or at least approached. I believe that evidence-based scientific ideas can be profitably applied to a human life to shed light on that life and to reveal truth and enhance understanding. And I value *truth* as much as I value anything.

Story

The strangest thing about the story of Donald Trump is that *there is no story*.

What I mean is that there is no coherent and elaborated story in Donald Trump's head about who he really is, how he came to be, and what his life means.

Still Trump has a few memories. And there are documented facts.

He was born on June 14, 1946, in the borough of Queens, New York City, the fourth of five children to Fred and Mary Anne (MacLeod) Trump. The oldest son, Freddy, drank himself to ruin, dead at age 43 from complications of alcoholism. The oldest daughter, Maryanne, became a federal judge, appointed to the U.S. District Court by President Reagan in 1983 and elevated to the Court of Appeals for the Third Circuit by President Clinton in 1999. Donald's younger brother, Robert, followed his father (and Donald) into the real estate business. Elizabeth, the third born, sandwiched between Freddy and Donald, went into banking. Of the five children, only Elizabeth has remained married to her first spouse.

Let us set the scene for the 1950s, the decade that marked Donald's childhood. The five children and their parents live in a stately, red-brick Colonial Revival home in Jamaica Estates, Queens. Parked in front are Fred's Cadillac and Mary's Rolls Royce. It is, say, a Saturday morning. But Fred Trump rarely takes a day off, despite the considerable wealth amassed from the apartment buildings erected and the rents collected throughout Brooklyn and Queens. The phone is constantly ringing this morning, business calls for Fred, deals to be made perhaps, or some trouble at one of the properties. There is no time to play catch in the backyard with his sons and probably no interest anyway. Instead, Fred heads off to one of the construction sites, or perhaps he drives over to an apartment building to collect delinquent rents. He takes Donald along.

"He would drag me around with him while he collected small rents in tough sections of Brooklyn," Donald Trump recalls, in his 2015 book, *Crippled America*. "It's not fun being a landlord. You have to be tough." On one such trip, Donald asks his father why he always stands to the side of the tenant's door after ringing the bell. "Because sometimes they shoot right through the door," Fred replies.

Did a disgruntled Trump tenant ever aim his gun at a rent collector? Did the tenant shoot through the door? Maybe. But if such a thing were likely to happen on that Saturday in Brooklyn, would Fred Trump have taken his children along

The Strange Case of Donald J. Trump. Dan P. McAdams, Oxford University Press (2020). © Oxford University Press.
DOI: 10.1093/oso/9780197507445.001.0001

to collect rents? Probably not. Fred Trump is one very tough guy, even ruthless in his business dealings, and he aims to instill toughness in his three sons. But he is protective, too, and he adores Donald—affectionately calls Donald his "killer" and his "king." Admittedly, those are odd appellations for a little boy. But they are terms of endearment in the mind of Fred Trump, and in the mind of his favorite son, as his son remembers it today. Let us assume that the event occurred as Donald Trump remembers it. Why did Fred Trump say what he said? And why does Donald remember the scene so clearly, if indeed he does remember it (and is not making it up), six decades later? Or, let us assume he is making it all up! Perhaps it never happened. Either way. It does not matter. The answer to all of these questions is the same: The story confirms that *the world is a dangerous place.* This is the great lesson from Donald Trump's childhood—and the bedrock assumption for his entire life.

But how can the world be so dangerous for a young boy living in luxury? Where are the threats coming from? The family is rich. The neighborhood is safe. The schools are good. As far as can be determined from the biographical record, there is no abuse in the family. Nothing bizarrely dysfunctional, on the surface at least. Family life seems consistent with the bygone standards of 1950s America, where the father is the hard-working breadwinner and the mother stays home to raise the children and to do good works in the community. Perhaps not *Leave It to Beaver* exactly, but stable enough, more-or-less normal enough.

His parents drop the three-year-old Donald off every weekday morning at the Carousel Pre-School. "Donald was a beautiful little boy, very blond and buttery," recalled the nursery school director, Shirley Greene. "He was a nice size for his age, very attractive, social, and outgoing . . . sturdy, and really quite jolly." By the time he is in the first grade at the Kew-Forest School, little Donald is exhibiting a highly rambunctious temperament. He is more outgoing than most of the other children and also more aggressive. "Growing up in Queens, I was a pretty tough kid," Trump writes today. "I wanted to be the toughest kid in the neighborhood." He punches his second-grade music teacher in the face, giving him a black eye. The reason: "I didn't think he knew anything about music." If the world is a dangerous place for the seven-year-old Donald Trump, *it is mainly because he makes it so.*

As teachers and principals send home more reports of bad behavior, Fred and Mary Trump begin to worry that their aggressive son may be headed down the path to delinquency. When they learn that Donald and a friend have been taking the subway into Manhattan to purchase switchblades (inspired by the Sharks and Jets of *West Side Story*), they decide to send their son to the New York Military Academy (NYMA), a boarding school for boys located on the Hudson River, not far from West Point. They hope that the strict regimen of a military school will help to alloy Donald's innate toughness with tough discipline.

Donald enjoys five successful years at NYMA, from eighth grade through high school. Yes, I say "enjoy," even though (actually, *because*) it was "a tough, tough place. There were ex-drill sergeants all over the place, and these people liked to scream and, above all, they liked to fight." As Trump tells it today, the instructors "used to beat the shit out of you; those guys were rough." But the teenaged Trump seems to thrive in this hard-nosed, competitive, supermasculine world, ever sensitive to (and excited by) the specter of danger it affords. NYMA reinforces the strong work ethic and sense of discipline Trump initially learned from his father. And it teaches him how to deal with other aggressive men, like his intimidating baseball coach, Theodore Dobias:

> What I did, basically, was to convey that I respected his [Dobias's] authority, but that he didn't intimidate me. It was a delicate balance. Like so many strong guys, Dobias had a tendency to go for the jugular if he smelled weakness. On the other hand, if he sensed strength but you didn't try to undermine him, he treated you like a man.

After attending college at Fordham and the University of Pennsylvania (where he graduates with a bachelor's degree from the Wharton School of Finance and Commerce), Donald Trump sets out to make his fortune, as his father did, in real estate. His dreams, however, are bigger than his father's. He is not content to build an empire in the outer boroughs. Against his father's advice, he focuses his efforts instead on Manhattan.

In 1971, Trump moves into a studio apartment on Third Avenue and 75th Street. While he continues to manage buildings and work on projects for the family business, Trump scours the Manhattan maps and walks the streets in search of new opportunities. It is a dismal decade for real estate in the Big Apple. Neighborhoods are decaying, crime is surging, and the city's finances are a mess. Rattled by a day-long power blackout in the summer of 1977 and the murder rampage of a man called Son of Sam, the New York tabloids run headlines like these: 24 HOURS OF TERROR and NO ONE IS SAFE. It is as if fear reaches a climax in the second game of the 1977 World Series, as the television announcer Howard Cosell observes smoke outside Yankee Stadium, and famously declares: "There it is, ladies and gentlemen, the Bronx is burning!" Yes, this does indeed resemble the kind of dangerous world that so thrills the mind and the imagination of Donald Trump.

Oh, to be young and handsome and very, very rich in Manhattan in the 1970s! Or any decade, I suppose, but the decade of the 1970s holds a special allure in Trump's biography, with its thrilling mix of danger and opportunity and the sense that life is about to explode with excitement and success. The young Donald Trump pursues (and presumably beds) gorgeous models and flight attendants. He cultivates important friendships with rich, older men, financial titans of the city, glamorous celebrities, politicians, men with connections and clout—like George Steinbrenner, the owner of the New York Yankees, and the inimitable Roy M. Cohn, a brilliant and ruthless attorney who defended organized crime figures. During the Red Scare of the 1950s, Cohn served as Senator Joseph McCarthy's legal counsel and hatchet man. Cohn was "a total genius," as Trump now remembers him, and unsparingly loyal. "He would kill for somebody that he liked."

An image is beginning to form, if not quite a story. A society columnist follows Donald Trump around town for a day as he wheels and deals and burnishes a persona of the James Bond of real estate. "He is tall, lean and blond, with dazzling white teeth, and he looks ever so much like Robert Redford," gushes Judy Klemesrud in the New York Times. "He rides around town in a chauffeured silver Cadillac with his initials, DJT, on the plates. He dates slinky fashion models, belongs to the most elegant clubs, and, at only 30 years of age, estimates that he is worth 'more than $200 million.'"

Klemesrud reports that Trump's chauffer and bodyguard is a former New York City police officer who always carries a loaded revolver. "As he [Trump] drove around the city, he exclaimed boyishly, 'Look at that great building [at 56th Street and Madison Avenue]. It's available! There are a lot of good deals around right now.'" Donald Trump is on the verge of completing real estate deals that promise to rejuvenate Manhattan, writes Klemesrud—a new convention center, reconstruction of the Commodore Hotel near Grand Central Station, and the construction of federally subsidized apartments on the Penn Central's 60th Street yards. Klemesrud quotes admiring colleagues who are boosters for these projects. They describe Trump as "bold, daring, and swashbuckling." Klemesrud quotes his 70-year-old father, Fred Trump: "'He has great vision, and everything he touches seems to turn to gold. Donald is the smartest person I know.'"

It is not true that everything Donald Trump touches in the late 1970s and early 1980s turns to gold. But he does enjoy notable successes. The city rejects his bid for what is to become the Jacob K. Javits Convention Center. But with the help of a 40-year, $400 million tax abatement deal, he turns the bankrupt and shabby Commodore Hotel into the sleek Grand Hyatt New York, which opens on September 25, 1980.

Construction of what is to become Trump Tower begins around the same time, on the site of the former Bonwit Teller flagship store, between 56th and 57th Streets on Fifth Avenue. Limestone bas-relief sculptures of seminude goddesses, designed in the Art Deco style and estimated to be worth $250,000, adorn the old store's entrance. An art dealer offers to arrange for their delivery to the Metropolitan Museum of Art. But Trump has no patience for the plan, and he worries that the transport will cost him precious time and money. He orders them destroyed. He also courts controversy by hiring undocumented Polish workers for demolition on the site and paying them scandalously low wages. Still, the building is completed in 1983, a 664-foot-high skyscraper that provides retail and office space on the lower levels and luxury condominiums for the ultrawealthy on its upper floors. Famous residents will include Johnny Carson, Sophia Loren, and Steven Spielberg, along with the building's namesake, who occupies the penthouse.

Trump's fame and influence continue to build in New York City, but he now longs to star on a larger stage. His is a distinctively American success story, he reasons. More Americans need to know about it. One day he receives a visit from the writer Tony Schwartz, who has been assigned by *Playboy* magazine to interview Trump. Like nearly everybody who has tried to get Donald Trump to open up about his inner life, Schwartz is flummoxed by his host's simplistic and unsatisfying answers to his questions. After about 20 minutes, Trump tells Schwartz that he does not want to reveal too much because he has just signed a lucrative book deal and needs to save his best material.

"What kind of book?" Schwartz asks.

"My autobiography," Trump replies.

"You're only thirty-eight—you don't have one yet!" Schwartz jokes.

"Yeah, I know," Trump admits.

"If I were you," Schwartz tells him, "I'd write a book called *The Art of the Deal*. That's something people would be interested in."

Trump immediately realizes the brilliance of this idea. But he has no interest in writing the book himself. "Do you want to write it?" Trump asks Schwartz.

A few weeks later, Schwartz agrees.

***

When Tony Schwartz joked that Donald Trump, at age 38, did not have an "autobiography" yet, his words held more truth than he realized at the time. And when Donald Trump conceded that Schwartz was probably right, he showed more insight about his own life than he arguably ever had before, or has since. In that fateful conversation in 1985, the two men thought they were talking about writing a book. But as I read Schwartz's account of their interaction today, I cannot resist the urge to see a deeper meaning, even if the two men never saw it at the time, and even if the conversation did not actually occur in exactly the way that Schwartz's memory, three decades later, reconstructs it.

Contra Schwartz, there was nothing especially odd in late-20th-century American society about a 38-year-old man's wanting to write a book about his own life and experiences, especially a man who had accomplished as much as Donald Trump had by age 38 and who was already the object of public fascination. The really odd thing, instead—the psychological strangeness that trumps all others in this strange case—is that Donald Trump never had a story to tell in the first place. "You don't have one yet," Schwartz said. At age 73, Trump still doesn't.

What does it mean to "have" a story?

Psychological research shows that children learn to tell little stories about events in their lives within a year or two after they begin to speak. They rely on what cognitive psychologists call their *autobiographical memory* to pluck out episodes worthy to tell. "Mommy took me to McDonald's yesterday," three-year-old Sarah says. "And what did you eat?" her grandmother asks. "Uh, hmm, it was raining," Sarah says. "Remember, honey? You had fries, and some of my milkshake," her mother interjects. "Milkshake!" Sarah exclaims.

Sarah's mother helps her tell the story to her grandmother, helps her get the facts right and arrange the story into a coherent pattern and sequence. Her mother is providing Sarah with what developmental psychologists call *scaffolding* for her narrative account. A scaffold is the temporary structure that goes up around a building as it is being built, providing a platform for the workers and the equipment. Once the scaffolding comes down, the building stands on its own. Older siblings, teachers, friends, and many others also provide scaffolding for the growing child's storytelling efforts. We learn how to tell stories about our experiences from each other. We watch and listen as others do it, and we adjust our own storytelling efforts accordingly.

By the time children are five or six years of age, they have typically developed a clear understanding of how a story should be told. Even though they cannot verbalize their formal knowledge, they implicitly know that a story should begin with a setting—where, when, once upon a time, yesterday at McDonald's. They know that there needs to be a main character—a protagonist—who initiates the action out of desire or belief. Little Red Riding Hood *needs* to get to grandma's house. The Big Bad Wolf *wants* to eat her up. They know that the plot needs to develop, that tension needs to build to a climax, and that the tension ultimately needs to subside as the story resolves. They know that stories are supposed to have a point. Research shows that when children hear stories that do not abide by the structural conventions they have internalized, they express confusion or lose interest. And if they do remember these faulty stories later on, children will often fill in the missing pieces and remember the stories as conforming more closely to what they should have been rather than what they actually were. Autobiographical memory works the same way—details are filled in; past events get selectively smoothed out and arranged into comprehensible patterns. Memories become stories.

There is every reason to believe that Donald Trump learned how to tell stories in pretty much the same way that most other children do. At the Kew-Forest School, Donald often occupied the center of attention. He was extremely outgoing and talkative, as he is today. He surely told his share of stories throughout his childhood and adolescent years, as he does today—about punching out the second-grade music teacher, maybe, or driving in the game-winning run for the NYMA baseball team, or triumphing over "Lyin' Ted" (Texas Senator Ted Cruz) and "Little Marco" (Florida Senator Marco Rubio) in the 2016 Republican primaries. In this sense, Trump is a master spinner of tales.

But the problem begins with the next developmental step. It is one thing to be able to tell stories about what happened last week. It is quite another to apprehend your entire life—the remembered past and the anticipated future—as an ongoing narrative, a big story that builds over time, that has a point, that makes your life make sense. The story, moreover, grounds your life in basic values and beliefs, providing a moral frame of reference for how you understand yourself and the world. Psychologists call this kind of story a *narrative identity*. It is an internalized and evolving story of the self, reconstructing the past and imagining the future in such a way as to provide the narrator's life with some measure of unity, moral purpose, and meaning. It is the story in your head about how you came to be the person you are becoming and what you hope to leave behind in the long run.

How do you get a narrative identity? First, you need to develop an understanding of how a human life is typically sequenced over time. This is pretty easy, although the process varies from one culture to the next. You look around, you talk to your parents, you listen to stories, you watch television, you read books (or consult the Internet), and eventually you develop a set of expectations about how a typical life unfolds—when people leave home to go off to college or work, for example, when people typically get married, have children, retire, and so on. You come to understand that your life story will be some variation of this pattern.

Next, you need to decide which events—from the past or anticipated in the future—should be included in your particular life story, what the high points and low points should be, how the events should be sequenced, how the main character (you!) should change over time, how the main character should stay the same, which subsidiary characters (allies and enemies) should get the big roles, what the overall arc of the story should look like, what the major themes should be, and what the entire narrative—beginning, middle, and end—should mean.

You need to "decide" these things, but I do not mean to suggest that you set time aside one afternoon to make the big decisions or that you consciously work it all out and type it all into a computer. The decisions are made subtly and unconsciously for the most part, over many years, as you live and make sense of your living, as you gradually become the author of your life. The process typically begins in adolescence and the young adult years, and it typically continues well into midlife and beyond. By the time you hit, say, age 38, you have probably been working on your narrative identity for at least two decades. By age 38, you most likely have a story to tell, even if (like most people) you never plan to write a book. My students and I have been studying people's life stories since the late 1980s. We focus mainly on men and women in their 30s, 40s, and 50s. Over the past three decades, we have met one or two people, at most, who do not seem to have a life story. People's narrative identities vary dramatically, in form and content, but nearly everybody has one by the time they are, say, age 38.

In authoring a narrative identity, you are sure to make good use of a cognitive tool called *autobiographical reasoning*. This involves deriving general, self-defining meanings from the key scenes in your life story. Let us say that your parents divorced when you were 10 years old. The divorce is a fact in your life story. But what does this fact mean? Perhaps, it means that you need to be really careful in choosing a life partner. Or maybe your parents' divorce helps to explain why your life took a downward turn around age 10, and why you have never felt good about yourself since. Or maybe it signals that you had to take charge of your life at an early age and that is why today you are such an admirably self-directed person. Or maybe it means very little at all: You got through it—no problem. You decide. Which meaning makes the most sense? Which one feels right?

A growing body of research in developmental psychology tracks how people begin, in their teenaged years, to make inferences like these about their lives and how the power and sophistication of autobiographical reasoning increases as we move into our 20s, 30s, and beyond. By age 38 (if you are that old), you probably had lots of experience with autobiographical reasoning—especially in America, where we expect everybody to have a life story that showcases their individual uniqueness, offers insights from their past, and explains how they came to be.

Barack Obama had a narrative identity, at age 38. And unlike Donald Trump, Obama *did* write and publish an autobiography in his 30s. In *Dreams from My Father*, Obama told the story of growing up with his white mother and her parents in Hawaii and Indonesia in the 1960s and 1970s and his longing to know the African father who abandoned the family shortly after he was born. His psychological search for his father became an animating theme for his early years, as did his unquenchable curiosity about the world around him and his confusion regarding his own identity as a young man who was both Black and not Black. In the most audacious use of autobiographical reasoning, Obama identified himself as an heir to the American civil rights movement, even as a Joshua to the Moses of Martin Luther King Jr. and other past advocates for human rights. Obama's personal story, as told in *Dreams*, is a progressive narrative of ascent that mirrors the nation's march toward equality and freedom—the long arc of history that bends toward justice, as King described it. Obama had already identified himself as a protagonist in this grand narrative by the time he married Michelle Robinson, at age 31.

George W. Bush had one, too, although he never went so far, in his 30s, to write the story down. By the time he married Laura Welch at age 31, Bush was already looking back, with considerable regret, upon the past decade of his life as a time of waywardness and squandered opportunities—his "nomadic period," as he later described it. He was beginning to see how the first draft of his narrative identity—that story about following dutifully in the footsteps of his extraordinary father—wasn't working out so well. Unlike George H. W. Bush, the fighter pilot who was a war hero, the scholar-athlete at Yale who would go on to make millions of dollars in the oil business and eventually serve his country as vice president under Ronald Reagan and then as the 41st president of the United States—unlike his father—the first-born son was mainly drunk throughout his 20s. But he was beginning to turn his life around when he met that cute librarian and married her—the "best decision I ever made," he instantly knew. He was beginning to develop a new narrative identity that resembled the prodigal son story in the New Testament. By the time he turned 38, Bush had experienced a significant religious conversion. Shortly after his 40th birthday, he gave up alcohol for good. In his mind, George W. Bush was creating a redemptive narrative to make sense of his life—a dramatic and ultimately inspiring story about paradise lost and regained, about getting a second chance in life and making the most of it. It was a story that many of his supporters knew and loved on the eve of the 2000 presidential election.

Donald Trump has never done this sort of thing with respect to his own life. You can examine all the interviews he has given and read every one of his speeches and tweets, and you will rarely find examples of Trump's crafting a narrative understanding for his own life through autobiographical reasoning. This is especially remarkable because Trump talks about himself all the time! He brags about his achievements. He proclaims himself to be the greatest president ever, the smartest man on the face of the earth, the winner of all winners. But each of these claims is no more than a proclamation of a generic trait: I am beautiful; I am great; I am a stable genius; I am this and I am that. These assertions are *statements* about the self, but they are not *stories* about the self. They do not explain how I came to be who I am and where my life may be going. They do not explain how I have changed over time, how I have developed, how I once was one thing and now I am another. They say nothing about what I value in life for the long run, beyond being the best now and winning in the moment. They do not offer any kind of long-term moral agenda for life. They do not acknowledge any failures or setbacks in life. They do not explain how I coped with those failures, how I learned from my mistakes, how I built my character, how I have evolved as a human being over the long term, and how I may continue to evolve. They do not convey any sense of humanity.

Sixteen years after George W. Bush rode his redemptive life story all the way to the White House, the Republican party's nominee for president had a grand opportunity to tell his own story to the world at the Republican National Convention in Cleveland. It was the night of his acceptance speech. It has become customary that presidential nominees—both Republican and Democratic—use their acceptance speech at the convention to convey a narrative about who they are, who they have been, and who they hope to become as president of the United States. As the long-time Democratic strategist Paul Begala put it after watching Donald Trump deliver his address, "the American people need to know their president's mythic arc."

But Donald Trump had precious little to say that night, or any night, about himself and his life, beyond boasting about his overall greatness. Covering the speech for the *New York Times*, one reporter wrote this: "After 40 years in the public eye, Mr. Trump decided on Thursday night that he was not interested in revealing himself to America with disarming tales of his upbringing, hard-earned lessons from his tumultuous career or the inner struggles masked by his outward pomposity." In what was, at that point in his life, the most important speech he had ever given, Donald Trump passed up the chance to "plumb his personal life and career for the kind of anecdotes that would turn him, in the eyes of his doubters, from a cartoon into a flesh-and-blood human being."

The reporter depicted Donald Trump as a "cartoon," rather than a psychologically full-bodied human being. The assessment seems harsh, until you realize that Donald Trump has described himself in almost the same way. In one of the very few instances when Trump actually seemed to recognize that his life might conform to an integrative narrative, he said, "I am the creator of my own comic book, and I love living it." At other times, he has described himself as a super-hero. With occasional exceptions, cartoon characters and comic book heroes are not especially deep. They are not known for bouts of self-reflection or rich inner lives. They are mainly known, instead, for their actions, and sometimes for their emotional displays. Donald Trump is a man of action and strong emotional display. Like Bugs Bunny or Bat Man, he is instantly recognizable by what he does and by the characteristic demeanor he portrays as he does it. Not the complex and multifaceted entity that we expect to find in a full-fledged "person." More like a "persona."

After meeting Donald Trump in 2006 to discuss a business transaction, Tom Griffin could not shake the impression that there was something unreal about him, that Trump was not quite a person. Griffin owned the Menie Estate, near Aberdeen Scotland. Over lunch at the Cock & Bull Restaurant, Griffin negotiated a sale of the property to Trump, who planned to convert the estate into a luxury golf resort. Griffin recalls that Trump drove a very hard bargain, refusing to give in on even the tiniest details. But his most vivid recollection pertains to the theatrics. It was as if the golden-haired guest sitting across the table were an actor on the London stage.

"It was Donald Trump playing Donald Trump," Griffin observed. He was like an actor playing a role.

Griffin recalls that Trump played the role really well. He had it down. This guy was good! He made all the right moves. He looked like Trump. Talked like Trump. Shouted, grimaced, and pounded the table—just like Trump does on TV. There is the old saying: "If it looks like a duck, swims like a duck, and quacks like a duck, then it probably is a duck." It really *was* Donald Trump, right? It had to be. He was just like the real thing. And yet he was always in character. Always enacting the persona. Never let his guard down. That is what made it so weird—that Trump remained the actor, through and through, for the entire lunch, reading his lines and sticking with the script, it seemed, deeply immersed in the role, as if he was *at one with* the role. As if he *was the role*, and *only* the role. He was so authentic, but fake, too. A truly authentic fake.

***

Donald Trump starred in the role of a lifetime for the reality television series, *The Apprentice.* He played himself, just as he does when he is not on television.

The first season of *The Apprentice* aired in the winter and spring of 2004. In each episode, contestants (called "candidates") competed to win Trump's favor as they worked in teams to accomplish various business tasks, such as selling a product, creating an advertising campaign, or raising money for a charity. The cameras followed the teams around various venues in New York City, beginning with Trump Tower (where they lived during the filming), as they struggled to accomplish the goals they were given, arguing, fighting, jockeying for position, and effectively doing the things, often very ugly things, that highly competitive human beings tend to do when they are forced to compete ruthlessly with each other, and sometimes to cooperate, to get ahead. At the end of each episode, the cameras would take the audience back to a Trump Tower boardroom, where Donald Trump would evaluate the activities of the teams and then, after consulting with a group of advisors on the scene, publicly target one unlucky candidate with those dreaded words: "You're fired!" The last candidate standing by the end of the season would win a one-year, $250,000 contract to work with one of Trump's companies.

The popular show burned Trump's indelible persona into the brains of millions of television viewers. Forceful, commanding, decisive, and showing flashes of wit, Trump was the personification of personal power and American business success. "With more than 27 million people watching the finale" of the first season, wrote Michael D'Antonio, "*The Apprentice* provided Donald Trump with publicity so valuable it would be impossible to calculate its worth."

In an article entitled "From *Apprentice* to President," the cognitive scientist Shira Gabriel reported an empirical study showing that viewers of the reality television show formed what Gabriel calls "parasocial bonds" with the host. These "one-sided psychological bonds with specific media figures such as favorite celebrities or fictional characters" leave the viewer feeling that he or she truly knows the star and enjoys a special relationship with the star. After statistically controlling for a range of other factors, Gabriel found that American television viewers who established parasocial bonds with the host of *The Apprentice* were disproportionately likely to vote for Donald Trump in the 2016 presidential election, even if they were Democrats. They were also more likely than others to report that they truly believed Mr. Trump's promises to bring back factory jobs to America, build a wall on the Mexican border, and defeat America's enemies in the Middle East. If it were not for *The Apprentice*, Gabriel suggested, there would be no President Trump.

Every week, the opening segment of *The Apprentice* transported the viewer to Donald Trump's dangerous world:

New York. My City. Where the wheels of the global economy never stop turning. A concrete metropolis of unparalleled strength and purpose that drives the business world. Manhattan is a tough place. *This* island is the real jungle. If you're not careful, it can chew you up and spit you out. But if you work hard, you can really hit it big, and I mean *really* big.

From the safety of their living room couches, the television audience vicariously experienced the world according to Donald Trump—a magnification and glorification of that same world that Trump had known since he was a child, where tenants shot at landlords through locked doors and only "killers," as his father would say, could become "kings." It is a tough, exhausting, overpowering world of high-stakes action, but irresistibly alluring, too, for the potential rewards are awesome. More likely than not, Trump's world will chew you up and spit you out. But there is always that slim chance that you will survive it. *Somebody* will win. It is guaranteed that one of the candidates, but only one, will hit it big, and I mean really big. The toughest or smartest killer will become king.

The opening segment from *The Apprentice* conveys, and perhaps exaggerates, a well-known sensibility about hard-driving American capitalism. More important, however, it also conveys Donald Trump's primal understanding of what life on this planet is fundamentally all about. For most human beings, life is likely to be nasty and brutish, the 17th-century philosopher Thomas Hobbes maintained. Humans are driven by greed and ego in an environment that invariably fails to provide sufficient resources for all. In a rare moment of philosophical reflection (back in 1981), Donald Trump expressed his philosophy of life to a reporter for *People* magazine: "Man is the most vicious of all animals, and life is a series of battles ending in victory or defeat."

Amidst the swirl of the millions of words uttered by Donald Trump in the 70+ years of his garrulous life, this is the foundational sentence for his psychological reckoning. There are two reasons I make that claim.

The first (and more obvious) reason is that Trump's 20 words, strung together as they are, succinctly express what he believes to be the nature of human life. They alert him, and us, to the signal Hobbesian warning: *Life is war.* Therefore, you must always be prepared to fight to win. You must never let your guard down. You must be willing to kill, or you will be killed. You must never be weak, not even for one millisecond, for as soon as you show a milligram of weakness, you will lose.

The second reason is subtler, but arguably more important. When I first read these 20 words, I inserted (in my unconscious mind) a comma between the words "battles" and "ending." I suspect you did, too. Inserting a comma makes it easier to affirm the conventional reading of the sentence, to suggest that it is "life" that ends in "victory or defeat." But it is possible, especially since there is no comma present at that critical point in the sentence, to infer that the word "ending" refers not to "life" itself, or at least not solely to life, but instead (or equally) to "battles." Indeed, it seems eminently reasonable to read the sentence in this alternative way, to suggest that it is each "battle" that ends in either victory or defeat. Accordingly, life itself may be seen as a series of battles, and each one of life's self-contained battles has an ending, and you either win that particular battle or you lose that particular battle. In episodic fashion, you fight one battle after another, winning or losing each, and on it goes, until you die.

Donald Trump is the episodic man. He moves through life, episode by episode, from one battle to the next, striving, in turn, to win each battle he fights. The episodes do not add up. They do not build to form a narrative arc. There is no life story, at least not the kind of coherent and integrative narrative identity that psychologists like me expect a life to convey. Every episode is a battle, but the successive battles do not really build to form a readily defined war, the kind of war that has its own narrative arc, with clearly defined foes, stable alliances, clear issues of contention that drive the antagonists apart, and the prospect that someday it will end—the war will be over, and we will look back on it and understand it as a story, as part of history. No. If life is continual warfare, if war never ends, then all there is to convey is the daily fighting, which, at most, produces an ephemeral victory here and there (and short-term defeat as well), but no ultimate direction. If there is no long-term resolution to the hostilities, then there can be no plot, no story line that makes sense in terms of how it all ends, because it never ends.

The episodic nature of Donald Trump's approach to life and the absence of any long-term narrative identity make up the psychological soil out of which his wildly unpredictable presidency has grown. It seems nearly impossible to predict what surprising thing he will do or outrageous thing he will say (or tweet) from one day to the next. Indeed, former Georgia congressman and Speaker of the House Newt Gingrich predicted during the Republican primaries that a Trump administration would function as a daily adventure: "If Trump does end up winning, you will have no idea each morning what's going to happen." For many of Trump's fans, the adventure is exhilarating. He is shaking the government up. He is changing the rules of the game. Another affirming interpretation comes from Ronald Kessler, in his account of President Trump's first year in office: Trump's "constantly shifting positions are a marketing ploy to see what sticks."

But many of President Trump's critics fear that the fluidity reflects a dangerous instability and confusion in the White House. *New York Times* columnist David Brooks characterized Trump's administration as the "Snapchat presidency." Snapchat is a mobile messaging app that enables users to share photos and texts. What made Snapchat unique at the time Brooks wrote his column was that the shared material disappeared from the recipient's phone after a few seconds. "Each time Trump says or tweets something, squads of experts leap into action, trying to interpret what he could have meant, or how his intentions could lead to changes in American policy," Brooks observed. But this is a waste of time, Brooks concluded, because what Trump asserts or intimates disappears shortly thereafter, without a trace. Brooks noted a direct connection between Trump's here-today-gone-tomorrow mindset on the one hand and his penchant for battle on the other: "When Trump issues a statement, it may look superficially like a policy statement," wrote Books, "but it's usually just a symbolic assault in some dominance-submission male rivalry game. . . . The primary thing is bashing enemies."

If each episode in life is a self-contained monad, a battle today that has absolutely no connection to the battle that may be waged tomorrow, then everything that exists at any given moment exists only for the purpose of winning the moment. What is *good* is what helps the protagonist prevail in the current battle. Likewise, what is *true* is what helps the protagonist prevail in the current battle. Throughout his life, but especially since he has become president, Donald Trump has been criticized (and sometimes praised) for being inconsistent and unpredictable. He may love you on Monday because doing so helps him win Monday's battle. But he may hate you on Wednesday because, again, doing so helps him win Wednesday's battle. On Friday, he may simply say hello to you in the West

Wing, as if he has forgotten what has transpired over the past week. Don't take it personally! Every episode is a different battle for Mr. Trump. Every battle has its own unique dynamics.

After he agreed to work with Donald Trump to write *The Art of the* Deal, Tony Schwartz sensed the same thing. "The Trump I met in 1985 had lived nearly all his life in survival mode," Schwartz recalled in a 2017 column for *The Washington Post*.

> [Trump] felt compelled to go to war with the world. . . . It was a binary, zero-sum choice for him: You either dominated or you submitted. . . . In countless conversations, he made clear to me that he treated every encounter as a contest he had to win, because the only other option from his perspective was to lose, and that was the equivalent of obliteration.

All that matters for the episodic man in a Hobbesian universe is winning the battle, so that he can survive to fight again. All that matters is what happens right now. Accordingly, truth and goodness are defined in the moment only, as those things, ideas, activities, and people that are useful for winning the battle in which the protagonist is currently engaged. To many critics, it may seem as if the episodic man has no consistent moral perspective and is, as a result, a chronic liar.

But the critics don't understand the terrible situation the episodic man finds himself in—or rather, has created for himself. They, by contrast, live in the world of narrative, where stories develop over time, from one episode to the next. In the world of narrative, which is the real world as perceived by most people who live on earth, it is expected that characters take something essential with them from one episode to the next, even as they develop over time. Characters have internal beliefs and values and long-term goals. To live out these values and accomplish these goals, they need to adhere to the facts of external reality, as generally understood by others, and the truths that transcend the exigencies of any given moment. But the episodic man living under the conditions of eternal warfare does not have that kind of luxury. If he starts worrying about trying to be truthful and consistent from one battle to the next, he will not be able to win the current battle. If he takes his eyes off the immediate goal of short-term victory, he believes, even for a moment, he could be dead.

Trump's incessant desire to win—to prevail in every battle—served him well in the 2016 Republican primaries and in the general election. A presidential campaign is a war of attrition. The goal is to survive each successive episode, be it a state primary or a campaign debate, and to outlast the opponents. It is the same goal pursued by the candidates on *The Apprentice*. The final act is a one-on-one prizefight against an ultimate rival, the member of the opposition who has also managed to outlast his (or, in the case of 2016, her) rivals. Winning is all that matters—the perfect life scenario for a man like Donald Trump.

When one of the two combatants finally wins, however, the campaign is supposed to end. The winner of the presidential election transitions then to what is supposed to be the main act of the drama—being president. It is generally assumed that being the president of the United States is a rather different task and experience than running for president of the United States. No longer a candidate, the new president faces the new and daunting challenge of serving as the chief executive of the greatest democracy on the planet and the commander-in-chief of its armed forces.

In the 2016 campaign, Hillary Clinton, Bernie Sanders, Marco Rubio, Ted Cruz, Jeb Bush, and nearly every other candidate in both political parties *wanted to win the election in order to become president*. The sentence I just wrote is ridiculously obvious. But I submit that in the strange case of Donald Trump, the reverse sequence captures better the psychological reality at play: Donald Trump *wanted to be president in order to win the election*. Winning was the only goal—sitting in the Oval Office and performing the functions of the president, well, that was/is effectively the after-the-fact means to the ultimate end of winning. The presidency turns out to be something of an afterthought.

A week or two before he was sworn into office, Donald Trump told his aides "to think about each presidential day as an episode in a television show in which he vanquishes rivals," as reported in a Trump interview with *The New York Times*. On his first day in office, President Trump filed papers to become a candidate for the 2020 presidential campaign. He needed to keep the war going, to keep moving from one battle to the next, to sustain the animating episodic psychology of victory-versus-defeat. "There has never been a more dangerous time," Trump repeatedly claimed during the presidential campaign, reprising a central assertion in his campaign manifesto, *Crippled America*. Once he was sworn into office, he reinforced the message in these stark and startling lines from his inaugural address:

> Mothers and children trapped in poverty in our inner cities, rusted-out factories scattered like tombstones across the landscape of our nation. An education system flush with cash but which leaves our young and beautiful students deprived of all knowledge. And the crime and the gangs that have stolen too many lives and robbed our country of so much unrealized potential. The American *carnage* stops here and stops right now.

In Trump's (and his speechwriters') defense, there is little doubt that the United States of America faced overwhelming challenges in January 2017, when President Trump spoke these words. Among the most difficult challenges was the erosion of high-paying working-class jobs in America, an issue that Trump underscored throughout the campaign. But the nation's crime rate had plunged to near historic lows by January 2017. The economy was recovering fairly well from the devastating recession of 2008. It is hard to believe that any other candidate in the 2016 election, Republican or Democratic, would have given a speech like this one, had he or she won the presidency. It is very unlikely that another president would look upon the nation and perceive raging chaos and carnage in January 2017. The origin of President Trump's imagery lies mainly in his own imagination, rather than in the world onto which he projects the imagery. Whenever or wherever he looks outside of himself, he sees the dangerous world that his mind conjured up for him so long ago. It is the same world his father perceived back in the 1950s when, accompanied by his favorite son, he paid visits to the apartment buildings he owned, determined to collect rents from delinquent tenants, who might shoot through the door.

Endless conflict. Chaos and carnage. A hypercompetitive vortex that swallows nearly everybody up, or chews them up and spits them out, even as a few of the fittest survive. The Hobbesian hell in which a small number of superheroes—indeed, maybe only one—still manage to make it big, and I mean really big. This menacing and melodramatic world view may frighten even Donald Trump, but it is also strangely appealing to him. It keeps him focused like a laser beam on the here-and-now moment, so focused that there is no time and no perspective to step back and apprehend a potentially larger story about what the fighting is ultimately for, what higher end he (and we) may seek to accomplish in the long run, no story for himself, no story for the country. In President Trump's episodic mind, there can be no overarching aspirational story for the nation he leads, because he has never been able, or inclined, to create such a narrative for his own life. For Trump and for Trump's America, it is solely about winning the battle we face today. And continuing to win.

Deal

"I guess I look at everything like a deal," Donald Trump told a television host long ago. "Deals are my art form," he once wrote. "Other people paint beautifully on canvas or write wonderful poetry. I like making deals, preferably big deals."

The Trumps have been making deals in America for over 120 years. It began with Friedrich Trump, a gangly 16-year-old boy from the German village of Kallstadt, as the *SS Eider* transported him and the 504 other immigrants in steerage, filthy and bedraggled, into New York Harbor, October 17, 1885. Approximately one million Germans immigrated to the United States in 1885. Most of them, like Friedrich, were trying to escape poverty. His father had died from a lung disease when Friedrich was eight years old, leaving behind a wife, six children, and a mountain of debt. As a teenager, Friedrich apprenticed as a barber, but job prospects were poor in Kallstadt. Moreover, Friedrich would soon be facing three years of mandatory military service—an outcome that did not appeal to him. Friedrich's oldest sister left for America a year before he did, settling with her new husband in a German section of New York City, on the Lower East Side. After he passed the inspection protocol at the Castle Garden immigration center, Friedrich moved in with his sister and brother-in-law. But he didn't stay long. There was not a lot of money to be made cutting hair, even in the New World. Lured by stories of striking it rich in the American West, Friedrich journeyed to Seattle.

The distinctively American road to the first Trump fortune was paved in gold, prostitution, and audacious deal-making. In 1891, Friedrich bought a cash register, an iron safe, 24 stools, and other fixtures of a seedy establishment called The Poodle Dog, changed its name to The Dairy Restaurant, and began serving hot meals to customers on Washington Street, along a strip filled with saloons, casinos, and prostitutes. He rented out rooms in the back, by the hour. A year later, Friedrich began investing in land. He falsely claimed to have found gold on a plot in the Cascade Mountains, which allowed him to seize control of real estate without shelling out a nickel. Capitalizing on the deal, he built a highly profitable boarding house on the site.

The Strange Case of Donald J. Trump. Dan P. McAdams, Oxford University Press (2020). © Oxford University Press.
DOI: 10.1093/oso/9780197507445.001.0001

After returning to Seattle and launching yet another profitable venture, Friedrich joined the Klondike gold rush in the Yukon, where he and a partner built a hotel and named it The Arctic. It wasn't exactly his grandson's Grand Hyatt, but the Arctic was an establishment that strived to offer the best a man could get. In 1900, a local journalist wrote: "For single men, the Arctic has excellent accommodations as well as the best restaurant in [town], but I would not advise respectable women to go there to sleep as they are liable to hear that which would be repugnant to their feelings and uttered, too, by the depraved of their own sex." Friedrich sold his shares in the hotel around the time that authorities began cracking down on drinking, gambling, and prostitution.

In 1901, Friedrich Trump went back to Germany. Sixteen years after arriving penniless in Manhattan, he was now a wealthy man. He had made his money by making good deals and by exemplifying many of the virtues, as well as the vices, that we Americans have always projected onto our immigrant heritage. Friedrich was ambitious, opportunistic, and supremely hard-working. He demonstrated the kind of relentless drive that is, more often than not, necessary for success among first-generation immigrants in the United States. Gritty and resilient, he did what he had to do to make a fortune.

But what he had to do sometimes violated the moral norms (and laws) that prevail in gentler environments, where life is more comfortable and settled than it was on the wild western frontier of North America in the late 19th century, or perhaps along parts of the southern border of the United States today. Friedrich was probably bolder than most, but there was nothing especially unusual back then and there for an ambitious man to lie about finding gold on a property to lay a claim to mineral rights. To encourage mining and economic development, the government effectively gave the land away if evidence for the presence of precious metals could be shown. The man with the fraudulent claim could, as a result, avoid the burden of having to pay money for the land. You would be an idiot to do anything else, one might argue. The attendant agreement required that the land be used only for mining. It was illegal, therefore, to build a restaurant or boarding house on the parcel. But the laws were not usually enforced. Should they, however, be enforced, Friedrich could quickly unload his shares and escape with the profits. By the time Friedrich left the Yukon behind, he had built up a considerable fortune. A self-made American success story, he planned now to settle down.

Friedrich returned to Germany to get a wife. He found his bride in his old hometown. Elizabeth Christ was only five years old back in 1885, when Friedrich had left Kallstadt for New York City. Sixteen years later she had grown into an attractive and marriageable woman. In the company of Elizabeth, Friedrich returned to the place where his American odyssey had begun, now a married man, planning to live a slower-paced and less-demanding life than he had endured out West and to start a family. But Elizabeth hated New York City and was desperately homesick for Kallstadt. So, the couple returned to Germany, planning to stay. But Kaiser Wilhelm II effectively kicked them back to the United States, threatening to imprison Friedrich because he had, in the German government's mind, dodged the military draft back in the 1880s.

The couple returned to New York City for good in 1905. While working as a barber and a hotel manager, Friedrich invested his Yukon riches in real estate, focusing mainly on the borough of Queens. Over the next few years and into the period of World War I, Friedrich enjoyed the pleasures of raising a family while maintaining and managing the wealth he had accumulated. But misfortune cut him down in the prime of midlife. Walking with his eldest son, Fred, to visit a real estate agent in March 1918, Friedrich began to feel sick. He was soon dead, one of 20 million human beings on the planet who succumbed to the Spanish Flu in the years 1918–1919.

Now a widow, Elizabeth made herself the head of the family real estate business, E. Trump and Son. The "Son" was the teenaged Fred, who showed the same kind of drive and passion to make money that his father had, along with a growing expertise in the building trades. By day, Fred labored on construction crews, developing skills in carpentry, plumbing, and other domains. At night, he took correspondence courses to learn the finer details of the construction business. Fred built his first house at age 17, and used the profits to finance his second. When a residential construction boom swept New York City in the 1920s, E. Trump and Son was ready to build. Fred started one house at a time, but soon the company was building groups of homes in the new subdivisions of Brooklyn and Queens. As the roaring twenties brought unprecedented wealth to many Americans, Fred built bigger houses, on bigger lots, and embellished them with architectural details that appealed to the upwardly mobile clientele. At a time when the average cost of a home in the United States hovered around $8,500, E. Trump and Son was building properties valued at $30,000 and more.

The stock market crashed in 1929, and the Great Depression brought devastation to the New York real estate market. But Fred Trump never lost his mojo. In 1931, he invested in a grocery store, which thrived throughout the Depression years. When law enforcement officials broke up the mortgage firm of Lehrenkrauss & Co. amid charges of fraud, Fred Trump and a partner, William Demm, struck a deal that enabled them to acquire the titles to many distressed properties. Fred used information obtained from the Lehrenkrauss records to buy houses facing foreclosure, buying cheap from sellers who had little choice but to sell. By the end of the 1930s, Fred Trump was piecing together lots in Brooklyn and Queens to create large tracts, building developments that ranged from a dozen houses to hundreds. Taking advantage of loans provided by the newly created Federal Housing Administration (FHA), many New Yorkers were back in the business of buying real estate. And Fred Trump was building many of the FHA subsidized homes they would buy.

Through the war years and after, Fred Trump methodically built a real estate empire. Fred became known in the business for his aggressive acquisition of properties, for the solid quality of the homes he built, his attention to detail, his penny-pinching ways, and his showman's flair. He advertised his properties on huge banners that were hoisted above city beaches. He promoted his housing developments from a 65-foot yacht that shot balloons high into the air. Each balloon contained a coupon for a discount on the purchase of a Trump home. Holding an ax, he once posed with four shapely bathing beauties who stood in the bucket of a bulldozer, a sexy photo by the standards of the day, pitching a Coney Island development.

At the same time, Fred cultivated critical relationships with politicians and other businessmen in New York, while staying on good terms with the mob. When the FHA turned to funding homes for veterans after World War II, Trump partnered with a mob-connected masonry contractor named William "Willie" Tomasello to build the huge Beach Haven project, near Coney Island. Bringing Tomasello into the mix assured that Italian gangsters would not disrupt the smooth supply of bricks, cement, lumber, and hardware. It also opened the door to hiring low-wage, nonunion workers.

We have now reached the 1950s—the decade of Donald Trump's youth. With their five young children and their beautiful home in Jamaica Estates, Queens, Fred and his wife Mary were living the American dream. All seemed to be going swimmingly, until the summer of 1954. On July 12, Fred Trump sat at a witness table in the U.S. Senate, summoned to answer for the $4 million he allegedly skimmed from the government through overcharging and other forms of cheating on FHA-backed housing deals. Indiana Senator Homer Capehart and a number of his colleagues believed that Fred was among a group of real estate developers who had swindled World War II veterans and their families, as well as the American taxpayer. For two grueling hours, Fred Trump explained how the methods he routinely used to squeeze the maximum profit from FHA projects were perfectly legal, if a bit convoluted.

For example, he explained how the land under his Beach Haven development was held in a trust assigned to his children but how six corporations owned the buildings on top. The six corporations paid annual rent to the trust. He explained how he paid himself a general contractor's fee that was included in the original estimate submitted to FHA and how he increased his own take by directing one of his corporations to do business with another. He provided justifications for the extra-high rents he charged and for keeping the extra cash left over from the

FHA building loan after he completed the project. For reasons I do not fully understand, these maneuvers were not technically illegal. They may have been unseemly, and they may have relied on interpretations of the FHA rules that the Roosevelt administration never intended, or perhaps never even imagined, when the FHA was established in the 1930s. But no laws were broken.

With supreme poise and a hint of indignation, Fred Trump told the senators that the windfall profits he raked in were fair compensation for his hard work and business acumen. And let us not forget that he created thousands of good jobs for American construction workers, and built first-rate homes in the process, beautiful homes for American families. The senators should've been thanking him for his service to the nation! Instead, their accusations were, in Fred's words, "very wrong"—"and it hurts me." In the end, the senators concluded that while Fred Trump may have violated the spirit of the FHA program, he had not committed criminal acts. Fred was exonerated, for the most part, but he was nevertheless barred from working with FHA ever again. From that day onward, Fred remained wary of the U.S. government. He never fully trusted the feds again, even to his death in 1999.

***

What is a *deal*? In simple terms, a deal is an arrangement made between different parties regarding an exchange of goods, be they tangible goods like products and services or intangible goods like promises to help, defend, cooperate, or retaliate. A deal aims to satisfy the competing interests of the parties. In business deals, something is always acquired or relinquished (typically bought or sold). For the Trumps, the art of the deal has always been framed in terms of business deals.

Friedrich Trump made deals to establish restaurants and hotels in the great Northwest, during the heady days of a gold rush. His son, Fred, made deals to acquire properties and to build and sell homes in New York, during the decades before and after the Second World War. Long before their famous descendant published *The Art of the Deal*, the grandfather and the father anticipated many of the deal-making guidelines that Donald Trump would embrace. Three basic principles come first to my mind. For each of the three, the pattern is established by his forebears but further elaborated, refined, and magnified, often in spectacular ways, by Donald Trump.

Principle #1: Fill a need

Sigmund Freud once remarked that a father's death is the most important psychological event in a man's life—and all the more important when the "man" is actually a boy. Friedrich lost his father when he was eight years old. The death thrust his family into poverty and sent Friedrich across an ocean. When he arrived in America, Friedrich seized the opportunity to make his fortune by catering to the needs of others, building restaurants and hotels, providing food, booze, and women for men in search of gold. Friedrich's son, Fred, lost his father when he was 12. In a heartbeat, Fred became the man of the family. He wasted little time in mastering the arts of real estate. Like his father, he saw a gaping need, and he rushed in to fill it. New Yorkers needed houses in the 1920s, and they had the money to buy them. E. Trump and Son was Johnny-on-the-spot, eager to give the client what the client needed, or wanted, and was now able to buy.

To fill a need, you first have to perceive that a need exists. The perception can be a creative act. In the 1890s, hundreds of thousands of American men rushed to the great Northwest in hopes of striking it rich. Most of them dreamed of finding gold or hoped to earn good wages in the business of mining. But Friedrich Trump saw it all from a different angle. Where would these men sleep? What would they eat? How might they find diversion? Friedrich rushed in to find a different kind of gold, meeting the basic needs of the miners themselves and others who moved to Seattle, the mining towns of the Cascades, and the Klondike. His son was even more creative in his perceptions. While other businessmen drowned in the tsunami of the Great Depression, Fred Trump kept himself afloat with his grocery store business and kept his eyes wide open for green sprigs of opportunity. He saw an opportunity in the dissolution of Lehrenkrauss & Co., and he rushed in to seize it. As the economy recovered and as the federal government began to involve itself in mortgage lending, Fred was perfectly positioned to fill the renewed need.

Like his father 40 years before, Donald Trump searched for glimmers of opportunities amidst the economic gloom. The decade of the 1970s was not as bad, of course, as the Great Depression, but New York City suffered from a severe real estate slump during the presidential administrations of Gerald Ford and Jimmy Carter. In *The Art of the Deal*, Donald Trump describes how he kept his eyes open, ready to pounce should he see an emerging need:

> I'm basically an optimist, and frankly I saw the city's trouble as a great opportunity for me. Because I grew up in Queens, I believed, perhaps to an irrational degree, that Manhattan was always going to be the best place to live—the center of the world. Whatever troubles the city might be having in the short term, there was no doubt in my mind that things had to turn around ultimately.

The emerging needs that Donald Trump ultimately filled turned out to be more grandiose and, in some cases, rather less tangible than those addressed by Friedrich and Fred. Perhaps because he grew up rich, unlike his grandfather and his father, Donald Trump was more tuned in to what rich people believe they need. And he understood better than nearly anybody else what Americans who aspire to be rich, in the 1980s and beyond, believe that they need, what they desire, what they dream about.

They need something to fulfill their fantasies. In *The Art of the Deal,* Trump scoffs at the detractors who were skeptical of Trump Tower even before it was built. The skeptics were convinced that the glitzy skyscraper on Fifth Avenue would turn out to be too gaudy and brash for sophisticated, wealthy New Yorkers. But Trump had a different clientele in mind: "I'm talking about the wealthy Italian with the beautiful wife and the red Ferrari." He was also talking about, or imagining in his mind's eye, the celebrities and sports stars who would love to own a condominium in such a glamorous building and at such a desirable address. And he was talking about the public who might feel just a little bit rich themselves, in a vicarious sense, simply by traveling up the grand escalator at Trump Tower and admiring the Italian marble and all the gold. In a nutshell, Trump writes, "I play to people's fantasies."

Some of Donald Trump's fiercest critics agree with the author of *The Art of the Deal* that a key to his success in business and in life has always been Trump's uncanny sense of how to fill a human need. The author of *The Confidence Game,* Maria Konnikova, likens Trump's skill to that of history's greatest con men. Believing in P. T. Barnum's adage that a sucker is born every minute, con men know that people need "to believe in something that gives life meaning." Men like Donald Trump are ready to sell that something at the highest price. "Their genius lies in figuring out what, precisely, it is we want, and how they can present themselves as the perfect vehicle for delivering on that desire." What is wrong with catering to people's desires? Critics answer with countless examples, from two-bit snake oil salesmen to Bernie Madoff, when con men promised things that ultimately failed to deliver the intended outcome, or when naïve and unsuspecting buyers agree, as we sometimes do, to deals that end up exploiting us.

Principle #2: Bend the rules

In the history of human deal-making, Friedrich Trump's claiming he spotted gold on a plot of land in the Cascades, when in fact he probably hadn't, hardly registers a blip. Ignoring the law that said he could then only use that fraudulently obtained parcel for the actual mining of minerals was yet another ho-hum event in that same long history. Friedrich was hardly a revolutionary. People have been bending the rules in deal-making, and ignoring them, for as long as deals have been made. Trace it back to the Book of Genesis, when Jacob made an unfair deal with Esau. Back from the hunt, the rather dim and impetuous older brother was nearly starving to death when crafty Jacob offered him a tasty meal in exchange for his birthright. Is it significant that God favors the cheater in this story?

Destiny seemed to favor Fred Trump, even when he bent the rules. Narrowly escaping censure from the U.S. Senate, Fred found ways to work around the express intent of FHA regulations, and he profited handsomely. Was he a cheater? Or did he merely find creative ways to get the maximum return due to him, without technically breaking the law?

In *The Art of the Deal*, Donald Trump never tells the reader to ignore the rules, whether those rules are enshrined in legal systems, moral codes, or basic tenets of decency. But he strongly endorses creative bending, especially when it comes to *norms*. Social norms are implicit expectations regarding how people should act in particular situations or with respect to particular roles. In many interpersonal situations, for instance, people are expected to treat each other in a civil manner and to be honest. If a co-worker smiles and says hello, I am expected to reciprocate in kind. Of course, I won't go to hell if I just walk on by, but the expectation of civility still holds, even if there are situations in life, and surely there are, when it is better to be rude. Regarding honesty, white lies and innocent exaggerations are usually fine, even desirable at times. But we expect people to tell the truth most of the time and in most situations, because if people did not follow this norm, even when it comes to trivial matters, we would find it very difficult to trust each other—and a world without trust does not work well.

What Donald Trump famously labeled "truthful hyperbole" proves to be one of his favorite means of bending the rules and defying the norms. In *The Art of the Deal*, Trump goes so far as to suggest that telling people that things are much bigger or better or more fabulous than, in fact, things really are—hiding the truth, deceiving the viewer—represents a virtuous act of kindness, even empathy! "People want to believe that something is the biggest and the greatest and the most spectacular," he writes. Bringing what I call Principles #2 and #1 together, Trump seems to be saying that bending the rules works in the service of meeting human needs. "That's why a little hyperbole never hurts."

Well, sometimes it hurts more than a little. In an iconic example from *The Art of the Deal*, Trump needed to convince the Holiday Inn board that he was making good progress in building an Atlantic City casino. The truth, however, was that virtually nothing had yet been accomplished. The construction site lay vacant. A week before board members were scheduled to visit the site, Trump hatched a plan:

> I called in my construction supervisor and told him that I wanted to round up every bulldozer and dump truck he could possibly find, and put them to work on my site immediately. Over the next week, I said, I wanted him to transform my two acres of nearly vacant property into the most active construction site

in the history of the world. What the bulldozers and dump trucks did was not important, I said, so long as they did a lot of it. If they got some actual work accomplished, all the better, but if necessary he should have bulldozers pick up dirt from one side and dump it on the other.

When the Holiday Inn board members observed the furious activity of the bulldozers and dump trucks, they concluded (erroneously) that good progress was being made on the construction site. (Apparently only one member noticed that trucks were filling up holes they had just dug! But he was still impressed with all the activity.) "The board walked away from the site absolutely convinced that it was the perfect choice," Trump writes. Three weeks later they signed a partnership agreement.

I admit that I love this story. I enjoy reading how Trump duped the board of directors of a major hotel chain. He did it by violating social norms, a form of rule-bending. At the same time, my reaction stirs up some unease in my emotional brain. After all, the casino in question ultimately failed. Long before its demise, Trump and the board members he had snookered fought each other in bitter court battles. To say the least, things did not work out so well for this deal, although the bulldozer antics probably had little to do with it.

Holiday Inn's CEO, Mike Rose, later reflected on his experiences with Trump: "Donald doesn't play by the rules." "He'll say those are the rules, but then right away he'll ignore them because winning is everything."

Throughout his career as a businessman, Trump has been both lionized and vilified for bending or, in many cases, ignoring the rules. Fans and supporters of his deal-making prowess marvel at the creative ways he circumvents inane or stifling regulations and defies conventional norms. Like successful entrepreneurs and cultural shape-shifters, Trump thinks outside the box. He makes his own rules. He does his own thing. Others may object to the means he has employed but acknowledge that the world described in *The Art of the Deal*—the world of New York real estate—is a very tough environment. Those who dutifully comply with the rules in that setting will lose the shirts off their backs, apologists claim.

But the deals you and I make every day are rarely made with reference to the New York real estate market. Therefore, we ask ourselves these timeless human questions: How much should we bend the rules? To what extent should we turn our backs on social norms? What would everyday social life be like if we were all like Donald Trump?

Finally, bending the rules shades easily into breaking the rules. Strong suspicions of illegality have shadowed Trump for most of his adult life. In 2017–2018, a team of journalists spent over a year investigating Trump's finances for the 1980s and 1990s, examining a vast trove of confidential tax returns and financial records. They uncovered substantial evidence of legally dubious practices and potential tax fraud on the part of Trump, his family, and his companies. As just one of many examples, Fred Trump loaned his son large sums of money in the 1980s, such that by 1987 Donald Trump's loan debt to his father was at least $11 million. Had Fred simply forgiven the debt, his son would have owed millions in income taxes. Instead, Fred and Donald came up with a different solution that, according to the journalistic team, "appears to constitute both an unreported multimillion-dollar gift and an illegal tax write-off." In essence, Fred Trump spent $15.5 million to buy a percentage share in one of his son's condo towers and then, four years later, sold that stake back to his son for a mere $10,000. Donald's resultant windfall effectively constituted a gift from his father, which Fred never reported to the Internal Revenue Service (IRS). Instead, Fred wrote off the loss, violating federal tax law that prohibits deducting any loss from the sale or exchange of property between members of the same family.

Principle #3: Put on a show

Like a late-night pitchman on cable TV, Fred Trump promoted his product with hoopla and hullabaloo. Ladies and gentlemen, do I have a deal for you! Act now, before it's too late! Just grab one of the thousands of balloons shot high into the air from the Trump Boat Show. Pop the balloon to get your coupon—a happy discount on a beautiful Trump home.

We often think of a "deal" as something that happens behind closed doors—the "backroom deal," the secret agreements formulated in "smoke-filled rooms." In the Broadway musical *Hamilton*, Aaron Burr wants desperately to be "in the room where it happens." He wants to be on the inside, where the political deals are made. The particular room referenced in this context is the place where Thomas Jefferson, James Madison, and Alexander Hamilton famously worked out a landmark compromise: The capital of the United States would move from New York City to the south, and in exchange the federal government would assume New York's debts and the financial burdens of all the other states in the union. A major conceit in the musical is that Hamilton repeatedly acts to keep Burr out of "the room," which is to say, *all* of the rooms, all of the clandestine places where the big deals are made. Burr cannot deal, so he resorts to a duel.

But Trump's way is different. Sure, agreements are made behind closed doors. The details of a real estate contract, or a deal to brand an enterprise with Trump's name, may be worked out behind the scenes. Specific arrangements may be hidden from sight. There is surely a clandestine side to Trump deal-making. He does hide things, as witnessed by the fact that President Trump is the first U.S. chief executive in recent history to refuse to release his tax records. But the social and emotional sensibility of a Trump deal often goes toward public extravaganza, even spectacle. My deals are "grander, more glamorous, and more exciting," Trump writes, in *The Art of the Deal*. They are like performance art, or a Broadway musical.

Trump reports that his mother had a dramatic streak, and a taste for elaborate pomp and celebration—"splendor and magnificence," as Trump describes it. He recalls her watching with fascination the 1953 coronation of Queen Elizabeth II, televised live from Westminster Abbey. As a young man, Trump himself briefly toyed with the idea of making a career in the movies, as a producer: "I was attracted to the glamour of the movies, and I admired guys like Sam Goldwyn, Darryl Zanack, and most of all Louis B. Mayer, whom I considered great showmen." Eventually he starred in his own television show.

Two decades before *The Apprentice* launched, Trump fully understood that staging an elaborate show was not merely something you did to announce or celebrate a deal after the fact, like traditional advertising. The show can be more than that—it can be part of the deal itself. The show frames the deal in terms most favorable to the producer of the show. The show may even make the deal happen. Parties to a possible agreement with Donald Trump may find themselves swept up in a publicity blitz, as Trump leverages for position in public. They are now on the Broadway stage, and all eyes are watching.

To frame a deal in the most extravagantly public way, Trump needs the press. In *The Art of the Deal*, Trump writes that the press "is always hungry for a good story, and the more sensational the better." With mild disdain, he tells the reader that newspaper reporters and the like are just doing their jobs. They can't help it, the fools. Given that we are stuck with the press, we might as well exploit them, Trump writes. Give them what they want: "The point is that if you are a little different, or a little outrageous, or if you do things that are bold or controversial, the press is going to write about you." This is far better than paying for a yacht to shoot paper advertisements into the air. It is free publicity. Trump writes, "From a pure business point of view, the benefits of being written about have far outweighed the drawbacks"—even if what they write is bad. For good deal-making, there is rarely such a thing as bad publicity, especially when it is free.

In sum, Donald Trump followed the leads of his grandfather and father when he built a career in deal-making around these three basic principles: (i) fill a need, (ii) bend the rules, and (iii) put on a show. In *The Art of the Deal* and through the countless deals he has made in the years that followed, Trump added two more.

Principle #4: Exert maximal pressure

Imagine that you knew nothing about Donald Trump except that he is a businessman who wrote a best-selling book entitled, *The Art of the Deal*. What

might you predict about the book? You might imagine that the author has specific expertise to impart about how to position yourself in negotiations with rival
parties, how to respond to different opening bids, what to do when deal-making
reaches an impasse. You might expect the author to write about different kinds
of deals that might be made, different strategies to employ in different situations,
and so on. The book might contain riffs on negotiation, persuasion, compromise,
trade-offs, and cost–benefit analyses. Deal-making is complex, right? So complex, so nuanced that it rises to an *art* form. There must be artistry in the art.

But you would be wrong. *The Art of the Deal* is mainly a treatise on *power*.

"My style of deal-making is quite simple and straightforward," Trump writes
at the beginning of Chapter 2 of *The Art of the Deal*, where he breaks the deal
down into its basic "elements." "I aim very high and then I just keep pushing
and pushing and pushing to get what I'm after." "Push" almost always comes to
"shove" in Trump deals. To get what you want in a deal, you must "use your leverage" and always "fight back." You must exert maximal pressure and never let up.

You begin a deal by projecting bigness. You "think big" in the sense of
envisioning an ambitious end. But you also need to *look big*. You need to come
across as fearsome and intimidating, and unshakable in your confidence. Make
the other side think that the deal at hand, even a very big deal, is of little importance to you. You don't really give a shit. You could take it or leave it. "The
worst thing you can possibly do in a deal is seem desperate to make it," Trump
writes. "That makes the other guy smell blood, and then you're dead." Instead,
you must "deal from strength, and leverage is the biggest strength you have." As
Trump defines it, leverage is "having something the other guy wants. Or better
yet, needs. Or best of all, simply can't do without." *Make him beg for it.*

In most deals, the "other guy" is, deep down, a "loser." "Most people think
small," Trump observes, "because most people are afraid of success, afraid of
making decisions, afraid of winning." You must exploit the loser's weaknesses
and thereby win. In many cases, this means calling the loser out, exposing his
pitiful impotence to the world. "Sometimes, part of making a deal is denigrating
your competition," Trump admits. He provides many examples. Sometimes the
"competition" is made up of the outside critics of the deal, like the architectural
critics who lampooned the gaudiness and the glitz of Trump Tower, or the city
officials who refused to give Trump a tax break for a particular property deal.
When those kinds of losers "treat me badly or try to take advantage of me, my
general attitude, all my life, has been to fight back very hard."

Trump projected bigness and force when he sat down with Tom Griffin at the
Cock & Bull restaurant in 2006 to work out a deal for the purchase of the Menie
Estate. Griffin owned the expanse of dunes and grasslands just outside Aberdeen,
Scotland. He was interested in selling the property. For his part, Trump wanted
to convert the estate into a luxury golf resort. In negotiating the terms of the sale,

Trump made one outlandish demand after another, bargaining hard on even the most trivial details. He never quit pushing. He applied maximal pressure throughout. Eventually, Trump wore Griffin down.

The same script had played out many times before. In *The Art of the Deal*, Trump describes the endless battles he fought with various committees and constituencies in the late 1970s in an effort to secure a deal for a new convention center in Manhattan. He writes: "In the end, we won by wearing everybody else down." "We never gave up, and the opposition slowly began to melt away." In the real "end," however, Trump lost the deal. Years later the city awarded the contracts for the Jacob Javits Convention Center to a rival group.

In Scotland, the deal for the Menie Estate did not end when Tom Griffin finally gave in and made the sale. Trump also needed to secure the sale of adjacent properties in the area, and a few of those local residents refused to sell. In retaliation, Trump ridiculed the losers in newspapers and on the *Late Show with David Letterman*, describing the locals as rubes who lived in "disgusting" ramshackle hovels. Sometimes, part of making a deal is denigrating the competition. Trump's attacks incurred the enmity of millions in the British Isles, inspired an award-winning documentary highly critical of Trump (*You've Been Trumped*), and transformed a local farmer and part-time fisherman named Michael Forbes into a national hero. After painting the words NO GOLF COURSE on his barn and telling Trump he could "take his money and shove it up his arse," Forbes received the 2012 Top Scot honor at the Glenfiddich Spirit of Scotland Awards. That same year, nonetheless, Trump successfully completed construction of the resort.

Principle # 5: Always win

This is the foundational principle, the one upon which the entire edifice of Trump deal-making is built. It is a principle, moreover, that applies beyond the realm of business deals per se. It is the bright lamp, the beacon that guides Trump forward on his episodic journey through life, one moment to the next.

In *The Art of the Deal*, Trump makes a clear distinction between winners and losers, and he is always a winner. When it comes to making deals, Trump was born a winner, he writes. Winning deals "is an ability you're born with. It's in the genes." Trump describes himself as obsessed with winning. "I think of it as almost a controlled neurosis, which is a quality I've noticed in many highly successful entrepreneurs," he writes. For Trump, winning is a zero sum game: If he wins, somebody else has to lose. To win a deal, he has to beat an enemy. The sweetest victories are those in which he beats the toughest enemies. In the New York real estate market, "you are dealing with some of the sharpest, toughest, and most vicious people in the world. I happen to love to go up against these guys, and I love to beat them."

For Donald Trump, winning is a perpetual way of being. "I win, I win, I always win," Trump told Timothy O'Brien, in an interview described for *TrumpNation: The Art of Being the Donald.* "In the end I always win, whether it's in golf, whether it's in tennis, whether it's in life, I just always win. And I tell people I always win, because I do."

In the decade that followed publication of *The Art of the Deal,* Donald Trump suffered a series of monumental financial setbacks. The Atlantic City casino project of bulldozer fame eventually became Harrah's at Trump Plaza. But the business never thrived. He developed a second casino in Atlantic City, Trump Castle, which ended up competing with the first. In 1988, Trump made a deal with the entertainer Merv Griffin and Resorts International to acquire yet another Atlantic City casino, the Taj Mahal. In total, the Taj cost more than $1.1 billion, and Trump personally guaranteed a loan for $75 million. Within a year, the project was hemorrhaging money, and Trump was unable to make the loan payments. During this time, Trump paid $30 million to purchase the largest yacht in the world, the *Trump Princess,* and paid $407.5 million to buy the Plaza Hotel in New York. He also purchased a fleet of planes from the failing Eastern Airlines, hoping to refurbish them for the Trump Shuttle, which would fly upscale passengers up and down the Atlantic seaboard.

In May 2019, Craig Buettner and Susanne Craig of the *New York Times* published a startling exposé of Trump's business losses for the decade running from 1985 to 1994. Based on printouts of tax transcripts from the IRS obtained by the journalists, Trump reported losses of $46.1 million from his casinos, hotels, and apartment buildings in the year 1985 alone. The business losses mounted, year after year: $68.7 million for 1986, $42.2 million for 1987, $30.4 million for 1988, $181.7 million for 1989, and even more in subsequent years. The total loss reported for Trump's core businesses for the 10-year period was a staggering $1.17 billion. Buettner and Craig concluded that from 1985 to 1994, Donald Trump "appears to have lost more money than nearly any other individual American taxpayer"!

At the lowest point in the spiral downward, Trump was $3.2 billion in debt and had personally guaranteed $900 million of that amount. What followed was one of the biggest financial bailouts in American business history. With banks on the hook for the massive loans they had made, Trump was effectively too big to fail. To save themselves, the banks had to save Trump. As Blair (2000) describes it, "nearly ninety financial institutions would be party to the bailout, and about one thousand bankers, lawyers, and accountants would participate in the marathon negotiations." Trump ultimately profited, or at least escaped ruin. The banks had no choice but to keep him going and simply to cut their own losses. Still, Trump did not escape unscathed. He gave up ownership interest in the three casinos, and he had to unload the Plaza, the yacht, and the Trump Shuttle. Also, the banks put Trump on an allowance. For a time, he was forced to limit his personal and household spending to $450,000 a month (which was not easy for him), and his annual salary was capped.

The key psychological point to take home, however, is that no matter how bad it got, no matter how humiliating it might seem to give up so many of your acquisitions and so much control in the wake of so many bad deals, Trump never stopped believing and proclaiming that he was a winner. He lost more money than nearly any other businessman in the United States during a 10-year period. And yet he proclaimed himself a winner throughout. *Always win*. Trump eventually came back from the brink. In the late 1990s and after, Trump rebounded in a big way, through lucrative branding deals, through his success with *The Apprentice*, and, in 2016, by winning the biggest political contest in the universe. As Trump sees it, his travails in the 1990s were solely due to the economic recession, not the bad deals he made, even though the losses began long before the recession kicked in. To this day, Donald Trump still wants you to know that, technically speaking, he never suffered personal bankruptcy in the 1990s. "If I had filed a personal bankruptcy, I don't feel that my comeback story would have been nearly as good a story," Trump told the press. "It would have been a tarnished story."

Let us pause for a moment to consider that last statement. Does it really make sense? Wouldn't it be a *better story* if he *had* failed miserably? If you were scripting *Trump: The Movie*, wouldn't you insist that your hero hit rock bottom in the 1990s, to magnify the dramatic significance of his subsequent ascent? In a great redemptive comeback story, shouldn't the hero *lose to win*? But Donald Trump cannot lose. He must always win—he must win every deal, every moment. The disastrous Taj Mahal deal in Atlantic City was a big win, as Trump sees it. Purchasing the world's biggest and probably most superfluous yacht (and virtually never setting foot on it, by the way) was a brilliant business move!

Trump believes that he would be "tarnished" if he ever had to admit a defeat—in any deal, in any battle, in any moment of his long life of winning. But Trump's self-serving take on all of this works only for the very strange sort of person who fails to see life as a story extended in time, with a plot that progresses from one scene to the next, building to create a narrative arc. As I argue throughout this book, Trump does not see his life as a story with a recognizable arc. Instead, life is a series of discrete scenes, each self-contained and divorced from the remembered past and the imagined future. Each moment presents the protagonist with a new deal to make, which is really a new battle to fight. The narrator of this account insists that the hero win each battle. In doing so, the narrator forfeits the opportunity to create a narrative out of life. There can be no comeback story, because when a hero wins every scene, there is nothing to come back from. There can be no comeback, because there is no story.

***

In the waning days of Bill Clinton's presidency, a North Korean senior military officer walked into the Oval Office to deliver a letter. Vice Marshal Jo Myong-rok had traveled all the way from Pyongyang to present Clinton with a personal invitation from the North Korean leader, Kim Jong-il. If Clinton were to travel to North Korea to meet one on one with Kim, the North Korean leader would negotiate an end to his nation's efforts to build a nuclear arsenal. Clinton turned the offer down. From the American perspective, the North Koreans had violated the terms of a 1994 agreement by secretly purchasing enriched uranium from Pakistan for use in building a nuclear bomb and by testing ballistic missiles. Recent efforts by Secretary of State Madeline Albright to resurrect the old deal, or make a new and better one, had failed. Clinton reasoned that meeting with Kim under these circumstances, before Kim agreed to end his nuclear build-up, would only serve to provide legitimacy for Kim's isolated and despotic regime.

Eighteen years later, President Donald Trump received the same invitation. He accepted it on the spot, even before consulting with aides. Trump reasoned that he could work out a grand deal with Kim Jong-un, the 34-year-old son of and successor to Kim Jong-il. When it comes to the art of making deals, there is simply nobody better, Trump figured. He told the press that previous U.S. presidents were amateurs who "got played" by North Korea, played "like a fiddle." I am a "different kind of leader," he boasted. "We're not going to get played, OK? We're going to hopefully make a deal." Looking forward to the one-on-one meeting, Trump predicted he would be able to tell "in one minute" if a deal with Kim would be successful. "Just my touch, my feel," he said. "It's what I do."

In the 18 years between the two invitations, relations between North Korea and the United States had gone steadily from bad to worse. After 9/11, President George W. Bush famously declared that North Korea, Iraq, and Iran were three outlaw states that comprise an "axis of evil." In 2002, North Korea expelled outside inspectors from the International Atomic Energy Agency and doubled down its efforts to build nuclear weapons. Between 2002 and 2009, negotiations between North Korea and a group of five other nations—China, Japan, Russia, Great Britain, and the United States—produced nothing. The Obama administration ramped up economic pressure on North Korea, but North Korea refused to slow down its nuclear build up.

In his first year in office, President Trump went on the verbal offensive. In response to increased nuclear and long-range missile testing on the part of North Korea, Trump mocked Kim and called him "Little Rocket Man." In August 2017, he declared that if North Korea continued to pose a nuclear threat to the United States, he would "totally destroy" the nation, unleashing "fire and fury like the world has never seen." Undeterred, North Korea became a credible nuclear threat: U.S. intelligence agencies estimated that as of early 2018 North Korea had developed between 20 and 60 nuclear weapons and a vast missile program that included intercontinental missiles capable of reaching the United States mainland and mobile missiles that could be hidden in tunnels.

Relations between North Korea and South Korea took a surprising turn for the better, however, in early 2018 when the two enemy nations, technically still at war, agreed to sponsor joint teams and activities at the Winter Olympics. A ruthless autocrat (he purged the government of officials not completely loyal to him, to the point of ordering the assassination of his own uncle), Kim Jong-un suddenly went on an international charm offensive. He signaled a willingness to suspend, and perhaps even dismantle, the North Korean nuclear program. He expressed enthusiasm about signing a treaty that would officially end the Korean War, suspended by a truce since 1953. He became the first North Korean leader ever to visit South Korea. Kim and the leader of South Korea, Moon Jae-in, developed a positive rapport. Moon began to serve as the main broker for an historic meeting between the leaders of the United States and North Korea.

The brief meeting took place on June 12, 2018, in Singapore. In a carefully choreographed encounter, Kim and Trump strode toward each other on a red carpet, arms extended. After posing in front of a wall of American and North Korean flags, the two leaders retreated with their respective interpreters to a private room to make a deal. A few hours later, they issued a joint statement. Kim and Trump agreed to work toward "denuclearization" of the Korean Peninsula. Trump also agreed to suspend joint military exercises with South Korea. They left the details to be worked out in future negotiations.

The president's approach to the North Korean case put on vivid display all five principles of Trump deal-making. For each of the five, however, there emerged a surprising twist or reversal.

Fill a need.

Upon receipt of the invitation from North Korea, Trump immediately saw a golden opportunity to strike a deal by providing his "customer"—Kim Jong-un—with something that Kim desperately needed. Years of economic sanctions had taken a terrible toll on the North Korean people. The impoverished nation was in desperate need of food, fuel, and economic resources. In response, Trump's team produced a slick, 4-minute video that showed Mr. Kim a gleaming vision of a prosperous, nuclear-free North Korea, complete with bullet trains and luxurious office towers. I "think of it from a real estate perspective," Trump quipped. The North Koreans "have great beaches," he told reporters. "You see that whenever they're exploding their cannons into the ocean, right? I said, 'Boy, look at that view. Wouldn't that make a great condo behind?' And I explained, I said, 'You know, instead of doing that, you could have the best hotels in the world right there.'"

The twist here is that Trump picked the wrong need, or at best a secondary need. The North Koreans needed resources, no doubt. But Kim's top priorities were, and always have been, *security* and *legitimacy*. "For them [the North Korean leadership] 'getting rich' is a secondary consideration," concluded William Perry, former secretary of state who negotiated with North Korea in the 1990s. "If I learned anything in dealing with them, it's that their security is pre-eminent." Jung H. Pak, a senior fellow at the Brookings Institution and an expert on North Korea, agreed. Trump imagined that Kim was a businessman who wants to get rich, Pak observed: "What he's forgetting is that Kim isn't looking for wealth," Pak said. "He has all the wealth in the country. He's looking for legitimacy."

Ironically, legitimacy is exactly what Trump gave Kim, by simply agreeing to a face-to-face meeting in the first place. Trump filled a vital need, although not the one he thought he was filling. Presidents Clinton, Bush, and Obama were never willing to grant legitimacy without first extracting concrete concessions from the North. Trump, by contrast, gave it away for free.

Bend the rules.

President Trump broke the diplomatic rules and shattered the norms when he agreed to meet face-to-face with Kim. Over 300 years ago, Francois de Callieres outlined the typical protocols that governments—or what de Callieres described as "sovereign princes"—should follow in formulating international agreements. Published in 1716, *The Art of Diplomacy* describes the process as slow and painstaking. Low-level diplomats should meet first to hammer out the details. Behind the scenes, experts should spell out all the complex contingencies before summoning forth the leaders, who then may arrive on the scene for the final, tri-umphant act, to affirm the big-picture agreement.

Trump turned the normative process on its head by skipping the details and rushing straight to the deal. Not only did he fail to consult with aides and allies be-fore accepting Kim's invitation, but he also refused to sit through detailed briefings in preparation for the Singapore meeting. He showed no interest in learning about the issues involved in dismantling and removing nuclear weapons, closing nu-clear test sites, halting uranium enrichment, ending hydrogen bomb production, disabling nuclear reactors, destroying chemical and biological weapons, or initi-ating and maintaining international inspections of North Korean sites.

It should not be surprising, therefore, that the joint statement issued by Kim and Trump at the end of their brief get-together presented the world with 391 words of vagueness—and nothing new, beyond the U.S. agreement to end military exercises with South Korea. For Kim's part, he merely reaffirmed the same hope to denuclearize that his father affirmed in the 1994 agreement with President Clinton. Indeed, the 1994 agreement, which followed a more conventional diplomatic process, contained a wealth of specific concessions on the part of North Korea, although ultimately, of course, the agreement fell apart.

The twist is that post-Singapore, the United States and North Korea reverted to the conventional diplomatic playbook. No more bending the rules. A week or so after the Singapore summit, they found themselves back to the same square one where they had consistently been over the past two decades, as experts and diplomats tried to hammer out detailed agreements. In July 2018, Secretary of State Mike Pompeo traveled to North Korea to begin the arduous task of working out a step-by-step framework for denuclearization of the Korean Peninsula.

As of mid-2019, the Trump administration still has nothing tangible to show for the North Korea deal. In violation of the spirit of the summit, North Korea has continued to manufacture new intercontinental missiles at a factory near Pyongyang and to produce nuclear fuel. Joseph Yun, a former State Department coordinator for North Korean relations, predicted before the Singapore meeting that President Trump's bending of the diplomatic rules would not be enough to usher in a breakthrough. "If Trump is truly expecting to see a handover of nuclear weapons in six months, without anything in return, that is very unrealistic," Yun said. He predicted that President Trump would be forced back to the conventional, rules-based, step-by-step process that all previous U.S. presidents have followed when it comes to North Korea, "because there is no other way."

Put on a show.

Whenever a U.S. president attends a summit meeting, there is pomp and pageantry. When it is the first-ever meeting with a traditional enemy, the drama is enhanced. Journalists from all over the world descended upon Singapore in June 2018 to witness a truly historic event. As Kim and Trump walked across the red carpet, as they extended their arms in a warm greeting, as Trump gently put his hand on the younger man's shoulder and they posed for photographs in front to their respective nations' flags, and as they then exited the stage with their interpreters to negotiate what might be a deal for the ages, the two leaders put on an exquisitely choreographed show, broadcast live around the globe.

Even before the event, moreover, Trump operated as the supreme showman he has always been, pitching the upcoming deal as the greatest show on earth. Whereas diplomats and world leaders typically tamp down expectations before they enter into delicate international negotiations, Trump ramped up expectations. He promised that he would form a special bond with Kim Jong-un. The leader he once derided as "Little Rocket Man" suddenly became "very honorable." The deal Trump would strike with Kim would be so great that Trump might even win a Nobel Peace Prize. "Everybody thinks" I deserve a Nobel Prize, Trump repeatedly said. At a rally in a Michigan sports complex, supporters began chanting, "Nobel! Nobel!" Knowing that Trump never tires of flattery, South Korea's President Moon Jae-in publicly encouraged the speculation about a Nobel Prize to promote the Singapore summit. The White House Communications Agency even minted commemorative coins, showing the heads of Trump and Kim facing each other to symbolize the "peace talks."

And then in an instant, it was all over. Poof! Promoted as the greatest deal on earth, the Singapore extravaganza turned out to be nothing more than a prime-time meet-and-greet. The show ended before the deal-making began. No second season. Not even a second episode for this Netflix special. Before he was president, Donald Trump put on gala shows to announce deals, cement deals, and make deals happen. The show itself was often an integral part of the deal-making process. In the case of North Korea, however, the show seemed to have no meaningful relation to any kind of deal, mainly because there was no deal to be made—at least not yet. At best, the Singapore show was an advertisement for a deal that might be made in the distant future, which itself might transpire as its own kind of long-running secret show, with different and sundry actors, and with a script so arcane and tedious that not even the most conscientious public broadcasting company would ever be interested in airing it. Or, if you want a more cynical and dangerous interpretation, Singapore may simply have been an elaborately produced one-off. One and done. There may be no second show.

Exert maximal pressure.

Following the leads of President Obama and the United Nations, Trump initially endorsed what he called a "maximum pressure campaign" for North Korea. Even China, the North's traditional ally and patron, cooperated with the international community in 2017 in applying crippling economic sanctions to Kim's regime. The mounting hardship for the North Korean economy, which struggled mightily even without the imposition of sanctions, surely had an effect on Kim Jong-un, and it may be the main factor that pushed him to make overtures to South Korea in 2018 and to the United States. Trump's verbal threats added to the pressure. No other American president had ever explicitly threatened to blow North Korea off the map. When Kim taunted Trump by declaring that he now had the capacity to shoot missiles at the United States mainland, Trump shot back that he, too, had a nuclear button on his desk, and his was "much bigger and more powerful" than Kim's.

As if they had just finished reading Chapter 2 of *The Art of the Deal*, Trump's aides and certain Republican politicians reinforced the idea that Trump needed to project bigness and toughness on the eve of the Singapore meeting. Just before traveling to Singapore, Trump met with leaders of the G-7 for economic talks in Canada. He clashed repeatedly with the American allies at the meeting and ultimately refused to sign a joint communiqué. On his way out of town, Trump accused Canadian Prime Minister Justin Trudeau of treachery in the negotiations, calling him weak and dishonest. On CNN's *State of the Union* program, Trump's economic advisor, Larry Kudlow, said that Trudeau had betrayed the United States, "stabbed us in the back." Mr. Trump "is not going to let a

Canadian prime minister push him around," Kudlow proclaimed. "He is not going to permit any show of weakness on the trip to negotiate with North Korea." Representative Peter T. King, Republican of New York, called the dispute with Canada "a warning shot to Kim Jong-un." By projecting toughness in Canada, King suggested, Trump was signaling to Kim that he better be careful: Don't mess around with an American president!

But Kudlow and King misread Trump's approach in Singapore. Weeks before, Trump toned down the rhetoric, and he compromised on his opening demands. Initially insisting that Kim agree to instant denuclearization without any reciprocal concessions from the American side, Trump softened his bid to allow for the possibility that scaling back Kim's arsenal might indeed take some time and further negotiations. Rather than exert maximal pressure, Trump was all sweetness and light by the time he met Kim on the red carpet. "He's a very talented man," Trump said of Kim. "He's smart, loves his people, he loves his country." And it was Trump, not Kim, who made concessions in Singapore—by agreeing to meet with Kim in the first place and then by agreeing to suspend military exercises with South Korea. Trump said he agreed with Kim that the exercises might seem "provocative" from the perspective of the North. If you give up leverage, you end up getting "played," Trump has always counseled. But in Singapore Trump put aside his maximum pressure campaign. Did he get played?

Always win.

Perhaps Duyeon Kim, a visiting senior fellow at the Korean Peninsula Future Forum in Seoul, read *The Art of the Deal*. Or else he simply observed Donald Trump on the campaign trail and in his first year as American president. Three weeks before the Singapore meeting, Duyeon Kim predicted that President Trump would declare victory at the summit meeting, no matter what: "The reality is that the summit will be a success because Trump will package, sell and call it a success to his supporters" he told a reporter for the *New York Times*. "It unfortunately won't matter what the experts think."

Duyeon Kim was right. Trump proclaimed victory even before he arrived in Singapore. "We're meeting with the chairman [Kim Jong-un] on June 12, and I think it's probably going to be very successful—ultimately a successful process," Trump said on June 1, after an uncertain couple of weeks during which he canceled and then uncanceled the summit. In Singapore, he said: "I feel really great. It's gonna be a great discussion and I think tremendous success. I think it's gonna be really successful, and I think we will have a terrific relationship, I have no doubt." On his way back home from Singapore, Trump announced that he had solved the North Korea problem: "There is no longer a nuclear threat from North Korea." The world "can sleep well tonight."

It is not clear, however, that the world slept any better in the month after the Singapore meeting. And if there was a winner in the "deal," the winner was Kim

Jong-un, many critics maintained. Insisting that the victory was his, Trump boasted in a July 3, 2018, tweet that there had been "no Rocket Man Launches or Nuclear Testing in 8 months. All of Asia is thrilled. Only the Opposition Party [Democrats], which includes the Fake News [mainstream American press], is complaining." "If it were not for me, we would now be at War with North Korea!"

***

Who really won in Singapore? Who lost? As of mid-2019, nearly one year after the historic Singapore summit, it is still too early to know. (A second summit meeting between Kim and Trump, held in Viet Nam in February 2019, was cut short because of lack of progress.) It would seem at first blush that Trump has given up plenty and gotten virtually nothing in return. But if the warm-up in the relationship between the two leaders eventuates in a reduction in the North's nuclear arsenal and the greater integration of that isolated nation into the global community, then Trump might be able to claim a legitimate win in the long run—and a win for the world as well.

For the most part, President Trump's effort to strike a deal with North Korea in the spring and early summer of 2018 showcased the general style of deal-making he first employed in the New York real estate market, features of which seem to have been passed down, as it were, from his father (Fred) and grandfather (Friedrich). During the 2016 presidential campaign, Trump sold himself to the American public as a master in the art of the deal. He lampooned international agreements worked out by previous administrations, such as the Iran nuclear deal and the Paris climate accord. Tapping into a deep vein of frustration and grievance, Trump argued that Americans were the victims of bad deals. Other nations, even our so-called friends (like Canada, Japan, and the European Union), have repeatedly taken advantage of us, Trump said. Moreover, Trump promised to make good deals in Congress. As a nontraditional Republican who effectively owed his party nothing, Trump promised to work with Democrats to pass legislation that would produce good deals for the American people.

In the mind of Donald Trump, the deal represents what psychologists call a *personal schema*, or a pattern of knowing the world. A schema is like a filter through which a person sees and interprets reality. "I guess I look at everything like a deal," Trump has admitted. But is *everything* really like a deal? More to the specific point, does the president of the United States function *mainly* as a dealmaker?

In the 1960s, President Lyndon B. Johnson used his formidable deal-making skills to cajole lawmakers into passing landmark legislation for civil rights and other social programs. Like Trump, Johnson knew how to bend the rules and exert maximal pressure. As with Johnson's efforts to catalyze the passage of legislation and Jimmy Carter's forging a peace treaty between Israel and Egypt in the 1970s, American presidents have sometimes found themselves in the position of trying to negotiate important deals, domestically and internationally. But when we think of consummate dealmakers in the world of politics, we typically first think of master legislators—senators and congresspersons—who twist arms and trade favors to get a law passed, or skilled diplomats (and other technical experts), who haggle and maneuver over long periods of time to work out the intricacies of an international deal, like a peace treaty or a trade agreement. Deal-making is just one thing that a president does and probably not the most common or important thing.

Outside the realm of deals, the president is the commander and chief of the nation's armed forces. The president is the nation's chief executive charged with implementing the laws that Congress has already passed. The president is also the ceremonial/psychological figurehead who is called upon to celebrate American achievements or to console the nation in the wake of tragedy, suffering, or defeat. Presidents appoint federal judges. Presidents set agendas, rally Americans around causes and initiatives, speak out against what they perceive to be wrong or even evil, speak up for those who they feel deserve a public champion, speak out for what they perceive to be good. To this last point, Americans have always perceived their president to be a moral force in the world and a symbol of what it means to be an American.

But let us stick with deals when it comes to Donald Trump, even though there is so much more to a presidency, and let us take stock of the deals he accomplished in the first two years of his presidency—through the spring of 2019. During that period, Trump was vastly more successful in tearing up old deals than making new ones. The book to be written for the first two years of Donald Trump's presidency might be entitled, *The Art of Destroying the Deal.* He took special aim at deals negotiated by the Obama administration. President Trump withdrew American support for the 2015 Iran nuclear deal, even as other signatories to the agreement—the United Kingdom, France, Germany, Russia, and China—held steadfast, insisting that Iran was complying with the tough directives of the agreement. The president took the United States out of the Paris climate accords. Adopted by the consensus of nearly 200 nations, the grand deal affirmed in Paris in December 2015 marked the first-ever international agreement to confront the mortal threat of global climate change. President Trump walked away from the Trans-Pacific Partnership (TPP) trade deal. From NAFTA to NATO, President Trump questioned the need and the very legitimacy of a number of other landmark deals forged by the United States since the end of World War II.

On the plus side, there was one major legislative achievement for the Republican-controlled Congress in 2017–2018. They passed a massive tax cut. Trump certainly supported the cut, but he was not intimately involved in the deal-making that went into the writing of the law and its passage. Nor were any Democrats, even though Trump promised as a candidate to involve members of both parties in pragmatic deal-making. For the most part, Trump ignored Democrats in the first two years of his presidency, except to blame them when deals could not be made. And the list of deals *not made* is very long: the Republican-controlled Congress failed to repeal the Affordable Care Act (Obamacare). Congress failed to pass immigration legislation. Congress failed to pass spending cuts. Congress failed to address the issue of gun control.

Back on the international front, President Trump assigned his son-in-law, Jared Kushner, the task of making a deal for peace between the Israelis and Palestinians. To date, there are no signs of progress on that intractable front. President Trump threatened trade wars against China, the European Union, and other nations who have perennially, according to Trump, taken Americans for suckers. At the same time, he offered to negotiate tough new bilateral deals with individual trading partners—a special deal with Canada on aluminum imports, say, yet another different deal with Japan regarding steel, and so on. Applying the rule of exerting maximal pressure, the administration has expended a great deal of energy in tough trade negotiations with China. Trump prefers bilateral deals, rather than more complex arrangements involving multiple parties. Keep it simple: One on one, mano a mano—as Trump displayed in the run-up to his meeting with Kim Jong-un in Singapore. In each unique case, Trump brings his own inimitable style of deal-making to the table—fill a need, bend the rules, put on a show, exert maximal pressure, and (most important) always, always win.

Is this a viable way to make deals when you are the president of the United States? Among the many critics who would answer "no" is Daniel M. Price, a former advisor on trade to President George W. Bush. When asked to evaluate President Trump's deal-making skills, Price remarked: "What the president seemingly fails to understand is that in foreign policy and in trade policy—unlike real estate transactions—the parties are all repeat players." "The country you insult or seek undue advantage over today you will have to work with again tomorrow." The same idea applies, I would argue, to nearly all opportunities for deal-making that any president of the United States confronts, even deals with Congress. *The parties are all repeat players.* There are no one-offs for presidential deal-making. The president is not trying to convince Kim Jong-un to buy a condo in Trump Tower; nor is he trying to outbid Kim for the rights to develop a vacant lot in Queens. The person who buys the condo or the person who loses (or wins) the bid for the lot in Queens may never see Donald Trump again. Their relationship is (probably) short-term and completely transactional.

When sovereign nations make deals with each other, the repeat players often include the putative leaders of the nations, as well as the particular diplomats and experts who work together to hammer out the details of the agreements. But the more important repeat players are the governments themselves and the various institutions that exist within the respective societies governed. For these repeat players, memory is long-term. If the United States exerts maximum pressure against Nation X when Nation X is at a disadvantage, Nation X will remember the insult for a very long time, long after everybody who was involved with the initial deal is gone. With a new cast of characters and a very keen collective memory, Nation X may turn the tables on the United States later, if it is ever to find itself in an advantageous position. Revenge diplomacy. An eye for an eye.

By contrast, to forge positive and meaningful agreements in these contexts, the various parties must establish the parameters of basic, long-term trust. Parties to the deal must trust each other to abide by the conditions of the deal, to play by the rules in the long run. They must also set up protocols whereby compliance can be verified. "Trust, but verify," President Ronald Reagan often said in discussing potential deals between the United States and the Soviet Union in the 1980s. Both trust and verification require a long-term perspective for deal-making. A long-term perspective in deal-making, and in life, pays homage to the past and the imagined distant future.

Donald Trump is a master, instead, of the short-term game. And here we see how Trump's art of making deals dovetails, psychologically speaking, with his overall understanding of life. If, as he says, Donald Trump "looks at everything like a deal," then he sees his own life as a series of deals, one following another, deal after deal after deal, extending indefinitely backward and forward in time. Psychologically speaking, each deal is a self-contained moment of combat in which he squares off against a tough opponent, determined to win the moment.

He is the episodic man. The central theme in this strange psychological case is Trump's inability or unwillingness to provide a narrative shape to life. He does not see his own life within the frame of a long-term narrative arc. Trump disregards the past and future, for the most part, to live exuberantly in the here-and-now moment. The same seems to follow for Trump's view of the world, which pays no attention to long-term historical trends and reveals very little interest in the formulation of a long-term vision for the future—except to win, and to keep winning. In the strange case of Donald Trump, there is no past, and there is no future. Instead, the hero of this nonstory moves from one contest to the next, moment to moment, deal to deal.

Fill an *immediate* need, *and don't worry about the long-term future consequences.*

Bend the rules, *because the past does not matter.*

Put on a show, *to celebrate the greatness of the here-and-now moment.*

Exert maximal pressure, *because you probably won't see these losers again, so they can't hurt you down the road.*

Always win—*and then move on, ever so quickly, to the next battle.*

Reward

About 5 to 7 million years ago, the evolutionary line that led ultimately to Donald Trump (and to you and me) split off from the one that led to present-day chimpanzees. As we went our own way, the forerunners to our strange species, *Homo sapiens*, evolved into bipedal creatures with big brains and an exquisitely *social* sensibility. In the endless struggle to survive and reproduce, the bygone ancestors of the human race had very little going for them. Compared to many other terrestrial species, we were not particularly strong or speedy. We were not blessed with especially acute sensory abilities, fine-tuned motor systems for capturing prey or avoiding predators, hardened coverings for resisting attack, or special skills of camouflage and perceptual deception. Instead, we survived and ultimately flourished by our wits and by living together in complex social groups.

It is our brainy sociality that distinguishes us from all other species. After we said goodbye to our chimp cousins, we began to adopt an upright posture, walking on two legs and liberating our hands to coordinate more intricately with our brains in the manipulation of physical objects. Approximately two million years ago, our forerunners invented simple stone tools for smashing, cutting, and grinding. These tools proved especially useful in scavenging and scraping meat off of dead animals. About a million years later, we figured out how to cook that meat—perhaps the greatest advance ever in the prehistory of our species. In the ancient Greek myth, Prometheus endured horrific punishment for giving fire to the humans. Zeus knew that the gift would elevate mortals to a position from which they might now threaten the gods. Zeus had a good point. Taming fire was a game changer in human evolution, for it led to cooking, and cooking ultimately led to a host of other developments, social and technological, that shaped human nature in decisive ways.

Our evolutionary ancestors were foragers and hunters who lived together in small groups, cooperating with each other in the group, and sometimes competing, to survive and reproduce. The groups migrated from one location to the next in search of edible plants and animals. With the advent of cooking, the social lives of these hominids gradually became more complex and more stable. The art of cooking became an avocation for certain specialists in the group. Others worked together in the hunt, bringing their bounty back to the group every day so that it could be cooked and shared in common meals. Groups began to

The Strange Case of Donald J. Trump. Dan P. McAdams, Oxford University Press (2020). © Oxford University Press.
DOI: 10.1093/oso/9780197507445.001.0001

organize themselves around campsites, which were the places where the cooking and the common meals happened, and where those not involved in the hunt nor in the gathering of consumable plants—children, those who tended the children, the elderly, and perhaps other specialists whose tasks kept them nearby—tended to gather together and, in our contemporary parlance, hang out. For the itinerant groups of hominids who crisscrossed the African savannah hundreds of thousands of years ago, the campsite became the origin of the human *home*.

When you have a home, you need to defend it. Throughout human prehistory, rival groups often clashed with each other. Putting down stakes for durable, long-term campsites may have ramped up intergroup conflict even more. Members of different groups might now raid each other's campsites. Specialists needed to be groomed—most likely, young men—to defend the site and to invade enemy sites. Other specialists fashioned primitive weapons to be used in hunting and for defending the group.

As the complexity of social life at the campsite intensified, different group members began to specialize in different roles. There were those who cooked, those who raised the children, those who hunted, those who gathered edible plants, those who defended the site against invaders, those who invaded rival sites, those who made weapons, those who fashioned other tools and implements, those who settled disputes among group members (because when has there ever been a human group in which everybody agreed with everybody?), and those who coordinated it all—proto-leaders, teachers, mentors, organizers, and so on. Different group members with their own unique skill sets and behavioral dispositions worked together to accomplish a wide range of group tasks and projects, each of which was too big or complicated for any individual member to accomplish alone. Especially successful and well-functioning groups grew in size and complexity. To accommodate the new cognitive demands that social complexity posed, human brains gradually became bigger, and their computational power increased. Bigger brains correlated with more sociality, and with greater nuance, differentiation, and organization in social life.

Within this intensely social context and amidst the proliferation of social roles, group members strived—as people strive today—to *get along* and to *get ahead*. They worked hard to get along because complex tasks required cooperation and because one's very survival was dependent on maintaining good relations in the group. Gaining the approval of others was, and always will be, a deeply ingrained motive, burned into human nature by the evolution of our ultrasocial species. You couldn't live without the group and without the approval of other group members. Still, group members also worked hard to get ahead, to compete with each other for limited resources, like food, mates, and shelter. There was rarely enough for everybody, and inequality in the distribution of resources was nearly always the norm, as it is today.

Striving to get along and to get ahead, the primordial humans who lived together in groups for the past million years were (and today still are) like *actors*
on a stage. Each performed his or her role in a unique and recognizable way.
As actors, they became known to each other through their *reputations*—by what
they could do in the various roles they performed for the group and the characteristic manner or style in which they repeatedly did it. The tall man with the
bad limp, say, was reputed to work hard, and group members tended to trust
him. Widely known to be ferocious in the hunt, the short man was also viewed
to be sneaky and dishonest. The slim woman who showed special affection for
the short man was known to be humble and sweet, but her sister was generally
viewed to be the most gregarious and socially dominant woman in the group.
Fearful and disoriented, the man with the scar on his forehead rarely left his spot
in the campsite.

On a psychological level, reputations of group members came to be captured
in the social attribution of *personality traits*—broad characteristics that varied
from one group member to the next, like friendliness, compassion, dominance,
anxiousness, courage, inhibition, and honesty. The predispositions that gave rise
to these traits may have resided, as they do today, in the group members themselves, but the differences did not become real and apparent (and the same is
true today) until they were manifest in social life. Each trait revealed itself as
a signature display of behavior and emotion. As they do today, actors in the
group performed behaviors and revealed emotions in ways that were observable
to others, who, in turn, formulated ideas in their minds about the actors they
observed. In this way, reputations were made and people became known to each
other, and to themselves.

Imagine traveling back in time 800,000 years to a campsite in Africa. You are a
member of the species *Homo erectus*, a forerunner to our own. You immediately
face the same challenge we all face today, whether we live in Queens, New York,
or a small village in India: How do I get along and get ahead? To meet the challenge, you need to align yourself with other group members to accomplish important group tasks. You need to develop relationships with different group
members in different role contexts. You need to be able to predict what other
group members will do. Who are the nice ones? Who are the ones you can de-
pend on? Who are the ones to avoid? But how can you tell?

Well, you might try to learn about people and get to know them by talking
to them. Imagine it like doing job interviews. But actually, you cannot do that!
I forgot to tell you that there is no language for *Homo erectus*. They do not speak,
although they probably do a lot of gesturing and grunting. If you are an actor on
this stage, the play is performed as a kind of pantomime. You need to watch the
actors carefully. You need to observe them over periods of time to detect regu-
larities in their behavior and emotional displays. You need to learn what their

reputations are in the group and thereby attribute to them personality traits, recurrent tendencies for which you have no words but which you nonetheless understand to be important features of psychological individuality. And you need to observe yourself as well and imagine what others see when they observe you. This is how you learn who you are in the group, which is who you are more generally, by the way, because human life is first and foremost group life, the life of a social actor.

Among the first things you are likely to notice in observing your fellow group members is that some seem to be even *more social* than the typical social actor. That is to say, some individuals develop reputations as especially outgoing, gregarious, and exuberant social actors—actors who consistently display a tremendous amount of social energy and social dominance, who seem to seek social reward with greater gusto than do the rest of the members of the group.

If you had language, you might label these people *extraverts*. If you were a personality psychologist studying this trait in the early part of the 21st century, you might call it *surgency*—the tendency toward seeking rewards in social contexts. All social actors seek social rewards, of course. But especially surgent social actors, the most extraverted ones in the group, seek out rewards with greater vigor and enthusiasm than do most others. These kinds of people are described (by observers who have language) as especially outgoing, gregarious, sociable, enthusiastic, and socially dominant. Social actors who show the opposite tendencies may be described as especially shy, withdrawn, private, taciturn, and inhibited. Whether the words exist or not, this quality of personality is recognized the world over, and it has probably been recognized in human groups for at least a million years.

Extraversion may be the most recognizable of all personality traits. It may be one of the first things that a social actor learns about another social actor upon an initial meeting. For an ultrasocial species like ours, after all, what could be more recognizable than the differences social actors display in the vigor of their socialness? We have evolved to notice this difference quickly, to make note of it, to accord it special significance in social life. And this all makes sense because extraversion performs an essential function in social life. The personality psychologist Michael Ashton has argued that extraversion's evolutionary function is *to attract and hold the attention of other social actors*. Whether we are talking about groups of *Homo erectus* nearly a million years ago or social life in contemporary London, social actors need to get noticed if they are ever to get along and to get ahead in the groups wherein their lives unfold. They need to attract and to hold the attention of others.

We all need this. And we all strive to attain it in one way or another, even those among us who are shy and socially withdrawn.

But some of us excel on this trait. Highly extraverted people are drawn to so-cial rewards like a heat-seeking missile. Dynamic and relentless, they engage the social world with more verve and vitality than do the rest of us. They are so so-cially dominant, so ebulliently out there in the social world, so energized by (and in) the group, that they cannot help but be noticed by nearly everybody, nearly every single minute. All eyes watch these supremely extraverted social actors, as they dominate the stage.

***

Donald Trump is one of the most extraverted human beings ever to walk the Earth. What gives me the authority to make that claim? Does it rest in my having spent the last 30 years of my life immersed in the scientific literature on personality psychology? Partly, yes. But mainly, my expertise is the same expertise that you have. Making attributions about other people's traits as social actors is not rocket science. It does not require deep psychological insight or any kind of spe-cial training, at least not for most people. Like you, I am a keen social observer. Like you, I am evolutionarily programmed to be that way, by virtue of being a card-carrying member of our ridiculously social species. This is what we do as human beings. We watch each other closely. We check each other out. Based on our observations, we make judgments about each other, judgments that often go in the direction of personality traits. The judgments are not perfect, but they are pretty good.

When you aggregate personality trait judgments to arrive at a consensus about social reputation, the result accurately reflects something important about the person being observed. It is like crowdsourcing—the collective assessment holds substantial validity. Moreover, the person being observed also observes himself or herself and, as a result, attributes trait labels to the self. It turns out that for most personality traits, how others see us (our reputation in their eyes) correlates fairly highly, although not perfectly, of course, with how we see ourselves (our reputation in our own eyes). For the most part, highly extraverted people tend to know that they are highly extraverted. And most people who have observed them over time agree.

Donald Trump knows he is an extravert. Nearly everybody who has ever known him well, or even observed him casually, would say the same thing. This goes for Trump's friends and his enemies alike. Whether you like him or hate him, you surely agree with me that Donald Trump is a very dominant social actor. You surely agree that he moves through life as a social dynamo, relentlessly seeking social reward and attaining high visibility. I challenge you to find me one sane member of our species who, with conviction and evidence, describes Donald Trump as "shy and retiring," or even just "*sort-of* outgoing."

In a 1976 feature story for the *New York Times*, Judy Klemesrud introduced the 30-year-old Donald Trump as a dynamic new force on the New York real estate scene: "*Energy* is a word that frequently pops up in discussions about Donald Trump. Besides being a fast talker, he is a fast walker, a fast eater, a fast business dealer," and a man who moves through life with tremendous social force.

A prominent New York real estate investor, Ben Lambert first met Donald Trump in the 1970s at Le Club, an exclusive Manhattan nightspot. Lambert described his first impression of the young Trump this way: "He was totally different [from other businessmen]. He had a flair. He had enormous creative spirit. He had a great deal of energy and incredible focus."

High levels of energy directed toward the attainment of social reward—that is what extraversion is fundamentally about. Highly extraverted social actors display a lust for social life. With exuberance and verve, they thrust themselves into the social fray, forever on the look-out for social opportunities that promise a positive, feel-good result. Like all of us, highly extraverted people want to feel good in the presence of others. They want approval; they want adoration; they want love; they want all the other rewards that a rich social life can confer upon members of our ultrasocial species. What makes them different, however, is the endless energy and the brio they display in the quest.

In *The Art of the Deal*, Donald Trump described a normal day in the life of an extraverted real estate developer, circa 1985: "There's rarely a day with fewer than fifty [phone] calls, and often it runs to over a hundred. In between, I have at least a dozen meetings." Trump would leave work around 6:30 PM, he wrote, but "I frequently make calls from home until midnight, and all weekend long." "It never stops, and I wouldn't have it any other way."

Back then and still today, Trump gets by with very little sleep. In the wee hours of the morning, he will often whip out his cell phone and, even in his pajamas, interact with millions of Americans via Twitter. On the campaign trail in 2016, Trump was a study in perpetual motion. No other candidate seemed to embrace campaigning with the kind of gusto Trump displayed. No other candidate seemed to have so much fun, as indicated in these early-morning tweets from April 2016:

3:13 AM April 12: "WOW, great new poll—New York! Thank you for your support!"

4:22 AM, April 9: "Bernie Sanders says that Hillary Clinton is unqualified to be president. Based on her decision making ability, I can go along with that!"

5:03 AM, April 8: "So great to be in New York. Catching up on many things (remember, I am still running a major business while I campaign), and loving it!"

Extraversion's emotional dynamism can be conveyed through words, but words are not always necessary. As social actors, our extraversion often comes across to others through facial expressions, body movements, and other non-verbal signs. Social psychologists have done experiments showing that outside observers watching nothing more than a 30-second tape-recording of a professor's lecture can accurately predict students' evaluations of that professor, and this is with the *sound turned off!* It does not seem to matter much what the professor says—only his or her style and demeanor in saying it. Linking these studies to Trump's performance at campaign rallies, one social psychologist remarks that people who watch Trump often respond to "dynamics, to force, to movement, to smiling, to facial expressions that convey authority." Trump "does it with more force. He does it with more energy. Energy is contagious."

When Dr. Jekyll first transformed himself into Mr. Hyde, he immediately felt a burst in energy and vigor. The tempo of his life increased. He found that he now moved more quickly than usual, with more power and exuberance. When inhabiting the persona of Hyde, "I felt younger, lighter, happier in body." "I stretched out my hands, exulting in the freshness of these sensations." Hyde experienced a surging "freedom of the soul," an emancipation of desire pushing him to seek reward.

Extraversion is indeed more about the seeking of rewards than it is about enjoying the rewards once you have obtained them. Prompted by the activity of dopamine circuits in the brain, highly extraverted social actors are driven to pursue positive emotional experiences, whether they come in the form of social approval, fame, or wealth. Indeed, it is the pursuit, more so than the actual attainment of the goal, that extraverts find so gratifying. When the television interviewer Barbara Walters asked Trump in 1987 whether he would like to be *appointed* president of the United States, rather than having to run for the job, Trump said no: "It's the hunt that I believe I love." Riding through Manhattan in his limousine, Trump once said the same sort of thing to journalist Timothy O'Brien, although in a decidedly different context. Admitting to O'Brien that he had some misgivings about his pending marriage to Melania Knauss, Trump said: "It's all in the hunt and once you get it, it loses some of its energy." "I think competitive, successful men feel that way about women. Don't you agree? Really, don't you agree?"

Let me add, however, that once Trump "gets" it, he is certainly capable of enjoying what he gets. Like most highly extraverted people, Trump may find the chase to be the best part of seeking rewards. The chase itself is rewarding. It is a contest to win. But there is still something to be said for enjoying what comes your way after the chase is over—after you win. To the victor go the spoils. Extraversion is one of the greatest gifts in human personality because it offers the recipient a double dose of social reward. First, there is the intrinsic reward of the hunt itself—the joy and exhilaration that are inherent in the process of seeking out social rewards, the appetitive thrill you feel in going after what you want, anticipating the fabulous consequences that may be just around the corner, feeling reward in seeking reward. Second, there is the consummatory joy you experience in savoring the achievement itself, the joy of having the rewarding thing, person, or moment that you sought to get when you first set out to get it. In many instances, moreover, extraverts do not have a precise goal in mind. They just jump in—because they like jumping in and because they figure that *something* good will probably come their way as a result.

The double dose of reward may be the main reason that extraverted people tend to be happier than people who fall on the more introverted end of the continuum. Yes, *extraverts tend to be happier*—this is one of the most well-documented findings in the science of personality psychology. To defuse the anger that my students express when I report this empirical finding to them, I am quick to add that there are always exceptions to the statistical rule. There are miserable extraverts out there, and there are many introverted people who report bliss and endless happiness in their lives. But the statistical finding still holds as a general trend.

The solid linkage between extraversion and happiness shows up in unexpected ways on occasion. For example, in one study that I always feature in extraversion lectures for my personality class, researchers found that people who score high on well-validated self-report scales of extraversion tend to report higher levels of happiness *even when they are alone*. Imagine two young women sitting on the same beach, a mile apart from each other. One happens to score high on an extraversion test, and the other scores low. They are each reading *this* book. Okay, it could be any book. Say it is *Pride and Prejudice*. Which of these two women enjoys reading the book more? Research suggests that the extraverted woman will report a slightly higher level of enjoyment. I swear it is true. You can look it up.

Whether they are sitting alone on the beach or mingling at a cocktail party, extraverted people carry with them more optimism and positive emotionality than do the rest of us. The reservoir of good cheer supports self-confidence, especially during difficult times. As his casinos failed and his debts mounted in the 1990s, Donald Trump faced the prospect of financial ruin. Throughout it all, nonetheless, he projected optimism and confidence. "I would have been looking for the nearest building to jump off of," remarked Stephen Bollenbach, one of Trump's associates during that dark period. But "he just remained upbeat all of the time." "He has this very optimistic approach to the world." As Trump himself describes it, "the mind can overcome any obstacle." "I never think of the negative."

Donald Trump believes in "The Power of Positive Thinking," which is the famous title of Reverend Norman Vincent Peale's self-help book, first published when Trump was six years old. Peale proclaimed his upbeat message on a radio show, as well, and in a magazine featuring inspirational stories for businessmen. Donald Trump probably did not need to read Peale's book, nor listen to his radio broadcasts, because Trump seemed to follow Peale's precepts on instinct, as many extraverts do. It is as if Peale set out to formulate a theology of American extraversion, tailored for 1950s American capitalism. Peale urged his readers to repeat this phrase over and over: "God gives me the power to attain what I really want." God will help you "actualize" your dreams of "prosperity, achievement, success." "Learn to pray big prayers," Peale wrote, for "God will rate you according to the size of your prayers." The Trump family had a special connection to Peale. They occasionally attended Manhattan's Marble Collegiate Church, where Reverend Peale presided. Peale also officiated at Donald Trump's first wedding.

The power of positive thinking urges the social actor to pray big, think big, to make bold plans, to take big risks. A long line of research in personality science documents strong links between extraversion and risk-taking. In gambling and in life, extraverted people place bigger bets, fully expecting they will win. They may throw caution to the wind when confronting risk. Impulsive and spontaneous, they eagerly embrace yet another opportunity for reward. Examples in Donald Trump's life are legion, too many to list. "Sometimes it pays to be a little wild," Trump advised in *The Art of the Deal*. Long before he wrote the book, Trump seemed to follow the advice. In grade school, he developed a reputation as a mischief-maker, willing to take risks to attract attention or to come out on top. One classmate recalls that Donald and his best friend, Peter Brant, got into mischief constantly, throwing spitballs, cracking jokes, and acting out in brash and unruly ways to get attention from their classmates. "They were extremely competitive and had to be on top whichever way they could. They really pushed the limits of authority and what they could get away with."

Every extravert deploys the trait in a unique way. In the strange case of Donald Trump, extraversion magnifies his emotional presence *in the moment*. He is a man without a story, bereft of an internalized and evolving narrative that explains (to himself and to others) who he is, how he came to be, and where his life may be going in the future. There is very little by way of a reconstructed past in the autobiographical mind of Donald Trump. There is very little by way of an imagined, long-term future. The consciousness of the episodic man is confined, instead, to the short-term, to the here and now. Donald Trump moves boldly from one scene in life to the next, striving with all his heart to win each scene. He is not linking the current scene wherein he finds himself to a narrative arc of previous scenes. He is not looking too far forward, either. Instead, he is with you now, in all his extraverted glory, brimming with dynamism and emotionality. There is no holding back for Donald Trump, no saving his emotional energy for the next chapter in the story, because there is no story going forward (or back). He is all there. And he is so much there, emotionally speaking, that he overwhelms the scene. You are riveted.

Trump's emotional resonance is mesmerizing, reported Branche Sprague, who worked closely with him in the 1980s. Back then, Trump "was very good looking; blond, thin, athletic. He could talk to you, and I saw him do it, to famous and important people, he could talk to you, and these people felt like they were the only person in the world. It was like he hypnotized them," Ms. Sprague recalled, in an interview with Timothy O'Brien for *TrumpNation*. "I don't know how he did it, and I never saw anybody replicate it. He didn't make it up, he didn't hone it, he was always that way."

While Sprague focused on small-scale social interactions, the same animal magnetism fills the arena at Trump's political rallies. Extraverts tend to project high levels of positive emotion, like joy and excitement. At Trump rallies, excitement spreads through the crowd like wildfire. And anger, too. Trump channels excitement and anger like no other politician in recent memory—and his supporters love him for this. Most people think of anger as a negative emotion, and there is truth in this belief. But psychological research, and perhaps your own personal experience, also attests to anger's positive features. It sometimes feels good, and deeply cathartic, to express anger. And anger often motivates people to act. Unlike the prototypical negative emotions of sadness and anxiety, anger pushes social actors to assert themselves forcefully, to attack. Extraverts sometimes use anger to energize their quest for social reward. But very few of them do it as masterfully as Trump does.

Unlike the crowds who flocked to hear Ronald Reagan give his speeches in the 1980s or Barack Obama just a few years ago, I submit that Trump's supporters do not attend his rallies because they admire the man, although many of them do. Nor do they attend because they want to be like Mr. Trump someday. I suspect that only a tiny minority of evangelical Christians, millions of whom voted for Trump in 2016, see Trump as a role model for their lives. Perhaps not a single one of them does; he is no Jesus. Trump supporters do not go to his rallies for inspiration. They do not go to learn where their candidate, now their president, stands on the issues. They attend the rallies, instead, because *they are thrilled to be there*. In ways that Reagan or Obama could never achieve, Trump brings the crowds in, and sends them home happy, by virtue of raw emotional resonance. One of his most effective tactics for winning the crowd is humor, biting and sarcastic, welling up from a vast subterranean cavern of anger. Trump entertains the crowd. He makes them laugh. He quickens the pulse and ignites their emotions.

In sum, sky-high extraversion is Donald Trump's greatest psychological resource. On this extraordinarily consequential dimension of personality, Trump is one of history's all-time winners. You would be making a very big mistake to underestimate the positive power of extraversion in the life of Donald Trump. As much as anything else, extraversion accounts for his success in business and in the entertainment world. I hesitate to state the obvious, because it is *so* obvious, but without his unique brand of unbridled extraversion, Trump would never have set foot in the Oval Office.

Psychologists know more about the trait of extraversion than they know about nearly anything else. And what they know, based on decades of research, is that extraversion is generally a force for good in the lives of social actors. Of course, you can have too much of a good thing. High levels of extraversion, for example, can sometimes shade into what clinicians call hypomania, a frenetic condition that keeps a person from settling into a happy and successful life. We can all name especially outgoing and sociable people, highly extraverted, who drive us crazy, or repel us. You may feel that way about Donald Trump.

In terms of overall trends, nonetheless, high levels of extraversion are associated with many good outcomes, not the least of which are higher levels of happiness, better social skills, broader and deeper friendship networks, greater success in business, higher ratings on leadership potential, and a lower likelihood of suffering from debilitating mental illnesses like depression and anxiety disorders. Consulting the research literature, I can also list a vanishingly small number of bad things that tend to be statistically associated with high extraversion, like juvenile delinquency and susceptibility to alcohol and drug abuse. But Donald Trump was never arrested as a juvenile. He does not drink, and he has never done drugs. So, there you have it.

***

Human beings have been attributing personality traits to each other for at least a million years. As social actors striving to get along and get ahead in complex groups, we have been checking each other out for a very long time, carefully observing and monitoring the behavioral and emotional displays expressed by our fellow group members and by ourselves. For much of that history, the social reputations that formed in our minds to make sense of group life were encoded nonverbally, as inchoate impressions stored in long-term memory. Somewhere along the winding path of evolution, human language emerged, which enabled us to assign words to trait impressions, words like "sociable" and "outgoing." Language made possible a greater level of precision and clarity in the articulation of social reputations. It also paved the way for *gossip*, which is the verbal transmission of reputation from one social actor to the next. Gossip may be the most distinctively human thing we do as ultrasocial animals.

In the years immediately before and after World War II, psychologists hit upon the brilliant idea of mining human language to reveal the structure of dispositional personality traits. In principle, each psychological trait that might be attributed to another social actor, or to the self, should correspond to at least one word in the lexicon, they figured. Therefore, psychologists decided to do this: (i) gather up all the trait words, (ii) sort them into piles based on similarity of content, (iii) develop simple items or questions reflecting the meaning of each pile, (iv) put those items or questions into surveys, (v) ask people to rate themselves or to rate specific other social actors on those items or questions, and (vi) do fancy statistical operations on the responses to the surveys to determine how the items group together. After doing this sort of thing over and over, and drawing from different language traditions, personality psychologists eventually arrived at a working consensus regarding the most basic dimensions of behavioral variability. While rival conceptions still exist, most experts have settled on a relatively simple taxonomy to describe the fundamental ways in which human social actors appear to differ from each other. They call it the Big Five.

> *Extraversion* (sometimes labeled *surgency*): gregariousness, social dominance, enthusiasm, reward-seeking behavior
> *Neuroticism*: anxiety, emotional instability, depressive tendencies, negative emotions
> *Openness*: curiosity, unconventionality, imagination, receptivity to new ideas
> *Conscientiousness*: industriousness, discipline, rule abidance, organization
> *Agreeableness*: warmth, care for others, altruism, compassion, modesty

Think of each of the five dimensions as a broad continuum, ranging from one extreme (say, *very high* extraversion) to the other (*very low* extraversion, or what we might call introversion). The distribution of social actors along each continuum is expected to resemble a bell-shaped curve. In other words, most people fall in the middle of any particular continuum (say, agreeableness), with fewer and fewer people appearing as you go further toward each extreme. Although we might speak of "extraverts" and "introverts" as absolute types, technically speaking there are no pure types; instead, everybody lies somewhere on each continuum. It is like height: Some people are taller than others, but there is no absolute cut-off—say five feet, nine inches—at which point people suddenly go from the short type to the tall type. Each of us has a position on the height continuum, ranging from the shortest person in the world to the tallest. The same logic applies to each of the Big Five.

Think of each of the five dimensions as a *family* of smaller traits. Extraversion, for example, is made up of many smaller dimensions, like gregariousness and social dominance. A person's relative position on each of the small dimensions is not exactly the same within the given family. You may score relatively high on the extraversion dimension, but your gregariousness (being friendly and people-oriented) may be *really* high and your social dominance (being forceful and commanding in social relationships) may be just a *little bit* high. Everybody has a unique profile, and there is considerable nuance within each of the five trait dimensions.

Decades of research findings show that people's relative positions on any given trait dimension are surprisingly stable over time. Donald Trump once said this about his traits: "When I look at myself in the first grade and I look at myself now, I'm basically the same. The temperament is not that different." Trump's claim is perhaps extreme, for children's scores on traits move around quite a bit. Nonetheless, there is some empirical truth in the overall idea that Trump is conveying. If you were one of the most extraverted people in your high-school graduating class, then you will probably find that you are still one of the most extraverted people in that group when you all get together for your 10-year re-union, and probably still at the 20th, although maybe not as much. The relative stability of traits is partly due to heredity. Although researchers have not yet iden-tified particular genes that correspond to particular personality traits, studies of twins reveal a relatively robust effect of genetic predispositions. Nonetheless, en-vironmental factors also play a strong role in shaping traits. And traits *can* and *do* change over time, especially in the early years of life (childhood through young adulthood) but even later (into midlife and beyond), albeit slowly.

In collaboration with 120 historians and other experts, the psychologists Steven J. Rubenzer and Thomas R. Faschingbauer rated all of the former American presidents, from George Washington to George W. Bush, on each of the Big Five trait dimensions. At the top of their list for extraversion were Teddy Roosevelt and Bill Clinton, with George W. Bush coming in at a very high rank as well (#5). Donald Trump out-extraverts them all, in my view. Compared to the general population, politicians have probably always been higher on extra-version. Still, interesting differences within a select population may be noted. At the bottom of the extraversion list was Calvin Coolidge, who served as president from 1923 to 1929. One story has it that a woman sitting next to the introverted President Coolidge at dinner one evening said to him, "Mr. Coolidge, I've made a bet against a fellow who said it was impossible to get more than two words out of you." His priceless reply: "You lose."

I am now going to rate Trump's reputation as a social actor for each of the other four trait dimensions. My long-term argument will be that Trump distinguishes himself dramatically on *two* of the five dimensions (high extraversion and *low* agreeableness), whereas for the other three (neuroticism, openness, and consci-entiousness) he gets mixed, middling, or ambiguous marks. This is not to say that the other three traits are not important in describing Donald Trump as a social actor. They do have bearing, and intimations of these traits will arise in various places in the chapters to follow. But when it comes to Donald Trump's profile on dispositional personality traits, sky-high extraversion and rock-bottom agreeableness are the Big Two (of the Big Five).

Neuroticism

A better name for the neuroticism dimension is *negative emotionality*. People who lie at the high end of this dimension experience high levels of negative emotions, such as sadness, anxiety, fear, shame, guilt, and a sense of vulnerability. Of course, everybody feels negative emotions at one time or another. Human beings evolved to experience negative emotions, so as to signal danger and threat. But some people experience negative emotions with more frequency and greater intensity, whereas others experience them rarely and in relatively mild forms. At one end of the continuum are social actors who are chronically plagued by negative emotional turbulence. At the other end are the stoic ones, the imperturbable social actors who never seem to lose their cool. Think: Barack Obama, preternaturally low on neuroticism, weirdly so, some would say. Ronald Reagan, too. The experts ranked Reagan as the lowest on neuroticism among the presidents. At the top of the list were John Adams and his son John Quincy Adams, along with Richard Nixon and Lyndon Johnson.

Neuroticism is a strong risk factor for mental illness, especially depression and anxiety disorders. Almost by definition, you could say, people at the very high end of the scale may be shading into the realm of psychopathology. High levels of neuroticism are also associated with chronic problems in interpersonal relationships—every kind of relationship you can think of, from casual friendships to relationships with one's boss to marriage. At strong statistical levels, high neuroticism predicts divorce. It is also associated with health problems.

If you try hard to be objective about this, you will see that Donald Trump presents a mixed picture on the trait of neuroticism. He is not calm. There is none of Reagan's or Obama's emotional tranquility. Instead, Trump is emotionally volatile. He seems to have trouble controlling his emotions, especially anger, although some would say that he uses his outbursts for tactical effect. People high in neuroticism often show high levels of hostility. Having said that, Trump rarely, if ever, admits to experiences of sadness or anxiety. If you scour the biographical record on Donald Trump, you will find very few, if any, examples of his expressing outright sadness. It is hard to imagine a depressed Donald Trump. And there are relatively few examples of explicit anxiety or fear. Still, some people might argue that anxiety lurks beneath the surface in Trump's personality, and perhaps they are right. But the traits we attribute to social actors pertain mainly to their widely observed social performance, captured in broad social reputations. With that in mind, I give him a medium score on neuroticism. Probably slightly above the mid-point.

Openness

Whereas extraversion and neuroticism tap mainly into the emotional features of social reputation, openness is more about thinking and cognition. At the high end of the spectrum are actors who are viewed (by themselves and others) to be especially imaginative, innovative, curious, cognitively flexible, and ready to embrace new ideas and experiences. They revel in complexity and ambiguity. At the low end are actors who appear to be more conventional, down-to-earth, cognitively steady and reliable, and resistant to change. They hold to simple truths and clear distinctions, like between right and wrong.

Both ends of the openness scale reveal human virtue: Highly open people may be more creative and nimble, but those low in openness may be more steadfast in their convictions. Which one would you vote for? Openness is the only trait of the Big Five that consistently predicts political orientation: Liberals tend to score higher than conservatives on openness. When it comes to presidents you have known, George W. Bush comes out near the bottom on openness. "I know what I believe, and I believe that what I believe is right," Bush once said, at a conference of world leaders in Italy. "I don't do nuance," he told reporters. The *New York Times* columnist Nicholas Kristof once wrote that George W. Bush was "less interested in ideas than perhaps anybody I have ever interviewed." At the high end of the openness continuum, we find Presidents Thomas Jefferson, John Quincy Adams (a very cerebral but emotionally troubled president), and Abraham Lincoln.

For Trump, the picture is mixed again. Like George W. Bush, he does not seem curious about the world. Trump appears decidedly uninterested in learning new things, even as president. He refuses to read detailed briefings in preparation for meetings with legislators or foreign leaders. He shows no interest in the specific details of social policy. With respect to his daily routines, he is a creature of strong habit, resistant to change. Even as a candidate who jetted all over the country during the presidential campaign, Trump preferred to return home every night, or to one of his resorts, to sleep in a familiar bed.

On the other side of the coin, Trump is a veritable revolutionary when it comes to his conception of the presidency. He refuses to abide by the conventions and norms of the office. To invoke a cliché that never seems to die, people high in openness tend to "think outside the box." And perhaps no president has ever thought so much outside the box as has President Trump. Moreover, people low in openness tend to adhere steadfastly to a core set of principles, rarely changing their basic beliefs and values. They are conventional. But Trump, married three times and alleged to have had numerous affairs, has hardly been conventional in his personal life. Moreover, for the past 30 years, Trump has been all over the map on the hot-button social issues in American society. For most of his adult life, he was pro-choice, but now he vehemently claims to oppose abortion, even going so far as to suggest that women who have abortions should be punished. When George W. Bush launched an invasion of Iraq in 2003, Trump supported the effort. Today, he claims he opposed the war all along. Critics may say that Trump is a hypocrite in these instances; others may chalk it all up to the kind of reputational maneuvering and flip-flopping that politicians often have to do, if they hope to win elections. Either way, these radical shifts in position are not the kind of thing that a person who is extremely low in openness typically does, even if he or she is a politician. My bottom line: relatively low on openness.

Conscientiousness

If you want to be successful and you can pick one trait to help you, pick this one. Social actors who are blessed with high levels of conscientiousness tend to work harder than everybody else. They persevere. They discipline themselves to control their impulses. They stay focused on their life goals. They are orderly. They play by the rules. Those who hold up the low end of the scale tend to be disorganized, undisciplined, undercontrolled, haphazard, inefficient, careless, negligent, undependable, and lazy. It is difficult to predict what they will do from one moment to the next. Their life lacks plan and purpose.

By a wide margin, conscientiousness is the strongest personality predictor of good grades in school and positive reviews at work. It is also the one consistent predictor, among the Big Five, of longevity. People high in conscientiousness live longer. In one famous study, conscientiousness scores obtained from teacher ratings of 10-year old children back in the 1920s turned out to be valid predictors of when those same children, who grew up to become adults, would die. Scoring in the bottom 25% on conscientiousness in that study proved to be a risk factor for an early death on par, statistically speaking, with having high blood cholesterol. We do not know for sure why people high on conscientiousness live longer, but it is probably linked to lower risk-taking and healthier lifestyles. On the list of American presidents, Jimmy Carter ranks very high on conscientiousness, along with the venerable George Washington and the dutiful Woodrow Wilson. Warren Harding, Bill Clinton, and John F. Kennedy rank as the bottom three.

When it comes to the broad domain of conscientiousness, Trump presents a contradictory profile. Throughout his adult life, Trump has been known to be a tireless worker. Going back to the 1970s, he would get up every morning, put on a suit and tie, and throw himself into his work. His dedication to achieving success in real estate and entertainment is a tribute to both sky-high extraversion and no small amount of conscientiousness. His well-known obsessiveness about cleanliness and order fits within the conscientiousness domain, as well.

Having said that, very few people would describe Donald Trump as self-disciplined, at least not with respect to his personal life and his emotional demeanor. Highly conscientious people tend to play by the rules, but Donald Trump does not play by anybody's rules. In his performance as president, moreover, he does not display the kind of serious focus and steady gravitas that highly conscientious presidents have tended to display. The wild disparities on this trait for Trump may reveal the limitations of trait psychology itself. Social reputations are oversimplified generalizations. By their very nature, they gloss over inconsistencies, contradictions, and nuances. Still, the Big Five sketch a broad outline that helps to situate a person, psychologically speaking, in the world of social actors. With all that in mind, then, let us put Trump somewhere in the vast middle when it comes to conscientiousness, shading more toward the low end.

That leaves us with *agreeableness*—to which we now turn.

Venom

As I write the first words of this chapter on August 26, 2018, let me report to you that John McCain died yesterday. Tributes have been pouring in from around the country for the six-term U.S. senator from Arizona, a war hero, and an American icon whom former President Jimmy Carter described today as "a man of honor, a true patriot in the best sense of the word."

McCain's grandfather was an elite naval officer in World War II, and his father served as commander of the entire Pacific fleet in the late 1960s and early 1970s. Following the family tradition, McCain graduated from the U.S. Naval Academy in Annapolis, Maryland, in 1958. He learned to fly attack jets at the Naval Air Station in Pensacola, Florida. He was promoted to lieutenant commander in early 1967, at which time he requested combat duty in the Vietnam War.

On October 26, 1967, John McCain took off on his 23rd bombing mission, part of a 20-plane attack on a heavily defended power plant in Hanoi. A Soviet-made surface-to-air missile tore off the plane's right wing. He was forced to eject. As he was exiting, McCain banged into the side of the plane, resulting in two broken arms and a shattered knee. He plunged into a lake and, with 50 pounds of gear, sank to the bottom. His broken arms useless, he managed to pull the pin of his inflating vest with his teeth. He rose to the surface, gasping desperately for air. North Vietnamese swimmers dragged him to shore, where a mob kicked him and spat upon him. He was bayoneted in the left ankle and groin, and a soldier struck him with a rifle butt, breaking a shoulder. Finally, he was taken to a compound for American prisoners of war, thrown into a cell infested with roaches and rats. Receiving only minimal medical treatment, McCain's injuries left him near death and permanently disabled.

McCain was imprisoned for over five years, two of which were spent in solitary confinement. He was fed only watery pumpkin soup and scraps of bread. He was repeatedly tortured. Eventually, the North Vietnamese learned that McCain's father was a high-ranking naval officer. As a result, they offered McCain the opportunity for early release. He steadfastly refused, adhering to a military code that prisoners be set free in the order captured. McCain was an inspiration for the other imprisoned American soldiers, who all knew that he refused special treatment and continued to defy his captors. Once a group of North Vietnamese dignitaries visited the prison camp, and McCain shrieked at them in furor. "Here's

The Strange Case of Donald J. Trump. Dan P. McAdams, Oxford University Press (2020). © Oxford University Press.
DOI: 10.1093/oso/9780197507445.001.0001

a guy that's all crippled up, all busted up, and he doesn't know if he's going to live to the next day, and he literally blew them out of there with a verbal assault," recalled Jack Van Loan, who witnessed the scene as a fellow prisoner of war. "You can't imagine the example John set for the rest of the camp by doing that."

Two months after the Paris Peace Accords ended American involvement in the war, John McCain was finally released. Upon his return to the United States, he was embraced by President Richard Nixon and California Governor Ronald Reagan and welcomed with celebratory parades. He received the Silver and Bronze Stars, the Distinguished Flying Cross, and other military decorations. McCain had always tried to live up to the high standards set by his illustrious father and grandfather. It was one of his happiest moments, therefore, upon his return from captivity, when John McCain joined his distinguished and greatly venerated father at a dinner one evening. Admiral McCain, in charge of the entire Pacific Theater, was introduced to the full assembly as simply John "McCain's father." That in itself was honor enough.

Donald Trump never served in the military. Less than a year after John McCain was shot down over Hanoi, Trump received a 1-Y medical deferment that kept him from being drafted for the Vietnam War. The Selective Service records do not spell out the nature of the condition. Trump has said that he suffered from bone spurs in his heels. Nonetheless, Trump has always professed strong support for American armed forces, and as president he pushed for hefty increases in defense spending. In the early days of his presidency, he stocked his administration with high-ranking military officers, including Defense Secretary James Mattis (Marine Corps), national security advisors Michael Flynn (Army) and H. R. McMaster (Army), and Chief of Staff John Kelly (Marine Corps). His tough-guy demeanor has generally found favor among military personnel and veterans.

But Trump's veneration of all things military has never extended to John McCain, a man with an independent streak who often spoke out against Trump's views. Shortly after he announced his candidacy for the Republican presidential nomination, Trump was interviewed at the Family Leadership Summit in Ames, Iowa. He asserted that John McCain was effectively a fraud, that he had never been a true war hero. "I like people who weren't captured," Trump said. He claimed that McCain had "done very little for veterans," during his time as a senator. He also belittled McCain for his loss to Barack Obama in the 2008 presidential election. "I don't like losers," Trump quipped.

Two years after Trump's interview in Iowa, McCain left his hospital bed and famously cast a "no" vote on a Senate bill aimed at repealing the Affordable Care Act (Obamacare). The move infuriated Trump: McCain's vote was "sad" and "a horrible, horrible thing." So intense was his animus toward McCain that when President Trump traveled to Fort Drum, New York, in the summer of 2018 to sign a defense bill named in McCain's honor, he refused to utter the senator's name. Even as McCain lay dying of brain cancer, Trump kept up a steady barrage of criticism. At various times, he called McCain a "dummy," "incompetent," and somebody who "let us down." Immediately after McCain's death, Trump stubbornly refused to issue a unifying tribute to the fallen hero, despite two days of desperate entreaties from White House aides, including Vice President Mike Pence and Chief of Staff Kelly. He also refused to fly the White House flag at half-mast during the full period running up to McCain's funeral. Only in the face of widespread and bipartisan outrage did Trump finally reverse himself, issuing a relatively tepid proclamation and lowering the flag.

John McCain occupies an honored place on what would be one of the longer lists to be found anywhere in the world, if such a list of human beings were ever to be compiled. They are the targets of Donald Trump's venom. Let us pause to remember a tiny few of history's more notable victims. I have chosen 11 of them.

1. *Serge Kovaleski.* On November 25, 2015, at a South Carolina campaign rally, Donald Trump mocked a disabled journalist who suffered from a congenital joint condition. Flapping his arms and contorting his voice to mimic Mr. Kovaleski's impairment, Trump expressed his anger over an unflattering story Kovaleski had written 14 years earlier.

2. *Omarosa and other women deemed to be "dogs."* For over a decade, Omarosa Manigault Newman was a loyal protégé of Donald Trump, whom she called her "mentor." An African-American woman who grew up in the housing projects, Omarosa achieved instant celebrity when she appeared in the first season of Trump's reality television series, *The Apprentice.* She served for a time as Director of Communications for the Office of Public Liaison for the president. Trump often expressed fondness for Omarosa, and she reciprocated by defending the president against charges of racial bias. After Omarosa was fired by Chief of Staff Kelly, she wrote a tell-all book about her experiences in the West Wing. On Twitter, President Trump lashed out at "that dog" Omarosa, calling her a "crazed, crying lowlife." The president claimed that Omarosa was hated by other staff members inside the White House and was known to be "vicious, but not smart."

   Going back to his school days, Donald Trump has deployed the word "dog" to target women (and some men) who have earned his wrath. The insult often goes to the woman's appearance. He once sent Gail Collins of the *New York Times* a copy of her own column with her photo circled and the words "The Face of a Dog!" scrawled on it. He has publicly called Arianna Huffington, founder of *HuffPost*, a dog. After the comedian Rosie O'Donnell described Trump as a "snake oil salesman" on television, Trump responded: "I'm worth billions of dollars, and I have to listen to that *fat slob*?" In the run-up to the Republican convention in 2016, Trump threatened to "spill the beans" regarding the mental health history of the wife of his opponent, Senator Ted Cruz. Later Trump posted an unflattering photo of Heidi Cruz alongside a glamorous shot of his own wife, Melania, tweeting: "No need to spill the beans, the images are worth a thousand words." He derided the appearance of a female Republican opponent, Carly Fiorina, by asking, "Can you imagine *that*, the face of our next president?" Moving from politics to Hollywood, Trump once declared on Twitter that Kim Novak, a reclusive elderly actress at the time, "should sue her plastic surgeon." The traumatized Novak went into hiding.

3. *Dusko Markovic.* In May 2017, President Trump attended a NATO summit in Brussels. So that he could position himself in the center for a group photograph, Trump shoved aside the prime minister of Montenegro, Dusko Markovic. When an aide privately told Trump that he may have come across as a little too aggressive with Markovic, Trump is reported to have responded, "Oh, he's just a whiny punk bitch."

4. *Mika Brzezinski and other "crazy" or "evil" women.* Upset with negative coverage he received on MSNBC's television show *Morning Joe*, President Trump lashed out at the show's co-host, Mika Brzezinski. In a series of Twitter posts in June 2017, the president described Ms. Brzezinski as "low IQ Crazy Mika" and as "bleeding badly from a facelift," the latter apparently referring to her appearance months earlier at a social event in Florida. (He described the show's other co-host, Joe Scarborough, as "Psycho Joe.") Trump has repeatedly described California congresswoman Maxine Waters as "crazy" and "low IQ." Complaining to a biographer once about "some nasty shit" that Cher, the singer and actress, once said about him, Trump bragged: "I knocked the shit out of her" on Twitter, "and she never said a thing about me after that."

   During his career as a businessman, Trump developed a special animus for the New York real estate tycoon, Leona Helmsley. (To be fair, Helmsley herself was no stranger to venom, known widely as "The Queen of Mean.") In a *Playboy* interview, Trump described Helmsley as a "vicious, horrible woman," "a truly evil human being," who is "out of her mind." According to Trump, Helmsley "treated employees worse than any human being I've ever witnessed, and I've dealt with some of the toughest human beings alive." "She is a living nightmare, and to be married to her must be like living in hell."

5. *Citizens of "shithole" countries.* In an Oval Office meeting with Senators Dick Durbin and Lindsay Graham in January 2018, President Trump said that he wished the United States would take more immigrants from nations like "Norway" instead of "Haiti" and other "shithole countries" in "Africa." The vulgar remark was greeted with worldwide outrage. A month earlier, an irate Trump complained bitterly that the United States had taken in too many

Haitians and Nigerians, grumbling that the Haitians "all have AIDS" and the Nigerians would, unfortunately, "never go back to their huts" once they saw America. To kick off his presidential campaign in June 2015, Trump famously characterized Mexican immigrants as "rapists" and drug dealers.

6. *Citizens of North Korea.* Donald Trump is the only U.S. president in history to threaten publicly to kill 25 million people, which was the approximate estimate of the population of North Korea when Trump uttered his threat to annihilate the country with nuclear weapons.

7. *Khizr Khan.* With his wife Ghazala by his side, the 66-year-old Khizr Khan, an American Muslim who lost his son in the Iraq War, spoke out against Donald Trump at the 2016 Democratic National Convention. (The son, Captain Humayun Khan, is buried in Arlington National Cemetery, killed at age 27 in an effort to protect his fellow soldiers from a suicide bomber.) Holding up a pocket copy of the U.S. Constitution, Khizr Khan challenged Trump to read it and to look for the words "liberty" and "equal protection of law." Rather than acknowledge the Khan family's tragic loss, Trump responded by suggesting that Hillary Clinton's speechwriters had probably written Khan's words (which is false) and that Ghazala Khan, who stood silent during the speech, was prohibited from speaking because she is a Muslim woman. In a television interview, Trump said: "She probably, maybe she wasn't allowed to have anything to say. You tell me."

8. *Professional football players.* In the fall of 2017, President Trump chastised National Football League (NFL) players who, protesting racial discrimination in American society, refused to stand for the national anthem. In a speech in Huntsville, Alabama, and a series of tweets, Trump called the African-American players "sons of bitches" and urged NFL owners to fire them. His critical remarks, which continued through the 2018 NFL season, ignited a hot controversy about race and sports in the United States.

9. *A fellow cadet at New York Military Academy and a kid Trump saw when he was riding his bike.* Hoping that the discipline of a strict boarding school would tamp down the young Donald Trump's aggressive tendencies, his parents enrolled him in New York Military Academy (NYMA) for his high school years. Authorized to inspect the living quarters of the cadets in Company E, Donald Trump ripped the sheets off of Ted Levine's unmade bed one day and threw them on the floor. This initiated a fight. Donald grabbed Levine by the throat and tried to push him out of a second floor window. Two other students jumped in to prevent Levine from falling. Going back a few years earlier in Trump's life, Steven Nachtigall remembered Donald's jumping off his bicycle and pummeling another boy. The attack must have seemed especially brutal to Nachitgall because six decades later he recalled it this way: "It's kind of like a video snippet that remains in my brain because I think it was so unusual and terrifying at that age."

10. *His second grade music teacher.* As I noted earlier, Trump confessed that he punched his music teacher in the face when he was a second grader. "Even in elementary school, I was a very assertive, aggressive kid," Trump wrote in *The Art of the Deal*. "In the second grade I actually gave a teacher a black eye—I punched my music teacher because I didn't think he knew anything about music and I almost got expelled." Shortly before he died in 2015, the recipient of the alleged punch, Charles Walker, recalled that Donald Trump was a "pain." "There are certain kids who need attention all the time," Walker stated. "He was one of those." When he learned in hospice that Mr. Trump was running for president, Walker told family members: "When that kid was ten, even then he was a little shit."

11. *Little Dennis Burnham.* He was but a toddler when his mother placed Dennis Burnham in a backyard playpen, a few houses down the street from the Trump home. Dennis's mother went inside for a few minutes. She returned to find Donald Trump—five or six years old at the time—hurling rocks at her son.

***

Human beings are social animals. We evolved to live in complex social groups, striving to get along and to get ahead. Like actors on a stage, we perform for each other, displaying characteristic emotional patterns and habitual actions. From an early age, we develop social reputations in our groups based on what others see when they observe our everyday behavior. We learn what those reputations are through interacting with those social actors who observe us. They tell us what we are like, or we deduce it based on how they respond to us. As we observe others, moreover, we also observe ourselves.

Social animals like us are always under surveillance. Long before cell phones and public cameras tracked our behavior, even as hunters and gatherers roaming the African savannah, we watched each other in real time. Long before humans invented language, even, we formulated impressions about each other's dispositions, so that we could cooperate and compete more effectively, so that we could attain success and survival in our self-sustaining groups. When it comes to the observed personalities of fellow social actors, these impressions coalesce into the five basic groupings I described in the last chapter—the Big Five.

There is *extraversion*—the most readily observed of all the traits, pertaining to the relative level of social energy, enthusiasm, and reward seeking a social actor displays. There is *neuroticism*, indexed by recurrent displays of negative emotion, like chronic anxiety and sadness. There is *openness*, which indicates how amenable a social actor is to social change and the degree to which he or she is eager to engage in novel or unconventional behaviors, emotional experiences, and thought patterns. There is *conscientiousness,* or the tendency to direct action and effort toward hard work, to discipline the self, to regulate behavior in accord with internal standards of excellence and goodness.

And there is *agreeableness*—the most valued trait of them all, the one that people across the world and for all time have considered to be the most important human disposition for actors who, for better and for worse, find themselves compelled by evolution to live together in groups. What is agreeableness? Little children know what agreeableness is, for it is so humanly simple and basic, so *humane*. Agreeableness is *how nice you are*.

When our two daughters were preschool age, my wife and I hosted a visiting professor from another university. He spent the night. The next morning, I was trying to settle a loud dispute that had broken out between our young girls. Somebody may have stolen the other's stuffed animal, or perhaps it had to do with different television preferences or just general taunting. Screaming and name-calling were involved. Trying in vain to calm the fracas, I finally yelled out: "Just be nice, damn it!" Our visitor was incredulous. Steeped in moral philosophy, he later joked with me about my parenting style: " 'Just be nice?' 'That's it?"

"Yeah, man!" I said. That's basically what it comes down to. I mean, you can read St. Aquinas or Kant for years. You can study moral enlightenment in a Tibetan monastery or at the Harvard library. You can get a doctorate in child development. But when it comes to raising children to be good social actors in the world, a lot of it is about being nice—being agreeable. A few minutes ago, I told my wife I was writing about the memory of the visiting professor. She immediately sent me a link to a web site advertising note cards, mugs, handbags, and T-shirts that all feature this simple quote: "In a world where you can be anything, be kind."

Donald Trump is not going to wear that T-shirt.

Words like "nice" and "kind" sound pretty namby-pamby. They fail to do full justice to the awesome scope and humanity of the agreeableness trait. Social actors who are seen by others and by themselves as especially high on the dimension of agreeableness are *more than* nice. Agreeableness incorporates the expressive qualities of love and empathy, friendliness, cooperation, and care. Indeed, the very term "agreeableness" may be too meek and mild for a clustering of human traits that includes concepts such as altruism, affection, and many of the most admirably humane aspects of human personality. Social actors at the high end of the agreeableness continuum are interpersonally warm, cooperative, accommodating, helpful, patient, cordial, empathic, understanding, courteous, and sincere. They are also described as especially honest, ethical, and selfless. They are peace-loving humanists, committed to their friends and family and to the social good. By contrast, social actors scoring especially *low* on this disposition receive some of the worst press in all of psychological science. They are antagonistic, belligerent, harsh, unsympathetic, disingenuous, scornful, crude, and cruel. They operate with wanton disregard of other people's feelings. They hurt other people. They constantly fight. In a fundamental sense, disagreeable social actors are *anti*social.

A large body of empirical research on agreeableness documents the wide purview of this seemingly simple trait. Studies show that people scoring high on well-validated measures of agreeableness enjoy happier marriages and a lower divorce rate, compared to those low in agreeableness. People high in agreeableness invest more of themselves into their roles as spouse, parent, and friend, compared to those scoring lower. Mothers who score high in agreeableness demonstrate warmer and more supportive parenting patterns with their children. High agreeableness is statistically associated with experiencing less conflict in interpersonal relationships and demonstrating higher levels of socially positive and altruistic behaviors, like community volunteering. People high in agreeableness are more likely to attend religious services and express stronger religious sentiment. Agreeableness is also an asset for certain occupations, such as customer service and the helping professions. Like any personality trait, however, high levels of agreeableness sometimes come with a down side. For example, one study shows that men (but not women) who score high on agreeableness tend to earn somewhat *lower* salaries than do men low in agreeableness. In some contexts, it pays to be disagreeable.

A little over a decade ago, a team of historians and psychologists rated all of the U.S. presidents—from Washington to George W. Bush—on the Big Five traits. Richard M. Nixon scored the lowest on agreeableness. But that was before Donald Trump. The dark and brooding Nixon was sweetness and light compared to the 45th president of the United States. Even President Trump's strongest supporters describe him as aggressive. President Trump describes himself in the same way, taking pride in his low level of agreeableness. "I have always loved to fight," Trump told one biographer, "all types of fights, including physical." "I love to have enemies," he said in an interview for *Time* magazine in 1989. "I fight my enemies. I like beating my enemies to the ground."

The enjoyment Trump has always experienced in pummeling his enemies—physically when he was a child and verbally as an adult—recalls Mr. Hyde's disagreeable sentiments in *The Strange Case of Dr. Jekyll and Mr. Hyde*. The suppressed persona inside the mind of Dr. Jekyll is the unbridled Donald Trump in the angry moment, with no supervising alter ego. "Instantly the spirit of hell awoke in me and raged," Hyde reported, as he burst forth into consciousness to confront a victim of his wrath. "With a transport of glee, I mauled the unresisting body, taking delight in every blow."

This is not to say that Donald Trump is incapable of being nice. We might point out, for example, that Trump loves his children. He is reported to be a generous and fair-minded boss. Regarding Trump's antipathy toward McCain, it is also true that he tried at one point to mend fences with the senator from Arizona by offering McCain's wife, Cindy McCain, a position in the administration's diplomatic corps. Going back a decade, there is also a famous story about Trump's meeting with a boy who was dying of cancer. A fan of *The Apprentice*, the young boy simply wanted Trump to reprise his famous line from the television show and to tell him, "You're fired!" Trump could not bring himself to do it, but instead wrote the boy a check for several thousand dollars and told him, "Go and have the time of your life." In his biography of Trump, Ronald Kessler writes: "Trump will hand out hundred-dollar bills to janitors or McDonald's cashiers and write checks for tens of thousands of dollars to people he has learned are in distress." Kessler argues that there are "two faces of Donald Trump." But Trump hides the kind and gentle face, Kessler insists, because he does "not want the public to see this side of him and know what he is like behind the scenes."

If Kessler is right, Trump has done a masterful job of hiding that face for over six decades. The Big Five traits, like extraversion and agreeableness, pertain to a social actor's overall style of relating to others and to the world, captured in the broad outlines of a social reputation. Exceptions to the rule on Trump's agreeableness, like the story of the young boy who wanted to be fired or Trump's handing out money to janitors, run against a lifetime tidal wave when it comes to the attribution of this broad personality trait. Trump is a tsunami of disagreeableness. If Donald Trump does not score low on agreeableness, rock bottom low, lower than probably anybody you know, then nobody does.

The venom of disagreeableness finds its daily expression, for President Trump, on Twitter. In regular morning tweets, the president seethes with rage and rails against his enemies. A favorite target of his incendiary outbursts is the press, but there are hundreds of others, including rival politicians (as well as members of his own cabinet), law enforcement officers and the institutions they work for, television celebrities, athletes, and even regular, nearly anonymous American citizens. No target is too big or too small.

On October 24, 2016, the *New York Times* listed "all the people, places, and things Donald Trump has insulted on Twitter since declaring his candidacy for president." On January 29, 2018, the same newspaper listed all targets of his Twitter insults "since being elected president of the United States." The lists, which each cover a period of about 16 months, are staggering, printed in tiny type and filling multiple pages for the newspaper's hard copy. From ABC news to a journalist with the last name of "Zuckerman," Trump employs his favorite words, again and again and again, to lambast his countless enemies: "clown," "crazy," "crooked," "disaster," "disgrace," "disgusting," "dishonest," "dog," "dope," "dumb," "dummy," "failing," "fraud," "hypocrite," "incompetent," "joke," "lightweight," "loser," "nasty," "phony," "rigged," "wacky," "waste," "weak," and "worst."

A month before he was sworn in as president, Trump sent out a tweet highly critical of a United Steelworkers union official named Chuck Jones. In a television interview, Jones had questioned Trump's claim that he had saved 1,100 jobs at an Indiana factory from being shipped overseas. Trump wrote that Jones "has done a terrible job representing workers." "No wonder companies flee country!" For a president-elect to go after a private citizen like this is beyond the pale, argued many at the time. Nicole Wallace, a former communications director for President George W. Bush and top strategist for other Republicans, described Trump's behavior as "dark and disturbing" and labeled it "cyberbullying." "When you attack a man for living an ordinary life in an ordinary job, it is bullying," she said. Robert Dallek, a presidential historian, called the verbal attack "beneath the dignity of the office." David Axelrod, former aide to President Barack Obama, said that Trump seemed not to realize how destructive his tweets could be, coming from the mouth (and fingers) of a U.S. president. "What you might think is a light tap is a howitzer," Axelrod said. "When you have the man in the most powerful office, for whom there is no target too small, that is a chilling prospect. He has the ability to destroy people with 140 characters."

Many of President Trump's admirers regret that he uses Twitter to lash out at his enemies. Even his wife, Melania, has urged him to quit tweeting. The assumption here seems to be that if the president were simply to refrain from typing out these 280-character insults, he would come across as a much more agreeable human being. Apologists are implying that Trump has a kind of "addiction" to Twitter, as if Twitter were the fundamental problem. But the truth is that Twitter is nothing more than an especially efficient tool for conveying the malevolent sentiments that Donald Trump has always held.

Before Twitter, he mailed nasty letters, or made phone calls, or did interviews, relentlessly denigrating his enemies. Richard Branson, the business magnate and investor, recalls a dinner he had with Trump back in the 1990s, a few years after Trump narrowly escaped personal bankruptcy. Trump provided a bitter account of the many businessmen and bankers who ignored him and refused to return his phone calls during the darkest days. "He said he had drawn up a list of 10 of these people and had decided to spend his life trying to destroy them." Branson told Trump that such a vendetta would be a waste of energy. But this kind of disagreeable behavior, through which Trump is able to direct his anger and contempt toward specific enemies, seems to energize him. When the biographer Timothy O'Brien asked Trump to nominate the "best person you've ever met," Trump named his father. When he asked him to nominate the "worst person," Trump responded this way:

> This list is too long to name. I've met more shit. I've met more scum. There are too many to name. I'd insult too many people by leaving somebody out. I can only say I know so many bad people, it's amazing.

One manifestation of very low agreeableness is *dispositional contempt*. A team of researchers led by Roberta Schriber and Rick Robins at the University of California–Davis recently identified dispositional contempt as a relatively stable tendency to look down on and to derogate others. People who score high on this dimension feel superior to other people, especially people deemed to be less powerful or competent. Rather than express compassion, pity, or tolerance for those perceived to be inferior to oneself, contemptuous people write them off as "losers." Contempt can be expressed through icy aloofness or raging fury. Either way, the contemptuous person refuses to waste psychological energy in trying to understand or make sense of those people deemed to be "shit" and "scum." As such, contempt proves to be a coping strategy for difficult interpersonal situations. It is hard work trying to empathize with human beings who fill you with disgust or offend you in some way. It is much easier to brush them aside.

In the extreme netherworld of low agreeableness, we encounter those tendencies and features assigned to the malevolent side of human nature. Violence may be the most notable feature, while empathy is notably absent.

Throughout his life, Donald Trump has been fascinated by violence and attracted to violent men. At NYMA, Trump developed a grudging rapport with the baseball coach Theodore Dobias, a former drill sergeant in the marines. "If you stepped out of line, Dobias smacked you and he smacked you hard," Trump wrote, in *The Art of the Deal*. Trump is awed by warriors, mobsters, and boxers, both real boxers (like Mike Tyson) and pretend (Sylvester Stallone, as Rocky).

Beginning in the late 1980s, Trump participated as a showman in that pretend world of violence known as professional wrestling, hosting WrestleMania IV and V at Trump Plaza in Atlantic City. In 2007, he "dueled" with the wrestling impresario Vince McMahon in "Battle of the Billionaires." The actual fighting was done by proxies—a bald African-American muscleman named Bobby Lashley for Trump and a tattooed hulk known as the Samoan Bulldozer for McMahon. But the real Trump and the real McMahon traded fake insults in front of frenzied crowds. One night, McMahon bragged that he would win their duel because of the size of his "grapefruits" (a reference to testicles, apparently). "Your grapefruits are no match for my Trump Towers," Trump yelled back. As the crowd roared, Trump pushed McMahon over a conference table, sending him into a backward somersault. The announcer shouted: "Donald Trump just shoved Mr. McMahon on his billionaire butt!" On another night, the real Trump smacked the real McMahon in the face, after the promoter playfully touched Trump's cheek. "I gave him a wallop," Trump boasted afterward. It was all fake, of course, as when McMahon later appeared on the *Today* show sporting a (fake) black eye from the "punch."

When it comes to violence, however, the line between fake and real is fuzzy in the life of Donald Trump. On the campaign trail and as president, he has seemed to incite violence, though sometimes his staff has claimed he was joking. In front of crowds as frenzied as WrestleMania, Trump encourages his supporters to rough up protestors. "Get them out of here!" he yells. "Knock the crap out of them." "I'd like to punch that guy in the face." At political rallies, Trump spews vitriol at journalists who are in attendance. He has repeatedly labeled the press "the enemy of the people." As Trump riles up the crowd, reporters covering these events begin to fear for their safety. At a campaign rally in August 2016, Trump famously intimated that guns rights enthusiasts might want to take matters into their own hands should Hillary Clinton win the election and then appoint judges seeking to reign in the Second Amendment. "If she gets to pick her judges, nothing you can do, folks," Trump said to a raucous campaign crowd, as they began to boo. He quickly added: "Although the Second Amendment people—maybe there is, I don't know."

Social actors who occupy the extreme low end of the agreeableness dimension often appear to lack the capacity for empathy, or they refuse to express it. To empathize with another person is to *feel* that person's emotional experience. Most young children experience rudimentary empathy, as when they show sadness in response to another child's pain. Empathy begins close to home, for it is easiest, especially early in life, to feel another's emotions if that other person is similar to the self. As social actors reach higher levels of development, their radius of empathy expands. In modern conceptions of human virtue and morality, we admire people who can empathize with others who are very different from themselves—people of a different gender, age, ethnicity, social class, religion, political persuasion, and so on. Love thy enemy, Jesus counseled in the Gospels. Or at least, try to feel what your enemy feels. Try to inhabit your enemy's emotional space, so that you can understand your enemy better. The more you do that, the fewer enemies you may have.

Donald Trump loves to hate enemies. It would make sense, therefore, that he might not waste empathy on *them*! But what about his friends? What about regular folks who have never offended Donald Trump? It is clear that Donald Trump enjoys being with people who like or admire him. But empathy seems to be a different matter. In his book *A Higher Loyalty*, former FBI director James Comey wrote that Trump seems to lack "the ability to imagine the feelings and perspective of another 'me.' . . . I got the sense that no one ever taught this to Donald Trump." In her book *Unhinged: An Insider's Account of the Trump White House*, Omarosa Manigault Newman observed that during her time as a White House official President Trump "had no empathy for anyone he offended, because he had no empathy for anyone, period."

It is easy to dismiss Comey and Newman as biased observers because both of these public figures were fired by and have become outspoken critics of

President Trump. But others have also noted a lack of empathy with Trump, including biographers as well as aides in his inner circle. Many have remarked that Trump approaches interpersonal relationships in a purely transactional manner—as a momentary exchange or transaction of give and take, a deal to be made. A good transaction is when I get more from the deal than I give. Trump's ghostwriter for *The Art of the Deal*, Tony Schwartz describes Trump as the "transactional man—it [is] all about what you can do for him." "People are dispensable and disposable in Trump's world," Schwartz says. Less cutting but still critical, a long-time associate once observed that Trump "absolutely cannot do small talk." What he meant, in part, is that Trump cannot slow down to focus on another person's mundane thoughts and feelings. Empathy requires a gentle patience, even when chatting casually with a co-worker on a Monday morning.

During the first year of his presidency, Hope Hicks served as communications director at the White House. She was one of Trump's closest aides. Hicks was worried that President Trump might not express the appropriate level of empathy in an upcoming meeting with parents, students, and teachers who had lost loved ones in a Florida school shooting. The president would need to be reminded, Hicks figured, to show compassion and understanding to the traumatized survivors. He would need to express gentle patience. He would need to know that the survivors of the horrific event were not visiting the White House for the purposes of a transaction. Therefore, Hicks prepared special note cards for the president with talking points written in bold letters. "I hear you," Trump was reminded to say. And, "What would you most want me to know about your experience?" Hope Hicks was not so naïve as to think she could teach Mr. Trump to feel what another person feels. But maybe she could teach him to say the right things, to mimic empathy.

***

How did Donald Trump become such a disagreeable person? How do we explain the development of this particular personality trait in the strange case of this particular social actor? A full answer can probably never be known. Personality development remains something of a mystery, involving countless factors and confounding complexities for any given life. Nonetheless, psychological scientists know enough about the development of agreeableness in general, and we have enough information about Trump's life in particular, to offer a reasoned interpretation. Let me take a stab at it now. My psychological story begins with temperament, and it ends with reading.

What he was born with

The broad personality trait of agreeableness develops out of a temperament base that may be recognized at birth, or shortly thereafter. Developmental psychologists use the term *temperament* to refer to broad, stylistic differences in responding to the environment that appear early in human life. These differences reflect genetic endowments, as well as effects on psychological development that may occur in the womb. As any parent who has had more than one child knows, babies are born different. Some of them come into the world chronically cranky and irritable. Others tend to show more positive emotions, exhibiting high levels of smiling and laughter and regularly bursting forth with joy. Some seem to be especially alert early on; others appear more lethargic or slow to warm up.

From all reports, Donald Trump was an active and high-spirited social actor from a very early age. His preschool teacher described him as especially "social" and "outgoing." What was to become Trump's in-your-face brand of ultra-extraversion in adulthood was foreshadowed in his energetic childhood temperament—ever ebullient, approach-oriented, seeking social reward, relentlessly on the make. Some especially sociable children draw their energy from the positive emotions of joy and excitement. Others draw from both positive and negative emotions. Little Donald Trump appears to have landed in the second category. *Excitement* and *anger* were his emotional calling cards. Therefore, by the time he entered Kew-Forest Elementary School, Donald Trump's sociability was beginning to reveal some rough edges. He was highly engaged in the social world, for sure. But he was also highly aggressive.

"I was a very assertive, aggressive kid," Trump wrote in *The Art of the Deal.* A teacher at Kew-Forest remembers him as "headstrong and determined. . . . He would sit with his arms folded, with this look on his face—I use the word *surly*—almost daring you to say one thing or another that wouldn't settle with him." His rambunctious style, moreover, often led to trouble. One fellow student recalled how Donald and his friends regularly disrupted classes with wisecracks and unruly antics. "We threw spitballs and we played racing chairs with our desks, crashing them into other desks," Paul Ornish recalled. Donald spent so much time in detention that his very name became synonymous with the punishment itself. Among his friends, "detention" came to be known as the "DTs"—short for Donny Trumps. At the same time, Donald's aggressiveness found a happier outlet in sports. He played basketball, football, and soccer, and he excelled in baseball, as a right-handed power hitter. On the baseball diamond, "he was fearless," recalled a classmate and good friend named Peter Brant. "If he stole a base, he came in all guns-a-blazing."

Agreeableness is about human warmth and kindness. But it is a *controlled* form of warmth or, to put it more precisely, *control in the service of warmth*. To be a caring and kind person, you have to be able to exert control over powerful urges—immediate and egocentric—that well up in the souls of all children and all adults. Self-control is arguably the greatest challenge that social actors face in their eternal quests to get along and get ahead in complex social groups. Thankfully, human nature comes equipped with a basic temperament disposition whose very job is to tamp down impulses. It is called *effortful control* (EC, for short). Emerging in the second and third years of life, EC is a child's capacity to ignore or postpone immediate urges to pursue a longer-term goal. Metaphorically, it is the ability to stop and take a deep breath, to step back from the emotional fray for just a tiny second, enough time to come up with a good strategy for achieving a valued end. EC enables us to resist temptation, or at least it helps us in our efforts to do so. The value of EC is obvious when it comes to school achievement, work, and other domains of instrumental success. EC promotes self-discipline, which, in turn, helps to build up the trait of conscientiousness.

But the power of EC is equally evident, I would argue, in the realm of agreeableness. It is very difficult to be *nice* to other people if you are unable to look away from the immediate urges of the self. As such, EC frees up enough time and psychological space to focus, perhaps for the first time, on the words or needs or consciousness of *another person*. A toddler is enraged when a peer encroaches on his play space. If EC kicks in, however, he may resist the urge to strike out at the intruder, perhaps pivoting to a different activity or simply asking the other kid to ease off. In writing this paragraph, I may experience boundless frustration and anxiety because I cannot get the sentences to sound just right. But if my wife calls me on the phone in the next minute, I will need to shift instantly to a positive emotional state to focus on her words. (Or just don't answer the phone, and wait for the bad mood to pass.) EC is not easy—if it were, psychologists would not label it as "effortful." Nonetheless, life would be immeasurably harder, impossible for most of us, if the better angels of EC did not come down from heaven and take up residence in our brains during the second and third years of our lives.

The consolidation of effortful control in early childhood is a necessary step along the developmental path toward flourishing agreeableness. Donald Trump followed a decidedly different path. One reason that his journey went the way that it did is that the EC angels seem to have passed him by. This particular temperament dimension never seemed to take hold in Donald Trump's personality development. Research shows that girls display a significant advantage over boys when it comes to EC. Many young boys struggle to resist momentary distractions, both those welling up from within and those presenting themselves as irresistible temptations in the environment. From preschool through the adolescent years, they have a difficult time ignoring the impulses that flood their awareness and distract their attention. Still, most boys, too, eventually learn to control the worst impulses so that they can attend to those things and people that transcend the self's immediate need. Despite their inborn nature, temperament dimensions can develop and strengthen with time. Even if it takes them a couple of decades, therefore, most boys and young men make decent progress in the strategic deployment of effortful control. But some don't.

The social environment: Grooming a killer

Donald Trump was the fourth of five children born to Fred and Mary Trump. When he arrived on the scene in the summer of 1946, the oldest daughter Maryanne was nine years old, Fred Jr. ("Freddy") was seven, and Elizabeth, four. Completing the set, Robert was born two years later. Around the time of Robert's birth, the family moved from a cramped two-story mock Tudor on Wareham Street to a spacious, 23-room Colonial. Fred designed the new home, which featured nine bathrooms, an intercom system, a library (which had few books but sported one of the neighborhood's first television consoles), and space for a maid and a chauffeur. From the domed-ceiling foyer, a formal curved staircase ascended to the second-floor landing. Fred also built a back staircase to be used by the children and staff.

Fred and Mary ran a tight ship. All five children were expected to work hard, to obey their elders, and to follow the household rules. No cookies or snacks between meals. No cursing. "You didn't utter a curse word in that house, or you'd get your neck broken," recalled Louis Droesch, who was one of Freddy's friends. When Fred returned home from work each evening, Mary provided him with a report detailing the children's misbehavior. Punishments included being grounded for a few days or being paddled with a wooden spoon. Despite the family's wealth, Fred insisted that the children learn the value of a dollar. They all worked summer jobs, and the boys had paper routes.

Both Maryanne and Donald remember their mother as fun loving and emotionally dramatic. She was the family entertainer. By contrast, Fred presented a serious and formal demeanor, and he was very stern. The overall emotional atmosphere in the family reflected Fred's sensibility more so than Mary's. Life was to reflect order and discipline. The children went to bed every night at an appointed time. Curfews were not to be violated. The children were told not to call each other by nicknames. The girls were forbidden from wearing lipstick. No pets allowed. One neighbor recalled that the Trump children often came over to her house to eat cookies and play with her family's kittens and rabbits. "The Trumps didn't have that [freedom] at their house, so they came over to mine," said Bernice MacIntosh.

The unbridled expression of emotion, positive or negative, was strongly forbidden in the Trump household. After Robert was born, Mary developed a severe abdominal infection, which required several surgeries. She almost died. Maryanne, who was a teenager at the time, later recalled that her father insisted she keep her emotions in check and soldier on, even during this dire situation: "My father came home and told me she [my mother] wasn't expected to live, but I should go to school and he'd call me if anything changed. That's right—go to school as usual!" (Mary Trump survived the ordeal and lived to age 88.)

Whereas Fred discouraged emotional expression, he urged his children to be fiercely competitive, especially the three boys. "Be a killer," he told them. He meant that they should always strive to beat the competition. Be the best in whatever you do. Let nothing and nobody stand in your way. Demolish your opponents. Maryanne competed successfully in school. She was an outstanding student. She grew up to be a federal judge. With respect to academics, Donald was in the bottom half of his grade school class. But he excelled in sports. More important, Donald internalized his father's life credo. For a child born to aggression, becoming a "killer" seemed the natural thing to do. "The most important influence on me growing up was my father," Donald Trump wrote in *The Art of the Deal*. Fred Trump was "a wonderful man" but "strong and tough as hell." "I learned a lot from him. I learned about toughness in a very tough business," and in life. Even in childhood, Donald pushed back against his father's strict codes. "I was never intimidated by my father, the way most people were," Trump recalled. "I stood up to him, and he respected that." Fred did more than merely "respect" Donald. He saw potential greatness in his favorite son. Donald was a natural-born killer.

The next critical step in the socialization of Donald Trump's aggression was his enrollment in NYMA, beginning in the eighth grade. Fred hoped that military training would serve to regulate and channel Donald's disagreeableness. He was not aiming to nurture his son's empathy or expand his perspective, however. The intent instead was to hone and channel the killer instinct to direct Donald's agonistic energy into productive work. At the time, Donald "wasn't thrilled about the idea" of attending NYMA, "but it turned out he [Fred] was right. . . . I stayed [at NYMA] through my senior year, and along the way I learned a lot about discipline, and about channeling my aggression into achievement."

Maryanne Trump described her brother Donald as "extremely rebellious" in his youth. But during the years when many young people rebel overtly against their parents and the status quo, Donald Trump was forced to conform. The regimented nature of life at the military academy made Donald's strict childhood home look like a Montessori school. In addition to taking classes and participating in sports, the cadets received strict instruction on folding their clothes, making their beds, and nearly every other detail of personal deportment.

Donald won medals for neatness and order. The cadets also learned how to clean an M1 rifle and fire a mortar. It was like five years of boot camp, complete with drill sergeants who kept order through mental intimidation and physical aggression.

The toughest authority figure at NYMA was Theodore Dobias. The barrel-chested Dobias had served in World War II and had seen Mussolini's dead body hanging from a rope. As a sports coach and tactical-training instructor, Dobias smacked students in the head if they showed any impertinence. "He absolutely would rough you up," Trump wrote in *The Art of the Deal*. "You had to learn to survive." Dobias regularly set up a boxing ring on campus and ordered cadets with poor grades to fight each other, whether they wanted to or not. Interviewed years later, Dobias reported, "I taught them that winning wasn't everything, it was the only thing." "Donald picked right up on this," Dobias recalled. "He would tell his teammates, 'We're out here for a purpose. To win.' He always had to be number one, in everything. He was a conniver even then. A real pain in the ass. He would do anything to win."

The nature/nurture conspiracy

In thinking about the origins of any psychological characteristic, people often wonder how much of that feature comes from a person's innate biology (e.g., genes) and how much comes from the environment. How much of Donald Trump's egregious disagreeableness is a direct effect of, say, his inborn temperament, and how much comes from social influences like growing up in Queens and his experiences in the military school? One answer might be that 50% came from nature and 50% from nurture. Another answer might be 70/30. But these hypothetical answers, and the question that prompts them, are 100% wrong. For the individual case, you cannot split biology and environment up in such a simple way, for every single moment of a person's life brings to the table all of a person's biology and all the environment that is present for the moment.

Okay. Let us try this: Donald Trump's remarkably low agreeableness is a result of an *interaction* between biology and environment. His (i) inborn tendencies combined with the (ii) environments he experienced growing up so as to produce one very, very antagonistic social actor. This way of putting it *is also wrong*—or at best, misleading. An "interaction" suggests that each of the two forces is independent. Nature arrives on the scene to meet nurture, and they combine their efforts to produce a certain kind of person. The problem with this framing is that nature and nurture are not independent. Metaphorically speaking, they collude and conspire, mixing themselves up with each other from Day 1 to the point where they can never be pulled apart again.

The conspiracy takes many forms. Let me highlight two of them. First, nature shapes nurture. Second, nurture works to shape the tendencies that owe their original manifestation to nature.

Imagine that you were born with a temperament tendency toward disagreeableness. Anger tends to be a predominant emotion for you, and you are behind the curve on effortful control. You carry this tendency with you from one situation to the next. People notice your tendency, and they react to it. Their reactions become part of your environment, going forward. Let us imagine that your disagreeable tendency brings out negative reactions on the part of others. You unwittingly provoke others to treat you in a more aggressive way than they might treat a social actor just like you who happens to be more agreeable. Their aggressive responses, in turn, serve to make you more aggressive.

At this point, the biologically driven tendency is being reinforced and shaped by the kinds of environments that it tends to evoke in the first place. Developmental psychologists use the word *evocation* to refer to this kind of environmental effect: a genetic predisposition that initially may push a person toward a particular trait *evokes* the kinds of social environments that work to shape the development of that same trait. After years of experiencing these kinds of events, you come out as a very aggressive person. Whose fault is it? Nature? Well, *yes*, because nature gave things an initial push. *But nurture may have done most of the work!* "If I hadn't been subjected to so many tough and aggressive environments growing up, I might not have turned out to be such an aggressive person," you may say. True! But those environments would never have come your way if you hadn't shown that initial, inborn tendency. Then again, if those environments hadn't come along just as they did, you might have turned out to be a very different kind of social actor. Or if you had *perceived* those environments in a slightly different way, the conspiracy might have taken a very different form.

In the strange case of Donald Trump, his *perception* of the environments he has found himself in throughout his life is, I believe, the most important factor in explaining how he became the famously disagreeable person he is today. For all intents and purposes, his perceptions *are* the environments. Why would a boy who grew up in a wealthy and more-or-less loving family, albeit a strict one, and in a safe neighborhood where people never locked their doors grow up to perceive the world as a ruthless and dangerous place and to believe that he himself is nearly constantly under attack? *Because he brought it on.*

The Kew-Forest school *was* a dangerous place when Donald sat down in the classroom or walked on to the playground. He made it dangerous by evoking aggressive responses from other children and from his teachers. He could not help but notice that others retaliated in response to his own provocative behaviors, even if they cowered in fear, and those responses—angry or fearful or encouraging from his peers, punitive from the authorities who sought to sanction him—came to occupy center stage in Donny Trump's social environment. Aggression breeds aggression, evoking excitement, anger, and fear. Growing up under these kinds of social and emotional conditions gradually moved this social actor further and further to the low end of the broad agreeableness continuum, exerting effects on both behavior and perception. Donald Trump began to perceive the world as a threatening place. He needed to be vigilant. He needed to fight back, even if he was the one, developmentally speaking, who started the fighting in the first place, a fact that he has never fully come to grips with. Donald Trump's experiences at NYMA reinforced his vision and strengthened his resolve to be tough, to fight back, and to admit no weakness.

The first two years of the Trump presidency provided an analog to the developmental sequence I have described. On the campaign trail and in many of his campaign speeches, Donald Trump repeatedly asserted, "There has never been a more dangerous time." His inaugural address portrayed the United States as an impoverished and ravaged nation, devastated by "carnage." America might as well have been—well, the Kew-Forest school, just before Donald Trump arrived in the morning. In the seventh year of an economic recovery with crime rates at historic lows, the nation was by no means a Shangri-La on the morning of January 20, 2017, when he delivered his address. But things were more or less okay, many would say.

Donald Trump walked in the door and immediately transformed the environment. He evoked strong, retaliatory responses from many others in that environment, stronger and more retaliatory than any new president has evoked in recent memory. The transformed environment further shaped President Trump's behavior. As Democrats, women, minority groups, foreign leaders, and the press attacked him, convinced that he was the initial aggressor, Trump fought back. It is developmental evocation all over again, a kind of unwitting conspiracy, or call it a vicious cycle, through which an initial force evokes strong responses from the outside world, which feed back to magnify and accentuate the force. Attack leads to counterattack, and on and on. Donald Trump's perception of the world as a threatening place is reinforced again and again in his mind because the world does indeed become more threatening *when he is in it.*

Many of President Trump's staunchest defenders argue that Trump has no choice but to be aggressive because he is constantly under attack. He is surrounded by enemies, who want to bring him down. Trump's defenders are correct! During the first two years of his administration, no president since Richard Nixon has incurred as much vehement opposition from the mainstream press, from former government officials, from intellectual elites of nearly all stripes, and from politicians on the other side of the aisle as has President Trump. Every president incurs strong opposition, of course. But Trump may be unique in modern times for his ability to evoke venom from others.

From the standpoint of his defenders, the best example of the antagonistic environment to which President Trump is constantly subjected was the 2017–2019 special counsel investigation, led by Robert Mueller. Mueller's team was tasked with determining the extent to which Mr. Trump's campaign may have conspired with Russians to influence the 2016 presidential election. From the beginning, President Trump labeled the investigation a "witch hunt." He described it as a political vendetta launched by angry Democrats. There is no doubt that the Mueller investigation contributed appreciably to the perception that President Trump was under attack during the first two years of his presidency. What the president's defenders may not quite realize, however, is that Donald Trump has lived in the same kind of venomous environment his entire life. The presidency is merely an extension of what he has always experienced—a fighter struggling to prevail amidst constant combat, one moment to the next. What President Trump himself may not fully realize is that this is the environment *he has created for himself.* It is the only world he has ever known—a world of his own making.

The weak and the strong: Freddy versus ROY COHN

As temperament tendencies develop into full-fledged personality traits in the first couple decades of life, they recruit a supporting cast of characters. In every life, traits like agreeableness and extraversion absorb role models to sustain and illuminate their respective trends. Fred Trump was Donald's first role model. Coach Dobias at NYMA may have been his second. Both were tough and disagreeable men. Both personified the success that men may achieve through aggression. Even as he competed with them, Donald identified with both his father and his coach. They came to occupy important positions in his *identity.*

In the 1940s, the famous psychoanalytic theorist Erik Erikson described identity as a person's psychological answer to the question, "Who am I?" Erikson theorized that people first confront this question in a serious way during their adolescent and young-adult years. A social actor's traits may become part of his or her identity at this time to the extent that he or she considers the traits to be self-defining. A particular trait may become self-defining in the mind of a social actor when he or she seeks to emulate a person whose behavior displays that trait—or when he or she seeks explicitly *not* to emulate a person whose behavior displays the trait's opposite. Erikson argued that coming to know who you are often involves first coming to know who you are *not.* From an early age, Donald Trump knew he was *not* his older brother. Long before he confronted Erikson's identity question, Donald Trump resolved that whoever he might become when he grew up, he would never become like Freddy.

Enter poor Freddy, the first bona fide *loser* in the saga of Donald Trump. The first-born son, Freddy was expected to follow closely in the footsteps of his father. But Freddy was no Fred, even though he tried to be. The biographer Gwen Blair describes Freddy as a "sweet lightweight, a mawkish but lovable loser, so anxious for attention and approval that he seemed [as a child and as a young man] almost desperate." Freddy tried to show his dad that "he could be a tough little street fighter," recalled one classmate. "But he was a real pussycat, not mean and aggressive, kind of pathetic, really." Freddy hung out with intellectual kids who aspired to attend Ivy League schools. Fred looked upon those friends with scorn. They reminded him of his own brother, an MIT professor who, as Fred saw it, was a "failure" because he made so little money. "I think Freddy's father feared that he would become an aesthete fairy, a little English gentleman," said a friend. He was worried that his first-born "was having the aggressive instincts schooled out of him and he was being turned into an Ivy League wimp."

After graduating from Lehigh University, Freddy worked in his father's business. But he never seemed to win his father's approval. He developed a serious drinking problem. Freddy moved to Florida and became an airline pilot. He married a stewardess, and they had two children. The marriage failed, and Freddy moved back to New York. In the months before his death from a massive heart attack at age 43, Freddy lived in his parents' home and worked on a maintenance crew for Trump apartment buildings.

From an early age, Donald Trump loved his older brother. As a teenager and afterwards, he heeded his older brother's warnings: don't drink or smoke, Freddy cautioned. Don't do what I do. From an early age, Donald observed Freddy's failures and his father's brutal responses to those failures. Blair describes the disagreeable dynamic this way: "Donald saw that cowering when his father got mad only made him angrier, that hanging around people who seemed more pointy headed than practical caused his father to fly into a rage, and that showing vulnerability around his father was a mistake." As the oldest sister Maryanne saw it, "Donald moved ahead as Freddy failed." Donald grieved Freddy's death. He has described it as the worst thing that has ever happened in his life. His older brother was "a wonderful guy who never quite found himself," Trump wrote in *The Art of the Deal*. But he was weak. His life and premature death were a cautionary tale. "Freddy just wasn't a killer," Donald concluded.

But Roy Cohn was.

In the fall of 1973, the U.S. Justice Department sued the Trump Organization for racial discrimination, citing the Fair Housing Act of 1968. The feds accused Fred Trump's company of turning away African Americans seeking apartments in Trump-owned buildings. Spurred by a conversation that the young Donald Trump had with the lawyer Roy Cohn at an exclusive New York nightclub, the Trumps hired Cohn as their attorney, vowing to fight back. Trump told Cohn,

"I'd rather fight than fold, because as soon as you fold once, you get the reputation of being a folder." Cohn told Trump he should tell the government "to go to hell." On January 12, 1974, Donald Trump and Roy Cohn called a press conference at the New York Hilton to announce that they were countersuing the Justice Department and requesting $100 million in damages due to the "irresponsible and baseless" claims. The judge threw the countersuit out. After nearly two years of legal battles, the Trumps agreed to a settlement.

In his late 20s when they met, Donald Trump was star-struck in the dazzling presence of the middle-aged Roy Cohn. After graduating from Columbia law school, Cohn landed a job with the U.S. Attorney's Office in Manhattan. He was assigned to write a memo about Alger Hiss, a State Department official suspected of spying for the Soviet Union. Cohn became convinced that hundreds of committed communists had infiltrated the U.S. government. In 1951, he worked on the prosecution of Julius and Ethel Rosenberg, who were convicted of espionage and passing on secrets regarding the atomic bomb to the Soviet Union. They were both executed. Cohn bragged that he was responsible for convincing the judge to send Ethel—not just Julius—to the electric chair. Later, Cohn signed up to work with Senator Joseph McCarthy, who launched a series of hearings, known as the Red Scare, alleging that many politicians, military officials, Hollywood actors, college professors, and other prominent citizens were deeply involved in anti-American activities associated with communism. McCarthy also sought to rid the government of suspected homosexuals. His paranoia and extremism eventually led to a Senate censure and his downfall. "McCarthyism" entered the English lexicon as a term denoting a "witch hunt."

After the Red Scare died down, Cohn returned to New York to become one of the most influential and notorious men in the city. Working out of a Manhattan townhouse, Cohn represented real estate moguls, prominent figures in the Catholic Church, entertainers, and mobsters. He proudly served as counsel for New York mafia families. Receiving payment for his services in cash, Cohn boasted that he never paid federal income tax. He was indicted on charges of bribery, extortion, and obstruction of justice, but Roy Cohn always beat the rap. His legal strategy was to attack opponents with all the fury and flamboyance he could muster, which was a considerable amount. *Esquire* magazine profiled him in a story entitled "Don't Mess with Roy Cohn." Ken Auletta wrote: "Prospective clients who want to kill their husbands, torture a business partner, [or] break the government's legs hire Roy Cohn. . . . He is a legal executioner—the toughest, meanest, loyalest, vilest, and one of the most brilliant lawyers in America. He is not a very nice man." What better role model might a young and aggressive real estate tycoon (who once punched out his second grade teacher) ever find, in New York City during the 1970s, to help build a personal identity around the trait of low agreeableness?

Cohn became a mentor for Donald Trump. As his lawyer, he provided a template for the many legal disputes that Trump would face in the decades to follow: Go on the offensive; admit to no wrongdoing; project yourself as the victim rather than the perpetrator of evil deeds; never, ever give in. Cohn also served as an informal advisor and publicist. He pulled strings and cashed in favors to make Donald Trump known to the city's most powerful men. Trump admired Cohn's audacious swagger and his gangster-like persona. His face made dark and leathery by too much exposure to the sun, his hair perfectly coiffed, Cohn never went out in public unless he was impeccably dressed in a fine suit and silk tie. He drove around town in a Rolls Royce, with his initials RMC etched on the vanity plates. He could often be found at the swankiest clubs sharing the latest gossip and hatching plots over drinks.

Donald Trump stored a photo of Roy Cohn in his desk. He would pull it out on occasion and thrust it in the face of a potential opponent, as an intimidation tactic. One viewer described the photo as the image of Satan himself. Roy Cohn "would kill for somebody he liked," Donald Trump said. Cohn epitomized the strength and aggression that a man must have to survive in a perilous and unforgiving universe, in a world where gentle weaklings like Freddy never stand a chance. Cohn was the killer that Fred Trump wanted all of his sons to be. In the mind of Donald Trump, Cohn continued to play that role until the fall of 1984, when he fell ill from HIV infection. The closeted gay man who worked with Senator McCarthy to rid the government of homosexuals knew that many Americans equated his sexual orientation with weakness. He refused to admit that he was stricken with AIDS. Shortly before his death in 1986, the state of New York finally disbarred Cohn for decades of "dishonesty, fraud, deceit and misrepresentation." Donald Trump attended the memorial service, standing silently in a back row.

Reading stories

Two kinds of environments shape the development of personality traits. There are first and foremost those things, people, and conditions that exist in reality, as we perceive them. Let us call them *real* environments. In the case of Donald Trump, these include all of the dynamics that played out as he grew up in a strict household in Queens, during the 1940s and 1950s. They include teachers and peers at the Kew-Forest school and NYMA. They include Freddy and Roy Cohn, and the other people who served as sources for his developing identity. They include all the material, economic, and social circumstances of Donald Trump's life. Second, there are *imagined* environments—make-believe worlds that play out in our fantasies and dreams. The sources of our imagined worlds are many, but chief among them is *reading* fiction, as well as related activities like watching movies and listening to music, through which we are transported to an alternative space and time.

I grew up in Gary, Indiana, a rough-hewn, working-class town with few cultural amenities. My father left my mother when I was five years old. She raised three difficult children on the salary of a telephone operator. My friends' fathers nearly all worked in the steel mills, unless they stayed home drunk. It was not until I was in high school that I ate in a sit-down restaurant—you know, the kind where the waiter brings you your check. But I was an inveterate reader. I imagined the 19th-century English countryside, the bloody streets of Paris during the French Revolution, the subways of New York at the turn of the 20th century, the land of milk and honey to which the ancient Israelites were drawn, the Roman empire during the time of Jesus, the make-believe towns and families in which the Hardy Boys solved mysteries or Danny Dunn embarked on his science adventures, and thousands of other imagined worlds, each of which presented imagined lives. I also read biographies of real people, like Willie Mays and Abraham Lincoln. The lives that I encountered through reading, and through other forms of fictive experience, were not *my* life. But in subtle ways, they taught me about human life, about how a human being *might* live.

A growing body of research in psychological science attests to the formative power of reading stories. The most important effects reveal themselves in the realm of agreeableness. Reading stories activates parts of the brain that are involved in what cognitive psychologists call *social cognition*, which refers to how we think (and feel) about people and our relationships with them. Critical components of social cognition include being able to imagine how other people see the world and being able to summon forth sympathy, empathy, and interpersonal understanding.

Reading is positively associated with social cognition and social skills. But not just any kind of reading. Reading *fiction* appears to be the key factor. In fiction, the reader explores the emotional states and intentions of characters whose experiences may be very different from the reader's own. The magical capacity of great literature has always been to give readers access to the minds of others. Sharing stories with others builds social bonds, bringing people together in communities of friendship and solidarity. In one particularly illuminating study, researchers compared reading fiction to reading nonfiction, statistically controlling for variables like intelligence and social class. They found that the amount of fiction a person has read over a lifetime strongly predicted empathy and social skills. Reading nonfiction, however, was not related to empathy and social skills. It is exposure to stories, rather than to general information per se, that seems to enhance characteristics that are simpatico with human agreeableness.

When one biographer asked Donald Trump to name his favorite book, Trump chose *The Art of the Deal*. His stated reason: "because I made a fortune from it." Perhaps Trump was making a joke. But I don't think so. It is well known that President Trump does not read books. His aides have a very difficult time getting him even to look over briefing reports in preparation for meetings.

Biographers report that very few books may be found in Trump's offices and homes. Tony Schwartz, who worked closely with Trump in writing *The Art of the Deal*, reported that he never saw a book on Trump's desk or in his office or apartment. "I seriously doubt Trump has ever read a book straight through in his adult life," Schwartz claimed. Still, Trump must have read *something* when he was a college student at Fordham University and the Wharton School. Maybe he read textbooks in economics, his academic major. But it is hard to imagine his ever curling up in a chair and reading a novel. Trump appears to have very little knowledge about what is arguably the most famous and widely read book in the history of Western civilization—the Bible. Reading from his notes for a speech delivered at Liberty University in early 2016, Trump referred to II Corinthians (Second Corinthians) as "Two Corinthians." If a speaker had made that mistake in the Baptist church I attended as a child, the congregants might have gotten up and left.

For the episodic man who must fight to win from one moment to the next, there is no time for books and stories and other artistic luxuries. Stories teach us perspective and empathy, and they also teach us how to *live our lives as stories*, how to create meaningful narratives for our own lives. For the pugnacious Donald Trump, there has never been enough time to learn about how to live in time, how to develop a long-term story for life. A boxer in the ring cannot let his mind wander into the realm of make-believe. If he tries to think about anything else but the next punch, he will get knocked out. He must focus on the aggressive moment. He must fight with all the force he can summon forth to survive the moment, to win the moment, which ends when the bell rings. He gets a one-minute interlude in his corner. That is not enough time to think about anything else except the next round of fighting, no time to read a book, no time to imagine a different story, no time to think about the perspectives of others, or to imagine a different perspective for one's own combative life. The bell rings again, and Donald Trump gets up to fight.

In an op-ed column written in June 2018, the novelist Dave Eggers observed that Donald Trump's is the only administration in recent memory to turn its back on literature and the arts. President Kennedy invited avant-garde artists to his inauguration and hosted literary greats like Arthur Miller, Tennessee Williams, and Robert Lowell at White House dinners. Ronald Reagan hosted White House concerts every few weeks. George W. Bush met Bono in the Oval Office and hosted a wide range of musicians, from Itzhak Perlman to Destiny's Child. Bush also competed with his aide Karl Rove to see who could read more books in a year. Barack Obama celebrated young poets and regularly reported on his favorite novels and nonfiction books.

By contrast, Trump actively scorns literature and the arts. He disparaged the hit Broadway play *Hamilton* and has aimed his venom at many Hollywood performers, including the acclaimed actress Meryl Streep. Lamenting Trump's rejection of all things literary and artistic, Eggers concluded his essay like this:

> With art comes empathy. It allows us to look through someone else's eyes and know their strivings and struggles. It expands the moral imagination to make it impossible to accept dehumanization of others. When we are without art, we are a diminished people—myopic, unlearned and *cruel*.

***

American politicians and dignitaries of all stripes attended the memorial services for Senator John McCain in the late summer of 2018. Former Presidents George W. Bush and Barack Obama delivered eulogies. They praised McCain's valor and his patriotism. They urged Americans to put aside their political differences and to transcend their animosities in the spirit of national civility and unity. The various tributes to McCain emphasized a pervasive theme: *Even when we disagree, we might still treat each other in a more agreeable manner*, with empathy and warmth and a shared sense of humanity.

Donald Trump was not invited to the funeral in the National Cathedral, nor to any of the other events celebrating Senator McCain's life. Instead, Trump attended a political rally in Evansville, Indiana. With the crowd cheering, Trump lambasted the press: "These are just dishonest, terrible people. I'm telling you that. Terrible people." As Republicans and Democrats came together to remember John McCain, Trump offered a venomous critique of his political opponents: "Today's Democrat Party is held hostage by left-wing haters, angry mobs, 'deep state' radicals, establishment cronies, and their fake news allies." He described immigrant gang members as "animals." "They want to slice people up! Young girls, walking home from school 16 years old. They died." It was not immediately clear whether Mr. Trump was referring to an actual murder, or if he was making the more general point that violent gangs make the world a more dangerous place.

As he nearly always does in speeches to supportive groups, Trump exulted in his 2016 victory over "Crooked Hillary" Clinton. "We love winners. We love winners. Winners are winners."

The enthusiastic Indiana crowd was the largest ever to attend an event at the Evansville Ford Center, surpassing all rock concerts held there and college basketball games.

Truth

I lie awake at night wondering what it is like to be Donald Trump. His over-mastering strangeness challenges my imagination like no project I have ever attempted. He is so utterly different from most of the rest of humankind, so different from who I believe myself to be and who I have been. I summon up all the empathy and perspective-taking I can muster to relate to his unique experience, to find a connection between my mind and his.

My effort to get inside Donald Trump's head is not without its successes. I can imagine the thrill he experiences in seeking social rewards, the dopamine-induced exultation of unabashed extraversion. I can imagine losing myself in the angry moment, as he does on a daily basis. I can sense what it would feel like to live without a synthesizing story for my life, from one moment to the next, without seeking any larger meaning to the arc of human existence. I once experienced life that way, as many of us did when we were children. I understand the logic of Trump's deal-making. I can imagine wheeling and dealing exactly as he has always done it, following in the footsteps of his father and grandfather. My father sold cars for a living, and I worked with him one summer. He would have loved Trump.

But it gets harder, I must admit, when I try to empathize with Trump's decided lack of empathy. How might a person move through life in such an unequivocally disagreeable manner? I don't think I could ever muster the venom, the cruelty. Then again, I have experienced rage in my own life and, occasionally, hatred. So maybe—yeah, maybe I can wrap my mind around the idea of a life dominated by the feeling of extreme animus every single day. If I water it down a bit, if I envision it as a repeating scenario wherein a hero who is constantly under attack lashes out at his enemies by day, sleeps for a few hours to refuel at night, and then wakes up the next morning and begins to lash out at them all over again—well, I can almost imagine living like that, for a few months, maybe. I can almost get there.

But then my imagination stops dead in its tracks, as if it has run smack into a concrete wall. It is a border wall, constructed by Trump to keep me out, to keep me from ever truly understanding him. No, it is not exactly a wall. It is more like an imposing apparition that turns me back. I lie awake completely stymied

The Strange Case of Donald J. Trump. Dan P. McAdams, Oxford University Press (2020). © Oxford University Press.
DOI: 10.1093/oso/9780197507445.001.0001

as I face the frightening specter of Trump's daily descent into *untruth*. I simply cannot imagine *the lying*.

I should be more precise: I cannot imagine continuing to lie when nearly the whole world knows you are lying. When the evidence of your lying is everywhere and for everybody to see. When the laws of physics and mathematics prove that you are lying. When even the people who love you and the millions who adore you, and would likely vote for you no matter what, know you are lying, too.

How can *he* sleep at night?

Let me now pose three big questions about the lying. For each, I will offer a brief answer to be developed in the pages ahead.

Question: Does Trump lie more than other politicians lie?

Answer: *Yes*. (That one is easy.)

Question: Why does Trump lie so much?

Answer: *Because he is the episodic man*. Because he does not experience his life as a *story*, but rather as a series of combative moments. Because "truth," for Donald Trump, is *whatever works to win the moment*.

Question: Why do his supporters put up with his lies?

Answer: *Because they do not see him as a person*. He is *more* than that—and *less*.

***

March 1, 2017 was a remarkable day in the presidency of Donald Trump. It was the first day of his administration in which he did not publicly utter a blatant falsehood. March 1 broke a 40-day streak.

But the lull was only temporary. On March 4, Trump tweeted out that former President Barack Obama had been spying on him, describing the former president as "a bad (or sick) guy." Parroting an unsubstantiated remark made by a talk radio host, Trump claimed that Obama had ordered the Federal Bureau of Investigations to tap his phones in Trump Tower during the month before the 2016 election. A week later, Trump went further, asserting that Great Britain's Government Communications Headquarters had conspired with Obama in the scheme. Spokespersons for both Obama and the British government strongly denied and condemned the claims. Since then, not a single shred of evidence has ever surfaced to support President Trump's false allegations.

Even as a candidate, Donald Trump showed a penchant for passing on false stories. During the heat of the primaries, he suggested that the father of his chief Republican rival, Texas Senator Ted Cruz, may have been involved with Lee Harvey Oswald in a Cuban-inspired plot to assassinate John F. Kennedy. Trump based his claim on a discredited story from the *National Enquirer* showing a photo of Rafael Cruz handing out pro-Castro pamphlets in New Orleans in 1963.

It is a truth universally acknowledged that U.S. presidents (and presidential candidates) do not always tell the truth. But some tell it less often than others. During the 2016 election, the independent, nonprofit watchdog PolitiFact kept track of how often (or infrequently) the candidates told the truth in their public campaign statements. In April 2016, PolitiFact calculated that only 2% of the claims made by Donald Trump on the campaign trail were completely true, 7% were "mostly true," 15% "half true," 15% "mostly false," 42% "false", and 18% "pants on fire." They save the last category for the most egregious and outrageous lies. Adding up the last three figures (from mostly false to flagrantly so), Trump scored a 75%. By contrast, the corresponding figures for John Kasich, Bernie Sanders, and Hillary Clinton were 32%, 31%, and 29%, respectively. The only rival candidate who even came close to Trump for the dubious honor of most deceitful was Ted Cruz, who scored 66%. (Donald Trump, therefore, was *not* lying when he famously gave Cruz the nickname "Lyin' Ted.")

After his surprise victory over Hillary Clinton in the 2016 presidential election, President-Elect Trump immediately began to make false statements about the election itself. Trump, of course, had won in the Electoral College, but the final tally for the popular vote gave Hillary Clinton a pyrrhic victory of nearly 3 million ballots cast. Trump alleged that voter fraud in numerous states kept him from winning the popular vote outright. He tweeted: "In addition to winning the Electoral College in a landslide, I won the popular vote if you deduct the millions of people who voted illegally." To date, no evidence has ever surfaced to support this amazing claim. It qualifies as a "pants on fire" by any objective standard. Nonetheless, President Trump has never renounced the false statement.

Despite the lack of evidence, furthermore, millions of Americans apparently believe that Trump's false statement about the election is *true*. According to a 2017 survey conducted by *The Washington Post*, 47% of Republicans erroneously believe that Trump *won the popular vote* in the 2016. And 68% of Republicans believe that millions of illegal immigrants voted.

With respect to Trump's assertions about the popular vote, defenders of the president might respond like this: Just because hard evidence of illegal voting has never been found, it does not strictly follow that the illegal voting did not occur. It *might have* occurred, one might claim. You can't prove a negative.

Fair enough. There is always a chance that evidence in support of Trump's claim could emerge, someday. But Donald Trump makes false statements even when the evidence against them is manifestly unambiguous—when the physical evidence is there for everybody's eyes to see. What may have been the first clear falsehood in the Trump presidency was his claim, made only hours after

he had been sworn in as chief executive, that the crowd attending his inauguration was the largest in history. Aerial photographs of the scene showed that the
mass of people spread out across the space in front of the capital building and on
the mall, although sizeable, was a considerably smaller crowd than the one that
attended President Obama's inauguration in 2009. There is simply no disputing
this fact, unless you believe that the photographs were doctored.

The day after the inauguration, President Trump's spokesperson, Sean Spicer,
followed his boss's lead and accused the press of making "false reports" on the
crowd size for the purpose of "delegitimizing" the new president. Another administration official, Kellyanne Conway, famously argued that Spicer was not
technically lying, even though the photographs proved him wrong. In Conway's
words, Spicer was simply offering "alternative facts." To date, President Trump
has not retracted his false claim about the size of the inauguration crowd.

In response to a steady stream of misleading statements and pants-on-fire
falsehoods coming out of the White House, mainstream news outlets in the
United States have hired fact checkers and initiated new journalistic practices
to separate fact from fiction. For example, *The Chicago Tribune*, which has traditionally slanted conservative and supported Republican policies in its editorial
outlook, now routinely evaluates White House statements for their accuracy, as
do local Chicago television stations. Many American newspapers now provide
a "fact check" section, explaining how specific statements made by President
Trump are "misleading," "mainly false," or "completely untrue." Just a few years
ago, television viewers might have been taken aback had they heard the friendly
local news anchor say this on the late-night report: "The president falsely claimed
today . . ." or "The statement from the White House is not true." Had CNN aired
the following commercial a few years ago, viewers would have scratched their
heads in puzzlement as they gazed upon the apple. Now, everybody knows the
meaning of the voiceover:

> *This is an apple.*
> *Some people might try to tell you that it's a banana.*
> *They might scream "Banana, banana, banana" over and over and over again.*
> *They might put BANANA in all caps.*
> *You might even start to believe that this is a banana.*
> *But it's not.*
> *This is an apple.*

The Washington Post calculated that President Trump made 2,140 false or
misleading claims during the first year of his presidency, averaging 5.9 per day.
A report from midway through Trump's second year suggested that the frequency increased, to 7.5 per day. Glenn Kessler headed a team of staffers at the

Post who kept the running tally. As reporter for *Newsday* years ago, Kessler covered Trump's real estate deals. Back then, he found Trump to be "boastful" and given to "laxity about the truth." If bank officials did not believe a false claim made by Trump regarding his business dealings, they might simply decline to provide him further loans. There would be no need to broadcast the lies. But now that Trump is president, the falsehoods become daily headlines across the world. "Most politicians, I find they exaggerate or stretch, but they don't want to out-and-out mislead people," Kessler told an interviewer. "The difference with Trump is that he doesn't really change what he says because you fact-check him. He'll double down and keep saying it." In comparison to the lies politicians sometimes tell, Kessler said that Trump is "in another realm completely."

There are many forms of untruth. A relatively common form among public officials is *concealing the truth*. For example, many American voters in 2016 reported that they did not trust Hillary Clinton—not so much because she uttered blatant lies but rather because she always seemed to them to be hiding something. According to many of her detractors, Hillary Clinton was deceitful in the sense of not being transparent. "Even when telling the truth, she sounded like she was lying to you," remarked Steve Bannon, Trump's one-time advisor and right-wing provocateur. Trump captured the sentiment well when he labeled his opponent "Crooked Hillary." By contrast, Trump appears to be more straightforward, many of his supporters have always claimed. What you see is what you get. It is true that Trump can be shockingly direct and straightforward. Nonetheless, Trump was the first presidential candidate in four decades to refuse to release his federal tax returns. Throughout his life, he has concealed information about his finances.

A more glaring form of untruth in the case of Donald Trump is *making unsubstantiated claims*. In many cases, the claims either go well beyond documented facts or are so sweeping and broad that no assessment of facticity can be made. These kinds of claims are common in the world of business and advertising, variations on what Trump deemed to be "truthful hyperbole" in *The Art of the Deal*. In his first presidential news conference on February 16, 2017, Trump said: "There has never been a presidency that has done so much in such a short period of time." On other occasions, he has claimed that his presidency is the greatest in American history. How do you assess the truthfulness of these assertions? They remind me of a drive-in restaurant that opened up a few blocks from our house in Chicago back in the early 1990s. In bold letters the restaurant advertised itself as having THE WORLD'S GREATEST FOOD. Were the owners of the restaurant lying? I guess they must have been, because the restaurant closed after a few months.

Another common practice in the art of Trumpian untruth is *spreading false stories*. The lies do not typically originate with him in these cases; instead, he is the main vehicle for their dissemination. As a candidate, Donald Trump claimed that the U.S. government had known in advance about the 9/11 attacks. He intimated that Supreme Court Justice Antonin Scalia had been murdered in his sleep. He spread a false story about Ted Cruz's father's being involved in the Kennedy assassination. As president, he has often retweeted information or stories that are based on unsubstantiated, and sometimes malicious, rumors.

The original sin of this nature, however, was Trump's promoting the false story that President Barack Obama was born in Kenya, rather than in the United States. The origins of the so-called birther tale go back to the 2008 election, during which a group of fringe conspiracy theorists alleged that Obama was not a natural-born American citizen and, therefore, ineligible to be president. In 2011, when Trump was considering a possible run for the White House against Obama, he began to question Obama's citizenship, demanding to see a birth certificate. By continuing to press the issue, Trump endeavored to confer legitimacy on a mendacious (and, many would argue, racist) claim. It was not until 2016 that Trump finally conceded the truth: "President Barack Obama was born in the United States. Period." At that point, Trump took credit for putting the birther controversy aside, blaming the whole thing on Hillary Clinton and claiming that it was Clinton who raised questions about Obama's legitimacy in the first place (also false).

Just a month into his presidency, Trump promulgated a false story about Sweden, based on a misinterpretation of a television show he watched. In a Fox News interview, a documentary filmmaker alleged that the Swedish "government has gone out of its way to try to cover up" terrorist activity and violence ignited by a recent wave of Muslim migration. The next day, President Trump made a speech in which he suggested that a terrorist attack had occurred in Sweden the night before. The Swedes were outraged. "We are used to seeing the president of the U.S. as one of the most well-informed persons in the world, also well aware of the importance of what he says," wrote Carl Bildt, a former prime minister of Sweden. "And then, suddenly, we see him engaging in misinformation and slander against a truly friendly country, obviously relying on sources of a quality that at best could be described as dubious." Bildt concluded: "We must all take responsibility for using facts correctly and for verifying anything we spread."

In the case of President Trump, it is not just about spreading false claims, failing to verify facts, and engaging in truthful and untruthful hyperbole. It is also about deliberately and systematically constructing lies. Based on hundreds of hours of interviews with White House officials and other witnesses to the Trump presidency, the veteran journalist Bob Woodward provided countless examples of President Trump's penchant for lying and other forms of untruth in his book, *Fear: Trump in the White House*. In one scene, President Trump was arguing with his advisors about trade policy. He wanted desperately to slap tariffs on China. He asked Treasury Secretary Steve Mnuchin why he was not declaring China to be a currency manipulator, which would help to justify retaliatory tariffs. Mnuchin replied, truthfully, that while the Chinese had routinely engaged in currency manipulation years ago, China was no longer a currency manipulator. That is simply a fact, Mnuchin emphasized.

Trump was incredulous.

"What do you mean?" he exclaimed. "Make the case. Just do it. Declare it."

The president was effectively telling Mnuchin to create alternative facts. Just make it up, damn it! Mnuchin and another advisor pushed back. They explained that U.S. law was quite specific regarding what constitutes currency manipulation and how such a claim must be justified. The claim required specific, verifiable facts.

"I don't want to hear that," Trump retorted. "It's all bullshit."

Woodward's book describes how cabinet members, lawyers, and other advisors to President Trump developed different strategies for coping with or getting around the president's proclivity for lying. Even his staunchest admirers concede that President Trump tends to lie about nearly everything—big issues regarding international relations and tiny issues, like his golf game. Gary Cohn served as Trump's chief economic advisor in the first year of his administration. He left the position over disagreements regarding trade policy. But Cohn left on good terms, and throughout Woodward's book, Cohn seems to enjoy a positive relationship with the president. "He's a professional liar," Cohn told an associate.

A Trump loyalist throughout, John Dowd, served as one of the president's top lawyers during the first 14 months of the Trump administration. In the strongest possible terms, he urged Trump not to agree to testify in Special Counsel Robert Mueller's investigation into Russian involvement in the 2016 election. Dowd told the president that testifying in person would be a "perjury trap." Dowd knew that President Trump was inherently unable to stick with the truth. He suspected Trump knew the same thing and that Trump would therefore come to realize that he should stay away from Mueller's team. Better to say nothing than to be caught in a lie. Look at what happened to Bill Clinton when he lied under oath! Dowd admired Trump greatly, and he strongly supported the president's policies. He believed that Trump was a great leader. But, as Woodward tells it in the final sentence of his book, channeling Dowd's angst: "Trump had one overriding problem that Dowd knew but could not bring himself to say to the president: 'You're a fucking liar.' "

The same sentiment was publicly voiced in dramatic fashion *from inside the White House*, on September 5, 2018, when the *New York Times* published an extraordinary opinion piece. The newspaper ran an anonymously authored essay entitled, "I am Part of the Resistance Inside the Trump Administration." The author of the essay claimed to represent a group of administration officials—"unsung heroes," endeavoring "to put country first"—who are "working diligently from within to frustrate parts of his [President Trump's] agenda and his worst inclinations." Among those worst inclinations, the author singled out an "impetuous, adversarial, petty, and ineffective" leadership style and "half-baked, ill-informed and occasionally reckless" decision-making. "The root of the problem is the president's amorality," the author asserted. "Anyone who works with him knows he is not moored to any discernible first principles that guide his decision making."

Near the top of any such list of "first principles" would be a commitment to truth. Trump's first Secretary of State, Rex Tillerson, offered a veiled rebuke of his former boss in a commencement address at Virginia Military Institute in May 2018. Tillerson warned that American democracy was threatened by a looming "crisis of ethics and integrity." "If our leaders seek to conceal the truth, or we as people become accepting of alternative realities that are no longer grounded in facts, then we as American citizens are on a pathway to relinquishing our freedom," Tillerson said. "When we as people, a free people, go wobbly on the truth even on what may seem the most trivial matters, we go wobbly on America."

Steeped in the thinking of the European Enlightenment, the framers of the American Constitution envisioned a democratic republic governed by the rule of law. For such a system to work, there needs to be some consensus or agreement among citizens regarding a consistent set of facts. Employing the power of human reason and appealing to empirical evidence in the world, free people living in a democratic society should ideally be able to make good decisions to promote their own well-being, as well as the common good. When a leader, however, blithely disregards the standards of truth to promote alternative facts, the cognitive infrastructure of a democratic society begins to erode. When the belief in truth decays, a society may become vulnerable to totalitarian rule. "The ideal subject of totalitarian rule," wrote the political philosopher Hannah Arendt in 1973, "is not the convinced Nazi or the convinced Communist, but people for whom the distinction between fact and fiction (i.e., the reality of experience) and the distinction between true and false (i.e., the standards of thought) no longer exist."

***

As social animals striving to get along and get ahead in complex groups, human beings evolved to have an ambivalent relationship with the truth. Our hunting and gathering ancestors who, for countless generations, roamed the African savannah managed to survive and to propagate because they were able to cooperate with each other to accomplish difficult tasks. For *Homo sapiens*, cooperation has always required a modicum of trust and transparency. Therefore, social actors who are widely perceived to be dishonest and untrustworthy are not likely to do well in the group. They may be shunned or punished. At the same time, group members compete with each other to get ahead in the group's status hierarchy and to obtain valuable resources. In some instances, therefore, it may be supremely adaptive to ignore or defy the truth—to lie or cheat or engage in deceitful behavior that promotes the social actor's well-being, even at the expense of others. If one can lie and get away with it, reputation unsullied, so much the better! But if one is caught lying, there may be reputational costs to pay.

For social actors like us, there is nothing more important than social reputation. We evolved to be obsessed with it. We sort each other out in terms of the basic traits that make up social reputation. As discussed in previous chapters, the fundamental psychological dimensions of social reputation fall into approximately five big groupings, widely known as the Big Five: (i) *extraversion* (vs. introversion), (ii) *neuroticism* (vs. emotional stability), (iii) *openness* (vs. dogmatism and closed-mindedness), (iv) *conscientiousness* (vs. lack of discipline and unreliability), and (5) *agreeableness* (vs. disagreeableness, cruelty, and mean-spiritedness). We have evolved to be especially sensitive to the differences we perceive in other social actors (and in ourselves) regarding various aspects of extraversion, neuroticism, openness, conscientiousness, and agreeableness.

Attributions regarding honesty and truthfulness tend to fall mainly within the agreeableness domain. In other words, ratings of how honest a person is tend to co-vary with ratings of how nice and kind and compassionate a person is. In our own minds and in social reality, agreeable people tend to be honest people. My guess, though, is that you can easily identify exceptions to this rule. There are surely many very, very nice people out there who are inveterate liars. And there are disagreeable and nasty people who are brutally honest. Nonetheless, research tends to show a general positive correlation between ratings of honesty, truthfulness, sincerity, and the like on the one hand and ratings of warmth, compassion, empathy, and the like on the other. Despite the many exceptions, agreeable people tend to be honest people.

In the case of Donald Trump, a highly disagreeable social actor turns out, as well, to be prone to lying, deceit, and various forms of untruth, in keeping with empirical findings.

The connection between general disagreeableness and lying seems to be especially close in Trump's case, according to the analysis provided by Bella DePaulo, a social psychologist who has studied lying for much of her career. Through anonymous surveys of community residents and college students, DePaulo has collected and analyzed the different kinds of lies that people tell. Her research shows that two categories are most common: (i) *self-serving* lies that aim to promote a social actor's self-interest ("I got the highest score ever recorded in the state of Indiana") and (ii) *kind* lies that aim to make other social actors feel better

("You look beautiful today, sweetheart"). Analyzing the content of falsehoods uttered by Mr. Trump, DePaulo found that he tends to utter more self-serving lies and fewer kind lies than do most other people.

But the big differences showed up in a third category of lies, a form of false statement that DePaulo rarely sees in her research. These are *cruel* lies, told to hurt or disparage others. In DePaulo's research, just 0.8% of the lies told by college students and 2.4% of the lies told by community members surveyed were categorized as cruel. For Trump, the score was 50%! DePaulo listed examples, such as Trump's proclaiming that former intelligence officials John Brennan and James Clapper were "political hacks," that foreign countries send their criminals and rapists to the United States to become immigrants, and that a Democratic candidate running for governor of Virginia was "fighting for the violent MS-13 killer gangs & sanctuary cities." In an op-ed piece, DePaulo wrote: "I study liars. I've never seen one like President Trump." He lies more than most human beings lie. And his lies are often laced with venom.

Donald Trump's reputation as a social actor who plays fast and loose with the truth was beginning to take root by the time he was 30 years old, when the society columnist Judy Klemesrud wrote a flattering portrait of the real-estate tycoon for *The New York Times*. Klemesrud described Trump as a bold and creative businessman and a swashbuckling man about town. When asked to identify any shortcomings that Mr. Trump might have, one person interviewed by Klemesrud said: "He's extremely aggressive when he sells, maybe to the point of overselling. Like, he'll say the convention center is the biggest in the world, when it really isn't. He'll exaggerate for the purpose of making a sale." Breaking into a smile, the respondent added: "That Donald, he could sell sand to the Arabs, and refrigerators to the Eskimos."

What Klemesrud did not know at the time was that Donald Trump told her at least four blatant lies, all of which she reported as facts in her article. First, Trump claimed that he finished first in his class at Wharton School of Finance, University of Pennsylvania. The claim is false. Second, he told Klemesrud that he was ethnically Swedish, a falsehood that Fred Trump also promulgated for many years. Fred Trump was German (and Mary Trump was from Scotland). Third, in reference to a federal suit brought against the Trump Organization in 1973, Donald Trump insisted that his father's company never discriminated against African Americans. The claim is highly dubious, at best. Finally, Trump told Klemesrud that he tends to be "publicity shy." I feel that I do not need to comment on that last claim.

During the 10 years between the publication of Klemesrud's article and the publication of *The Art of the Deal*, Donald Trump's reputation in New York City grew exponentially. A highly extraverted and disagreeable social actor, Trump was known for outlandish bouts of untruth as much as he was known for anything else. Even his buildings lied. Trump Tower claims to be 68 stories high, but it is really 58 stories high because the numbering system skips 10 stories. By the abysmally low standards of New York City real estate developers in the 1980s, Donald Trump stood apart for his unabashed embrace of wild exaggeration and out-and-out lying. While many New Yorkers admired Trump's penchant for "truthful hyperbole," many others were disgusted. "I wouldn't believe Donald Trump if his tongue were notarized," quipped Alair Townsend, when he served as deputy to New York Mayor Ed Koch.

The fellow real-estate magnate Steve Wynn was even more cutting, as quoted in a 1998 interview for *New York* magazine: "No sane or rational guy would [or should] respond to Trump" and his lies, Wynn said, after Trump had publicly questioned Wynn's mental health. "His statements to people like you [the press], whether they concern us and our projects, or our motivations, or his own reality, or his own future, or his own present, you have seen over the years have no relation to truth or fact. And if you need me to remind you of that, we're both in trouble. He's a fool."

Trump believed that Wynn was probably angry because of golf: "We used to be friendly. Had a good relationship, would play golf. Which was always the problem. I kicked his ass in golf," Trump told *New York*. "He thinks he's a good golfer, but he's terrible. Not that I give a damn."

"What is the matter with him?" Wynn asked in response. "How deeply is he disturbed? When he was a kid growing up—who did this to him? I mean, a psychiatrist would know all this."

I doubt any psychiatrist knows for sure.

But Tony Schwartz, who was Trump's ghostwriter for *The Art of the Deal*, has hinted at what I believe to be part of the truth behind Trump's penchant for untruth. In a 2016 interview with Jane Mayer for *The New Yorker*, Schwartz said this about Trump: "Lying is second nature to him. More than anyone else I have ever met, Trump has the ability to convince himself that whatever he is saying *at any given moment* is true, or sort of true, or at least ought to be true."

Schwartz reveals a critical insight about the nature of *time* in the strange case of Donald Trump. The past is gone (and mostly forgotten), and the future is unknowable. For Donald Trump, there is only the immediate moment. He must win the moment.

What does the moment feel like? It feels like war. For Donald Trump, the present moment is nearly always a battle to be won (or lost). "The world is a horrible place," Trump wrote in a book entitled *Think Big*. "Lions kill for food, but people kill for sport." "The same burning greed that makes people loot, kill, and steal in emergencies like fires and floods, operates daily in normal everyday people. . . . People will annihilate you just for the fun of it or to show off to their friends." The journalist Mark Singer wrote of what it was like, back in the 1990s, to watch a movie with Donald Trump while airborne on Trump's private 747. Trump chose the action movie *Bloodsport*. Using the VCR, he fast-forwarded through all the plot development sections of the film to focus exclusively on the discrete fight episodes, which Trump played over and over.

As the episodic man who is constantly under siege, Trump lives in the bloody, combative moment—outside of time, outside of plot, outside of narrative. This is why history has no meaning for him; why he knows virtually nothing about U.S. history; why he once suggested that President Andrew Jackson (who died in 1845) was somehow involved in the American Civil War (1861–1865); and why he once intimated that the 19th-century escaped slave and abolitionist, Frederick Douglass, was still living and writing in the year 2017. When an economic advisor tried to give President Trump a short history lesson regarding tax cuts that occurred in the Reagan administration, Trump reportedly shouted, "I don't give a shit about that!"

As with the past, so goes the future. During the 2016 presidential campaign, Trump refused to develop a transition planning team. As a result, his administration got off to a very slow start with respect to hiring key people and developing policy. As described in Woodward's book *Fear: Trump in the White House*, President Trump refuses to engage in long-term strategic planning. He does not even prepare for important meetings, trusting that his instincts will enable him to master the situation and address issues as they arise. Trump loves to quote the boxer, Mike Tyson: "Everybody has a plan until they get punched in the mouth." Like Tyson, Trump punches his way through life, one moment to the next. But he rarely leaves the ring. Day in and day out, he continues to punch and to be punched. The threats of annihilation never go away. No time for planning or looking back. The emergency of the moment blots out the past and the future. Trump cannot see beyond the current fight—or, at most, the anticipated next one.

Under the psychological conditions that envelop the episodic man, truth is reduced to whatever works to win the moment. *What is true is what helps me to win*. But we are not talking here about a long-term victory. *There is no long-term*. The battle is upon us, and *we must fight it now*. To imagine truth as something loftier and more enduring than what helps the episodic man to win the moment is to imagine a psychological luxury that the episodic man can never know. His response to the conventional conceptions of truth, honesty, and interpersonal trust probably goes something like this: *Yeah, dude, that's a nice idea—truth as consistency from one moment to the next, truth as consensus among rational agents who share the same reality, eternal truths that are good for all time and all situations. But I don't give a shit about that. I don't live in that world. I have a fucking battle to win.*

One of the most glaring examples of President Trump's refusal to tell the truth involves the 2017 hurricane that devastated Puerto Rico. Shortly after the storm hit, the president began to boast about the success his administration enjoyed in leading the recovery initiative. A year later, he continued to brag about "the incredible, unsung success" of the federal government's effort. The truth, however, is that Hurricane Maria was profoundly devastating, and the administration's recovery effort failed in many key respects. For example, it took nearly a year to restore power to the entire island.

Researchers at George Washington University conducted a systematic study of the tragedy. They found that the hurricane resulted in nearly 3,000 deaths in Puerto Rico, which is nearly twice the number who died in 2005 from Hurricane Katrina. The researchers based their findings on sophisticated statistical procedures that calculated how many more deaths than expected occurred in the aftermath of the storm. The same procedures have been used to assess fatalities in other disasters. President Trump has rejected the findings and claimed that the entire study was the result of a conspiracy by Democrats "to make me look as bad as possible."

Despite the empirical findings and without any countervailing evidence of his own, Trump insisted, "3000 people did not die" as a result of Hurricane Maria. "When I left the island, AFTER the storm had hit," he said, "they had anywhere from 6 to 18 deaths. As time went by it did not go up by much. Then, a long time later, they started to report really large numbers, like 3000."

For Mr. Trump, the hurricane was a discrete moment in time—a demarcated episode. Once the hurricane passed over the island, the episode was done. Freeze frame: How many died? Six? Eighteen? Maybe 50, at most? Given how strong the winds were and how fragile the Puerto Rico infrastructure was to begin with, the American response was "one of the best," Trump concluded. I win the moment. The reality, though, is that a hurricane's effects may be felt for days, months, even years. A disaster is not a discrete episode. It is, instead, a sequence of interlaced and ramifying events, playing out over a long period of time. It is an ongoing *story*. Trump does not think of life that way. The findings from the study, like history itself and like the long-term prognostications of climate scientists as they try to envision the future of the globe, make no sense to Donald Trump.

Abraham Lincoln once said, "No man has a good enough memory to be a successful liar." Lincoln's point was that lying is hard cognitive work. To be really good at lying, you need to keep track of all the lies you have told, so that you can continue to deceive people going forward. But Lincoln did not anticipate Trump. Trump is a successful liar because he does not let memory get in the way. The episodic man does not need a good memory—far from it! A *bad* memory is what he really needs. And just as he ignores the past, the episodic man needs to ignore the future, too. Trump lies shamelessly in the here-and-now moment. And it would be a lie to say that he has *not* been successful in doing so.

***

Truthfulness is a valued quality of human behavior the world over. Honesty, sincerity, and integrity are hallmarks of an ethical person in religious traditions, philosophical systems, and the minds of common folk who go about their daily business, striving to get along and get ahead. Honest people are nearly always praised and trusted. In the United States, our most admired president was known as "Honest Abe."

With that in mind, why do so many Americans tolerate Donald Trump's renunciation of truth? After all, dishonesty is hardly a *minor* character flaw, akin to forgetfulness or bad table manners. Most Americans consider themselves to be honest and good people. And yet nearly 63 million American adults voted for Donald Trump in the 2016 presidential election. Perhaps most of them were not aware at the time of Trump's problems with truth. But two years into his presidency, the vast majority of Americans probably know. While Trump's approval ratings for the first two years of his presidency were relatively low by historical standards (hovering around 40%), he still retained the strong support of tens of millions, including the overwhelming majority of self-identified Republicans (around 85% in polls at the end of 2018).

How do President Trump's strongest supporters come to terms with his lying? I believe they employ at least five different strategies. Each is like a coping mechanism that enables a person to make sense of a potentially fatal character flaw on the part of the president and to justify continued, and even enthusiastic, support. In many cases, the mechanisms his supporters use to continue to affirm the president are implicit or unconscious: People are not fully aware that they are using the mechanism. Most likely, people can use a number of different mechanisms, even when different mechanisms seem to contradict each other. For all of us, political allegiances and voting decisions are never purely rational. We don't typically know all the reasons behind our political actions. Still, we *do* have reasons, sometimes buried deep in our minds. Let us consider, then, each of the five mechanisms as a "reason" for continuing to support a chief executive who has been shown to be a chronic liar.

Reason #1: He doesn't lie

In an interview with a CNN reporter on July 24, 2017, presidential advisor Kellyanne Conway asserted that Donald Trump "doesn't think he is lying" when, for example, he alleges that President Obama tapped his phones and when he claims that millions of illegal immigrants voted in 2016. Conway's logic is simple: If you don't know that your statement is false, then the statement cannot truly be called a "lie." Variations on this idea abound among President Trump's supporters. They all suggest that, in reality, President Trump does not lie very much, if at all. They downplay or deny the lying.

This general strategy may stem from inattention or cynicism. Many Americans are simply not paying much attention to what goes on in Washington, DC. They like President Trump, and they trust him to tell the truth, more or less. The media outlets they tune in to, if they do indeed tune in, tend to gloss over Trump's problems with untruth. To the extent some supporters are aware of the negative reports about President Trump's truthfulness, they may dismiss the allegations as politically partisan attacks or as the wailings of an unreliable, left-wing press. Or else they may simply assert that all politicians are liars, and President Trump is no worse than anybody else. In the latter case, they may be admitting that Trump does indeed lie but insisting that lying does not matter in the realm of politics.

Reason #2: He lies, but his emotions are true and authentic

Many of President Trump's strongest supporters admire his authenticity. He says what he thinks. He tells it like it is. In a sense, these supporters believe that President Trump is *more truthful* than other politicians and, indeed, more truthful than many other Americans, especially more truthful than those "politically correct" people who regularly censor themselves so as not to offend others. This general strategy pits veracity against authenticity. Sure, the president may lie about the details. He may exaggerate and even deceive. But his feelings and instincts are true. His broad intentions are good. His heart is in the right place.

Corey Lewandowski, who worked as a top aide on the Trump presidential campaign, channeled this sentiment in a critique of the mainstream press: "You guys took everything Donald Trump said so literally. The American people didn't." Lewandowski suggested that the American people, unlike many journalists, don't focus on, and really don't care about, the misstatements and exaggerations Donald Trump routinely makes. They see through all that to a deeper truth, a truth that is more about human emotion and sentiment and about big ideas, rather than trivial details.

Lewandowski's take is consistent with what many people see as the ethos of the business world. Donald Trump, after all, originally came to fame as a real estate developer. He promoted his projects with boundless energy, often employing what he called "truthful hyperbole." Trump was an amazing salesman. In business and advertising, we expect people to exaggerate, to stretch the truth, even to utter wild falsehoods. We see it every day in television commercials and on the Internet. Why should we worry about this? Instead, we should celebrate President Trump's untruths, as harmless as they may be, because he is forthrightly engaged in the bigger business of promoting America, of promoting *us*.

Reason #3: He lies, but what he says "could be" true

The social psychologist Daniel Effron conducted a study of 2,783 Americans from across the political spectrum (including Trump supporters and Trump opponents) to examine how they respond to politically relevant statements that are demonstrably false but *could be true*. Effron called these statements "counterfactuals." Let us imagine that you are a research participant in Effron's study. You are presented with a series of counterfactuals. You are told that each counterfactual statement is indeed false, and you are asked to rate how "unethical" it would be for a person to knowingly utter that falsehood. Some lies are certainly worse than others, warranting a higher rating on unethicalness. It is probably more unethical, for example, to lie about your SAT scores to a prospective employer than it would be to lie about what you ate for dinner last night.

Let us imagine two counterfactuals. Counterfactual A is this: *President Trump's inaugural crowd was the largest in American history.* Counterfactual B is this: *President Trump removed a bust of Martin Luther King Jr.(MLK) from the Oval Office.* Both statements are factually *false*, and you, as a participant in this study, are explicitly told that they are false. As an overall finding, Trump supporters tended to rate a person telling Counterfactual A as less unethical than did Trump opponents. Conversely, Trump opponents tended to rate a person telling Counterfactual B as less unethical than did Trump supporters. No surprises there.

Now, here is where it gets a little more complicated, but much more interesting. Before they made their ratings on the unethical scale, half of the participants in the study (let us call them the "experimental group") were asked to imagine how the counterfactual they had just read *could have been true* if circumstances had been different. The other half (the "control group") were not given these instructions. The results of the study showed that participants in the experimental group—those asked to imagine how the falsehood could have been true—tended to rate a hypothetical person who would utter the falsehood as *less unethical* than did the participants in the control group, *but only when the falsehood was consistent with their initial political opinions about President Trump.* In other words, among Trump supporters, those who imagined how Counterfactual A (the false claim about the inauguration crowd) could have been true (even though they knew it was not true) tended to rate telling such a falsehood as even less unethical than did those Trump supporters who were not asked to imagine its being true. Similarly, among Trump opponents, those who imagined how Counterfactual B (the false claim about removing the MLK bust) could have been true (even though they knew it was not true) tended to rate telling such a falsehood as even less unethical than did those Trump opponents who were not asked to imagine its being true. Imagining how the counterfactual could have been true had no effect, however, when Trump supporters evaluated a lie against Trump, or when Trump opponents evaluated a lie that was designed to support Trump.

The take-home message from Effron's study is that imagining how a lie could be true helps a person discount the lie, but only when the lie is consistent with what a person believes in the first place. On an everyday basis, some of President Trump's supporters are quite willing to excuse his falsehoods, even when they know that he is lying, because the falsehoods could have been true.

When President Trump retweeted a video falsely purporting to show a Muslim migrant committing assault, his press secretary Sarah Huckabee Sanders defended him by saying, "Whether it's a real video, the threat is real." On another occasion, Sanders conceded that the president made up a story about how Japanese government officials drop bowling balls on American cars to test their safety, but she argued that the false story still "illustrates the creative ways some countries are able to keep American goods out of their markets." When asked about Trump's false claims regarding the size of his inauguration crowd, Kellyanne Conway suggested that bad weather had kept people away. In each of these three cases, imagining how the false claim could be true does not make it any less false. But psychologically, it may make the falsehood seem more innocent and less untruthful and, thus, less unethical to tell.

Reason #4: He's a con man, but he's our con man

The proverbial con man is known for his ability to trick or deceive people into believing that falsehoods—sometimes, outlandish falsehoods—are true. The con man gains the "confidence" of unsuspecting people through guile and trickery. His disingenuous methods work in the service of enriching or advancing the con man himself. In the popular imagination, con men are brash swindlers who operate with charm and even charisma. They are masters of deceit who win the trust of gullible victims.

Critics have long accused Donald Trump of operating like a con man. Many of the business principles that Trump outlined in *The Art of the Deal* may be viewed as instructions for how to be a successful con man: "play to people's fantasies," "promote bravado," engage in "truthful hyperbole." "People want to believe that something is the biggest and the greatest and the most spectacular," Trump wrote. Con men make big promises, but they often fail to deliver in the end. Insidiously, they know from the get-go that their promises will never be met. When their targets finally realize that they have been duped, the con men have absconded with the ill-gotten gains.

When it comes to making the case that Donald Trump fits the con man designation, Trump University is Exhibit A, many critics would argue. Trump University promised to make its students rich. A for-profit education company that ran a real estate training program in the years 2005 to 2010, Trump University was the subject of an investigation by the New York Attorney General's Office for illegal business practices. The investigation led to a lawsuit filed in 2013. Trump University was also the defendant in two class action lawsuits brought in federal court. The claimants alleged that Trump University defrauded unsuspecting students by using misleading marketing practices and aggressive sales tactics. Trump professed his innocence and his good faith all along, and he insisted that he would never settle the lawsuits. But in November 2016, he settled all three cases, agreeing to pay $25 million in restitution.

A professor of English at the University of Virginia, Emily Ogden wrote an essay comparing President Trump to 19th-century American hypnotists and other con men. Using sleight of hand, the powers of suggestion, and other tricks, hypnotists mesmerized their gullible audiences into doing all sorts of bizarre things. Skeptics of the day resoundingly criticized what the hypnotists were doing. But even when the fans knew that the hypnotists were frauds, they still flocked to their performances. In a similar manner, Ogden argued, some of President Trump's supporters are supremely cognizant of his conniving ways. Rather than condemn him for deceit, they applaud. "Great con men feed off accusations of dishonesty," Ogden wrote. "They mesmerize us *because* we suspect them of deception, not in spite of the fact." His supporters appreciate the fact that President Trump is a "master of the deceptive arts."

In the Hobbesian world that has always captured Donald Trump's imagination, swindlers and con men run rampant, along with cheaters, thieves, rapists, killers, and all manner of malevolent actors. In this kind of world, you want the tough guys to be on your team. Even for those who do not ascribe to Trump's sinister world view, peril and uncertainty may appear to be ubiquitous in modern life. It can be very difficult to know what the truth is, and to know whom you can trust. "When no one is trustworthy, you might as well trust a con artist," Ogden wrote. "Innocent lambs may be admirable, but they're not the defenders you want in a dog-eat-dog world. Better to have a sly fox on your side."

Reason #5: He is a different kind of being

Observers of the current political scene often express wonderment regarding Donald Trump's uncanny ability to survive one self-inflicted crisis after another. Imagine if evidence had emerged that either Barack Obama or

George W. Bush had once (i) cruelly mocked a disabled reporter, (ii) bragged on camera about grabbing a woman's genitals, (iii) paid a porn star $130,000 to keep quiet about a sexual escapade, (iv) refused to release his tax returns, (v) condoned violence at political rallies, (vi) suggested a moral equivalence between white supremacists and those protesting white supremacy, (vii) sided with a Russian dictator over his own intelligence agencies, (viii) publicly made 2,140 demonstrably false statements in the first year of his presidency, and (ix) shot and killed a man in the middle of Fifth Avenue. That last one did not happen. But Trump famously imagined that it might: "I could stand in the middle of Fifth Avenue and shoot somebody, and I wouldn't lose voters," Trump said at a campaign rally in Sioux City, Iowa, in January 2016. His point was that his supporters will stick with him no matter what. When it comes to the issue of truth, it does not seem to matter how much he lies, or how outrageous his lies may be. It is as if Trump's supporters hold him to a different moral standard than they impose on other people, as if he is fundamentally different from other people.

"Everything about Mr. Trump is strange." In this book's prologue, I marked this statement, from an admiring personal butler who worked for Donald Trump for 30 years, as the starting point for my psychological interpretation of Trump's life. We must never lose sight of the strangeness. Trump himself never loses sight of it—nor do many of his supporters, I believe. They see him as a very different kind of person, as indeed Trump sees himself. He is special. The rules do not apply to him.

The sense that many people have regarding Donald Trump's unique ontological status—his unique being-ness—is expressed in many different ways. Some of his admirers relate to him as if he were a *superhero*, and indeed Trump has characterized himself as such. In early 2016, just when Trump's campaign was starting to gain traction, the columnist David Brooks observed: "Trump's supporters aren't looking for a political process to address their needs. They are looking for a superhero." Superheroes have special, superhuman powers. They can do things that other human beings cannot do.

In a related vein, Trump has been described as the personification of a primal force in human nature. Kent G. Bailey, a professor emeritus of clinical psychology at Virginia Commonwealth University, has characterized Trump as an *archetype*: "Donald Trump is the prototypical, archetypal and testosterone-driven alpha male who rules by the sheer force of his personality, imposing physique, quick wit, mastery of repartee and almost hypnotic control over his gathering masses of adoring followers." He is "our fearless leader against the pagan forces of progressiveness and political correctness," "a quintessential warrior male of yore capable of vanquishing any and all opposition in his way." Archetypes are one-dimensional mythic figures. Often represented as gods in ancient mythologies, they personify, or put into personal form, a particular set of qualities—like power in the case of Zeus, wisdom in the case of Athena, or love in the case of Aphrodite.

Superheroes and archetypes enjoy extraordinary personal powers. They are, however, not quite *persons*. Instead, they are idealized *types*. Superheroes and archetypes take a small subset of attributes that human persons are expected to have and magnify those attributes into an exaggerated form. In the process, however, they leave behind a host of other human attributes that do not fit the type. For this reason, we do not expect superheroes and mythic figures to experience a rich and varied inner life, of the sort that a normal person is expected to experience. We do not expect them to experience the full gamut of human emotions and desires. We do not expect them to suffer in the way that real persons suffer. Importantly, we do not expect them to be moral agents in the way that normal people are. While superheroes and mythic figures may perform good actions and bad actions, we do not expect them to deliberate long and hard about their moral choices. We do not expect them to muddle through moral dilemmas, to make tough moral decisions amidst uncertainty. Clark Kent was a fallible person who knew what it meant to feel angst and ambivalence. But the moment he stepped into a phone booth and became Superman, he lost the psychological and moral messiness that comes with being a person, even as he gained superhuman powers to defend truth, justice, and the American way. Faster than a speeding bullet, more powerful than a locomotive, he became more than a person—and less.

Of course, most people do not literally believe that Donald Trump is superhuman. Even Donald Trump does not think this—or at least I think he doesn't. But many people, nonetheless, project mythic qualities onto him, I believe. I include in the count a growing number of white evangelical Christians. Political observers have always found puzzling the strange hold Trump has on white evangelicals. Divorced twice and alleged to have had multiple affairs, Trump has never been a model of Christian piety. Moreover, the man who spoke to a Liberty University audience about "Two Corinthians" appears to be nearly bereft of knowledge about Christianity and bereft of Christian faith. According to the Reverend Jerry Falwell Jr., however, many evangelicals see Trump as a kind of *savior*. "All the social issues—traditional family values, abortion—are moot if ISIS blows up some of our cities or if the borders are not fortified," Falwell told *The New York Times* in February of 2016. Rank-and-file evangelicals "are trying to *save* the country," Falwell said. Being "saved" has a special resonance among evangelical Christians—saved from sin and damnation, for sure, but also saved from the threats that come from a corrupt and dangerous world. Christian America is under siege, as some see it. And Donald Trump may be the mythic figure destined to defend traditional Christian America against radical Muslim terrorism and the more subtle threats that come from secularism and the erosion of traditional Christian values.

I grew up in the Christian evangelical tradition. In Baptist Sunday School, we learned that the Lord often works in mysterious ways. Why were an impoverished teen-aged virgin and a humble carpenter chosen to be the earthly parents of the Son of God? Why would Jesus choose a prostitute to be one of his loyal followers? Who can ever know why God chooses whom God chooses to deliver and personify God's message of redemption? The most joyous moments in my Baptist upbringing were the altar calls that occurred at the end of the Sunday service. Who might come forward today to accept Jesus as Lord and personal savior? Who might walk to the front of the church to confess all his sins and let Jesus into his heart? For ten years or more, a gigantic lady whom I can still picture in my mind sang every Sunday in the alto section of the choir. Rumor had it she was married to a drunken scoundrel. The prodigal husband showed up one Sunday morning, 100% sober and dressed in a tattered suit that he must have purchased from the Salvation Army store. With the congregation singing "Just as I Am," he stumbled to the front of the sanctuary to accept the gift of Christian salvation. The big lady could not hold back her tears. Nor could anybody else.

Is Donald Trump that drunken husband? Is the Lord working through a man who told 2,140 lies in the first year of his presidency? Many evangelical Christians are simply thankful that Trump seeks their counsel and listens to their concerns, as he expressly does, and that he supports policies that they tend to support. But some may push it further, sensing that Trump may indeed be part of a divine plan, that he may be an unwitting vehicle for God's will. For example, Trump's Attorney General Jeff Sessions, a devout Christian, may fall into that category. Bob Woodward relates the gist of a conversation that Sessions had with Steve Bannon, as told by Bannon:

> Bannon turned to what was perhaps the fondest memory of their [Bannon's and Sessions'] political lives—when Trump had won the presidency on November 9. Victory was as sweet as it got.
>
> "Is there any doubt in your mind on the 9th, when it was called, that it was the hand?" Bannon asked, dipping into a shared religious belief system. "That divine providence that worked through Trump to win this?"
>
> "No," Sessions said.
>
> "You mean that?"
>
> Sessions said he did.
>
> "It was the hand of God, right? You and I were there. We know there's no other way it could've happened than the hand of God."
>
> "Yes."

We do not hold superheroes, mythic gods and goddesses, and characters whose actions are dictated by the hand of God to conventional standards of morality. Superheroes make their marks through their superhuman deeds. It is their actions and their powers that we consider relevant in making sense of their being—not so much their moral choices and motivations. Archetypes exist to exemplify one or two extraordinary traits. We do not imagine them as full-bodied persons who experience life the way you or I experience it. Instruments of God's will are closer to the person ideal, as perhaps Jesus was as depicted in the New Testament, but there is still a difference. We often do not see them as exercising free will in the way that other persons exercise it. Their actions seem to be beyond their personal control, reflecting a higher reality. If Donald Trump's lies are in the service of God's higher plan, a plan that a mere mortal like me can never hope to understand, then who am I to criticize him? Donald Trump may be a scoundrel. But he is God's scoundrel! He has been chosen for a destiny that neither you nor I nor Donald Trump can alter. Therefore, Donald Trump may not be responsible for his actions and his falsehoods to the extent that other people are.

I believe that a sizeable number of Donald Trump's supporters unconsciously project superhuman qualities on to him, and this projection slightly alters in their minds his status as a person. The projection helps them to justify or rationalize or simply ignore Trump's descent into untruth. This is not an unusual thing for enthusiastic political supporters to do. It could be argued that some Democrats may have done something similar vis-à-vis Barack Obama. In their cases, the projection may have also served the psychological purpose of rationalizing away President Obama's shortcomings. But Obama was not a professional liar. And Obama did not participate in the myth-making, person-transforming process with the same kind of gusto that Donald Trump exhibits. At the end of the day, Obama saw himself to be a normative person. By contrast, Donald Trump has expressly endeavored to cast doubt on his own personhood for much of his adult life. He has done this by suggesting that there is something about him that goes beyond being a person.

"It's a feeling, an aura you create," Trump told *Time* magazine in 1989. Being "Trump" became more than a matter of walking down the streets of Manhattan as a famous flesh-and-blood person. It was more even than being a celebrity. It involved creating a golden penumbra around his personhood, a shimmering sensibility that evoked awe and desire in the eyes and minds of others. It involved creating a *brand* that expanded Trump's personhood to encompass Trump Tower, Trump University, Trump Casinos, Trump Steaks, Trump Wine, and on and on. As the Trump biographer Michael D'Antonio observed, "the facts of his life didn't matter as much [to Trump] as *the idea of him*."

In a 1997 profile for *The New Yorker*, Mark Singer wrote that Trump's greatest talent was "being 'Trump' or, as he often referred to himself, 'the Trumpster,' looming ubiquitous by *reducing himself to a persona.*" Singer noted that as the *persona* expanded outward, the inner life of the real *person* contracted, becoming smaller and smaller. Becoming a persona, an image, an idealized form, a brand, an idea in the minds of an adoring audience—all of this "exempted him from introspection," Singer observed. Trump would seem to agree. "When you start studying yourself too deeply, you start seeing things that maybe you don't want to see," Trump said in the 1989 interview with *Time.* "And if there's a rhyme and reason, people can figure you out, and once they can figure you out, you're in big trouble."

In the minds of many Trump supporters, I believe, Trump cannot be "figured out" in the way most persons are typically figured out. The conventional norms of morality and psychology that human beings typically apply to persons do not quite apply to a persona. They do not quite apply to him.

In a 1990 interview for *Playboy* magazine, Trump said that his yacht, his glitzy casinos, and the other glimmering objects that were associated at the time with the idea of him, with the aura and the penumbra, were all "props for the show." "The show is 'Trump' and it is sold-out performances everywhere." In the following decade, the show became even more literal, through *The Apprentice.* Trump's persona expanded to become a reality TV star. Becoming president of the United States in the following decade kept the show rolling, in Trump's mind. On the eve of becoming the most powerful person in the world, Trump told his aides to think of every single day in his presidency as an episode in a reality TV program, wherein the superhero fights to vanquish his foes.

By what standards do we evaluate the stars of reality TV programs? By their morality? Their truthfulness?

No. We judge them by their ratings. And ratings are based on viewership, which ultimately derives from entertainment value or other qualities personified by the persona—who is not quite a person—to attract our rapt interest.

This is why President Trump believes he will win re-election in 2020. In an impromptu interview with the *New York Times* on December 28, 2017, the president predicted that he will "win another four years" "because newspapers, television, all forms of media will tank if I'm not there because without me, their ratings are going down the tubes."

It was vintage Trump—over-the-top outlandish, beyond anything that any president would ever say, or even think, and yet weirdly authentic, and maybe just a little bit *true.*

Love

In principle, even the most disagreeable and dishonest human beings are capable of genuine love. This is because the experience of love for *Homo sapiens* is an inevitable result of our extreme sociality. Compared to many other species, we are intensely social throughout our life cycles, and this is evident from day one. Human infants form bonds of love with their caregivers, as naturally as they suck at the breast to obtain nourishment. Natural selection has mandated that human babies do this. Any baby that might come into the world with a different plan—say, an "I-can-go-it-alone" plan, no need to waste time with love—might as well forego food and water, too. The plan would be an evolutionary loser. Even severely autistic children, known for their difficulties in forming interpersonal relationships, experience some form of love for their caregivers. Every conscious human being, Donald Trump included, knows what love feels like, at some level.

The Big Five dispositional traits that describe differences between human beings as social actors—extraversion, neuroticism, openness, conscientiousness, and agreeableness—do not fully capture the experience of human love. As indicators of broad social reputations, individual differences in these traits are related to love, and related to things that are related to love, but none of the traits is up to the psychological task of revealing the complexities of human love. The Big Five traits are too broad and superficial for that. For example, social actors who, like Donald Trump, are characterized as especially extraverted tend to have more romantic involvements and more sexual partners, compared to those who score toward the introverted end of the scale. At least, that is what the scientific research shows. But what does love feel like to people high in extraversion? What do they want in love? How do they make sense of love? We do not know, probably because each love relationship contains its own unique features.

In study after study, high scores on the trait of neuroticism are associated with a host of emotional problems in romantic relationships, in family relationships, and in friendships. All other things being equal, people high in neuroticism are significantly more likely to get divorced than those who score low on the trait. When it comes to the Big Five trait of openness, there is almost nothing we can say regarding love. Research draws a blank. Knowing a person's relative position on the openness continuum, therefore, probably tells you nothing about what that person's experiences with love might turn out to be. Research on the trait

The Strange Case of Donald J. Trump. Dan P. McAdams, Oxford University Press (2020). © Oxford University Press.
DOI: 10.1093/oso/9780197507445.001.0001

of conscientiousness is a bit more instructive: People high in conscientiousness tend to enjoy relatively stable family and romantic relationships, compared to those scoring low on conscientiousness. They are less likely to have extramarital sexual affairs. They report secure and especially loving bonds with their parents.

Of all the Big Five traits, the broad dimension of agreeableness would seem to be the closest to love per se. But even here, research reveals only statistical associations on the surface—nothing deep or specific. Thus, people high in agreeableness tend to report less conflict in their relationships and a stronger sense of security, compared to people who, like Donald Trump, find themselves on the low end of the agreeableness dimension. Statistically speaking, agreeableness is positively associated with experiencing marriage, friendship, and parenting relationships in an especially warm and caring manner.

It is probably fair to say that people low in agreeableness, like Donald Trump, are more difficult to love than are nicer people. Many human beings may shy away from forming close relationships with social actors who are widely seen to be rude, callous, arrogant, cruel, dishonest, and malicious—but not completely, because many human beings also suspect, for better and for worse, that most people out there, even mean people, might turn out to be gentle and loving "inside." Indeed, many people may believe that they, and perhaps they alone, can bring out or stimulate that elusive quality of love in the most disagreeable person, especially if that person holds attraction in other ways. Western literature is filled with disagreeable characters who ultimately reveal themselves to be capable of genuine love—think of Scrooge in *A Christmas Carol* or the beast in *Beauty and the Beast*. We tend to expect that buried deep within the mind of even the most misanthropic human being lies a soft kernel of love. We expect this because we are members of the species *Homo sapiens*, which means we all experienced infancy once upon a time as a profoundly dependent state suffused with longing and love.

Not only is human love first experienced in the infant–caregiver bond, but the quality of that primal connection may establish a basic pattern or model for future love relationships, as well. Over 100 years ago, Sigmund Freud wrote that the earliest bond of love between the infant and mother is "the starting-point of the whole of sexual life, the unmatched prototype of every later sexual satisfaction, to which phantasy often enough returns in times of need." Love begins, Freud believed, with sucking at the mother's breast, a highly sensual experience that results in the mother's becoming the first object of the infant's sensual desire. "I can give you no idea of the important bearing of this first object," Freud wrote, "upon the choice of every later object, of the profound effects it has in its transformations and substitutions in even the remotest regions of our sexual lives."

In the 1960s, John Bowlby and Mary Ainsworth developed modern attachment theory, blending certain Freudian insights with evolutionary theory and

research in developmental science. Through eye contact, smiling, vocaliza-
tion, clinging, following, and, yes, sucking, too, Bowlby and Ainsworth argued,
infants develop an attachment bond with a very small set of caregivers in the first
year of life, the mother typically being most central. From an evolutionary standpoint, the development of attachment helps to protect the infant from predators
and other dangers in the environment by assuring that the caregiver and infant
remain in close physical proximity. Compared to nearly all other animal species, human infants are absurdly needy when they enter the world. Setting it all
up such that infants and mothers cannot help but fall in love early on is natural
selection's brilliant strategy for maximizing the chances that caregivers will protect and provide for their helpless infants' needs, and will continue to nurture
them going forward, through childhood and beyond.

Every attachment bond is unique. Some mother–infant pairs establish highly
secure bonds of love. In these cases, the infant may experience an abundance
of trust in the presence of the caregiver, freeing him or her up to explore the
environment with confidence and aplomb. Other mother–infant pairs establish bonds that are perhaps not quite as secure, although still loving. In the
cases of *anxious* attachment, babies may feel some degree of ambivalence and
nervousness in the presence of their caregivers. In the cases of *avoidant* attachment, babies may sometimes keep their mothers at a distance, psychologically
speaking, to tamp down strong feelings that threaten to overwhelm them. Other
patterns may be observed as well, including the rare and troubling instances of
disorganized attachment, wherein babies seem disoriented and confused in the
mother's presence.

Each of these patterns may lay down in the brain of the baby what attachment
researchers call a *working model* for love. A working model is an unconscious
set of expectations regarding how love works. It is what Freud referred to as "the
unmatched prototype" of later relationships, carried forward in the mind of the
lover. While many factors surely impact how love develops over the course of a
human life, the early bond with the mother is believed to be one of the more important influences.

With all that said, what do we know about Trump's early relationship with his
mother?

Mary Anne (MacLeod) Trump is the mystery woman in the strange case of
Donald J. Trump. The youngest of 10 children, Mary was born in 1912 in the
village of Tong on the rugged Scottish Isle of Lewis. Her father was a fisherman,
and the family kept a small plot of land for "crofting," which was a local term for
subsistence farming. Going back generations, many adults living on the island
were crofters, and many were evicted from their tenant farms in the 19th century,
throwing their families into dire poverty. One account from the time described
the landless people of Tong as living in "human wretchedness." The Isle of Lewis

sent 6,000 young men to war between the years 1914 and 1918. Nearly 1,000 of them perished in the conflagration, and another 205 died, perhaps even more tragically, when a small ship transporting them home struck rocks and sank, within sight of the island's shore. The men who survived World War I returned to a landscape that was even more impoverished than it had been when they left.

Mary spoke Gaelic as a girl, learning English as a second language in school. She completed eighth grade. With few prospects for work and few marriageable men in sight, Mary left Scotland shortly before her 18th birthday, following three of her sisters to America. She boarded the SS Transylvania in Glasgow on May 2, 1930, arriving in New York City on May 11. She planned to live with one of her sisters in Astoria, Queens, and to work as a domestic. It was the middle of the Great Depression, so work as a maid or nanny was difficult to find in New York. Still, she did manage to garner employment with a wealthy family. In her book Golden Handcuffs: The Secret History of Trump's Women, Nina Burleigh reported that Mary settled in at 2 East 91st Street in Manhattan, working as a maid to the widow of Andrew Carnegie.

Five-foot-eight, with fair hair and blue eyes, Mary got her big break when she met Fred Trump at a party. Six years her senior, Fred had managed to stay financially afloat during the Great Depression, and he was on the verge of reigniting his family's real estate business. Fred and Mary were instantly drawn to each other. When Fred came home from the party, he told his mother he had met the woman whom he would marry. In a trip back to Scotland, Mary told her parents that she and Fred were likely to wed. The wedding happened in January 1936 at a Presbyterian Church on the Upper East Side of Manhattan. She wore a "princess gown of white satin and a tulle cap and veil," and her bouquet featured "white orchids and lilies of the valley," reported Scotland's Stornoway Gazette, in a short article entitled, "Tong Girl Weds Abroad." Twenty-five guests attended the reception at the Carlyle Hotel. The couple spent a honeymoon weekend in Atlantic City. Fred returned to work on Monday, and Mary began her new life as a different kind of "domestic," a mid-20th-century American housewife.

She would soon be a mother. The first child, Maryanne, arrived in 1937, followed by Fred Jr. ("Freddie") in 1938, Elizabeth in 1942, Donald in 1946, and Robert in 1948. Robert's birth was complicated, and Mary experienced severe hemorrhaging. She underwent a hysterectomy. Mary also suffered from a life-threatening case of peritonitis. After several surgeries, she recovered her health and resumed her busy household role. That role involved being a mother to her five children, of course, but also significant volunteer work at a local hospital and regular luncheons and social engagements with other ladies, to say nothing of the emotional support she provided for her hard-driving husband. A middle-aged live-in maid, Emma, did the cooking and cleaning, and she served as a second mother for the Trump kids. One of Donald's childhood friends recalls that he rarely interacted with Mary, but Emma made "the best hamburgers I'd ever tasted."

In her biography, *The Trumps*, Gwenda Blair concluded that Donald Trump's family of origin provided him with "a source of warmth and security that nothing else in life could ever match." Blair almost seems to be channeling Freud here, suggesting that something in Trump's early environment set down the "unmatched prototype" of love and trust, the working model of a secure attachment scenario. Blair does not explicitly identify Mary as the source of the warmth and security, but it would be hard to argue that Mary was not significantly involved, given her emotional centrality in the family.

Donald Trump idolized his father, for sure, but he also consistently praised his mother, albeit in vague terms. In response to a question from Timothy O'Brien regarding who is the "best person you've ever met," Trump remarked: "I've always said that the best person is my father, but it's *my mother and father*." On Twitter, he has described Mary as "fantastic," "tremendous," "a wonderful person," "a great beauty," and "very warm." In *The Art of the Deal*, Trump wrote that his mother had an artistic and dramatic streak, and he partly credited her for his own skills as a public performer. Friends and acquaintances consistently described Mary as cordial, friendly, pleasant, and unassuming. A long-time colleague of Donald Trump, Louise Sunshine told a journalist that Mary "was a very strong woman." She was "quiet," "not aggressive" and "very low-key," but "loving" and "embracing." A friend from Donald's childhood reported that the Trump children "always spoke well of their mom" and "never had a harsh word" to say about her.

While these general comments about Mary's personality traits speak to her social reputation, they do not directly address the quality of her relationships with her five children. We cannot blithely assume that a woman known to be a generally warm and pleasant human being formed a caring and secure attachment bond with her fourth child. Nor can we assume that she did *not* form such a bond. We simply do not know.

Donald Trump's childhood relationship with his mother remains a mystery. This remains stubbornly true even though Trump has been the subject of public fascination and scrutiny for nearly five decades. Biographers and journalists have interviewed him ad infinitum, and interviewed his siblings, childhood friends, and anybody else who feels they have something illuminating to say about the strange case. Very few facts about the mother–child bond have come to the fore—and what we do know seems to suggest that the relationship may have been surprisingly *non*strange.

Many people who have strong negative feelings toward President Donald Trump assume that the qualities in his personality that they abhor *must* be derived from a dysfunctional relationship with his mother or, more generally, from family turmoil and pathology. Otherwise, they ask, how could he have turned out to be such a terrible person?! In a psychological profile I wrote on Donald Trump for the *Atlantic* magazine in early 2016, I noted that the Trump children seemed to enjoy a relatively secure family environment growing up and that I could find very little that was explicitly dysfunctional or rabidly abusive. In response, one licensed clinical social worker (presumably a psychotherapist) wrote to the magazine to say that my analysis was "amazingly shallow," "irresponsible," and "laughable from a psychological point of view." "Donald Trump isn't who he is because he hasn't suffered severe developmental trauma."

This response reveals a very common form of mushy thinking when it comes to human psychology. Many people, including some mental health experts, presume that a specific cause they have imagined (for which there is no direct evidence) must be true in light of an observed consequence. In the case of my critic, the licensed clinical social worker observes (correctly) that Donald Trump often lashes out at people who disagree with him, that he does not trust many people, that he sees the world as a dangerous place, and so on. Like me (and presumably you), my critic then asks the question, "Why is Donald Trump like this?" Answer: He must have suffered "severe developmental trauma." The critic seems to be suggesting that some kind of psychologically menacing and devastating experience involving the mother and/or father of the Trump children was at play. *It must be true*, otherwise Trump would not be the way he is! As further "proof" of developmental trauma, the critic adds, "The older brother, Freddy, didn't drink himself to death because he felt secure." (It is hard to argue with that—probably nobody has ever died from complications of alcoholism because they felt *too secure* in the world.) But Maryanne, the first-born daughter, grew up to be a venerated federal appeals court judge. How do we explain her? Why did the toxic family environment that the critic imagines fail to wreck Maryanne's life?

We cannot help but search for the specific causes of observed psychological consequences in people's lives, especially in a life as strange as Donald Trump's. But if we are to make a defensible claim about a cause, I believe, we need to find solid evidence for it—that is, evidence for the cause itself. Otherwise, we are just making things up.

Determined to find causation in the early attachment bond, some psychologists have hypothesized that the health problems Mary suffered after the birth of Robert may have compromised her relationship with Donald. When Donald was a little more than two years old, Mary gave birth to her last child and then nearly died from a serious abdominal infection (peritonitis). She was hospitalized for at least two weeks, and we may assume that she convalesced at home for a significant period after that. Therefore, Donald and the other three older children were separated from their mother for a period of time. Might the short-term separation from his mother help to explain why Donald Trump ultimately turned out the way he turned out?

In an interview with a journalist for *Politico*, one psychotherapist said this: "A 2½-year-old is going through a process of becoming more autonomous, a little bit more independent from his mother. If there is a disruption or a rupture in the connection, it would have had an impact on the sense of self, the sense of security, the sense of confidence." In a similar vein, a psychiatrist noted that, from the child's perspective, the separation may be experienced as "the withdrawal of a mothering figure. It might evoke ways of acting that are increasingly bombastic and attention-seeking. The child becomes almost exaggerated in the ways they try to court attention."

Well, *maybe*. This line of thinking does seem to heave a weighty burden of causation, however, onto a short separation from the mother, even as siblings, other relatives, and the household maid likely rallied to make up for the loss. I might also add that there is no evidence in the research literature in developmental psychology to support the idea that a two-week separation from one's mother in the third year of life leads to the subsequent emergence of any particular set of personality traits, let alone bombastic attention-seeking. Had Donald Trump been forcibly abducted from his parents at this time, kidnapped by terrorists, or sent to live with complete strangers in a detention camp—well, that might have had some long-term effect. Still, one cannot completely rule out the speculation about a brief separation from his mother at age 2½, even if the second expert (the psychiatrist) ultimately qualified his claim in this way: "I'm not speaking specifically about Donald Trump," mind you. Well, *I am*, and it seems to me that if this speculation is true, people might have noticed a sudden change in Donald Trump's personality around the age of 2½, immediately following the separation. I have seen no such evidence.

What can we safely conclude regarding Donald Trump's early relationship with his mother and the possible effects that relationship may have had on his subsequent psychological development? Unfortunately, *not much*—or perhaps it is more accurate to say, *not as much* as many people would like to conclude. There is no direct evidence that Donald Trump did not develop a more-or-less normal, loving attachment bond with his mother, and perhaps other caregivers, in the first year of life. The bond may have been especially secure, or perhaps it went slightly more in the direction of anxious attachment or avoidant attachment. We cannot know for sure, but there is no direct evidence for anything psychologically bizarre or pathological in this realm.

The parents were strict, especially Fred, but they also seem to have expressed love for their children. None of the Trump children has ever said, nor even hinted at the possibility, that he or she felt unloved as a child. Instead, they have tended to talk in vague but highly positive terms about their mother, Mary Trump. People outside the family tend to describe Mary in the same way, as relatively warm, caring, and nice. Because of her significant involvements in charity work and social clubs, Mary may have been away from the home for more extended periods of time than many other stay-at-home moms were in the 1940s and 1950s. But these activities were consistent with the expected script for women of ample financial means in her social set, who typically hired household help so that they could be more active in the community.

Donald Trump has always professed that he loved his mother and that she loved him. Maybe this time he is telling the truth. Through evolution's magnificent protocol whereby babies and their mothers bond to each other in the first year of life, Mary was probably Donald's first love. At some level, as Freud suggested, she may have represented an "unmatched prototype" of later love relationships. Yet it is all shrouded in soft and gauzy mystery.

***

At the New York Military Academy during his senior year in high school, Donald Trump was *not* voted "Most Likely to Succeed." But he did garner the most votes for the honor of "Ladies Man." In college at the Wharton School (University of Pennsylvania), he had more than his fair share of dates with attractive members of the opposite sex. "Every time I saw him, he had a pretty girl on his arm," remembered one classmate. One of those pretty girls was the actress Candice Bergen, who recalled a blind date with him: "He was wearing a three-piece burgundy suit, and burgundy boots, and [he drove] a burgundy limousine. He was very coordinated. . . . It was a very short evening."

Living in Manhattan in his 20s, Trump developed a reputation as a playboy. In her 1976 article for *The New York Times*, Judy Klemesrud reported that Trump dated "slinky fashion models" and regularly frequented the most glamorous night clubs. His experiences at the clubs left an indelible impression on Trump. He later recalled seeing "things happening there that to this day I have never seen again." Trump said: "I would watch supermodels getting screwed, well-known supermodels getting screwed on a bench in the middle of the room. There were seven of them and each one was getting screwed by a different guy. This was in the middle of the room." Despite the company of slinky fashion models and the libidinal rush of the club scene, Trump found surprisingly little satisfaction in his relationships with women during this period in his life. He often complained that many of the beautiful women he spent time with were short on brains and personality. And then along came Ivana.

Ivana

Wearing a red minidress with three-quarter-length sleeves and high heels, Ivana Zelnickova was standing in a long line at Maxwell's Plum, a New York restaurant famous for its burgers and celebrity clientele, when a young man with blonde hair tapped her on the shoulder.

He said, "I am so sorry to bother you. My name is Donald Trump, and I noticed that you and your friends are waiting for a table. I know the manager and I can get one for you fast."

"That would be great," Ivana replied. "Thank you." He went off to take care of it. Ivana turned to her friends and said, "I have good news and bad news. The good news is that we are going to have a table soon because of that man over there."

"What's the bad news?" one of the friends asked.

"He's going to sit with us."

Raised in Czechoslovakia under Communist rule, Ivana was the only child born to Milos (affectionately known as "Dedo") and Marie ("Babi") Zelnickova, an engineer and telephone operator, respectively, in Zlin, which was a factory town about 190 miles from Prague. As a teenager, Ivana skied with the Czech national team. They traveled beyond the Iron Curtain to ski in Italy and Austria. Enamored with the prosperity of the West, Ivana solicited the help of an Austrian skier named Alfred Winklmayr. Their sham marriage enabled her to obtain an Austrian passport, which was her ticket out of Czechoslovakia. Eventually, she moved to Montreal, Canada, where she lived with a boyfriend named George Syrovatka, who had defected from Czechoslovakia during a ski meet in the West. Ivana did modeling for Montreal department stores and posed for furriers. In 1976, she traveled with a group of models to New York City to participate in a fashion show designed to promote the upcoming Winter Olympic Games in Montreal. Hoping to catch a glimpse of Warren Beatty or Barbara Streisand, or maybe, as Ivana remembered it decades later, to "meet some sexy American men," Ivana and her group headed over to Maxwell's Plum, went to the back of the line, and then—.

Donald Trump picked up the tab for dinner and arranged to drive Ivana's group home in a limo. The next day, he sent three dozen roses. Over the next couple of months, he wooed Ivana incessantly. "I found the combination of beauty and brains almost unbelievable," Donald said, in reference to Ivana. At first, Ivana saw Trump as nothing more than "a nice all-American kid, tall and smart, lots of energy: very bright and good-looking." But after she learned of his growing prominence in the world of New York real estate, magnified enormously by Judy Klemesrud's article in the *Times*, her interest accelerated. He proposed marriage on New Year's Eve of 1976. They were married on April 7, 1977, at

Marble Collegiate Church in Manhattan. The Reverend Norman Vincent Peale presided, and Donald's older brother, Fred Jr. ("Freddy"), was best man.

Ivana got pregnant on the honeymoon. The first son was born on December 31, 1977. When she suggested that they name the firstborn after his illustrious father, Donald Trump wavered. "What if he's a loser?" Donald mused. Ivana prevailed. The first daughter arrived in 1981. This time it was Ivana's turn to pass her name down to the next generation. She named their girl "Ivana," known to the world today as "Ivanka," which translates as "little Ivana." Eric was born in 1984.

The children grew up in one of the most opulent domiciles in the western hemisphere. The triplex penthouse at Trump Tower was 30,000 square feet of extravagant luxuriousness, in the heart of midtown Manhattan. On weekends, the family often retreated to a large but quieter home in Greenwich, Connecticut. Later, Mar-a-Lago functioned as yet another palatial destination for relaxation and fun, in West Palm Beach, Florida. Ivana supervised a staff of nannies, housekeepers, chauffeurs, and other assistants who together made up the interpersonal infrastructure tasked with raising the three Trump children. Her parents, Dedo and Babi, also played key roles. For example, Dedo taught Don Jr. and Eric how to fish and hunt.

Donald Trump pitched in as father, when he felt he could. He attended parent–teacher conferences. He enjoyed having his children play in his Trump Tower office, as he took telephone calls and conducted business. Ivana reported that when the children were little, Donald "would kiss them and hold them, but then he would give [them] back to me because he had no idea what to do."

Don Jr. recalled,

It wasn't a "Hey, Son, let's go play catch in the backyard" kind of father–son relationship. It was "Hey, you're back from school, come down to the office." So I would sit in his office, play with trucks on the floor of his office, go trick-or-treating in his office. So there was a lot of time spent with him, and it was on his terms. . . . He never hid from us, he never shied away, but it was on his terms. You know, that tends to be the way he does things.

Like his own father, Fred Trump, Donald's interactions with his children revolved mainly around his own work. Still, he expressed genuine love for them. Ivana wrote:

Donald loved his children, was affectionate, and was a good provider. He took them to Elton John concerts at Madison Square Garden or to Yankee Stadium to hang out with George Steinbrenner. But he'd be the first to admit that he had no idea how to engage the kids at their respective ages and converse on their level. The children didn't know how to relate to him, either. Ivanka always said that her big breakthrough with Donald happened when she was old enough to talk about business.

Ivana learned how to talk about business with her husband, too—and this may have marked the beginning of the end in their love relationship. Brash and highly competitive, Ivana was never suited to play the behind-the-scenes role that Donald Trump's mother, Mary, had played in her marriage to Fred. Beginning in the late 1970s, Ivana assumed official positions in the Trump Organization, first overseeing interior design at the Grand Hyatt and Trump Tower. In 1985, she was dispatched to Atlantic City to manage the Trump Castle casino. Like her husband, she could be imperious and dictatorial in her relations with her employees, but in many cases, like her husband again, she also won their devotion. "Donald and Ivana were cut from the same cloth," said Louise Sunshine, a long-time Trump associate. "They were just exactly the same kind of people—very, very determined, laser focused, very sharp . . . very synergistic and very much alike, too much alike. It was hard to tell them apart. They could have come from the same sperm." Pushing the (vaguely creepy) genetic analogy further, Ivana would later remark that Trump called her "his twin as a woman."

In the early years, Trump seemed to be happy with his wife's involvement in the business. But by the time she was running Trump Castle, the conflicts between them turned ugly and went public, as Trump repeatedly castigated Ivana in front of the casino's vice presidents and managers when the casino's performance did not satisfy him.

"Without me, you're nothing!" he ranted. "You're doing a shitty job down here. If you don't get your act together, you're gone."

Yes, that is *his wife* he is talking to.

And then, after shaming Ivana in public, Donald would later call her on the phone and tell her, "I love you." The bizarre pattern reprises a life strategy that Trump has repeatedly employed in many other contexts. As the episodic man, Donald Trump engages life in the moment, and he does whatever needs to be done to win the moment. Because he was angry and wanted to motivate his managers to improve the performance of Trump Castle, he chastised and humiliated his own wife in front of other employees. Later in the day, however, he might find himself in a different episode, thinking about Ivana for the moment as a wife rather than a business partner. To win the new moment, he would call her up and whisper sweet nothings into her ear. Complicit in the strangeness, Ivana always replied, "I love you, too."

What began as a romance gradually morphed into an emotionally fraught business partnership. In his book, *Love Is a Story*, the social psychologist Robert Sternberg identifies a number of common narratives that give shape to love relationships. One of these is what Sternberg calls *the business story*—a relationship between lovers wherein "economic considerations, social status, and business sense" strongly influence how the two partners perceive the relationship and interpret its development. A major danger in this story is that one or both of the partners may "quickly become bored with the relationship and look for interest and excitement outside the marriage."

For Donald's part, that is exactly what happened. He lost his sexual interest in Ivana in the mid- to late 1980s, as he tired of being married to a business partner. Looking back on that period a decade later, Trump wrote,

> [My] big mistake with Ivana was taking her out of the role of wife and allowing her to run one of my casinos in Atlantic City, then the Plaza Hotel. . . . When I got home at night, rather than talking about the softer subjects of life, she wanted to tell me how well the Plaza was doing, or what a great day the casino had. I really appreciated all her efforts, but it was just too much. . . . I soon began to realize that I was married to a businessperson rather than a wife.

Ivana described the same dynamic:

> My huge professional wins came at a personal cost. My husband and I became more like business partners than spouses. We'd talk about work all the time, about the bottom line, the high rollers coming in that weekend, what was going on at the Plaza. He loved what I did for his company, but, on the other hand, he was frustrated that I spent so much time working.
>
> Behind every successful woman, there is a man in shock. I was *too* successful to be Mrs. Trump. In our marriage, there couldn't be two stars. So one of us had to go.

A turning point: 1989

If Donald Trump apprehended his own life as a coherent and integrated story explaining how he has come to be the person he is becoming, he might mark the year 1989 as a dramatic turning point. But the episodic man does not understand his own life in that way. He does not operate in accord with an internalized and evolving story of the self, a morally grounded, long-term tale that brings the reconstructed past together with the imagined future. The strangest feature of Trump's very strange case is that he does not seem to have a narrative identity. Perceiving himself, instead, to be more like a superhero than a fully formed person, Donald Trump has never been especially introspective, retrospective, or prospective. When it comes to 1989, then, let me do the psychological work for him.

It is the spring of 1989, and Donald and Ivana Trump have gone well over a year without having sex. He repeatedly complains that her breasts are too small and that she is beginning to look old and haggard. Desperate to win back her husband's ardor, Ivana undergoes extensive plastic surgery. Dr. Steven Hoefflin adds collagen to her lips, tightens her face, resculpts her cheekbones, and amply augments her breasts. But the makeover fails to turn her husband on. Now, he recoils from touching her fake, implanted breasts. At the same time, Donald is struggling to come to terms with his own midlife changes. At age 43, he is no longer as trim and fit as he once was. His body is plumping out, and he is beginning to lose his hair.

"The worst thing a man can do is go bald," Trump has recently warned one of his top executives.

But there are bigger problems, of course. Trump's casinos are losing massive amounts of money, and he is sinking further and further into debt. Although he does not know this yet, it will be nearly a decade before he recovers his financial footing. Complicating his personal life, he has been carrying on an affair with a 26-year-old actress named Marla Maples. Their relationship is not exactly a secret; some of his friends and associates in the Trump Organization know about it. Thankfully, Ivana is in the dark, for the time being. Still, Marla is an expensive habit to keep, and she requires high maintenance on the emotional front.

And let us not forget that the economy is beginning to tank. In October 1989, the stock market plunges. During the week immediately preceding the most precipitous drop for the Dow, three of Trump's closest business associates die in a helicopter crash. In a bid for more attention from the press, Trump falsely claims that he almost boarded the helicopter on that fateful day. Still, the loss hits him hard, both personally and professionally. He considers one of the passengers to have been a close friend, and the three dead men were his top experts in the casino business. The crash seems to remind Trump of his own mortality, urging him to disregard social conventions even more than he has before. Although it is hard to believe that Donald Trump ever did otherwise, he resolves going forward always to do only what he wants to do, fearlessly and shamelessly, and to ignore the negative consequences of doing so.

What happens next depends on whom you believe. As described in Harry Hurt's 1993 book, *Lost Tycoon: The Many Lives of Donald J. Trump*, Donald makes a visit, in late October, to the office of Dr. Steven Hoefflin, the same plastic surgeon who transformed Ivana's look. Hurt's account is based, he has always claimed, on transcripts of testimony given by Ivana Trump at a legal deposition in the early 1990s. Donald has always denied that the visit and resultant events occurred.

Following Hurt's account, Dr. Hoefflin performs a liposuction procedure to suck some of the fat out of Donald's midsection and his chin. He also performs a scalp reduction operation to cover the creeping bald spot on the back of Donald's head. As part of the procedure, Hoefflin injects a tattoo dye into Donald's scalp to match the color of his hair, which should help to camouflage the baldness. The medical ordeal is painful and requires a period of convalescence. Donald is not happy about the pain, and he feels that the results are not satisfactory. He telephones Hoefflin to express his venom.

"I'm going to kill you," Donald cries. "I'm going to sue you. I'm going to cost you so much money. I'm going to destroy your practice."

Next, he turns on Ivana. It is her fault, too, he thinks. She brought this idiot doctor into their lives.

Back in the triplex at Trump Tower, Ivana is relaxing in the master bedroom, thinking about the trip she is going to take to Tahiti. Suddenly, according to Ivana, Donald bursts into the room.

"Your fucking doctor has ruined me!" he screams.

In a rage, he throws Ivana to the bed and pins her down. He begins to pull her hair out. He rips her clothes off and forces her into sexual intercourse. It is the first sex they have had in 16 months. But to Ivana, it feels like rape. She escapes the bedroom and runs upstairs to her mother's room. She locks the door and spends the rest of the night crying.

"He raped me," Ivana tells her friends.

But later, Ivana alters her terminology. After *Lost Tycoon* had already been printed and was awaiting shipment, the publisher (W. W. Norton) received a communication from Donald Trump's lawyers, the text of which was subsequently pasted into the front page of Hurt's book:

> During a deposition given by me in connection with my matrimonial case, I stated that my husband had raped me. I wish to say that on one occasion during 1989, Mr. Trump and I had marital relations in which he behaved very differently toward me than he had during our marriage. As a woman, I felt violated, as the love and tenderness, which he normally exhibited toward me, was absent. I referred to this as a "rape," but I do not want my words to be interpreted in a literal or criminal sense.
>
> Any contrary conclusion would be an incorrect and most unfortunate interpretation of my statement which I do not want to be interpreted in a speculative fashion and I do not want the press or media to misconstrue any of the facts set forth above. All I wish is for this matter to be put to rest.
>
> This statement can only be released and used in its entirety.
>
> Approved: Ivana M. Trump
> Date: April 6, 1993.

(The publisher noted that Ivana Trump's new statement did "not contradict or invalidate any information contained in the book.")

Let us continue the story, rushing to the end of 1989.

It is late December. Ivana and the Trump children are taking their annual ski vacation in Aspen, Colorado. Donald joins the family at Little Nell's, a newly opened luxury hotel with an emerald green oval roof and a gourmet restaurant. Ivana and the children do not know, however, that Donald has flown his girlfriend, Marla Maples, and Marla's friend (Kim Knapp) to Aspen, too. Marla and Kim are staying just down the road in a condominium. Donald plans to rendezvous with Marla on the slopes. I ask you: Is this a wise plan? Remember this: Ivana still does not know about Marla. She gets her first inkling, however, when Charles Weaver, an Aspen realtor who helped to arrange the accommodations for Marla and Kim, calls Donald on the hotel suite phone. Both Donald and Ivana pick up when they hear the ring.

"That Marla sure is a piece of ass!" Weaver exclaims.

After the call is completed, Ivana asks Donald: "Who is this Moolah?" mispronouncing Marla's name.

"She's someone who has been chasing me for about two years," Donald replies, which is not a complete lie. But then he tells Ivana that there is absolutely nothing going on between him and Moolah.

On December 30, the Trump family stops for lunch at Bonnie's Beach Club restaurant, tucked beside a rocky ledge halfway down one of Aspen's ski slopes. This is where Ivana and Marla finally confront each other, on the next-to-last day of 1989. Exactly how it all transpires depends again on whom you believe. According to Ivana's memory, Marla walks right up to her, as she and the children are waiting in line for food, and says: "I'm Marla, and I love your husband." Ivana tells her to get lost. In Marla's version, Ivana charges up to *her* and accuses Marla of trying to steal her husband. What follows is a great deal of yelling and screaming, according to witnesses at the scene, and the chaos continues when Donald returns to the group. "It was horrible," one local Aspen woman recalled. "The words were flying back and forth so fast, and I felt really sorry for the kids. For the whole family, really, I felt so badly." Don Jr. is 11 (his birthday is the next day); Ivanka, 8; Eric, 5.

Marla, and then Melania

Looking back on 1989, Ivana has always insisted that she knew the marriage was over the moment she met Marla. "I didn't file for divorce until March, but as far as I was concerned, the marriage ended that day at Bonnie's." It took two years of legal wrangling and the renegotiation of terms that were originally set forth in their 1977 prenuptial agreement, but the divorce was finalized in 1991. The settlement provided Ivana with a one-time payout of $14 million, the Greenwich estate, and $650,000 annually as spousal and child support. She was also entitled to stay at Mar-a-Lago rent-free for one month out of every year.

Importantly, the divorce agreement barred Ivana from publishing or broadcasting "any diary, memoir, letter, story, photograph, interview, article, essay, account or description of any kind whatsoever . . . concerning her marriage to Donald or any other aspect of Donald's personal business or financial affairs . . . without obtaining Donald's written consent in advance." Through what was effectively a gag order, the episodic man put a clean end to this episode in his life, a pattern he would repeat with Marla years later. In business and in his personal life, the nondisclosure agreement became one of Donald Trump's most powerful tools for erasing the past. By paying off potential informants, he created autobiographical black holes, from which no damning information about the past could escape. It is impossible to know, therefore, what really happened between him and the women he claimed to love. Like the fog of amnesia surrounding his early relationship with his mother, the nondisclosure agreements conceal details of Trump's relationships with the most important women in his life. Much of what we think we know is what he wants us to know.

Still, Trump has not been able to exert complete control over the flow of information. This became especially apparent in the months following the Aspen confrontation between Ivana and Marla. When the Trumps returned to New York, the tabloids caught wind of the marital intrigue. Donald, Ivana, friends of Marla, and a host of other informants fed gossip to Liz Smith at the *New York Daily News* and Cindy Adams at the *New York Post*. The two competed to unveil the most sordid secrets and produce the most outlandish headlines. Based on an interview Ivana did with Liz Smith, the *Daily News* broke the first story on February 11, 1990—EXCLUSIVE: LOVE ON THE ROCKS. Reporting on an alleged statement made by Marla Maples to a friend regarding her sexual experiences with Donald Trump, the *Post* ran the famous headline on February 16—BEST SEX I'VE EVER HAD.

In February 1990, the *Daily News* plastered Trump items on the front page for 12 straight days. The *Post* sported an eight-consecutive-day streak, this during a month in which major news stories from across the world included Nelson Mandela's release from prison, Vaclav Havel's visit to the White House, and the accelerating deterioration of the Soviet Union—all relegated to the inside pages of the tabloids. The spectacle went on through the winter and spring of 1990, as Donald and Ivana competed in the press to win the public relations war. Both claimed that they were mortified by the scandalous coverage and were especially concerned about the negative effects it might have on their children. At the same time, they fed the beast, regularly providing interviews and revealing scoops.

For a while, Marla hid out in the Hamptons and later Guatemala to avoid the cameras and reporters. She emerged to do a *Prime Time Live* television interview with Diane Sawyer. Marla told Sawyer that she did not consider herself to be the main reason for the dissolution of the Trump marriage. "Only the two of them know what really went on with their marriage," Marla said. "But I am not the reason for that marriage having problems." When Sawyer asked her if she loved Donald Trump, Marla responded, "I can't lie about it. You know I do." Around the same time, Ivana took the three children out of school for a few months and escaped to Mar-a-Lago. Homework was sent through the mail. Throughout it all, Donald basked in the press attention, even as he lashed out against it. The tabloid wars showed the world that he was a coveted object of beautiful women's desire. What could be better than that?! "This is prime time for me," Trump exulted.

Prime time, however, was mainly the worst of times for Donald Trump, as the 1990s proved to be his most challenging decade on both the business and personal fronts. But if we wish to measure it in terms of the sheer number of glamorous women he is rumored to have dated, then the 1990s were not shabby. These women included the models Rowanne Brewer and Carla Bruni-Tedeschi and the actresses Kim Basinger, Catherine Oxenberg, and Robin Givens. The rumors about Givens came to light during the period she was married to the heavyweight boxing champion Mike Tyson. In *TrumpNation*, Timothy O'Brien described the story Trump told him about a confrontation with Tyson in his office in Trump Tower.

"Everyone's telling me that you're fucking my wife and I think you're fucking my wife," Tyson said.

"Mike, let me tell you something: I never even thought about it. And I heard those rumors and they're disgusting. In fact, I called you a couple of times to tell you that I heard those rumors and it pisses me off. And I never, ever thought about it. She's your wife, she's with you, she's loyal to you, and it's total bullshit."

Apparently, Tyson accepted Trump's response, because he then asked if he might take a nap on Trump's couch!

"Sure, go ahead."

Trump joked with O'Brien about his life's "passing in front of his eyes" when the greatest boxer in the world accused him of sleeping with his wife. "Now I froze, I'm dead," Trump remembered.

When an assistant later reported to Trump that Mike Tyson was drooling on his couch, Trump said, "*You* wake him and tell him." We may assume that Tyson finished his nap in peace.

Pretending to be a publicist named John Miller, Trump called the *Post* in 1991 to report that beautiful women were besieging Donald Trump. Attempting to disguise his voice, "Miller" claimed that Madonna was among the long list of women who had expressly professed a desire to date Trump. In the early years of his career, Trump occasionally called reporters under the fake name of John Miller, or more often, John Barron, to spread self-aggrandizing gossip and news.

Despite brief affairs—real and rumored—with other women, Trump focused his main romantic attention during the early to mid-1990s on Marla Maples. Born and raised near Dalton, Georgia, Marla Maples took third place in a 1985 beauty pageant sponsored by the Hawaiian Tropic suntan lotion company. One of the judges happened to be Jerry Argowitz, the president of the New Jersey Generals, which was the team that Trump owned in the new upstart United States Football League (USFL). Argowitz was smitten with Marla and wanted to help her launch a career in acting or modeling. He offered to take her to New York and show her around. Marla met many of the New Jersey Generals players and employees, and she was briefly introduced to Donald Trump. The first meeting did not register for either of them. A year later, they met again, when Trump spotted the blonde beauty standing in front of the Pierre Hotel on Fifth Avenue.

"Hello," she said. "My name is Marla Maples. I'm a friend of Jerry Argowitz."

It dawned on Trump that they had met before. He would not forget her this time. Trump arranged for her to attend a book party celebrating the publication of *The Art of the Deal*. The man who escorted Marla to the event (her ex-boyfriend) told a friend, "You could see the fireworks go off the second Donald and Marla set eyes on each other." They arranged a lunch date. Dinner dates followed. Whereas Trump had sent roses to woo Ivana, this time around he sent Marla press clippings about his business successes and rave reviews of his book. She must have been impressed and not too concerned about the fact that Trump was, in 1987, a very married man. As the relationship developed into a full-fledged romance, some of Marla's friends warned her of trouble ahead. To allay the concerns of one confidante, she said, "When Donald's around me, he doesn't act like a big bad businessman. . . . He's always so sweet and so kind. And he wants to help me with my career."

The publicity she garnered did promote her career. Marla appeared as "Ziegfeld's Favorite" in the Broadway production of *The Will Rogers Follies*. On opening night, Trump packed the house with guests, including the singer La Toya Jackson, television newsman Mike Wallace, and talk show host Maury Povich. In a reciprocal sense, Marla hoped to promote Trump's personal growth. Deeply immersed in popular psychology and New Age spiritualism, Marla saw in Donald the reincarnation of a former monarch. She hoped to nurture the benevolent side of the "king . . . a ruler of the world, as he sees it." She would promote his greatness by bringing to the fore a kinder and gentler version of Trump, an inner humanitarian who would soothe "the little boy that still wants attention." Marla believed that there was a soft and loveable core inside Donald Trump's armored psychological frame. Once she actualized his inner potential, the two of them together would be able to promote philanthropy and make the world a better place.

While she never succeeded in transforming Trump into Mother Teresa, Marla did play a comforting and supportive role during a difficult period in Trump's life. She was "loyal and patient and, mostly, nothing but kind and forgiving of his many sins," wrote Emily Jane Fox in *Born Trump: Inside America's First Family*. In her biography of Trump, Gwenda Blair wrote that Marla seemed to be Trump's "only refuge from a world spinning out of control. In the middle of conversations he would pull out her picture and rhapsodize about her physical endowments." Timothy O'Brien remembered that in 1996 Trump had a life-size cardboard cutout of Marla, clad in a bikini, standing up in his office. A source of comfort, perhaps—but also an erotic stimulus and a symbol of his midlife virility. Trump had little use for Marla's dreams of improving him, but he appreciated that she was nice and loving, and he never seemed to tire of her body. "Nice tits, no brains," he told his friends.

The tabloids obsessively chronicled the ups and downs of Trump's relationship with Marla as it developed in the post-Ivana years. In July 1991, Trump gave her a 7.5-carat diamond ring. Months later what Marla thought was an engagement was off. Then back on again. Donald believed that Marla was using birth control, but she got pregnant anyway. Their child, named Tiffany, was born in October 1993. Finally, they were married, in December 1993. A thousand guests joined the couple in the Grand Ballroom at the Plaza. Few of them thought the marriage would last for very long. "I give it four months," remarked the radio celebrity Howard Stern. "There wasn't a wet eye in the place," quipped a reporter from the *New York Times*.

The marriage lasted six years. Whereas Trump's relationship with Ivana degenerated into what the social psychologist Robert Sternberg identifies as a business story, the Marla chapter resembles what Sternberg calls a *game story* for love, at least from the perspective of Trump. The idea that romantic love can be playful and game-like goes back to Ovid's *Erotic Poems*, written over 2,000 years ago. Lovers engage the game for the purpose of enjoyment and diversion. Whereas Ivana became a business partner, Marla was more like a plaything for Trump, a life-size, three-dimensional toy with "nice tits, no brains."

Sternberg argues that the game can often turn competitive. As one partner begins to win, the other begins to lose. In the case of Donald and Marla, the world was able to watch as the game played out in the press. Trump seemed to be winning early on as he captured and controlled his sexy prize. But Marla enjoyed big victories in gaining a child from her king and finally convincing him to marry her. Trump won again when he finally managed to get rid of Marla. For Trump, the fun had begun to wear off even by the time of the wedding: "I was bored when she was walking down the aisle," he said. The divorce was finalized in 1999, with the usual nondisclosure agreement. Trump won the settlement, too, for Marla received a relatively paltry compensation for playing the game—a lump sum of $2 million and ongoing support for living expenses for herself and for Tiffany.

Enter Melania, at long last. She turns out to be the first romantic partner to be created in the image of Trump's mother—beautiful, yes, but low maintenance, content to hide mysteriously behind the scenes and behind her inscrutable persona, happy (it would seem) to play the domestic role without competing and without playing games. Melania is content to live out the *house and home story*, in Sternberg's taxonomy of love narratives. And Trump loves it this way. Whether it is Trump Tower, Mar-a-Lago, or the White House, Melania is confined to the domestic sphere. And it is in the domestic sphere—and only here—where the love relationship between Trump and his third wife plays out, completely private, behind closed doors.

Like Ivana, Melania Knauss hailed from eastern Europe. She grew up in a concrete apartment building in the village of Sevnica, within the multiethnic federation that comprised the former Yugoslavia. Like Ivana, she longed to escape from the drab confines of her socialist world. Whereas Ivana got out through skiing and a sham marriage to a fellow skier, Melania became a fashion model, working in Milan, Italy, at first, and then, in the mid-1990s, in New York. She met Donald Trump at a party hosted by her modeling agency at the Kit Kat Klub, in 1998. Although Donald was technically still married to Marla at this time, he attended the event with Celina Midelfart, a gorgeous Norwegian heiress. When he saw Melania, however, he forgot about the woman he brought. He asked Melania for her phone number. She resisted, but eventually the two of them began dating.

Trump was over-the-moon thrilled when Melania was featured in the *Sports Illustrated* swimsuit edition. Even better was her appearance in *GQ* magazine, for the month of January, 2000. The headline read: "Sex at 30,000 feet. Melania Knauss earns her air miles." The cover photo showed Melania lying on a fur throw in Trump's Boeing 747, apparently naked except for a diamond choker and matching bracelets. Open up the magazine, and you would see Melania pointing a pistol as she stood on an airplane wing, clad in a red bra and matching thong. In a rare public statement, Melania once called a radio talk show to tell listeners that she and Donald enjoyed tremendous sex on a daily basis. For episodes of Trump's reality television show, *The Apprentice*, Trump gave the contestants tours of his lavish condominium in Trump Tower and sometimes introduced them to Melania.

They were wed at the Episcopal Church of Bethesda-by-the-Sea, in Palm Beach, Florida, on January 22, 2005. The reception was at Mar-a-Lago. Among the 350 guests were Hillary Clinton and Oprah Winfrey. Their son, Barron, was born the following year. Melania continued to do some modeling, but she mainly devoted herself to raising their son and providing a secure base of emotional attachment for her husband. Has Trump finally found, in Melania, the realization of what Freud described as the "unmatched prototype" of human love and security? "I think Donald is so happy with her, and she dotes on him and their son, and they're such a beautiful couple," remarked Norma Foerderer, a long-term friend and associate of Donald Trump. "I've never seen Donald like this," she added. "They're just darling together, and they tease and they laugh. I think I've seen this more now with Melania than with any other wife."

In sharp contrast to the other two wives, Melania has remained an extraordinarily private person, even in her role as wife to a man who has now become the most famous human being on the planet. It is as if she is wearing a mask. It is the mask of a fashion model, and she never seems to take it off—a beautiful but emotionally enigmatic mask, icy-blue eyes and a flawless complexion, high cheekbones befitting the most glamorous 21st-century models, staring straight forward as if she were walking down the runway, sometimes offering an angry glare, sometimes showing a slight smile. As First Lady, Melania has rarely spoken in public. She has kept a remarkably low profile. From the East Wing of the White House, she initiated a vaguely defined program called "Be Best," which encourages children to put kindness first in their lives, particularly on social media. The irony of the initiative, given her husband's regular rants on Twitter, has not escaped the press. In 2018–2019, the Be Best program remained ill-defined and enigmatic, like Melania herself. The world wonders: *Who is she?*

Nobody really seems to know, least of all her husband. "She's a very private person," Trump says. "But a very smart person; and considered one of the great beauties." Not an especially illuminating psychological portrait, there. Friends describe Melania as fiercely independent and emotionally stoic. She can be warm and lively once you get to know her, some claim. She is a doting and demanding mother for Barron, and she shows real affection for her husband, although always when the cameras are off, when the two of them are together in the loving domestic mode of what Sternberg calls the house and home story.

In the public eye, however, Melania is the other great mystery woman in Donald Trump's life, following in the distant wake of his mother. Melania is the supermodel, who married the superhero. They are an archetypal couple, as if a goddess were to marry a god. From the outside, both appear to be superhuman, and for that reason, somewhat *less than* human, as well, like single-minded action heroes who personify, respectively, ultimate beauty and ultimate power, and not much more. Early on, the three older Trump children nicknamed Melania "the Portrait." She did not seem quite real to them. She does not seem quite real to me, either. But she must be real, right? She is a real human being, and so is Donald Trump. The strangeness lies in their seeming to be not fully realized, psychologically recognizable human beings—and in the related sense that each of them seems to live outside a humanly coherent and discernible life narrative. He has no inner story for his life, and she hides hers.

***

Does Donald Trump have a woman problem?

Any discussion of his love life and the three wives he has known leads naturally to the topic of how Trump has tended to think of women more generally and how he has treated women throughout his life. Many women (and men) believe that Donald Trump is a malignant and misogynist sexist who routinely exploits, demeans, and belittles women. Many other women (and men) hold a somewhat more benign view, seeing him more as an exaggerated case of how heterosexual men have, for better and largely for worse, historically related to women as objects of desire. Whereas the first group condemns Trump, the latter group is more forgiving, tending to excuse his indiscretions as an unfortunate product of human nature. The two viewpoints are not completely contradictory.

In the 2016 presidential campaign, Trump's woman problem exploded like a nuclear bomb on October 7, four weeks before the election, when the *Washington Post* broke the story of the infamous *Access Hollywood* tape. In footage shot in 2005 when the 59-year-old Trump was on his way to film an episode of the NBC television show, *Access Hollywood*, he is seen bragging about groping women and grabbing their genitals in a riotous conversation with Billy Bush, who worked as a host for the show. "I moved on her like a bitch," Trump says in describing one effort to seduce a married woman. "You know I'm automatically attracted to beautiful [women]—I just start kissing them. It's like a magnet. Just kiss. I don't even wait. And when you're a star, they let you do it. . . . . Grab 'em by the pussy. You can do anything."

Within hours of its release, the *Post's* story became the most-read online article in the history of the newspaper's website. The publication's servers went offline for a short period that day due to the surge in web traffic. Reactions from the public, and from politicians, were swift. Hillary Clinton, who would be meeting Trump for their second presidential debate two days later, tweeted, "This is horrific. We cannot allow this man to become president." Her running mate, Senator Tim Kaine, said of the tape, "It makes me sick to my stomach." Republicans also criticized Trump. Mitt Romney, who was the 2012 Republican candidate for president, tweeted this: "Hitting on married women? Condoning assault? Such vile degradations demean our wives and daughters and corrupt America's face to the world." Ohio governor John Kasich called the remarks "indefensible." Former Florida governor Jeb Bush deemed them "reprehensible."

John McCain and a number of other Republican politicians withdrew their support from Trump.

On the collateral damage front, the hapless Billy Bush, who is seen on the tape laughing and encouraging Trump's outlandishness, was fired from his position as host of NBC's *Today* show.

The firestorm unleashed by the tape prompted one of the rare apologies ever offered by Donald Trump: "I said it, I was wrong, and I apologize." He went on to "pledge to be a better man." However, he also defended the remarks as "locker room banter, a private conversation that took place many years ago." And by the way, "Bill Clinton has said far worse to me on the golf course—not even close."

As everybody in the world knows, Trump still won the election in November. And he received 53% of votes cast by white women. Yes: Over half of the white women voters in the United States in 2016 refused to support the first white woman ever to run for president and cast their votes instead for a man who boasted of grabbing pussy. It is hard to figure.

But one thing that Donald Trump said in this sordid scenario was probably true: His crude remarks *were* like locker room talk—men's locker rooms, circa high school and college. Some of the responses to the *Access Hollywood* tape may have been more hysterical than authentic. Have you ever been around young American men when they gather in packs outside the purview of female recognizance? Think of these settings: Football locker rooms. Fraternities. Hunting trips. Bars. Prisons. The steel mills in Gary, Indiana, where I worked for two summers to pay for college. Even church youth retreats, when the girls are not around. This is how some young men talk in these sex-segregated settings. Not *all* young men, for sure. But enough of them to make this quintessentially male form of discourse deeply familiar to most American men, even surely Mitt Romney and Tim Kaine. Moreover, many American women may suspect such a thing to be the case, as yet another example of boys' being boys. It is disgusting, no doubt. And Donald Trump was a late-middle-aged man when he regaled Billy Bush, not a young adult. But many women may still simply let it go, like those tens of millions who voted for Donald Trump in 2016 instead of Hillary Clinton.

Those Americans who tuned in to Howard Stern's nationally syndicated morning radio show in the 1990s might not have been so shocked to see the *Access Hollywood* video. Between 1990 and 2005, Trump appeared more than 20 times on the raunchy talk show, discussing with Stern such weighty topics as the merits of oral sex and whether or not either of the men would "bang" Mariah Carey, Cindy Crawford, or Princess Diana. Regarding Diana, Trump said he would have had sex with her, "without hesitation." "She had the height, she had the beauty, she had the skin. . . . She was crazy, but those are minor details." The two men made it a habit to rate the tops and bottoms of female celebrities. Regarding one particular actress on a popular TV soap opera, Trump opined: "A person who is very flat chested is very hard to be a 10." Regarding the reality TV star Kim Kardashian, he said: "Does she have a fat ass? Absolutely!" And "her boob job is terrible. They look like two light posts coming out of a body."

The locker room banter, broadcast live across the country, even extended to the subject of Melania. Stern asked Trump if he would stay with his wife should she be disfigured in an automobile accident, emerging with her arm and leg damaged, and with "100 stiches on her face."

"How do the breasts look?" Trump asked.

"The breasts are okay," Stern said.

"That's important," Trump said.

Talk is one thing; action, another. Which brings us to the subject of Trump's alleged physical mistreatment of women. At least 22 women have publicly and formally accused Donald Trump of sexual misconduct, including assault, groping, and unwanted sexual touching. Most of these cases came to light after the publication of the *Access Hollywood* tape.

For example, Jessica Leeds accused Trump of groping her when they were seated next to each other on an airplane in the late 1970s. In October 2016, Leeds told the *New York Times* that Trump "was like an octopus. His hands were everywhere." She fled to the back of the plane. In a subsequent television interview, Leeds claimed that she ran into Donald Trump three years after the airplane incident, at a gala in New York. Trump recognized her and called her a "cunt." When asked about the accusations from Leeds, Trump responded that he would never have groped a woman who was as unattractive as she. At a political rally in October 2016, he said, "Believe me, she would not be my first choice."

Jill Harth and her husband, George Houraney, partnered with Trump in the early 1990s on a business venture that involved putting on beauty pageants. It did not go well. The couple sued Trump for $125 million, alleging that Trump failed to uphold his end of the business deal and that he sexually harassed Harth. In a deposition, Harth alleged that Trump groped her and made a series of threatening and unwanted sexual advances at a 1993 party at Mar-a-Lago. "He was relentless," Harth said. "I didn't know how to handle it. I would go away from him and say I had to go to the restroom. It was the escape route."

Included among the 22 sets of accusations are examples of Trump's forcing himself on unsuspecting women, grabbing their breasts and buttocks, propositioning them with money or favors, and insisting that they go with him to a condo or hotel room to have sex. Six of the women who have leveled accusations were participants in beauty pageants that Trump sponsored. An especially disturbing pattern involved Trump's penchant for walking unannounced into the dressing rooms while contestants were naked. At the 2001 Miss USA contest, Trump entered the dressing room and began ogling the girls, according to two contestants who expressed their disgust in interviews years later. He hugged the girls, they alleged, running his hand very low down their backs. They described Trump as akin to a "creepy uncle."

Samantha Holvey was a 20-year-old student at a private Baptist college when she was chosen to be a contestant in the 2006 Miss USA pageant, which Trump owned. In an interview with CNN, she described how Trump individually inspected each woman in the pageant.

"He would step in front of each girl and look you over from head to toe like we were just meat, we were just sexual objects, that we were not people," Holvey said. It was "the dirtiest I felt in my entire life."

Regarding sexual relations of a more consenting nature, at least two women have claimed notable affairs with Trump from the year 2006, during which time Melania was pregnant with the couple's son. A former *Playboy* model, Karen McDougal has alleged that she and Trump had numerous dates and sexual encounters over a 10-month period in 2006–2007. She expressed considerable affection for Mr. Trump and found him to be charming and solicitous. Because she felt so much guilt about betraying Melania, however, McDougal broke off the relationship. According to a report in the *Wall Street Journal*, American Media Inc. (AMI), the owner of the *National Enquirer*, paid McDougal $150,000 for the exclusive rights to her story about the affair with Trump. David J. Pecker, the chairman of AMI and a good friend and political ally of Trump's, then refused to publish the story, apparently to protect Trump in the run-up to the 2016 election.

Stephanie Clifford, a pornographic film star who goes by the name of Stormy Daniels, famously alleged that she and Trump had sexual relations in 2006 and that she was subsequently pressured to keep quiet. Weeks before the 2016 election, Trump's personal lawyer, Michael Cohen, paid Daniels $130,000 for the written promise that she not disclose the brief affair. With her flamboyant lawyer, Michael Avenatti, at her side, Daniels became a media sensation in 2018. She sued Trump, arguing that the nondisclosure agreement was invalid. In August 2018, Michael Cohen pleaded guilty to a series of criminal charges that were not technically related to the Daniels' affair, including bank fraud, tax fraud, and campaign finance violations. He effectively admitted, however, that the hush money for Daniels was indeed paid and that the funds came from Trump.

To date, Donald Trump has denied it all—the many accusations regarding sexual misconduct, the alleged affairs with Karen McDougal and Stormy Daniels, the payments to McDougal and Daniels, all of it. Given that many of the claims came to light after the *Access Hollywood* revelations, Trump has chalked them all up to political vendettas promulgated by Democrats and the liberal press. He has also accused some of the women of seeking cheap publicity by fabricating salacious stories about the President of the United States.

Characterizing the women as gold-diggers and liars, Trump draws from a deep personal reserve of emotional ambivalence regarding woman. In

Trump: The Art of the Comeback, he describes women as manipulative and dis-ingenuous: "Women have one of the great acts of all time. The smart ones act very feminine and needy, but inside they are real killers. . . . There's nothing I love more than women, but they're really a lot different than portrayed," he writes. "They are far worse than men, far more aggressive, and boy, can they be smart."

One of the reasons that the world is such a dangerous place in Donald Trump's mind is that women are scary, even as they entice and delight. Trump admits to being attracted to but also repulsed by women. They can be beautiful, but they can also be gross and repugnant. After Megyn Kelly of Fox News asked Trump a series of tough questions in a 2015 Republican debate, he said, "You could see there was blood coming out of her eyes, blood coming out of her wherever." It was widely assumed that the second mention of blood was a reference to men-struation. On the theme of women's bodily fluids, he repeatedly remarked upon Hillary Clinton's taking a bathroom break during a Democratic debate, calling it "disgusting."

To be fair, it should be noted that a small number of Trump's female friends and associates have routinely come to his defense on the issue of the woman problem. Barbara Res was a top construction engineer in the 1980s. Trump tapped her to supervise construction at Trump Tower. The fact that Trump would choose a young woman for this job was remarkably progressive, Res notes. At the age of 31, Res became the first woman to run a major construction project in New York City. Looking back from the perspective of retirement, Res says: "Donald, for all of his commentary and womanizing, was the least sexist boss I ever had as far as trusting me and viewing me equally with all the men he encountered in our mu-tual dealings. . . . He wanted me to be like him on the job. He said I would be like a 'Donna Trump.'"

Others have noted that Trump has worked hard to promote the careers of women he likes (or loves). This was true for all three wives. According to Kate Bohner, who was Trump's co-writer on *Trump: The Art of the Comeback,* Trump's reputation as a serial womanizer and philanderer was always more mythic than factual. It was part of his shtick, part of his brand. Bohner remarked: "I saw Mr. Trump being more paternal toward women than playboy"—more like a father than a seducer. And of course, he could be both, at the same time. The object of his sexual desire could also function, in his mind, as a product of his own creative power, something to be cultivated and nurtured. In an uncharacteristi-cally insightful observation, Trump analogized two of his wives to the buildings he has created. In a 1994 interview, he said this: "I create stars. I love to create stars. And, to a certain extent I have done that with Ivana. To a certain extent, I have done that with Marla." Trump added: "I've really given a lot of women great opportunity. Unfortunately, after they're a star, the fun is over for me. It's like a creation process. It's almost like creating a building."

Be they beautiful, disgusting, enticing, manipulative, sexy, ruthless, smart, malevolent, or merely competent, *women are objects* in the mind of Donald Trump. The operative relationship with the opposite sex is built on *objectification*. To treat a person as an object is to deny some feature of that person's subjectivity. It is to treat the person as something that is not quite human. To be fair again, many of us engage in objectification on a daily basis, especially in the realm of sexuality. To see another person as an object of desire involves suspending or putting aside, at least for the moment, certain other features that make that person a full-fledged human being. This is not necessarily a bad thing. A man may deeply respect his lover's empathy and intellect, but these laudable features of the lover's being may not be on his mind when he reaches for his lover in bed. Substitute the word "woman" for "man" in the preceding sentence, and I think it will still run pretty true.

But Donald Trump takes objectification significantly further than most men (or women) take it, I believe. In his behavior and in his words, he has repeatedly and flagrantly reduced women to one-dimensional objects—not all women, perhaps, but many. When Donald Trump inspected her body, Samantha Holvey felt as if she had been reduced to a mere "sexual object" rather than a "person." She and the other contestants in the 2006 Miss USA pageant *were* pieces of "meat" in Donald Trump's eyes, just like Kim Kardashian's "fat ass" and Melania's magnificent breasts. Women are *things*, comprised of things like faces, asses, breasts, pussies, and sometimes even brains.

How do we relate to things? How do we evaluate objects? We mainly evaluate them in terms of their *appearance* and their *function*. An object—that is, a thing—is good for me to the extent I like the way the thing looks or feels or sounds. An object is good for me to the extent it does something for me, to the extent it serves a function that I value. I love the car I bought a few years ago. I love the way it looks and performs. I love my wife, too. But I love her in a different way, as a person rather than a thing. I am not convinced that Donald Trump makes the distinction I just made.

Among the desirable objects that have populated Donald Trump's world over the past 40 years are his buildings, his wives, his mistresses, and competent coworkers like Barbara Res. These objects are good objects to the extent that they continue to meet his needs, by virtue of appearance and function. When they no longer perform as good objects, he typically discards them. I will trade my beautiful car in some day, for a better model.

Here is the stranger part: It is not only women who are objects in Donald Trump's mind. The woman problem is about 51% of a larger problem. With a few possible exceptions (e.g., his children), Donald Trump objectifies nearly everybody in his world, women and men alike. Relationships are contractual for him, episodic deals to be made regarding the exchange of products and services—products as objects, services as the functions objects perform.

Stranger still is the disquieting possibility that Trump's objectification extends not only outward but inward, too. Among the most supremely objectified of all persons in Donald Trump's world, I believe, is *Donald Trump himself*. Remember: He sees himself as akin to a superhero, more than human, and *less than* human, too. In his own mind, Donald Trump is more like an object than a person, a beautiful, brilliant, awesome, omnipotent *thing*. Donald Trump thinks of himself, and longs for himself, as a larger-than-life object, an object of desire, an object to be loved, *the* "unmatched prototype" of every desirable love object, to recall Freud's memorable expression. And *he*—Donald Trump as an object, as a thing—is the object that Donald Trump *loves* most.

Me

For psychologists, it is almost impossible to talk about Donald Trump without using the word *narcissism*.

In 2015, a few months after Trump announced that he would run for the Republican presidential nomination, the magazine *Vanity Fair* asked prominent psychologists to comment on Trump's personality. Howard Gardner, a renowned developmental psychologist at Harvard, summed up his response in two words: "Remarkably narcissistic." George Simon, a clinical psychologist who conducts seminars on narcissism, said that Trump is "so classic that I'm archiving video clips of him to use in workshops because there's no better example" of narcissism. "Otherwise I would have had to hire actors and write vignettes. He's like a dream come true."

Texas Senator Ted Cruz, a Republican ally of Trump's, may have never taken a psychology course in college. But the characterization he made of Trump when the two were competing against each other in the 2016 Republican primaries echoes what Gardner, Simon, and many other psychologists and psychiatrists have said: Donald Trump is "a narcissist at the level I don't think the country's ever seen."

In the ancient Greek legend, the beautiful boy Narcissus falls so completely in love with the reflection of himself in a pool that he resolves never to leave his beautiful lover. But the reflected image—forever outside his embrace—fails to reciprocate, and as a result Narcissus melts away, a victim of the passion burning inside of him. The story provides the mythic source for the modern concept of narcissism, which is typically conceived as *excessive self-love*, with the attendant qualities of grandiosity and a sense of entitlement.

On an interpersonal level, highly narcissistic people are forever trying to draw attention to themselves. Repeated and inordinate self-reference is a distinguishing hallmark of their behavior. Inside their heads, highly narcissistic people are obsessed with themselves, to the point of self-addiction. They love themselves almost as if they were objects, external to themselves. Narcissus fell in love with his *reflection*. He saw it outside of himself, the self reflected in the environment. It was so beautiful, so alluring. He felt helpless in the presence of his love object, desperate to unite with the most desirable thing he had ever seen. It did not end well for the young boy.

The Strange Case of Donald J. Trump. Dan P. McAdams, Oxford University Press (2020). © Oxford University Press.
DOI: 10.1093/oso/9780197507445.001.0001

When I walk through downtown Chicago and head north on State Street, I sometimes pause to gaze at the gleaming tower that Donald Trump built on the Chicago River. I know he built it because the letters T-R-U-M-P are stenciled on the south-facing side, 20 feet tall. It is not quite like seeing his face reflected gargantuan on the gleaming facade—but almost. To see the omnipresent face, I need merely to glance over at the screens hanging on the first floor of the ABC news studio, just south of the river. Unless they are doing the sports or the weather, chances are high that Trump's face will appear—and if not there, on the covers of multiple magazines, newspapers, and books at the newsstand across the street. His name and his image are everywhere.

It is as if I am now living in the world that Donald Trump has lived in for most of his life—a world reflecting the glory of his name, his face, and his brand. Magazine covers and photographs of Trump plaster the walls at the Trump Organization headquarters. For years, Trump maintained an electronic clipping service that alerted him to how often his name appeared in the media each day. Before that, his staff made copies of every Trump photo or news story they could find every day and presented the file to him each morning. It was the first thing he looked at when he arrived at work. Now, he simply turns on the television when he wakes up in the White House. His face will be there, reflected in the 21st-century version of the Narcissus pool.

Beginning with Trump Tower in New York City, Donald Trump has attached his name to more things, and more different kinds of things, than nearly anybody else on the planet. There are/were seven Trump Towers around the world; nine Trump hotels, including the Trump International Hotel in Washington, DC; various Trump casinos and resorts; at least a dozen Trump golf courses; the DJT restaurant in Las Vegas (guess what the initials stand for); the Donald J. Trump fashion collection (formerly sold at Macy's); Trump talking dolls (also sold at Macy's); Trump airplanes (the Trump Shuttle, which went out of business in 1992); Trump Model Management (a model agency); Trump steaks; Trump wine; Trump vodka; Trump water; Trump cologne; a Trump board game; Trump campaign paraphernalia, including Make America Great Again (MAGA) hats and campaign pins; *Trump* magazine; and Trump University. I do not claim that this list is exhaustive. Moreover, Trump's name appears on his books—not just as author, but also *in the titles: Trump: The Art of the Comeback; Trump: Think Big; Trump: Never Give Up*; and so on. To convey just how strange this is, imagine that Leo Tolstoy gave his greatest novel this title: *Tolstoy: War and Peace*. Trump once expressed interest in providing funding for a new Broadway play. I am not even going to tell you what the title of the show was to be.

It is not enough, however, for Trump to be seen and to be known—his face, his name, his identity. He must be seen as big and wonderful and known to be *the greatest*. Not even a month into his presidency, Donald Trump publicly proclaimed that his administration was arguably the greatest of all time. In a wild 77-minute press conference in February 2017, his first as president, he lambasted the press for failing to celebrate his greatness and claimed, "There has never been a presidency that has done so much in such a short period of time." He went on to make the false claim that his Electoral College victory was the largest since Ronald Reagan's, when in fact he won fewer electoral votes than did three of the four presidents since Reagan. In an interview with a British newspaper in July 2018, Trump criticized British Prime Minister Theresa May for failing to take his advice on policy, claiming that he knows more than May does about British politics because he is a "stable genius." He did not make the remark in jest. He was serious, as he was when he made the following public remarks:

"The greatest builder is me, and I would build the greatest [border] wall you have ever seen."

"If I were a liberal Democrat, people would say I'm the super genius of all time. The super genius of all time. If you're a conservative Republican, you've got to fight for your life. It's really an amazing thing."

"I think apologizing's a great thing, but you have to be wrong. I will absolutely apologize, sometime in the hopefully distant future, if I'm ever wrong."

"I get along with everybody. People love me, and you know what? I've been very successful; everybody loves me."

"All of the women on *The Apprentice* flirted with me—consciously or unconsciously. That's to be expected."

Self-promotional self-references have always peppered Donald Trump's speech, public and private, going back at least to his 20s. When he is talking to friends, strangers, or the general public, there appears to be nothing nearly as fascinating to Donald Trump as the topic of Donald Trump. Whatever idea or person or thing comes in second on the list of Donald Trump's top conversational topics is miles behind the winner. Trump will inject the idea of his own greatness into almost any kind of social setting, no matter how much his words violate social norms. When, in the summer of 1999, he stood up to offer remarks at his father's funeral, Trump spoke mainly about himself. It was the toughest day of *his own life*, Trump began. He went on to talk about Fred Trump's greatest achievement: raising a brilliant and renowned son. As Gwenda Blair wrote in her biography of the Trump family, *The Trumps*, "the first-person singular pronouns, the I and me and my, eclipsed the he and his. Where others spoke of their memories of Fred Trump, [Donald] spoke of Fred Trump's endorsement."

As president, Donald Trump has received resounding criticism for boasting about himself and his administration in situations that call for a more serious, somber, or self-effacing approach. He has great difficulty expressing empathy for people who are suffering, even when his staff schools him on how to do it. When he made a phone call to console the widow of a slain American soldier in October 2017, Florida Congresswoman Frederica Wilson, who witnessed the call, described it as insensitive and disrespectful. Trump didn't even seem to know the soldier's name.

Rather than offer sympathy to the victims of a devastating hurricane in Puerto Rico in September 2017, President Trump boasted of the great job his administration was doing in response to the emergency, and he lashed out at the mayor of San Juan, Puerto Rico, accusing her of poor leadership. When a mammoth storm hit Houston just days later, dumping 40 inches of rain on the city and causing untold suffering, Trump immediately sent out tweets marveling at the storm's awesomeness: "Wow!" "Historic." "Biggest ever." "Epic." The *New York Times* columnist Frank Bruni characterized Trump's response as full of "self-impressed wonder," "childishly intent on superlatives, puerilely obsessed with size, laden with boasts and lavish with discordant asides." Moreover, Trump admitted that he timed the public release of a controversial decision to coincide with the height of the storm, to maximize publicity: "In the middle of the hurricane, even though it was a Friday evening, I assumed the ratings would be far higher than they would be normally." The Houston hurricane "didn't blow away the opportunism and narcissism at Trump's core," Bruni wrote.

It is Trump's narcissism, probably more than anything else, that leads his critics to describe him as immature and childish. But even friends have occasionally described him that way. Many years ago, the *New York Daily News* columnist Liz Smith remarked: "There's something about him that's ever juvenile. It's hard to believe he's a grown-up person who went to college." Smith added: "He's like a kid, and he's got the brash, narcissistic thing that works for him. He has enormous appeal to the masses because of that." Smith recalled that Trump once threatened to buy her newspaper and fire her in response to a story she wrote— and yet, she said, "I still go on liking him."

Smith's mixed feelings about Trump reveal an important insight: For certain audiences in certain situations, narcissism can be very appealing. Trump's expansive self-promotion gets rave reviews from the thousands of Americans who attend his political rallies. Cheering crowds find his boasting to be entertaining and inspiring. Basking in the aura of his reflected glory, they are transfixed by his greatness and his charm, like Narcissus staring into the pool. In a paper on Trump's narcissism, the psychiatrist Tom Singer summarized the uplifting message that Trump conveys to the adoring crowds. In Singer's words: "I am the Greatness to which America may once again aspire. By identifying with how great I am, you can rekindle your wounded American dream and make yourself and America great again." Another way to express the same sentiment, Singer wrote, goes like this: "I have achieved the American dream; I am the American dream; I am the incarnation of the Self that the country aspires to."

In a similar vein, the psychiatrist Leonard Cruz has deconstructed the basic message that Trump transmits to his admiring audience through narcissistic display. The key concept in Cruz's conception is *narcissistic injury*, which refers to a wounding of the self. According to Cruz, many of Trump's most ardent supporters have experienced serious setbacks in life and feel disrespected or left behind. Psychologically speaking, they are the walking wounded. In Trump, they see a comrade in arms. Even though he is the most powerful man in the world, Trump has been disrespected again and again, his supporters know. Despite his being a superhero, he is also like them, and like America itself, which once was a great nation but has since been disrespected and mistreated. Their identification with Trump reinforces a readiness to believe the following promise that Trump has made to the American people, a promise that plays out in a logical sequence, beginning with Trump's inspiring narcissism: I am great → I've been mistreated → Americans have been mistreated → I obliterated my competitors → I will obliterate America's competitors → I will make America great again → I am great . . .

And the cycle repeats.

***

The first psychologically minded scientist to draw explicit inspiration from the ancient story of Narcissus may have been Havelock Ellis, a British sexologist. In 1898, Ellis used the term "narcissism" to refer to a state of absorbed contemplation on the beauty and greatness of the self, which could shade into an erotic self-admiration. Ellis quoted two 19th-century women who wrote about their narcissistic experiences in private correspondence: "I love myself; I am my God." The women found enrapturing "this unique and marvelous *me*, by which I am enchanted, and which I adore like Narcissus." As Ellis saw it, the self's adulation of itself provided the emotional impetus for certain autoerotic ecstasies, wherein the self takes its own body to be its most desired object.

In his paper, "On Narcissism," published in 1914, Sigmund Freud sought to normalize narcissism and give it a more general meaning. Freud argued that the infant first loves the self, as Narcissus did, but quickly switches affection to the mother because she is the source of nourishment. As Freud saw it, narcissism marks an early developmental stage in life, through which nearly all individuals pass on their way to establishing more-or-less normal relationships with people and objects in the outside world. Nonetheless, a residue of narcissism remains psychologically active for many people throughout the course of their lives. Those with the strongest narcissistic inclinations tend to be strongly focused on their own self-preservation while exhibiting characteristics of aggression, fierce independence, and leadership. In Freud's view, narcissism is a mixed blessing, incorporating both positive and negative features.

For a good part of the 20th century, the concept of narcissism lay dormant and neglected in mainstream psychological discourse. Nobody seemed to be much interested in it. But in the 1970s, it burst forth as a cultural and psychological phenomenon. Psychotherapists noted a large uptick in cases wherein patients seemed to be suffering from narcissistic injuries and related disorders—deficiencies in or inflations of—self-esteem, self-regard, and self-worth. Cultural critics observed that Americans were becoming increasingly self-preoccupied. The values of hard work and self-sacrifice were giving way to a consumerist culture in which people placed an inordinate emphasis upon feeding the self with objects, products, and experiences, to the neglect of mature interpersonal relationships and civic commitment. Tom Wolfe famously labeled the 1970s "the Me Decade."

Christopher Lasch summarized a wide range of what he believed to be dangerous psychological developments and societal trends in an extraordinarily influential book, *The Culture of Narcissism*, published in 1978. What Lasch described as "the narcissistic personality of our time" "sees the world as a mirror of himself and has no interest in external events except as they throw back a reflection of his own image." The narcissistic person is adept at manipulating others for his own ends, but he has no genuine feeling for other people because he is too caught up in the love affair with self. He is unable to identify with other people. He is unable to internalize the values and norms that others may extol. At the same time, American society increasingly rewards and reinforces narcissism, Lasch argued. Among the corrupting forces that were aiding and abetting the rise of narcissism, Lasch contended, were the breakdown of traditional mores regarding sexuality and gender and the 1970s human potential movement, which urged Americans to contemplate and reflect obsessively upon the self through Eastern meditative practices, New Age spiritualism, and hallucinogenic drugs. Lasch also blamed television, advertising, Hollywood, self-help groups, autobiographical fiction, and many other givens of modern American life. Lasch died in 1994. One shudders to think of the judgments he might have made regarding selfies and Facebook.

Meanwhile, also during the 1970s, two very different portraits of narcissism were beginning to crystallize, as expressed in the writings of prominent psychoanalysts, the intellectual descendants of Freud.

Otto Kernberg was the leading theorist behind the first view, which emphasized the dark and malevolent features of narcissism. Kernberg depicted certain patients whom he had seen in therapy as *malignant narcissists*, deeply unsatisfied people who, like Narcissus himself, are destined to experience frustration and rage in failed self-love. According to Kernberg, malignant narcissists often exhibit a superficial but seductive charm, a glittery fascination in the eyes of others, and what may appear to be an inflated self-regard. At the same time, they are interpersonally ruthless, incapable of expressing empathy and suffering from fragile self-esteem. They have an impoverished inner life, to the point of feeling empty inside, and they are roiled by anger, resentment, and grandiose fantasies of revenge. In a book entitled, *The Americanization of Narcissism*, the historian Elizabeth Lunbeck provided a vivid capsule summary of Kernberg's view:

> Kenberg's pathological narcissists inhabit a landscape without laws, in which brutality, aggression, and predation reign. By his telling, envy, sadism, and corruption, all forms of "rationalized aggression," course through social and organizational life. Relations among individuals constitute an unending contest for supremacy; better to sadistically exploit, the narcissist thinks, than to risk exploitation and the humiliation of defeat. Most other people are but "lifeless shadows," unreliable and crooked, ready at all times to attack and enforce submission. Those few whom narcissists admire are but idealized extensions of themselves, devalued and "dethroned" if they disappoint in any way. Those whom narcissists enlist to admire them are but "slaves" to be casually tossed aside and mercilessly mistreated but not freed. Weakness—financial, social, sexual—is to be callously exploited.

A second and less menacing view of narcissism appeared in the writings of Heniz Kohut, who tended to take a more developmental approach. Kohut conceded that immature, and indeed pathological, narcissism can resemble the dark portrait painted by Kernberg. But many highly functioning people show a more mature form of narcissism. In Kohut's developmental theory of narcissism, young children regularly express grandiosity and feel pleasure in exhibiting their own strength and efficacy. There is nothing wrong with this, Kohut said. What matters is how the parents respond to the early narcissistic display.

Adopting a relatively traditional view of family dynamics, Kohut deemed it the mother's role to function as a "mirror" to the child, warmly affirming and reflecting back the child's greatness, beauty, and ambition. The child is literally able to see, Kohut believed, the gleam of praise in the mother's eyes. Perceiving her affirmation bolsters the child's self-esteem. At the same time, the father's role is to function as a human "ideal," providing values to guide the child's ambitions and projecting a sense of calm. The father helps the child channel narcissistic energy into productive and creative activity while soothing the child's anxieties. Affirmed by the mother's love and guided by the father's ideals, the self-promoting child should become, over the course of life, a well-functioning adult blessed with mature narcissism. Mature narcissists can become forceful and generative leaders, Kohut asserted. They are loved and admired by many others, even as they love and admire themselves.

While clinicians like Kernberg and Kohut provided rich anecdotal accounts of narcissism as experienced by patients in therapy, contemporary social and personality psychologists have taken a more scientific route, focusing their attention on quantifiable research. Building on the insights of Lasch, Kernberg, Kohut, and other cultural and clinical accounts, the research literature on narcissism has grown very large over the past couple of decades. There exist many different, and sometimes conflicting, empirical findings, as well as many different theoretical approaches for making sense of the findings. Amidst it all, however, there are some important common themes and take-home points. Let me highlight four of them that, in one way or another, bear on the strange case of Donald J. Trump.

Point #1: Narcissism is not a personality "type"

Many people think of narcissism as an all-or-nothing category that applies to certain "types" or "kinds" of people. If you are a narcissist, then you have certain recognizable psychological features. If you are not a narcissist, then you do not have those features. You are either a narcissist, or you are not a narcissist.

By contrast, most social and personality psychologists see narcissism as a continuous dimension, upon which people differ. Some people are more narcissistic than others, but there is no strict dividing line on the continuum separating "the narcissists" from the "nonnarcissists." It is simply a matter of degree. Scores on narcissism measures form a bell-shaped distribution, like variation on height or weight, or like differences that people show on basic personality traits such as extraversion and conscientiousness. We may all have some narcissism in us, but some of us have more than others. Thinking of narcissism as a dimension, moreover, reminds us that narcissism is merely one feature of personality, rather than the whole picture. The dimension of narcissism combines with a host of other variables in personality—everything from temperament traits to narrative identities—to comprise the psychological uniqueness of an individual person.

Point #2: Narcissism contains contrasting elements

Clinicians have long noted that highly narcissistic individuals exhibit an assortment of different psychological qualities, some of which seem to conflict with each other. They may be brimming with confidence and deeply insecure at the very same time. They may be charming and manipulative, solicitous and cruel. They may have high self-esteem at one level, but low self-esteem at another.

Two research psychologists at Iowa State University, Zlatan Krizan and Anne D. Herlache, recently developed an integrative theoretical model for narcissism that incorporates many of the different features that have been proposed, going back even to Freud. At the core of narcissism, argue Krizan and Herlache, is *entitled self-importance*. But this core feature expresses itself in variable ways across a spectrum, running from approach-oriented qualities to avoidant-oriented qualities. On the approach-oriented side of the spectrum, narcissism may reveal itself in bold and grandiose ways. The highly narcissistic person may shamelessly exhibit an inordinate level of hubris—boasting and preening, extolling awesome power or matchless beauty, manipulating the world to feed his or her grand ambitions. On the avoidance-oriented side of the spectrum, narcissism may reveal itself as defensiveness, vulnerability, and seething resentment. The highly narcissistic person may suffer painful bouts of insecurity, motivating him or her to lash out against those who fail to appreciate and applaud. The distinction between approach-oriented and avoidance-oriented manifestations of narcissism captures two different factors that often appear in self-report scales designed to measure individual differences in narcissism—grandiosity and vulnerability.

Other approaches divide narcissism up in different ways. For example, one group of researchers distinguishes between narcissistic *admiration* and narcissistic *rivalry*. Highly narcissistic individuals praise themselves (admiration) and derogate others (rivalry). In romantic relationships, the researchers show, the admiration feature may attract potential mates. But over time, the rivalry component drives them way. This interpersonal dynamic plays out in many kinds of relationships for highly narcissistic people. Research in social psychology repeatedly shows that people who score high on narcissism measures can be extraordinarily charming and appealing early on in relationships but that over time potential friends and lovers grow weary of them.

Point #3: Narcissism can be good or bad, but maybe more bad than good

Reflecting the contrasting perspectives offered by Kernberg and Kohut, the research literature provides evidence for both narcissism's costs and its benefits. People high in narcissism tend to show more anger and hostility when challenged or insulted, compared to people low in narcissism. They tend to show sharper mood swings, oscillating between exuberance and negativity. They tend to make more enemies than do people who score lower on narcissism measures. Having said that, some studies show that highly narcissistic people are more popular. They are also judged to be more physically attractive. In this case, the causal arrow probably goes in the reverse: Physically beautiful people, like

Narcissus, cannot help but think highly of themselves. And, perhaps you wanted to know that highly narcissistic men tend to be flashy dressers and highly narcissistic women tend to wear blouses that show more cleavage. A statistical review of many different studies has shown that narcissism tends to be associated with leadership emergence, but not leadership effectiveness. In other words, highly narcissistic men and women tend to rise to positions of leadership. But they are no more effective as leaders than are less narcissistic men and women.

On the topic of leadership, a team of researchers recently compared U.S. presidents, running from George Washington to George W. Bush, on the dimension of grandiose narcissism. On first blush, you might expect that narcissism would be part of the job description for anybody aspiring to become the chief executive of the United States. The expectation makes sense, especially in this day and age: A person probably has to possess tremendous audacity to think he or she might ascend to the presidency, a status position that has been attained by only 45 human beings in history. Nonetheless, American presidents appear to have differed considerably from each other on narcissism, if the scientists' and historians' ratings are to be believed.

Lyndon Johnson scored the highest in the ratings made for grandiose narcissism, followed closely by Teddy Roosevelt and Andrew Jackson. Franklin Delano Roosevelt, John F. Kennedy, Richard Nixon, and Bill Clinton were next. Millard Fillmore ranked lowest. Correlating these ranks with objective indices of presidential performance, the researchers found that narcissism in presidents is something of a double-edged sword. On the positive side, grandiose narcissism is associated with initiating more legislation, public persuasiveness, agenda setting, and historians' ratings of presidential "greatness." On the negative side, it is also associated with unethical behavior and congressional impeachment resolutions.

In business, government, sports, and many other arenas, people will put up with a great deal of self-serving and obnoxious behavior on the part of highly narcissistic individuals as long as those individuals perform at high levels. Take Steve Jobs, for example—one of the most narcissistic public figures in America during the last few decades of the 20th century. As the co-founder and CEO of Apple, he routinely heaped abuse on colleagues, subordinates, and friends. At age 27, he cried when he learned that *Time* magazine had not chosen him to be Man of the Year. He went into a rage after receiving a phone call congratulating him for the release of Apple's I-Pad, in 2010. The call came from President Obama's chief of staff, Rahm Emanuel. Jobs felt that President Obama himself should have called. He never got over the slight. Jobs was so self-absorbed that he effectively ignored his wife and children, to the point of refusing to acknowledge for some time that one of those children was in fact his.

Yet, like many narcissistic people, Jobs could be witty and charismatic. Narcissists may attain high levels of popularity and esteem in the short term.

As long as they prove to be successful and brilliant—like Steve Jobs—they may be able to weather criticism and retain their exalted status. In other words, if you really are a stable genius, you can probably get away with being a flaming narcissist, too. More often than not, however, narcissistic individuals wear out their welcome. Over time, people become annoyed, if not infuriated, by their self-centeredness. When narcissists begin to disappoint those whom they once dazzled, their descent can be precipitous. There is still truth today in the ancient proverb: Pride goeth before the fall.

Point #4: Narcissism is mainly about motivation

Within the first few months of life, human infants begin to show traces of the temperament dispositions that will ultimately shape the kind of social actors they will become. By three or four months of age, some babies show signs of a broadly positive emotionality, expressed as general cheerfulness and an energetic engagement of the social world. Others appear somewhat more timid and diffident. By age 1 year, babies show clear differences with respect to tendencies toward aggressiveness and anger. In the second and third year of life, they reveal variation in self-control and perseverance. Strongly driven, we assume, by genetic effects and early gene by environment interactions, these early emerging differences in emotional and social display foreshadow the full-fledged variations we will later observe in adult personality traits—that is, those basic dispositions captured in the Big Five dimensions of extraversion, neuroticism, agreeableness, conscientiousness, and openness.

But narcissism is different. Compared to the Big Five traits, narcissism waits longer to show its face. This is because narcissism requires a psychological infrastructure that is rather more sophisticated than what traits require. It requires that a person has developed a characteristic *motivational agenda*, by which I mean a set of beliefs, goals, plans, and values that speak to what a person wants in life and to what a person fears or hopes to avoid. Of course, babies want things. They want to be fed when they are hungry. They want to be comforted when they are upset. But these basic and pervasive wants are not psychologically articulated and do not comprise meaningful psychological differences between babies. Babies don't wake up in the morning with a plan for the day. They do not have a list of goals and values in their head. They do not have an agenda. They are social actors, but not yet motivated agents.

To become a motivated agent one must have an internal agenda that guides thought and behavior going forward in time. Beginning in later childhood and adolescence, people show marked individual differences in their motivational agendas. One person's goals and values may go in the direction of achieving success in school and work. Another's may focus on cultivating intimate relationships with family and friends. Yet another person's agenda may revolve mainly around having fun and making the most out of every moment in life.

A highly narcissistic person develops an agenda that centers on the *promotion and protection of the self*, to the exclusion of most other goals. The agenda is developed in service of what Krizan and Herlache identify as entitled self-importance. As a highly narcissistic person, "I" (the subject) reflexively see "me" (the object) as being especially grandiose and vulnerable. I see myself (me) as great, but I feel threatened, too. I must assert and defend my greatness. This is the first thing that I worry about when I wake up in the morning. This is the last thing I think about before I fall asleep. I even dream about it. This is what I want in life, what I value. This is what I care about more than anything else.

A person's motivational agenda is different from his or her dispositional personality traits. In the case of Donald Trump, high extraversion and remarkably low agreeableness capture the main contours of his trait profile. By all accounts, he is, and pretty much has always been, a bold, hard-charging, high-energy, reward-seeking, sociable, gregarious, and dominant social actor (high extraversion), who also happens to be remarkably tough, aggressive, contentious, norm-violating, and disagreeable, and lacking in gentleness and empathy (low agreeableness). He is socially energetic, and he is mean. These trait attributions, however, do not speak directly to his motivational agenda. High extraversion and low agreeableness do not tell much about what a person wants in life, or what he fears. When an extraverted, disagreeable person wakes up in the morning, what kind of a plan does he have? We can't really know based solely on his traits. We need to get inside his mind.

It is true that *some* highly narcissistic people, like Donald Trump and Steve Jobs, tend also to show high extraversion and low agreeableness. Indeed, research shows that self-report measures of narcissism are, in a general sense, positively associated with self-report measures of extraversion and negatively correlated with agreeableness. But it must also be emphasized that many highly narcissistic people do *not* show this particular trait profile, and many people who show this trait profile do not harbor highly narcissistic motivational agendas. As social actors, narcissistic people come in many different shades and forms. They have different styles. For example, one of the most narcissistic people I know is relatively introverted, very warm and caring, and shows high levels of conscientiousness and openness. She is a leading scholar in her academic discipline. She is obsessed with her self-image, which is both grandiose and fragile. She believes that every research article she writes is a game changer, destined to transform her field of study. She believes that her work is the most important scholarly work being done on the planet today. When people criticize something she writes, she is crushed. As a social actor, she comes across as a nice person—and she really *is* nice, and generous, and kind. But her motivational agenda is all about narcissism, about *me*.

***

How did Donald Trump become such a highly narcissistic person? I do not have a satisfying psychological answer. Any psychologist who claims to have one either has lower standards than I have for what counts as a good explanation or has access to a treasure trove of information on Trump that has never before been revealed. In truth, the psychological research literature does not offer many clues regarding the developmental roots of narcissism more generally. There are many theories, of course, but very few well-documented and replicated empirical findings.

In the absence of a definitive developmental answer to my question, let me propose instead a life-course account of Donald Trump's *career in narcissism*. Let us follow him over time, from infancy through the presidency, as he develops a motivational agenda centered on promoting and protecting a grandiose and fragile self-concept. Let us see him advance and expand that agenda over time, as he moves up in the ranks, as it were, from an amateur narcissist to a master. Let us try to imagine what it feels like to articulate and live out a narcissistic agenda during each epoch of his life. What goes on in the narcissistic mind of Donald Trump? What has it been like to be him?

Infancy

We begin at the mysterious beginning. Both Kohut and Kernberg argued that problems in narcissism stem ultimately from cold and detached parenting. Kohut singled out the mother's mirroring relationship. Does she affirm and reflect back the infant's exuberant grandiosity? If not, the infant may have to compensate by becoming both the mirror and the image reflected back. Like Narcissus, he may be destined to hover near the pool for the rest of his life, forever gazing at his magnificent reflection, lest he lose confidence in his greatness and beauty.

Despite the fact that Kohut's developmental story enjoys little, if any, empirical support in the scientific literature, it has proven to be a compelling account, and useful in therapy. In the case of Donald Trump, however, we have virtually no relevant information to assess its applicability. There is no evidence to suggest that Mary Trump was *not* a supportive and affirming mother to her five children, the fourth of whom went on to become president. Looking back on their childhoods, all five of her offspring lavished praise on her, although they tended to speak in vague terms about her role in the family. She was warm, they have said. She was there for them, even though she suffered some health problems after her last child was born and even though she spent considerable time outside the home, doing volunteer work and attending social events in the community. Both Mary and Fred were strict parents. They enforced rules regarding proper behavior, and they discouraged the unbridled expression of strong emotions.

As consciousness gradually dawns in the second and third years of Donald Trump's life, he finds himself to be an energetic and high-spirited social actor, expressing his emotions in a family environment that discourages outbursts. He nonetheless feels a strong engagement with his environment, driven by inborn temperament dimensions. He enjoys playing with his toys—trucks, blocks, toy soldiers, and other gender-typical implements that boys played with in the 1940s. Life is exciting. But his daily experience is tinged with anger, too, and not a small amount of aggression. A few years later, when he is around five years of age, he will find himself throwing rocks at a toddler, little Dennis Burnham sitting in his backyard playpen, as reported decades later by Dennis's mother. Where does the anger come from? Why does he lash out? Does it stem from the frustration Donald feels when his parents ignore his entreaties and withhold emotional support? Maybe. But probably not so much. We don't know where his anger comes from. And maybe the question is silly. Does anger need to *come from* somewhere? In many cases, anger simply *is*. Research shows that temperament differences in the experience of anger and the expression of aggression begin to appear by the time parents celebrate their child's first birthday.

Christopher Lasch once speculated that narcissism may arise in family situations wherein the child feels emotional neglect but is nonetheless told that he is the favorite. It is an interesting idea. In Lasch's scenario, the child knows in his head that his parents think he is the greatest show on earth, but the child does not *feel* it in his heart because his parents do not back up their statements with emotion. Because he does not *feel* special but knows that he is supposed to *be* special, the child develops a grandiose but emotionally vulnerable self. From an early age, Donald Trump was reminded that he was effectively the family favorite. Fred called Donald his "killer" and his "king." Therefore, one half of Lasch's scenario appears to have been in play when Donald Trump was very young. He may have *known* he was great. But did he *feel* it? We don't know.

Childhood

Endowed with temperament dispositions at the very start, human beings are social actors from birth onward. But they do not begin to become motivated agents until age 4 or 5, and even then but gradually. The first step forward is the emergence of what developmental psychologists call *theory of mind*. There are many different ways to define theory of mind and many subtle nuances, but let me strip it down to the basics: Theory of mind is the child's understanding that people have minds within which reside their desires and beliefs. These desire and beliefs *motivate* behavior.

Let me illustrate it.

When my younger daughter was in kindergarten, she asked me what my profession was. She needed to report my response to her class.

"I am a professor of psychology," I said, or something to that effect.

"What is that?" she asked.

"I study why people do what they do."

"Well, why *do* people do what they do?" she asked, with mild scorn in her five-year old voice.

"I don't really know, sweetheart. I guess that's why I study it."

"*I* know why people do what they do."

"Oh, you do? Why?"

"Because *they want to!*"

And she walked away in disgust. Her father must be an idiot.

Amanda's insight is the folk-psychological key to theory of mind: Why do people do things? *Because they want to do them.* Because they have *desires* in their *minds* that they translate into motivated, goal-directed *behavior.* Common sense! Still, children do not grasp this common sense until around age 4, studies have repeatedly shown. It is a developmental breakthrough. Once you realize that people have desires and beliefs in their heads that motivate their behavior, it is a small step forward to realize that you have them, too—to realize that you are a motivated agent, albeit a rather simple one at first.

Motivated agency gets more complicated as the child moves through elementary school. What some developmental psychologists call *the age 5 to 7 shift* ushers in a suite of cognitive and social advances in human development. Prompted by changes in the brain and structured by the educational environments that schools provide, children become increasingly rational, organized, and future-oriented in their thinking about themselves and the world in which they live. They develop what the famous cognitive psychologist Jean Piaget termed *concrete operations*, which effectively enables them to classify objects and ideas in the world into logical categories, to sort and organize things into seriated patterns, running from high to low, most to least, best to worst, and so on. The evaluations they receive from their teachers, coaches, parents, and other socializing agents reinforce an emerging status hierarchy. Some kids are smarter than other kids. Some kids are better at sports. Some kids are nicer, and some are really mean. These differences are not apparent to the kids themselves at age 3. By age 8 or 9, however, they are (sometimes painfully) clear. The rational and organized minds of fourth and fifth graders can sort it all out. It is within this cognitive and social context that *self-esteem* walks onto the motivational stage.

Research suggests that children begin to show meaningful individual differences in self-esteem around the age of 7. To make a self-esteem judgment, you must be able to step back from yourself and make an assessment. You must be able to gaze into the pool and evaluate what you see. Like Narcissus, the judgment can, and often does, involve a person's physical attractiveness as observed by the person himself or herself. But more than that, self-esteem typically involves *valued goals*. Now that I know I am a motivated agent who does things because he wants to do them, I begin to organize my wants and desires into goals, plans, and programs; that is, I begin to articulate a personal motivational agenda. The agenda includes short-term and long-term goals, more long-term goals as I get older. This week's goals are to get Jennifer, the cutest girl in class, to like me and to get an *A* on my arithmetic test. In the long run, I would really like to improve my batting skills in baseball and to quit fighting so much with my sister. And wouldn't it be great if my parents got back together? Talk about a big goal! My self-esteem is largely a product of how well I think I am doing on my motivational agenda. Am I achieving the goals I set out to achieve? Am I getting what I want out of life?

Some psychologists define narcissism as *excessively high self-esteem*, resulting from motivated agency run amok. The highly narcissistic person believes that he or she deserves the grade of *A*+ in all of the valued goal domains in life. I am the best at everything, or at minimum, the best at everything that is worth being the best at. The social psychologist Keith Campbell developed an *agency theory of narcissism*, which depicts narcissism as resulting from a strong and abiding motivational emphasis on pursuing goals of power, status, personal perfection, and the like, to the exclusion of love and intimacy goals, and a relentless focus on enhancing self-esteem. People who score high on measures of narcissism fantasize about power and status to a greater extent than do people low in narcissism. Importantly, their fantasies involve an imaginary audience. For the highly narcissistic person, it is not enough to be successful in achieving goals. One must be widely recognized for the achievement, glorified and honored by others. The highly narcissistic person needs other people, not as friends and lovers but rather as fawning admirers, who serve to affirm agency and boost self-esteem.

At the Kew-Forest Elementary School, Donald Trump seems to be achieving some of his valued goals and not achieving others. It is becoming clear that the young boy who will one day declare himself to be a stable genius is, at best, a slightly above-average student when it comes to classroom performance. Does this bother him? Probably. Does it negatively impact his self-esteem? Maybe. His sister Maryanne seems to be the good student in the family. But Donald compensates in sports, which is a strongly valued goal arena for him. He is among the best in baseball, a right-handed power hitter. He excels in basketball, too, and enjoys football and soccer. He is a physically powerful boy. He is developing a reputation, moreover, as a fighter, and he is admired for this. Getting into fights with other boys may not be central to his motivational agenda, but when he finds himself in a fight, he must win. His goal is always to win. His self-esteem is tied up with winning. He is beginning to form the belief that the world contains a few big winners and throngs of countless losers.

Adolescence

Self-esteem typically takes a huge hit in the early teen years. The drop is demonstrably steeper for girls than boys, the research suggests. The brutal social environments of junior high school and high school establish pecking orders and status hierarchies that leave many teenagers feeling frustrated and inferior. So many losers, for only a few can truly be number one. The fear of social rejection overwhelms many young teens, exacerbated by bullying and so many Machiavellian maneuvers among peers that I would rather not write anything more about this. It is the best of times for a chosen few; the worst of times for many more.

Donald Trump probably does not experience the normative dip in self-esteem that many teenagers experience. He continues to feel good about himself, continues to perceive himself to be a winner, as he makes the transition to the New York Military Academy (NYMA), in eighth grade. The hypermasculinized culture at NYMA is precisely the kind of social environment wherein the adolescent Donald Trump can rise readily to the top. He is big; he is strong; he is extremely tough and disciplined; he is aggressive; he is good-looking; and he is a formidable athlete. His fellow cadets generally admire Donald, although he has no really close friends. It is difficult for others to get close because he is so competitive. He sees himself as apart. He is better than others. His baseball coach, Theodore Dobias, recalled that Donald "just wanted to be first, in everything, and he wanted people to know he was first." "He was always proud of himself," Dobias said. "He believed he was the best."

It is indeed at NYMA, as he moves through puberty and grows to be a strapping young man, where Donald Trump begins to resemble Narcissus himself. He falls in love with his body and appearance—the imposing physique, the hair, the regal bearing, the handsome young man in military uniform, reflected in a mirror and in photographs from the time. There he is in one school photo, taken at a high school military parade in Manhattan, as told by one biographer, "smartly uniformed, down to his bright white gloves, right in front of Tiffany's iconic store on Fifth Avenue." Dobias remembered that Donald "was very conscious of how his uniform looked—he always wanted his shoes to be shiny and he wanted to look sharp."

As he marvels at his own beauty and power, Donald Trump begins to note that others are looking at him, too. It is intoxicating to be seen and admired and commented upon. In his third year at NYMA, Trump's heroics on the ball field merit a headline in the local newspaper—TRUMP WINS GAME FOR NYMA. The experience is "electrifying," as one biographer characterizes it. "It felt good seeing my name in print," Trump said 50 years later. "How many people are in print? Nobody's in print. It was the first time I was ever in the newspaper. I thought it was amazing."

Emerging adulthood

The developmental psychologist Jeffrey Arnett popularized the term *emerging adulthood* to refer to that period in life running from the late teens through the 20s. In modern societies, emerging adulthood is marked by the continuation of education and job training for many, floundering and uncertainty for many others, and the provisional exploration of adult roles. It is a period in which young people are still trying to "find themselves," striving to develop an identity in the adult world. It can be an exciting time in life, full of promise and expectation.

Thankfully, self-esteem begins to recover (on average) in the early 20s, for both young men and young women. As emerging adults develop their identities, they ideally settle into motivational agendas that are both appropriately aspirational and more-or-less realistic. They make plans to pursue valued long-term goals that promise to bring them meaning and happiness in their adult years. They begin to crystallize their ethical, religious, and social values and beliefs. They begin to make commitments in love and work. They begin to see their lives as extended, self-authored narratives, the reconstructed past giving birth, in their narrating minds, to an imagined future, providing life with some sense of temporal continuity, unity, and purpose.

For Donald Trump, emerging adulthood comprises his time at Fordham University and the University of Pennsylvania (the Wharton School) and his early years as a fledgling real estate developer in Manhattan. In college, he has a clear motivational agenda, but it bears little resemblance to the goals, plans, and values running through the heads of most of the other students on campus. Despite his extraverted nature, young Trump is not especially interested in cultivating friendships and developing social networks among his college peers. He believes that they are of very little use to him. He plays on the squash team at Fordham, but beyond that, he keeps his distance, goes home on weekends.

He is not interested in campus parties. No drinking. No drugs. He is not interested in his classes, except for those related to real estate at the Wharton School.
He is not interested in expanding his mind or gaining new experiences. As the
war in Vietnam heats up and tens of thousands of students mobilize to protest
America's involvement, Trump stays away, expresses no opinion. Instead, he is
focused on plans for the family business, imagining how he will someday make a
fortune in real estate, how he will develop an empire that vastly exceeds what his
father achieved. "He really wanted to be a success," recalled one person who occasionally spoke with Trump back then. "He was already focused on the future,
thinking long-term more than present. He used to talk about his dad's business,
how he would use him as a role model but go one step further."

On a crisp and cloudless Tuesday morning during the fall of Donald's
freshman year at Fordham, he accompanies his dad to join hundreds of
New Yorkers at the opening public ceremony for the Verrazano-Narrows
Bridge, the largest suspension bridge in the world. Connecting Brooklyn to
Staten Island, the great bridge is 70 stories high and more than a mile in length.
Robert Moses, the legendary New York builder, summons politicians and other
dignitaries to the dais to deliver speeches and offer accolades for the project. The
original designer of the bridge, however, is ignored. Standing alone in the crowd
and completely forgotten is the 85-year-old Othmar Hermann Amman. Trump
notices the slight. Imagine you are Trump in this moment. How might you
react? Maybe you feel pity for Amman. Maybe you are outraged by the oversight.
Maybe you just shrug it off as simply another sorry example of how life is not
fair. But no. Donald Trump directs his antipathy and disgust *toward* Amman.
The 85-year-old designer standing alone *is a fool*, Trump concludes, because he
fails to stand up or speak out for himself. He is a *sucker*. This becomes a cardinal
lesson in narcissism, which Trump will remember for the rest of his life: Never
cede attention. Never let the spotlight shine anywhere but on the self. "If you let
people treat you how they want, you'll be made a fool. I realized then and there
something I would never forget: I don't want to be made anybody's sucker."

Many of Trump's emerging-adult peers in the 1960s, like emerging adults
today, scan their environments to find examples of lives worth living, people
worth emulating, and futures worth envisioning, as they address the big identity
questions: Who am I? Who will I become? What kind of life is worth living? The
young Donald Trump does not scan his environment, except to find examples
of losers and weaklings, like poor Othmar Amman. He already knows who he
is, who he will become, and what kind of life is worth living. He is Fred Trump's
son, born to wealth and greatness. Like his father, he will immerse himself in the
world of real estate. He will become a master builder. He will become greater and
richer and more famous than his admired father. There are no other options in

his mind. He never questions the fundamentals. He never seriously considers an alternative life, one outside the orbit of his father's influence.

The psychologist Erik Erikson attained his greatest fame during the 1960s, which roughly correspond to Donald Trump's emerging adulthood years. Erikson documented the different paths that emerging adults follow in their quest to create identity. A common path tracks the move from what Erikson called *psychosocial moratorium* to *identity achievement.* During a period of moratorium, the young person explores various occupational and ideological options in the world. He or she questions beliefs and values that were established in childhood and often rebels against what is perceived to be the status quo. In moratorium, the young person questions the motivational agenda developed in childhood and experiments with different life styles and conceptions of the self, trying out different identity solutions to see which ones fit. Moratorium eventually gives way to identity achievement when the emerging adult commits himself or herself to a new motivational agenda, a new plan for life that builds, in some way, on the systems of goals, values, beliefs, and perspectives developed in the childhood years. In the process, the emerging adult begins to articulate a story to explain how the self of the past will lead to a new self for the future. It is a story about how I have become the person I am becoming—who I was, who I am now, and who I will be in the future.

Donald Trump takes a different route. He follows the path of what Erikson called *identity foreclosure.* In foreclosure, the young person never breaks from the past. The motivational agenda of childhood remains intact, unsullied and unquestioned. Rather than opening Donald Trump up to new ways of thinking about himself and the world, his college years merely provide him with a credential. He will forever show pride in graduating from the University of Pennsylvania Wharton School of Finance and Commerce. He will falsely claim that he graduated first in his class. Going forward, he will link his self-esteem to the progress he makes in fulfilling a motivational agenda inherited directly from his father, as if it were a set of genes. The college experience irrevocably changes many young people, but it seems to have virtually no effect on Donald Trump. Psychologically speaking, he comes out looking pretty much the same as he looked going in.

Even in identity foreclosure, most emerging adults begin to construct a story about how their childhood years prepared them to take on the challenges that may lie ahead. Even if they never seriously question the past, they seem to draw upon it for lessons and insights. In making their lives into stories, they begin to develop a narrative identity. But the young Donald Trump does not seem to do this—or, at most, he seems to develop a thematically impoverished story to live by, barely a story at all: *I was my father's son: I am my father's son; I will continue to be my father's son, but I will be greater than my father.*

Trump's motivational agenda for the future will expand as he moves through adulthood, but it will tie back to no more than a vanishingly tiny number of life-story scenes to be remembered from the past, and those mainly about either being a winner or not being a loser. For example, he remembers clearly winning that game at NYMA and seeing his name in the newspapers. He remembers the scene featuring the pathetic 85-year-old designer of the Verrazano-Narrows Bridge. But not too much else gets incorporated into an ongoing, meaning-conferring self-narrative. Perhaps the personal past—replete with those specific autobiographical memories of childhood and adolescence around which a coherent narrative identity is usually fashioned—is not so important for a young man, not something that needs to be pondered and processed very much, when, psychologically speaking, that very strange young man never truly grows out of it, never truly leaves the past behind.

You don't need to create a meaningful story about your past if you remain locked within the past. You don't need to create a retrospective account of childhood if you never, psychologically speaking, graduate from childhood. If life stories are fundamentally about change and if, in a deep psychological sense, you have never really changed, then there is no story to tell about who you were, are, and will become. There is no need to construct a narrative identity for your life because who you are today and who you will be tomorrow are the same as who you were yesterday. Nothing changes, so there is no story to tell. Instead, you stay close to the pool, forever gazing on the unchanging, forever-great, and beloved self. Narcissus had no story for his life once he gazed upon his reflection. From that point on, he was fixed in time. Mr. Hyde had no story for his life either, once he emerged into consciousness. He simply was—the eternal id, blindly seeking the gratification of the moment, moment by moment. The episodic man, who is really a ferocious and self-magnifying *man-child*, striving to win and, then, to win again.

Through midlife

From his early 30s through his mid-60s, Donald Trump enjoys many triumphs in his professional and personal life, and he endures many setbacks, too. By age 30, he is widely recognized in New York City as an ambitious real-estate developer and an attractive man about town. By age 40, he has built Trump Tower, and he is about to publish *The Art of the Deal*, which will make him a household name in the United States. He lives in the most luxurious homes with a beautiful wife and business partner—Ivana Trump—and their three children. By age 50, however, Donald Trump is on the verge of abject failure: Much of his fortune is in jeopardy; his casinos are failing; he has divorced Ivana and temporarily alienated at least one of his children (Donald, Jr. does not speak to his father for a year following the split); and he is involved in an on-again off-again relationship with Marla Maples, which will result in a very unsatisfying and short-lived marriage. By age 60, he has rebounded, expanding his branding empire worldwide, attaining even greater fame through his reality television show, *The Apprentice*, and basically settling down, to the extent Trump can settle down, with Melania, who will soon become his third (and probably most compatible) wife.

Throughout it all, from peak to valley to peak, Donald Trump's self-esteem soars. This is not to say that Trump is immune to suffering. He admits unhappiness and angst when things do not go his way. During one of his worst arguments with Ivana, for example, he is reported to have screamed: "Why don't you just shoot me!" His mood may fluctuate violently, from euphoria to rage within minutes, but his conscious assessment of himself never seems to waver. Self-esteem is closely tied to a person's motivational agenda, to a person's strongest values and goals. Trump's strongest value and goal come down to one thing: *Me*. The agenda is thoroughly narcissistic. He values *me* above all else; he lives to glorify *me*. From 1976 to 2011, from age 30 to age 65, he continues to pursue the agenda, dogged and flamboyant. How well does he do? From the outside, it would seem that his record is mixed: Sometimes he is up, and sometimes he is down. But that is not how he sees it. Donald Trump believes that he has never failed. He believes he is the greatest. He is the best. He is a winner. He has always been a winner. He believes he will always be a winner.

And yet the nature of winning changes. Narcissism develops, morphs over time. In his 30s, Trump's method for glorifying the self is to build things and acquire things that redound positively upon the self. His buildings and his possessions become reflections and extensions of *me*. He *is* Trump Tower. He *is* the yacht, the airplanes, the sports team, the casinos, the books, and the money. He loves these things as if they are the self, because they *are* the self. Later, Trump's narcissism expands to encompass something more abstract—the brand, the aura, the persona of Trumpness. In the early 1990s, Louise Sunshine observed that the transition had already begun: "When I first went to work with him in 1974, Donald was very hands-on, in total control, and on top of everything, leaving no stone unturned." "But as his figure began to loom larger and larger in the press, he became distracted by the idea of becoming a celebrity, a presidential candidate, and a movie star." Sunshine lamented the transformation, which in the early 1990s seemed ridiculous in her mind. Donald Trump as a media star?! Donald Trump as *the president*?! What Sunshine mischaracterized as a "distraction" represented instead a major midlife promotion in narcissism's career.

Even as it changes its focus in midlife, Trump's is a decidedly primitive form of narcissism, very much akin to the original experience portrayed in the ancient

Greek myth. Like the beautiful young boy, Trump must *see* himself in the re-flected pool—literally, in the visual sense, and somewhat less literally, but still vividly, in the mind's eye. One of his ways of achieving the visualization of *me* is to create a recurrent tableau. A tableau is an idealized setting or scene that visually depicts the most valued features of the motivational agenda. As I try to visualize what Trump visualizes, I come back again and again to three successive tableaus.

The first is a dashing Donald Trump, in his late 20s, 30s, or 40s, strolling through Manhattan with a beautiful woman on each arm. The tableau celebrates glamour, wealth, and sexiness. The second is a more serious scene—Donald Trump, in his 50s or 60s, sitting in the boardroom on an episode of *The Apprentice*. He exudes power and decisiveness, and there is a flash of wit. He gives sage advice to the contestants, and he famously utters, "You're fired!" The third tableau is the political rally. Trump is on stage in front of an appreciative crowd of thousands. He is the candidate now, or the president, in his early 70s. He is riffing on the events of the week, trashing his rivals, accusing the press of being "the enemy of the American people," as the crowd chants "Lock her up" (in reference to Hillary Clinton) or "CNN sucks" (in reference to the media). The faces in the crowd are almost beatific. They feel that he understands them. Trump is inspiring—and inspired. He feels as if he is God.

In the photo gallery of self-portraits that crowd out nearly everything else in Donald Trump's mind, the three perfect tableaus, representing three stages in the career of Trumpian narcissism, stand out as favorites. But there are surely many more, each a visual display without the accompanying text that might connect them into a life narrative. In those moments when he cannot see his image on television, or inspect the letters T-R-U-M-P as they may appear on the façade of a building or on the branding insignia of a Trump-inspired product, when he is not holding forth in front of a rapturous crowd in a small-town bas-ketball arena or reading a flattering puff piece written by a right-wing blogger, Trump can still gaze into the pool inside his head and, like Narcissus, bask in the beautiful reflection of the envisioned tableaus. He is never alone, for he never leaves *me*.

As President

At the end of President Trump's first year in office, a team of reporters aimed to depict a typical day-in-the-life for the 45th president, basing their account on interviews with White House aides.

After just 5 to 6 hours of sleep, the president wakes up around 5:30 AM and im-mediately turns on the television in the White House master bedroom. Toggling back and forth between CNN and MSNBC for news, and switching over to his favorite show, *Fox & Friends*, for comfort and affirmation, President Trump gets oriented for the day. The news shows fire him up for the day's battles. Sometimes energized, sometimes infuriated, he grabs his mobile phone and begins to tweet about the topics that obsess him, like these:

- *Special Counsel Robert Mueller*—his investigation (which the president repeatedly labeled a "witch hunt") into a possible collaboration between Russia and the Trump campaign in the 2016 presidential election, as well as possible obstruction of justice on the part of the president (Mueller ended his investigation in the spring of 2019 and submitted a report, but issues remained unresolved and Trump continued to obsess over the investigation and its aftermath in the third year of his presidency);
- *Attorney General Jeff Sessions*—his recusal from the investigation into Russian collusion, which set in motion a process leading to the appointment of Robert Mueller and left the president feeling betrayed (Trump fired Sessions after the November 2018 midterm elections);
- *Hillary Clinton*—her defeat at the hands of Donald Trump in the 2016 election, although tarnished by her victory in the popular vote and her very presence as a forever enemy to Mr. Trump and somebody who, Trump believes, should be "locked up" because she engaged in inappropriate email activity and other serious crimes;
- *Other terrible Democrats*—that is, nearly all Democrats, but especially California Congresswoman Nancy Pelosi, New York Senator Chuck Shumer, Massachusetts Senator Elizabeth Warren, California Congresswoman Maxine Waters, Connecticut Senator Richard Blumenthal, Montana Senator Jon Tester, and Chicago Mayor Rahm Emanuel;
- *Republicans who disagree with him about something, anything*—depending on the day or the topic, but especially Senate Majority Leader Mitch McConnell, former Speaker of the House Paul Ryan, and, before he died, Arizona Senator John McCain;
- *The "fake news" media*—by which the president means the mainstream press, including the *New York Times*, the *Washington Post*, most major daily newspapers, CNN, and network news, except for Fox News.

Despite the president's professed hatred for the media, he remains fixated on his press coverage for much of his day. The president's day is filled with meetings and appearances of various sorts, but he still regularly squeezes in four hours during the day, if not more, to watch television, sometimes with the volume muted, repeatedly checking his image on the screen and monitoring what is said about him. A large television screen is visible in the dining room. "No one touches the remote control except Mr. Trump and the technical support staff," the team of reporters wrote. "During meetings, the 60-inch screen mounted in the dining room may be muted, but Mr. Trump keeps an eye on scrolling headlines. What he misses, he checks out later on what he calls his 'Super TiVo,' a state-of-the-art system that records cable news." Twice a day, President Trump receives a folder filled with flattering news clips, admiring tweets, transcripts from glowing television interviews, and photos of him, as president, looking powerful.

The reporters wrote: "To an extent that would stun outsiders, Mr. Trump, the most talked-about human on the planet, is still delighted when he sees his name in the headlines. And he is on a perpetual quest to see it there. One former top adviser said Mr. Trump grew uncomfortable after two or three days of peace and could not handle watching the news without seeing himself in it."

The comment from the former top advisor is remarkable and disquieting. And yet it resonates with a general expectation that many Americans now have regarding the president and the news. Two or three relatively quiet days may go by, with the predictable reports of world crises, wars, disasters, political intrigue, human interest stories—a coup here, a display of heroism there. The world turns and people live their lives, almost as if there were no Donald Trump. But not for long. Donald Trump cannot keep himself on the periphery of our attention for long. And not only because he is the president of the United States, which means that nearly everything he does is at least mildly newsworthy. It is much more than that. He must say something outrageous, break precedent in some dramatic way, insert himself into a situation that no other president would ever touch just, it seems, to get back into the headlines—just, it seems, so he can see again his reflection in the pool.

It is as if Donald Trump is *addicted to himself.* He wakes up every morning in need of a fix. He cannot go long without an injection or infusion of the *me.* He cannot get enough of himself. He never grows tired of seeing his face in the pool. Well, that is just human nature, you may say. We all love to see ourselves. We are all narcissists at heart. To a certain extent, you may be right. But Donald Trump is stranger. Try to imagine what it is like to be him. You wake up every day to see yourself reflected back at you, in so many different ways. Over and over and over. Your face is everywhere. Your name is on everybody's lips. This might feel good for a while, a few days, a week, a month, maybe a year or two. But it goes on for decades, for your entire adult life. It never ends. You never get away from yourself.

For the vast majority of humanity, I would submit, the full-bore narcissistic experience, Trump style, would eventually get old. We would tire of it. We would habituate. We would get bored with ourselves. Unwavering self-focus becomes oppressive over the long haul. Nobody is beautiful enough or powerful enough or interesting enough to warrant eternal, undivided self-attention. Human beings evolved to be social animals, facing outward as well as inward. We are not designed to gaze into the pool all day, every day, for eternity. Narcissus tried to do it, and he melted away.

But Trump succeeds where Narcissus ultimately failed. He stays focused on *me*. How does he do it? Psychologically speaking, how does Trump manage to achieve what even the young hero of the ancient Greek myth could not achieve?

There are at least two reasons, I believe, both of which reflect themes I have underscored throughout this book. First, Donald Trump is the episodic man, bereft of a life narrative that might provide long-term meaning and purpose. Second, Donald Trump loves himself the way human beings love objects, rather than the way human beings love persons. In his mind, he is not quite a person— more than a person, but less than, too.

Regarding the first reason, fashioning a coherent life story would seem to be the easiest thing in the world for a narcissistic person to accomplish. The challenge of narrative identity, as it first arises in the emerging adulthood years, is to create an integrative narrative out of the scattered episodes in one's life. You look back on the past and you try to order events into a meaningful sequence to explain how you have become the person you are today. You look forward to the future and try to imagine events that are yet to occur. You connect the reconstructed past to the imagined future to make a story out of your life. The story situates your motivational agenda within a meaningful narrative context. It explains how your goals and values came to be; it gives them justification and meaning. People with motivational agendas centered on narcissism should, in principle, find it natural and satisfying to accommodate their lives to a broad narrative arc. They should love to tell stories about the self! And most narcissists *do* have a narrative identity.

But Donald Trump does not, or at best, his narrative identity is vague and nondescript. Rather than see his life as an ongoing story, Donald Trump lives in the emotional moment, from one moment to the next. He refuses to be retrospective, prospective, or introspective. He never looks back; he never looks very far forward; and he never looks inside. One after another, each life episode involves a battle of some kind, a struggle to triumph over an adversary because, as he sees it, the world is a dangerous place, filled with vicious people. Without the luxury of a life narrative, each episode arises as a new event, disconnected from all others. Over the course of a day, a week, and indeed much of his life, Donald Trump has awakened anew to each new event, as if there were no distant past and will be no long-term future. Therefore, the beautiful self-image, the cherished name, the gorgeous and inspiring tableau—they never grow old. They are refreshed and reinvigorated with each new episode in life, each new battle to win, to win for and as the beloved self.

Regarding the second reason, the object of his overmastering love is the self, as is always the case with narcissism. Trump loves other things, too, of course. He has loved numerous women in his life. He loves his children. He loves Trump Tower and his golf courses. As projections of self, he loves his face and his name. He loves the tableaus in his head. But with the possible exception of his children, Trump loves all of these objects *as objects*, as things. They are beautiful in his eyes, or they are useful to him in some way. *His love of self has the same quality.* Trump characterizes himself as a superhero, as something that is larger than life, more than human, qualitatively different from the everyday persons that you and I are. He is an aura. He is a brand. He is a beautiful and beloved *thing*, to be loved and desired as something separate from the self, as a thing outside the self even though it is the self.

In the normal case, people love people in ways that are different from how they love things. At some level, we know that people hold a certain primacy and sovereignty in the world, whereas things are ultimately dispensable and replaceable. People are ends; things are means to an end. Importantly, people can be loved, and ideally should be loved, categorically—that is, in an unconditional manner. But love for things is always contingent, no matter how wonderful or beautiful the thing is.

Should you find that you are a thing rather than a fully formed person, you can never rest secure. There is always a chance that you will be replaced, that a better thing will come along, something more beautiful, more powerful, or more useful than you. Because unconditional love cannot be conferred upon you as a thing, given that you are not fully a person, you must always rely on your positive qualities, which can never grow old or melt away. You must always win.

Let us extend the logic further. If your very self, the sense of *me* that you love more than anything else in the world, is truly a *thing* in your mind, rather than a fully formed person, then there will always be a tentativeness and a fragility in your self-love. You can continue to love yourself for only as long as your self lives up to its billing as the most beautiful, powerful, or useful thing in the world. *It* must always win. And you can never afford to grow tired of it. You must affirm the self anew, from one episode to the next, as *the next great thing*, and the next, and the next.

***

In late November 2018, President Trump celebrated Thanksgiving weekend with his family at Mar-a-Lago. When asked what he was most thankful for, he said this: "For having a great family and for having made a tremendous difference in this country. I've made a tremendous difference in the country. The country is so much stronger now than it was when I took office that you wouldn't believe it." On the one day of the year when most Americans set aside their self-promotional agendas to enjoy turkey, watch football, and give thanks for their blessings, President Trump refused to follow the normal human script.

On behalf of Donald J. Trump and the American people, the president gave thanks for *himself*.

Goldwater

(A Clinical Interlude)

"He's just a *psychopath*, Dan."

The remark came from a good colleague of mine whom I met at a conference in the early summer of 2016. The colleague told me he liked an article I had just written for *The Atlantic* magazine, entitled "The Mind of Donald Trump." He appreciated my effort to get inside Trump's head and to elaborate on a number of different features of Trump's personality and psychological make-up. But he also wondered, out loud and only half joking, why I had gone to so much trouble. Just call him a psychopath, he suggested. And be done with it.

My colleague's remark anticipated a number of other responses I have received since then, either in reference to the 2016 magazine article or to the idea that I am writing a book on President Trump.

"What's your diagnosis going to be?" "He's crazy, right?" "Doesn't he have some kind of narcissistic personality disorder?" "I think he's psychotic." "Are you going to talk about his dementia?"

The words "psychopath," "diagnosis," "crazy," "disorder," "psychotic," and "dementia" come from the language of *medicine*. Whether they are loose and colloquial (e.g., crazy) or diagnostically precise (e.g., narcissistic personality disorder [NPD]), terms like these refer to the realm of mental illness and mental health. We visit mental health professionals—psychiatrists, clinical psychologists, counselors, clinical social workers, and therapists of various other kinds—when we perceive that there is something wrong with us, something disordered that requires treatment. Regardless of which professional we see, we tend to relate to them as if they were "doctors," even if they are not. In doing so, we experience ourselves as patients who are a under a doctor's care. In fact, only psychiatrists are medical doctors. And although many clinical psychologists have doctoral degrees (PhD), it is professionals without doctoral degrees who provide the lion's share of psychotherapy in the United States.

When we visit a medical professional, or someone to whom we relate in the same way, we expect a diagnosis first, followed by treatment. The professional must first determine what the disorder or malady is before he or she can provide a therapy or intervention designed to resolve the disorder and alleviate the

The Strange Case of Donald J. Trump. Dan P. McAdams, Oxford University Press (2020). © Oxford University Press.
DOI: 10.1093/oso/9780197507445.001.0001

suffering that accompanies the disorder. A patient may suffer from hypertension (diagnosis); the treatment of choice may be a prescription drug that lowers blood pressure. A patient may be diagnosed with breast cancer; the treatment may involve radiation, chemotherapy, or some other therapy regimen. In general, therapies—whether they are applied to the body or the mind—are designed to cure, alleviate, reduce the effects of, or, at least, manage the illness. For mental illness, there are talking therapies of many kinds, there are drug therapies, and there are therapies that combine both.

In the realm of mental health, professionals make diagnoses with reference to the *Diagnostic and Statistical Manual of Mental Disorders* (DSM) published by the American Psychiatric Association (APA). The most recent edition of this mammoth manual (DSM-5) contains hundreds of diagnostic categories. Among the most severe conditions are various manifestations of schizophrenia and manic-depressive (bipolar) illness. My colleague's term "psychopath" is a common expression that corresponds closely to the DSM's *antisocial personality disorder*. The disorder is defined by a pervasive and long-term disregard for morals, social norms, and the rights and feelings of others. The cardinal "symptoms" of the disorder are callousness, lack of emotional connection to other people, immorality, aggression, recklessness, impulsivity, and general social deviance. It is often, although not always, accompanied by criminality and substance abuse.

When clinical psychologists and other mental health experts talk about clinical labels they might apply to President Trump, they are typically more likely to reference the diagnostic category of NPD. According to traditional criteria from the DSM, NPD involves "a pervasive pattern of grandiosity (in fantasy or behavior), need for admiration, and lack of empathy." NPD is indicated if at least *five* of the following nine indices are clearly manifest:

1. An exaggerated sense of self-importance (e.g., exaggerates achievements and talents, expects to be recognized as superior without commensurate achievements);
2. Preoccupation with fantasies of unlimited success, power, brilliance, beauty, or ideal love;
3. Believes he is "special" and can only be understood by, or should associate with, other special or high-status people (or institutions);
4. Requires excessive admiration;
5. Has a sense of entitlement;
6. Selfishly takes advantage of others to achieve his own ends;
7. Lacks empathy;
8. Is often envious of others or believes others to be envious of him; and
9. Shows arrogant, haughty, patronizing, or contemptuous behaviors or attitudes.

NPD is a rare condition in the mental illness realm. Yet, looking over the nine criteria, some readers may conclude that if Donald Trump does not have NPD, then nobody does. Others might demur. In her book, *Mad Politics*, the psychologist and talk show host Gina Loudon argued that Trump suffers from no mental illness whatsoever but instead is the paragon of mental health. If he is "crazy" at all, Loudon writes, he is crazy like a fox—that is, "crazy" in a good way.

In the case of Donald Trump, however, the toughest call to make on NPD may involve the cardinal presupposition that lies behind the nine specific criteria. A person "suffering" from NPD must first show actual signs that he or she is *suffering*! There must be distress and impairment. The disorder must be interfering with his or her overall adaptation to life, messing his or her life up in a way that the individual afflicted with the disorder finds aversive. If Mr. Trump feels great about his narcissism, if he is moving through life without debilitating distress and achieving his life goals in a successful manner (he did achieve the presidency, after all), then can we really say that he is suffering from any psychiatric disorder at all? It is a tough question, and mental health experts differ in their responses to it.

In the chapter immediately preceding this one ("Me"), I argued that Trump has long cultivated a narcissistic motivational agenda. Beneath the traits of high extraversion and low agreeableness resides an elaborate amalgam of goals, motives, values, and beliefs all dedicated to promoting the glorious self. Trump loves himself as the ancient Greek boy Narcissus loved his beautiful image reflected back at him in the pool. Trump's excessive self-love, strangely objectified and dependent on his always being the winner, energizes and directs his daily behavior in the absence of a self-defining, long-term narrative identity. He is the narcissist without a story, the episodic narcissist whose self-love must be repeatedly renewed and affirmed in each successive episode, as he moves from one discrete battle to the next in a life of war.

But does that all mean that Donald Trump is a textbook case of NPD? Why don't I just identify a clinical label and be done with it? Why not just play the doctor role and give him a medical diagnosis? Although I do have a doctoral degree in Psychology and Social Relations, with a specialization in personality and developmental psychology, I am not trained as a clinician. I am not licensed to do psychotherapy. I do not diagnose patients.

But what if I did? What if I were a trained clinical psychologist who diagnoses people according to the DSM every day? Would it be professionally appropriate for me, as a practicing clinical psychologist, to diagnose Trump with NPD? Would it be ethical? Don't forget: In this scenario, he is not my patient, and I have never done a diagnostic interview with him. Let us imagine, nonetheless, that I did offer such a diagnosis. What would be the utility of that? What would the diagnostic label tell us that we did not know before? Would American voters be better informed if they received diagnostic information regarding political candidates' mental health? What would the implications be for American political life if psychologists were routinely called upon to diagnose elected public officials? Which brings us to the so-called Goldwater Rule.

***

The 1964 U.S. presidential election pitted Barry Goldwater, the Republican senator from Arizona, against the Democratic incumbent Lyndon Johnson. Assuming the presidency after the assassination of John F. Kennedy, Johnson rallied liberals and political moderates around an agenda of expansive social programs, civil rights, and an activist foreign policy. By contrast, the Republican Party took a sharp turn to the right at its 1964 convention in San Francisco, nominating the arch conservative Barry Goldwater. A libertarian who pushed for massive tax cuts and a balanced budget, Goldwater had voted against the U.S. Senate's Civil Rights Act. He was widely perceived to be a hawk on defense. In one of the most famous political ads ever made (the "Daisy Ad," televised on September 7, 1964), a lovely 3-year-old girl wearing a simple dress and standing in a bucolic meadow plucks the petals off of a daisy as a nuclear bomb is about to explode overhead. The ad ends with the solemn instruction to vote for Lyndon Johnson on November 3 because "the stakes are too high for you to stay home." Reflecting the sentiment of the day and of the ad, many mainstream politicians and journalists believed that Goldwater was dangerous and ideologically too extreme for the presidency. In sharp response to his many detractors, Goldwater famously proclaimed, "Extremism in the defense of liberty is no vice."

A significant number of American psychiatrists also believed that Goldwater was too extreme. In the months leading up to the election, *Fact* magazine published a survey of psychiatrists, who were asked to pass expert judgment on Barry Goldwater's mental health. The survey was sent to 12,356 psychiatrists. From that total, 2,417 of them (approximately 19% of them) responded. From the respondents, 1,189 deemed Goldwater to be mentally "unfit" for office, while 657 deemed him to be mentally fit. The other 571 reported that they did not have enough information to render a definitive assessment. The magazine, under the direction of its avowedly liberal editor, Ralph Ginzburg, published the results of the survey under the cover headline: "Fact: 1,189 Psychiatrists Say Goldwater Is Psychologically Unfit to Be President."

In addition to the quantitative results, the article reported verbatim commentary from some of the psychiatrists, depicting Goldwater as "emotionally unstable," "immature," "amoral and immoral," and a "dangerous lunatic." One psychiatrist wrote that a "megalomaniacal, grandiose omnipotence appears to pervade Mr. Goldwater's personality, giving further evidence of his denial and lack of recognition of his own feelings of insecurity and ineffectiveness." A number of respondents offered formal diagnoses, such as "schizophrenia," "paranoia," "obsessive-compulsive disorder," and "narcissistic character disorder" (now, NPD). One of the most prominent psychiatrists of the day, Dr. Jerome Frank, wrote in the survey that the "ill-considered, impulsive quality of many of Goldwater's public utterances is, in my mind, sufficient to disqualify him from the presidency."

Johnson won in a landslide. Barry Goldwater's resounding defeat probably had little, if anything, to do with the article in *Fact*, an obscure magazine that went out of business just a few years later. But Goldwater was incensed by the way the magazine portrayed him, so he sued Ralph Ginzburg and *Fact* for libel. He alleged that the magazine had published "false, scandalous, and defamatory statements" about him. On the witness stand, Goldwater insisted that his mental health was impeccable. The court effectively ruled in the senator's favor, awarding him just $1 in compensatory damages but $75,000 in punitive damages. The ruling on damages suggested that while Goldwater probably incurred relatively little by way of pain and suffering (public figures are often criticized, and the article surely did not cost him the election), the magazine had nonetheless engaged in irresponsible behavior. Upon appeal, the Supreme Court upheld the original ruling, 7–2. Justices Hugo Black and William O. Douglas, however, dissented. Explaining the minority position, Black wrote that the "public has an unqualified right to have the character and fitness of anyone who aspires to the Presidency held up for the closest scrutiny."

The psychiatric community was shamed by the *Fact* affair. Many observers concluded that the left-leaning psychiatrists had disguised their political animus in medical garb, unfairly stigmatizing a public figure whom none of them had ever treated as a patient. In addition, the psychiatric establishment came under pressure from the larger American Medical Association, whose members had tended to support Goldwater over Johnson in the 1964 election. The APA issued several statements warning members against making diagnostic pronouncements regarding politicians and other public figures. Finally, in 1973, the APA enshrined Rule 7.3 into its first-ever formal code of ethics. Known since then as the Goldwater Rule, the APA's statement prohibited psychiatrists from offering a "professional opinion" regarding the mental health and fitness of a public figure unless the psychiatrist "has conducted an examination and has been granted proper authorization for such a statement." Although the exact meaning of the Goldwater Rule has been debated ever since, the notion of "professional opinion" has typically been interpreted to mean *psychiatric diagnosis*—that is, offering a professional judgment regarding the extent to which a public figure may be afflicted with a recognized form of mental illness.

For the 52 years that spanned the presidential administrations from Lyndon Johnson to Barack Obama, psychiatrists mainly abided by the Goldwater Rule, even if there were occasional grumblings. Clinical psychologists followed suit, even though their corresponding professional organization (the American Psychological Association) does not have a specific analogue to the Goldwater rule. Of course, professionals and laypersons alike have sometimes questioned the mental fitness of presidents, without offering formal pronouncements. President Nixon's staff was concerned about his heavy drinking in the last months of his presidency and his bouts of paranoia. Many observers feared that President Reagan may have suffered from early stages of dementia in his second term. Moreover, biographers and historians have sometimes offered diagnoses of past presidents, long dead. In *Lincoln's Melancholy*, for example, the journalist Joshua Shenk argued that Abraham Lincoln suffered from serious depressive illness during his presidency but that he managed to draw creatively upon his chronic sadness to expand his empathy and broaden his vision for the United States. Shenk's provocative thesis held that a mental disorder may become an asset for a leader, under certain conditions and in the presence of certain character strengths.

Then, along came Donald Trump. Within months of Trump's declaring his candidacy for president in 2015, mental health professionals began to express concern about his suitability, and some psychiatrists began to question anew the Goldwater Rule. Rival politicians, journalists, and laypeople began to throw around all kinds of diagnostic terms in reference to Trump, but the Goldwater Rule prohibited those who arguably had the greatest professional expertise in mental health from joining the conversation. In the midst of it all, the leadership of the APA doubled down. In 2016, the president of the APA wrote that "the unique atmosphere of this year's election cycle may lead some to want to psychoanalyze the candidates, but to do so would not only be unethical, it would be irresponsible."

Still, some psychiatrists and clinical psychologists rebelled, arguing that they had a higher duty to warn the public of a clear and present danger. In January 2017, clinical psychologist John Gartner, a former part-time assistant professor of psychiatry at Johns Hopkins University, told *U. S. News and World Report* that Trump suffers from "malignant narcissism" (not technically a DSM category, but presumably a combination of NPD and strong antisocial tendencies) and that he is "dangerously mentally ill and temperamentally incapable of being president." Gartner launched an online petition entitled "President Trump is Mentally Ill and Must Be Removed." Similar initiatives appeared in other psychiatric and psychological venues. For example, Bandy Lee, a professor of psychiatry at Yale Medical School, sent letters to Congress warning that Trump's "severe emotional impairments" pose "a grave threat to international security." In August 2017,

Representative Zoe Lofgren, a Democrat from California, introduced a House resolution mandating a psychiatric examination for President Trump. (The bill went nowhere.) Lofgren pointed to "an alarming pattern of behavior and speech causing concern that a mental disorder may have rendered him unfit and unable to fulfill his Constitutional duties." She asked, "Is the President mentally and emotionally stable?"

While some have questioned the Goldwater Rule from the standpoint of civic and moral urgency, others have argued that the rule should be abolished on scientific grounds, no matter who the president is. In an influential paper published in 2018, Scott O. Lilienfeld, Joshua D. Miller, and Donald R. Lynam (all clinical psychologists) argued that the Goldwater Rule is based on out-of-date and dubious scientific assumptions. The bedrock assumption of the rule is that psychiatrists obtain unique and invaluable information regarding psychopathology from their personal examination of a patient. Whereas in other realms of medicine the examination might involve the doctor's doing an X-ray or evaluating a blood test, in psychiatry the examination is mainly an in-person *clinical interview*. The patient tells the psychiatrist about his or her symptoms, and then the conversation may go in many different directions, as the two discuss a range of issues bearing on the patient's emotional life, family, work, interpersonal relationships, and so on. The bottom line of the Goldwater Rule is this: If you don't do the interview, you can't do the diagnosis.

Lilienfeld and his colleagues reviewed the extensive research literature that has accumulated since the 1970s exposing the problems and limitations of clinical interviews. They contended that other methods of data collection, including repeated observations of people in public and the assessment of social reputations, are at least as valid as, and often much more valid than, interviews for making inferences regarding mental health. Mental health experts who may wish to diagnose candidates from afar have at their disposal a wealth of valuable information in the public domain. They don't need to interview President Trump, or Hillary Clinton, or other highly visible public figures—because high-quality information already exists in many cases, from which valid inferences can be made, and because interviews themselves are deeply flawed anyway.

Lilienfeld and his colleagues recommended that the Goldwater Rule be abandoned when it comes to evaluating and diagnosing public officials holding positions of substantial power over others, such as high-profile politicians. Such individuals potentially wield immense power, the ramifications of which bear on the public welfare and national security. The authors suggested that professionals with significant expertise in mental health should be free to exercise a "duty to inform" the citizenry regarding those who run for high public office. They should exercise the duty with caution and humility, and they should offer their diagnoses only when they have amassed substantial supportive evidence and made sound medical or scientific inferences.

In an interesting twist, however, Lilienfeld and colleagues argued that mental health experts should stop short of answering the question first posed by *Fact* magazine in 1964: Is the person mentally *fit* for office? "Rarely if ever are mental illnesses absolute disqualifications for serving in office," they wrote, and "many politicians with clear-cut mental illnesses have surely served capably in positions of high authority." In other words, the public should be informed about the presence of mental illness, but mental health experts should not conclude that the presence is grounds for disqualifying a person from public office. Psychiatrists and psychologists have important expertise to share with the American people. They should be empowered to offer well-documented mental health evaluations of men and women who occupy positions of high power in American society, as well as those seeking such powerful positions, as long as they do so while upholding the highest standards of medicine and science and as long as they refrain from offering an up-or-down verdict on fitness.

Like most mental health professionals who have written about the Goldwater Rule, Lilienfeld and his colleagues tend to blur a distinction in psychological discourse that I believe should be sharpened. It is the distinction between the language of medicine (which dominates psychiatry and clinical psychology) and the language of human personality (which guides my own interpretation of Donald Trump's life).

As we have seen in the controversy over the Goldwater Rule, the language of medicine is the language of *sickness* and *health*. Within this framework, people suffer from mental *symptoms*, *illnesses*, and *disorders*. To alleviate their suffering, they go to *therapists*, who play the role of *doctors*. *Patients* hope to experience a *cure* for their illness. Therapists consult the DSM to arrive at *diagnoses*, for which suitable *treatments* are set forth. Part of a treatment protocol may involve exploring the *etiology* of the illness—what caused it in the first place, what *risk factors* were involved. The therapist may offer a *prognosis*, or prediction regarding the anticipated course of the illness. When all goes well, the patient may be restored to full *mental health*.

When applied to human behavior, the language of medicine shrouds itself in a mystique and authority that virtually no other realm of human enterprise can match in the 21st century. While many Americans may doubt the authority of religion, science, technology, and government, medical doctors are viewed to have an almost unimpeachable expertise. Many Americans may disagree with scientists when they argue that global warming is a threat or that human beings evolved from apes, but very few of them will disagree with their doctor when told they have cancer, especially if a second opinion confirms the diagnosis. The medical diagnosis of a discrete mental illness may carry the same kind of weight in the public's mind. In addition, mental illness still carries a considerable stigma in the minds of many Americans, unlike cancer or measles. There is still something embarrassing about it for many people. As such, the diagnosis of a mental illness, made by a professional under what the public views to be the imprimatur of medicine, conveys the message that the patient not only has a discrete "sickness," but a shameful sickness.

If the Goldwater Rule were to be abolished, or if mental health professionals decided en masse to disregard the guidelines it sets forth, the attribution of psychiatric diagnoses might well become a new weapon of political campaigning. Accordingly, the presidential elections of 2020 and 2024 might feature dueling teams of mental health experts. Drawing upon the expertise of medicine, candidates might now recruit their own "doctors" to diagnose the opposition. Like negative attack ads, the temptation to engage in this kind of escalation in the political arms race might be too strong to resist. In arguing for the abandonment of the Goldwater Rule, Lilienfeld and colleagues are betting that the noblest intentions of mental health professionals will prevail. Are they being naïve?

Even if psychiatrists and psychologists were to operate with restraint and integrity in diagnosing public officials, the attribution of psychopathology is problematic in other ways. Diagnosis leads to either/or thinking. The candidate either *has* the mental illness or does not. Donald Trump either suffers from NPD, or he does not. These kinds of attributions are appropriate in many realms of medicine. A patient needs to know if he has cancer or does not, is infected with HIV or is not. A woman is either pregnant (a medical condition of sorts, although not an illness), or she is not. But psychological characteristics, as they appear in flesh-and-blood human lives, are rarely either/or. Even the most severe forms of psychopathology, such as schizophrenia and autism, seem to manifest themselves on a continuum, or spectrum. When it comes to NPD, for example, the boundaries between having the disorder and not having the disorder are arbitrary. The DSM simply dictates that if a person has five or more of the nine criteria listed, then he or she "has" NPD, as if there were some magical Rubicon that a person crosses when he or she gets to the fifth criterion.

Finally, the attribution of medical diagnoses threatens to strip away personal responsibility for human behavior. In this regard, I am reminded of Tina Redsie, a woman who once dated Steve Jobs. When it comes to having a narcissistic motivational agenda, Jobs was a worthy match for President Trump. Redsie felt mistreated by Jobs for many years, and she was continuously amazed, and dismayed, by his arrogance. When Tina Redsie later read the DSM description of NPD, she was thunderstruck by how well it captured her experience with Jobs: "It fits so well and explained so much of what we had struggled with, that I realized expecting him to be nicer or less self-centered was like expecting a blind man to see."

As comforting as Redsie found the diagnosis, how comfortable are *you* in explaining away arrogance and abuse as merely the manifestation of an illness? Broad diagnostic labels may fill a human need to categorize people into neat and tidy types, and there is cognitive satisfaction and perhaps some comfort in that. But they usually oversimplify people's lives, and they can undermine the concept of responsibility for one's actions. Now that Redsie has found a suitable diagnostic category to affix to her former lover, should his misbehavior be excused in the same manner as a blind man's failure to see? If yes, then perhaps his critics should excuse President Trump's indiscretions and his shortcomings as chief executive because they follow readily from his NPD, or because, in the words of my colleague, he is "just a psychopath." He has a mental illness. He can't help it!

In contrast to the language of medicine, the language of human personality frames human lives with concepts such as temperament, values, goals, motivation, self-conceptions, attachment dynamics, narrative identity, and related ideas from the fields of personality, social, and developmental psychology— the guiding concepts that I have applied to the strange case of Donald J. Trump throughout this book. Rather than searching for the most suitable diagnostic category, my effort is to understand who Donald Trump is and how he came to be. Rather than a civic duty to inform the public about a politician's possible mental illness, my goal is to *make sense* of an inscrutable individual who, as I write these words, strides across the world's stage as a goliath. I am also hoping that my psychological portrait will contribute to a more enlightened conversation about the role of personality in politics today. With these goals in mind, to reduce Trump to a category in the DSM would be to cut the conversation short by glossing over the manifold facets of his psychological uniqueness. *Moreover, he is so much stranger than any diagnosis you can find.*

Unlike the language of medicine, the language of human personality mingles easily with traditional concepts for understanding human beings as social animals. Quintessentially human concepts for evaluating persons—such as character, morality, integrity, honesty, competence, wisdom, and virtue—go a long way in providing us with standards for determining the value and worth of people. Voters who evaluate President Trump in a negative way with respect to these standards do not need a medical diagnosis to justify their decision. Voters who evaluate President Trump in a positive way with respect to these standards are probably no more likely to do so if they learn that a psychiatrist gives him a clean bill of health.

At the end of the day, I find myself to be hopelessly conflicted about the Goldwater Rule. Part of me is convinced by the arguments made by Lilienfeld and his colleagues, as well as the dissenting Supreme Court opinion in the original case. Psychiatric diagnosis of a powerful public figure, when it is conducted in a responsible way, does provide the public with potentially useful information.

Democracy thrives best when diverse ideas are exchanged in a free and unfettered manner, I believe. It seems to me that mental health experts should be part of the political conversation. At the same time, I do worry that without the Goldwater Rule political partisans would quickly enlist armies of mental health experts to weaponize diagnosis.

On January 10, 2018, the *New York Times* published an editorial entitled "Is Mr. Trump Nuts?" The editorial board wrote: "The language of mental health and illness is widely used yet poorly understood, and it comes loaded with unwarranted assumptions and harmful stereotypes." The editorial went on to argue that there is little to be gained by diagnosing Donald Trump. It is enough to consider the man from the standpoints of temperament, character, morality, beliefs and values, judgment and wisdom, basic competence, achievements in office, and his positions on public policy—criteria that human beings have always applied to evaluating their leaders. When it comes to the psychology of President Trump, they suggested, the subject of mental illness is effectively beside the point. I tend to agree.

With respect to the language of human personality, however, I feel absolutely no ambivalence about undertaking a thorough psychological reckoning when it comes to the life and the presidency of Donald Trump. Rather than diagnose the president, the intent throughout this book has been to develop a *psychological commentary* on him, and on the phenomenon that is/was the Trump presidency. Historians may formulate their own perspectives on President Trump by comparing his presidency to those of the past. Economists may use their expertise to evaluate his economic and fiscal policies. Political scientists may be best positioned to understand what his presidency means for the future of democracy.

As a personality psychologist, I see *my* task as trying to understand the unique psychological makeup of the 45th president of the United States, employing the best analytic tools at my disposal and drawing upon the best research findings and evidence-based theories in psychological science. As I try to wrap my mind around the utter strangeness of Donald J. Trump my goal is to develop something sensible and psychologically illuminating to say about who he is, and how he came to be who he is. I want to understand the man. I want to explain him to you, and to myself.

Us

In the presidential contest of 1824, Andrew Jackson won the most electoral votes, edging out John Quincy Adams, Henry Clay, and William Crawford. Because Jackson did not have a majority, however, the election was decided in the House of Representatives, where Adams prevailed. Adams subsequently chose Clay as his secretary of state. Jackson's supporters were infuriated by what they described as a "corrupt bargain" between Adams and Clay. The Washington establishment had defied the will of the people, they believed. The elite insiders who resided in the nation's capital and in its major cities along the eastern seaboard had stolen the election from the common folk—hard-working, God-fearing men who toiled in the small towns and on the farms that filled the great expanse of rural America.

Four years later, Andrew Jackson rode the wave of public resentment to victory, marking a dramatic turning point in the history of American politics. Jackson was our first populist president. Born to Scots-Irish colonists somewhere near the border between North and South Carolina, a land of swamps and forests, Jackson endured a harrowing childhood, imprisoned at age 13 by the British, orphaned by age 14. Eventually, though, he rose to become a lawyer and a prosperous landowner (and owner of slaves) in Tennessee. As a military general, he attained national prominence by winning the Battle of New Orleans in the War of 1812. The first nonaristocrat to hold the highest office in the United States, Jackson was a beloved hero of western farmers and frontiersmen. He was the first to invite everyday folk to the inaugural reception. To the horror of the political elite, throngs tracked mud through the White House and broke dishes and decorative objects.

Washington insiders reviled Jackson. They saw him as intemperate, vulgar, and stupid. Opponents called Jackson a jackass—the origin of the donkey symbol for the Democratic Party. In a conversation with Daniel Webster in 1824, Thomas Jefferson described Jackson as "one of the most unfit men I know of" to become president of the United States, "a dangerous man" who cannot speak in a civilized manner because he "choke[s] with rage," a man whose "passions are terrible." Jefferson feared that the slightest insult from a foreign leader could impel Jackson to declare war. Even Jackson's friends and admiring colleagues feared his volcanic temper. Jackson fought a number of duels in his life, leaving him with

The Strange Case of Donald J. Trump. Dan P. McAdams, Oxford University Press (2020). © Oxford University Press.
DOI: 10.1093/oso/9780197507445.001.0001

bullet fragments lodged throughout his body. On the last day of his presidency, he admitted to only two regrets: that he was never able to shoot Henry Clay or hang John C. Calhoun (who had briefly served as Jackson's vice president).

Similarities between Andrew Jackson and Donald Trump do not end with their aggressive temperaments and their respective positions as Washington outsiders. The similarities extend to the dynamic created between these domi-nant social actors and their adoring audiences—or to be fairer to Jackson, what Jackson's political opponents consistently *feared* that dynamic to be. They named Jackson "King Mob" for what they perceived as his demagoguery. They saw him as a potential tyrant, a wild-haired mountain man who channeled the crude sen-sibilities of the masses. Just as his fans had trashed the White House on inau-guration day, so too might the common hoards, inspired by Jackson's charisma, trample over the fine-tuned norms and institutional conventions that held the young republic together. Jackson was a charismatic strongman, his detractors believed—the kind of would-be autocrat that the framers of the Constitution most feared.

At the emotional heart of Jackson's popular appeal was the widespread per-ception among his supporters that Jackson was "one of *us*"—and, therefore, *not* one of *them*. The *them* meant many different things in 1828, including corrupt Washington insiders, the descendants of moneyed Brahman families in Boston and New York, literary and cultural elites, and the big banks. Importantly, the *them* also meant Native Americans, who represented a paramount threat to the livelihood of the "us." Many white Americans living in rural areas resented the federal government for not adequately protecting them from what they per-ceived to be a mortal threat from savage infidels. Jackson sympathized with their plight. He sought peaceful resolutions that would protect both the white settlers and the native people. His envisioned solutions, however, disenfranchised the Indians. Jackson ignored a Supreme Court decision that rendered unconstitu-tional a Georgia law seizing all property from Native Americans. He pushed through Congress the Indian Removal Act, which eventually led to the forced re-location of 45,000 Native Americans. At least 4,000 Cherokees died on the Trail of Tears, which ran from Georgia to the Oklahoma territory.

Like Jackson, Donald Trump railed against the forces of the establishment who sought to deny him the presidency in 2016. As president, he continued to rail against them. For Trump, the *them* includes 21st-century versions of the Washington insiders who bedeviled Jackson nearly 200 years ago. In 2017–2019, these were political liberals (mainly Democrats) and all of those conservatives (mainly Republicans) who traditionally accommodated to Washington's ways, along with the tens of thousands of civil servants who work in various capacities in the federal government and who constitute what some Trump supporters ominously refer to as "the deep state." Trump famously pledged to "drain the swamp" in Washington. The *them* also included cultural elites, from Hollywood to Broadway to Silicon Valley, as well as the mainstream press, academia, the legal establishment, the scientific establishment, environmentalists, feminists, advocates for African-American rights (such as the Black Lives Matter movement), the president's own Justice Department, the Federal Bureau of Investigations and Central Intelligence Agency, and, on any given day, anybody or any institution that defies the president's stated will, whatever that will is on that particular day.

The *us* is the Trump base, which is widely perceived to trend toward older, white Americans, especially those living in rural areas, more male than female, not well-educated, generally fundamentalist or evangelical Christian. The *us* also includes many wealthy white Americans. These are better-educated traditional Republicans who have made their fortunes through business and entrepreneurship, and more libertarian-leaning voters who do not appreciate the government's meddling with what they perceive to be their God-given liberties and self-chosen lives.

The peculiar position that Native Americans represented for Jackson's base in the 1820s and 1830s is filled today for many of President Trump's supporters by Muslims and immigrants. Muslims are feared because they have become linked, in the minds of some Americans, with Islamic groups in the Middle East who promote terrorism. Immigrants, especially those from Mexico and Central America, are resented because they are perceived to take jobs away from those who have lived in the United States for a longer period of time. Immigrants living in the United States today, particularly those who are undocumented, are the *them* who live among "us." Their Latin American brothers and sisters who have not yet crossed over, but desperately want to enter, are the *them* who are still on the outside, clamoring to get in.

In the speech he gave on June 16, 2015, announcing his run for the Republican nomination for president, Donald Trump promised to crack down on illegal immigration from Latin America. He characterized Mexican immigrants as "rapists" and "drug dealers." "When Mexico sends its people, they're not sending their best," Trump said, as if the Mexican government were rounding up its most dysfunctional citizens and shipping them north. "They're sending people that have lots of problems, and they're bringing those problems with them. They're bringing drugs. They're bringing crime. They're rapists." In one of the most audacious suggestions ever made by a presidential candidate, Trump promised to build a wall on the southern border to keep *them* away from "us." As president, he promised, "I will build a great, great wall on our southern border, and I will make Mexico pay for that wall. Mark my words."

Watching the speech on television or reading about it the next day in the news, many Americans thought that Donald Trump, always controversial and prone to outlandish claims, had finally lost his mind. *Build a wall?* In terms of engineering, such a thing would not even seem to be possible. After all, the border is over 2,000 miles long and is interrupted by rough terrain and bodies of water. Moreover, hadn't Ronald Reagan captured the prevailing American sentiment when, in reference to the Berlin Wall, he famously proclaimed: "Mr. Gorbachev, tear down this wall!"? That wall—despised worldwide—eventually came down! Doesn't the United States pride itself on being a nation of immigrants? Don't the words at the base of the Statue of Liberty urge other nations to send *us* their "huddled masses yearning to breathe free"? "I lift my lamp beside the golden *door!*" The operative metaphor is America as a *door* through which the "homeless, tempest-tossed" people of the world enter. Not a wall to keep them out.

But the laugh was on *them*. Trump's railing against Mexican immigrants and his promise to build a wall coursed through the American electorate like a lightning bolt. His appeal to protect *us* from *them* galvanized Trump's candidacy. At political rallies, his supporters chanted, "Build the wall! Build the wall!" A promise that many of Trump's critics have always chalked up as ridiculously impractical and fundamentally un-American carried him to the presidency.

Trump's us-versus-them sensibility continued to shape policy during his first two years in office. Right out of the box, he took first aim at Muslims by issuing an executive order, in late January 2017, banning travel from seven Islamic countries: Iran, Iraq, Yemen, Somalia, Sudan, Libya, and Syria. When District Court Judge James Robart halted the travel ban, Trump tweeted: "Just cannot believe a judge would put our country in such peril. . . . If something happens, blame him and the court system."

Throughout his campaign, Trump warned of the dangers stemming from what he called "radical Islamic terrorism." For example, in a speech to supporters in Youngstown, Ohio, Trump called for a "total and complete shutdown" of Muslim immigration. "The hateful ideology of radical Islam," he told the crowd, must not be "allowed to reside or spread within our own communities." Influential advisors to Trump provided intellectual arguments for Trump's nativist instincts. Michael Flynn, who served as Trump's first (and short-lived) national security advisor, wrote that "fear of Muslims is RATIONAL." "Islam is not necessarily a religion but a political system that has a religious doctrine behind it," he told an interviewer. An ardent foe of all immigration, Steve Bannon ran Trump's campaign in the late summer of 2016 and served as a senior advisor during Trump's first year in office. Bannon has argued that Western Christianity is engaged in an epic war with Islam.

As president, Trump returned again and again to the problem of the southern border. In 2017, it was estimated that approximately 11 million undocumented immigrants were residing in the United States. In an effort to protect the children who accompanied their undocumented parents when they crossed the border,

President Obama established the Deferred Action for Childhood Arrivals (DACA) policy in 2012. DACA mandated a two-year period of deferred action on deportation of such children. The policy allowed grown children of undocumented immigrants to obtain work permits, as long as they had clean legal records. In 2017, President Trump announced he would suspend DACA. He went even further in October 2018, announcing that he would sign an executive order stopping children of undocumented immigrants *born in the United States* from becoming American citizens. The conventional reading of the Fourteenth Amendment renders all children born on U.S. soil to be citizens of the United States. Both Democrats and Republicans denounced Trump's threat to defy the Constitution.

In 2018, Trump also called for depriving all undocumented immigrants of due process rights. Any individuals who cross into the United States illegally, including refugees fleeing violence in their home countries, should be sent back immediately, rather than appearing before a judge. "We cannot allow all of these people to invade our country," Trump proclaimed. He also announced a "zero tolerance" policy regarding families attempting to cross the border. With the new policy, children were separated from their parents once they arrived in the United States. Over 2,300 children were taken from their parents and detained, leading to a national outcry in June 2018. Even members of Trump's Republican party expressed horror at the images of crying children being taken from their distraught parents, who were then incarcerated. Trump eventually suspended the policy, and many of the families were reunited.

In the fall of 2018, a wave of potential refugees and immigrants began a long trek to the United States from Central America, through Mexico. Conservative commentators labeled the group "the Caravan" and described its steady movement north as an imminent threat to the security of the United States. One radio host estimated the Caravan's size at 14,000 and predicted that its eventual arrival would spell "the end of America as we know it." Hinting at a worldwide conspiracy underwritten by Jewish sources, some argued that the Caravan was organized and funded by George Soros, a Hungarian-Jewish philanthropist and perennial supporter of liberal causes.

President Trump enthusiastically joined the chorus of alarm. Without evidence, he claimed that the Caravan contained "many Gang Members and some very bad people," along with terrorists from the Middle East. Trump sent 5,000 military troops to the border to counter what he characterized as an "invasion of our country." (Critics suggested that the call-up of troops was mainly designed to fire up Republican voters for the upcoming midterm elections.) An ardent Trump supporter living in Sparta, Illinois, Alicia Hooten told reporters that the Caravan was a "ploy to destroy America and bring us to our knees." "I feel like we're fighting for our freedom when it comes to our boarders. I'm not going to take it—not going down without a fight."

Alicia Hooten never had to fight. And, thankfully, "the end of America as we know it" never came to pass. Nor was any evidence ever unearthed regarding the possible involvement of George Soros. A rag-tag collection of unarmed men, women, and children, the Caravan was never a threat to begin with. When some of the marchers eventually arrived peacefully at the border, there were very few gang members or criminals to be found, and no Middle East terrorists.

***

During and after World War II, social scientists sought to explain the rise of German Nazism and other fascist movements in Europe. They developed the idea of an *authoritarian personality* as a pattern of attitudes and values revolving around adherence to society's traditional norms, submission to authorities who personify or reinforce those norms, and antipathy—to the point of hatred and aggression—toward those (the *them*) who either challenge group norms or lie outside their orbit. People who show characteristics of the authoritarian personality are hypothesized to be especially accepting of autocratic leadership that aims to protect *us* from *them*.

Heavily influenced by Freudian ideas, early researchers argued that the authoritarian personality stemmed from a highly repressive family environment. They claimed that the child represses strong biological impulses because of overly punitive conditions experienced early on, ultimately projecting those impulses onto others in a defensive way. The original developmental claims about authoritarianism have never received empirical support in the scientific literature. There is, however, some evidence that people who grow up to be highly authoritarian may have experienced insecure attachments with their mothers. More particularly, they show signs of what developmental psychologists call *avoidant attachment*, or the tendency to keep a cautious distance from the potential source of love and support in childhood, leading to general mistrust of other people.

Ask yourself how much you agree with each of these two statements:

> *The only way our country can get through the crisis ahead is to get back our traditional values, put some tough leaders in power, and silence the troublemakers spreading bad ideas.*

> *What our country really needs is a strong, determined leader who will crush evil, and take us back to our true path.*

These are two items from the Right Wing Authoritarianism Scale (RWA), which is the most well-validated measure of the authoritarian personality used in research today. Many studies show that people who score high on RWA, strongly endorsing items like the two previous statements, tend to cherish the values and conventions of their own ethnic or religious group, tend to reject strongly the values and conventions of rival groups, and tend to show highly prejudiced attitudes toward those whom they perceive to be "deviants"—that is, those who, by virtue of their race, religion, sexuality, gender, or perceived values, deviate from the "us." Among white Americans, high scores on RWA are associated with overt racism and anti-Semitism, with strong antagonism toward what are perceived to be rival religions and political ideologies, and with heightened distrust of foreigners, immigrants, people with AIDS, people with mental illness, gays and lesbians, and the homeless. High scores are also associated with the endorsement of traditional gender roles, rejection of science and the arts, militaristic sentiments, Christian fundamentalism, cognitive rigidity, the belief that complex problems have simple solutions, and the tendency to embrace conspiracy theories.

In the 2016 presidential contest, high scores on authoritarianism strongly predicted political support for Donald Trump's candidacy. In the months before Trump secured the Republican nomination, the political scientist Matthew MacWilliams conducted a survey of 1,800 registered voters across the country to parse out the main variables that might account for Trump's support. He found that the strongest statistical predictor of support for Trump was not gender, age, income, race, or religion but instead self-reported authoritarianism. In other words, those voters who scored highest on items like those in the RWA tended to prefer Trump over the other candidates who were then in the race, both Republican candidates (like Marco Rubio, Ted Cruz, John Kasich, and Jeb Bush) and Democratic candidates (Hillary Clinton, Bernie Sanders). Those Republicans who scored highest on authoritarianism, moreover, tended to express strong support for Trump's proposals to deport 11 million undocumented immigrants, prohibit Muslims from entering the United States, shutter mosques, and establish a nationwide database that tracks Muslims.

Authoritarianism represents a personality constellation that exists, as it were, inside the person, as part of a person's basic make-up. But authoritarianism is more than that. There exists an *authoritarian dynamic*, through which a person who is subject to authoritarian tendencies relates to a powerful leader. In a sense, *authoritarianism happens in the space between the person and the leader*. It is about how members of *us*—the *in-group*—relate to our leadership, which depends greatly on how we (and our leaders) perceive *them*, or the various *out-groups* in our world. People who are dispositionally inclined toward authoritarianism feel a strong sense of loyalty to the in-group and its leaders.

Importantly, under conditions of threat (real or perceived), even members of the in-group who are not especially inclined toward authoritarianism may temporarily become authoritarian. When out-groups strongly threaten the well-being of the in-group, as in times of war or overwhelming economic hardship, it is natural to feel strong attachments to the in-group, to glorify the in-group's leadership, to uphold the conventions of the in-group, and to despise those forces that threaten the in-group's very existence. These are basic social psychological processes that derive from the human proclivity to identify with groups.

To a certain extent, then, authoritarianism is malleable. It can well up in nearly any human being, if the threat to the in-group is strong enough, or scary enough. Human beings evolved to live in groups. When our groups face a mortal threat, we can readily feel fear, anger, contempt, and disgust for those out-groups who threaten us. *We evolved to fear and to hate them.* If we had not evolved as such, then we would not be here today to read about it. Without the combination of strong allegiance to the group and enmity toward competing groups, humans would never have formed groups strong enough to survive and flourish. And without groups, we are nothing—we would never have made it this far. Authoritarianism, therefore, is as natural as nearly any other characteristic that defines the species *Homo sapiens.* We are all potential authoritarians. Part of Donald Trump's appeal, therefore, springs from the deepest recesses of our shared human nature.

Saying that authoritarianism is natural, however, is not the same thing as saying that it is *good.* One of the strongest empirical findings in all of psychology is the unassailable connection between authoritarianism and overt prejudice. Granted, there is probably no person on earth today who is completely free of prejudicial feelings toward one group or another. Subtle racial prejudice is pandemic. But people who score high on RWA consistently demonstrate blatant and emotionally raw prejudice against many different out-groups. The prejudice may express an abiding fear, but it also recruits strong emotions of anger, contempt, and disgust. The emotion of disgust appeals to ancient fears of contagion. Out-groups are like parasites, poisons, or other impurities that threaten to contaminate the in-group. We must expel them from the body. We must destroy them as if they were germs that infect us and make us sick.

The social psychologist Jesse Graham has argued that Donald Trump has a peculiar obsession with disgust and impurities. In an interview in early 2016, he stated, "More than any other Republican nominee, Donald Trump has been appealing to a particular combination of in-group loyalty and moral purity." Graham remarked that Trump often uses the word "disgusting" to refer to everything from women's bodies to public policies he finds offensive, but "his purity appeals are most commonly in the context of group boundaries, like building walls on our national borders to prevent contamination by outsiders, who are cast as murderers and rapists, both morally and physically dirty."

Authoritarian sentiments lead to dehumanization. The threatening out-groups are perceived to be so dirty, so poisonous, so contaminating, so utterly loathsome, that they are barely human at all. When others are dehumanized, they are no longer entitled to the respect and the empathy that human beings typically receive. They are no longer people; they are instead the disgusting enemy. As such, aggression against the enemy is permitted. Our foes—be they rapists, criminals, or radical Muslims—deserve no less. Donald Trump has considerable expertise in dehumanization, appealing to the authoritarian sentiments of his audiences. In his book *Crippled America*, Trump stoked fears of radical Islamic terrorism through an especially lurid depiction of the ISIS group, or Islamic State: "These people are medieval barbarians. They cut off heads, they drown people, they torture people, and we can't allow them to ever gain a safe foothold anywhere. . . . So defeating them requires real commitment to go after them relentlessly wherever they are, without stopping, until every one of them is dead."

A 2017 study by the social psychologists Nour Kteily and Emile Bruneau demonstrated widespread derogation and dehumanization of Muslims and Mexican immigrants in the United States. The researchers showed that the tendency to dehumanize these two groups was especially strong among Republican voters who support Donald Trump. American Muslims and Latinos do indeed feel the effects of dehumanization, the study suggested. But their responses to what they feel are hardly submissive and instead point to a strong backlash. When American Muslims and Latinos feel especially dehumanized, they are more likely to endorse hostile behaviors in response to what they feel, including support for violent collective action. What may transpire, Kteily and Bruneau warn, is a vicious and self-fulfilling cycle: Aggressive policies that dehumanize out-groups may motivate those out-groups to respond aggressively against their foes, reinforcing the original fears and escalating hostilities between groups.

On the campaign trail in Raleigh, North Carolina, in December 2015, Trump stoked fears in the audience by repeatedly saying that "something bad is happening" and "something really dangerous is going on." A 12-year-old girl from Virginia asked him: "I'm scared—what are you going to do to protect this country?"

Trump responded: "You know what, darling? You're not going to be scared anymore. *They're* going to be scared."

***

White nationalists had long planned to converge on Charlottesville, Virginia, for the weekend of August 11–13, 2017. Members of the Ku Klux Klan, neo-Nazis, neo-fascists, advocates for the alt-right agenda in American politics, and others vowing to "take our country back" gathered for the weekend rally under the banner of "Unite the Right." They chose Charlottesville to protest that city's decision to remove a statue of Robert E. Lee, the military leader of the Confederacy in the American Civil War.

Friday night, several dozen of the protestors marched on the campus of the University of Virginia. Carrying torches and semi-automatic rifles, they chanted slogans like "White Lives Matter" and "Jews Will Not Replace Us." One of those in attendance was David Duke, the former imperial wizard of the Ku Klux Klan. He told reporters that protestors were "going to fulfill the promises of Donald Trump" to "take our country back." Another protestor said, "I'm tired of seeing white people being pushed around." The group encountered a gathering of about 30 counterprotestors, mostly students at the University of Virginia, who locked arms around a statue of Thomas Jefferson. A brawl ensued, with several people on both sides sustaining minor injuries. The Virginia State Police were summoned to quell the disturbance. Meanwhile, a group of clergy, who strongly opposed the white nationalists, led an ecumenical prayer service at St. Paul's Memorial Church nearby.

The next morning hundreds of protestors and counterprotestors gathered at Emancipation Park. Some protestors waived Confederate flags while others chanted slogans targeting Jews and African Americans. Dozens of protestors wore Donald Trump's "Make America Great Again" campaign hats. Among the counterprotestors were religious and academic figures, like the Harvard professor Cornel West, as well as members of antifascist groups. The protestors and counterprotestors squared off and began kicking, punching, hurling water bottles, and deploying chemical sprays against one another. With injuries and chaos mounting, Virginia governor Terry McAuliffe declared a state of emergency. Riot police attempted to clear the scene. In the early afternoon, a self-identified white supremacist drove his car into the crowd of counterprotestors, injuring 19 and killing Heather Heyer, a 32 year-old paralegal who came out Saturday morning to voice opposition to white supremacy. The 20-year-old driver, James Alex Fields Jr., would later be convicted of murder.

On Saturday, expressions of outrage aimed at the white supremacists poured into newsrooms and flashed across television screens. Both Democratic and Republican politicians denounced the blatant racism, anti-Semitism, and outright fascism expressed by protestors in Charlottesville. For example, Republican Senator Cory Gardner of Colorado tweeted this: "Mr. President—we must call evil by its name . . . There were white supremacists and this was domestic terrorism." Mike Huckabee, the highly conservative former governor of Arkansas and father to the president's press secretary, called the behavior of white nationalists in Charlottesville "evil." Republican House Speaker Paul Ryan said, "The views fueling the spectacle in Charlottesville are repugnant. Let it only serve to unite Americans against this kind of vile bigotry."

But President Trump remained uncharacteristically mute. From his golf club in New Jersey on Saturday afternoon, he put out a milquetoast statement calling for the "swift restoration of law and order" in Charlottesville. He refused to call out the protestors. He suggested that there was blame "on many sides" for the violence, and he urged calm. After two days of relentless criticism for his weak response, the president finally issued a formal statement condemning the white supremacists who incited the bloody weekend. On Monday, August 14, he read from a prepared text and said, "Racism is evil, and those who cause violence in its name are criminals and thugs, including the KKK, neo-Nazis, white supremacists and other hate groups that are repugnant to everything we hold dear as Americans."

Then, he took it all back on Tuesday. Speaking to reporters in the lobby of Trump Tower in Manhattan, he said that there were "some very fine people on both sides" and insisted that both the white supremacist protestors and their opponents were to blame for the violence in Charlottesville. "I think there was blame on both sides," he said in a combative exchange with reporters. "You had a group on one side that was bad. You had a group on the other side that was very violent. Nobody wants to say that. I'll say it right now." He went on to criticize the counterprotestors and other leftist groups, suggesting a moral equivalency between them and the KKK. Regarding the protestors gathered together for Unite the Right, he pointed out that many of them were in Charlottesville simply to object to the removal of the Robert E. Lee statue. Then he explicitly compared Lee to Presidents George Washington and Thomas Jefferson, who both, like Lee, were slave owners. "This week it is Robert E. Lee and this week it is Stonewall Jackson [another hero of the Confederacy]. Is it George Washington next? You have to ask yourself, where does it stop?"

Donald Trump has always claimed that there is not an ounce of racism in his psychological make-up. He once told a journalist, "I am not a racist. I'm the least racist person you will ever interview." He is, nonetheless, the darling of white racists throughout the United States. Just 12 days after he announced his presidential run, Trump received the endorsement of the Daily Stormer, America's most popular neo-Nazi site. "Trump is willing to say what most Americans think: It's time to deport these people [Mexican immigrants]." The Daily Stormer urged white men "to vote for the first time in our lives for the one man who actually represents our interests."

One of the white men who heeded the call was Jared Taylor, a 64-year-old editor for white supremacist publications. Taylor had never supported a presidential candidate before: "I mean, for heaven's sake, was John McCain ever going to do anything useful as far as the legitimate interests of whites are concerned?" But in 2016, Taylor made robocalls to voters across Iowa and New Hampshire, urging them to support Donald Trump. "We don't need Muslims," he said on the call. "We need smart, educated, white people who will assimilate to our culture." When Donald Trump received the endorsement of the KKK's David Duke, he initially refused to renounce Duke and his white supremacist ideology. In response, the Daily Stormer exulted, "God bless this man." When President Trump tweeted an unfounded accusation that the Jewish philanthropist George Soros was paying women to protest against Trump's judicial nominations, white supremacists basked in the "I-told-you-so" moment. "Trump has officially named the Jew," wrote one man on 4chan, an online message board known for hosting extreme speech and graphic imagery. Another added, "Trump knows." Wrote another white supremacist, cheering Trump's characterization of Mexican immigrants as rapists and drug dealers, Donald Trump is "the glorious leader."

Groups loosely affiliated with the white power movement in the United States have long operated on the margins of mainstream society and in the shadows. They have long shared common beliefs about the world: that white Americans descendant from Northern Europeans are a superior race; that African Americans are intellectually and morally inferior; that immigrants from Latin America should be thrown out of the country; that worldwide conspiracies, especially those involving Jews, threaten to undermine the achievements of Christian white people; that the federal government is somehow linked to these perceived conspiracies; and that white people need to arm themselves and organize to defend white culture against its many enemies. Ku Klux Klan members, neo-Nazis, skinheads, and white militias aspired to organize a guerrilla war on the federal government in the 1980s and 1990s. Operating with discipline and clarity, white power activists trained for warfare in paramilitary camps, and undertook assassinations, mercenary soldiering, armed robbery, counterfeiting, and weapons tracking. They inspired Timothy McVeigh to explode a Ryder truck filled with fertilizer in front of the Alfred P. Murrah Federal Building in Oklahoma City, killing 168 people, including 19 children, on April 19, 1995.

During the Obama presidency, the growth of social media enabled far-flung groups espousing white supremacy and related ideas to communicate with each other more readily, and to build their support. Members of these groups generally despised Obama and saw the election of the first black president to be the fulfillment of their worst nightmares. When Trump began, in 2011, to claim that Obama was not born in the United States, the result was like beautiful music to their ears. They were enraptured when he stoked their fears about murderous Mexicans and radical Islamic terrorism. When he hired Steve Bannon, an avowed right-wing extremist and long-time supporter of white supremacist views, to be his campaign director, and later a top presidential aide, white supremacists began to sense that they no longer dwelled in the political wilderness. They now had a seat at the table. They had managed to make their voices heard at the highest echelons of American government. They were now legitimate.

Many white nationalists fear that someday Americans of European descent will find themselves outnumbered in the United States. Their fears are legitimate. The year 2013 marked the first year that a majority of U.S. infants under the age of one were nonwhite. The median age of white Americans today is 58; for Asians, it is 29; for African Americans, it is 27; and for Hispanics, it is 11. In 2018, white deaths outnumbered white births in 26 states. Moreover, demographers predict that by 2030 immigration will overtake new births as the dominant driver of population growth in the United States, and most of that immigration will come from Latin America, Asia, Africa, and the Middle East. These trends all predict that black, Hispanic, Asian, and mixed-race segments of the American population will continue to grow in the years to follow, while the relative population of whites will decline. Around the year 2045, America will transition into a majority–minority position—for the first time in the nation's history, non-Hispanic whites will no longer constitute the majority of the population.

Most Americans are not explicitly aware of these statistics and projections. But they sense that the demographic nature of the United States is changing, and with it shifts in culture and power. The shifts may be felt especially acutely among working-class white Americans, many of whom voted for Donald Trump in 2016. Since the 1970s, manufacturing and mining jobs have declined in the United States, as has the influence of labor unions. While the good wages from jobs in the steel mills and automobile plants could sustain a middle class life in the 1950s, most of these jobs have vanished in recent decades (lost to automation or shipped overseas). The jobs remaining for unskilled blue-collar workers now pay a small fraction of what they once paid.

As a candidate, Donald Trump promised to bring high-paying blue-collar jobs back to America, a promise that held a strong appeal for working-class white males living in Ohio, Michigan, Indiana, and Wisconsin and other regions where manufacturing was once king. (It should be noted, however, that the loss of manufacturing jobs over the past few decades hit African American workers just as hard as it hit whites, or perhaps harder. In principle, Trump's economic message should have appealed to working-class blacks as well.) Trump's promise to restore America's manufacturing glory was presumed to be one of the biggest ways in which he would make America great again.

Economic anxieties surely played a major role in the 2016 election. But many social scientists believe that status anxiety and issues of cultural identity were equally important in motivating white Americans to vote for Trump. After all, Trump defeated Clinton not only among working class whites (where he enjoyed his biggest margin), but also among college-educated and professionally employed white Americans as well. Moreover, race proved to be the biggest demographic factor in predicting voting patterns in the 2016 presidential election, swamping gender, income, and education. Exit polls estimated that Trump won

58% of white votes, while Clinton won only 37%—a whopping difference of 21 points. Among African Americans, Trump won 8%, while Clinton won 88%!

The social psychologists Maureen Craig and Jennifer Richeson have argued that concern about their declining status in American society is a pervasive issue for white Americans today, spanning the socio-economic spectrum. Even subtle reminders of their diminishing power can prompt fear and affect political behavior. In a study published two years before Trump won the presidency, Craig and Richeson asked 360 white, self-identified political independents to complete one of two different surveys. Half of the participants received a survey that informed them that California had become a majority-minority state—that is, a state where non-Hispanic whites no longer make up more than 50% of the population. The other half were not told this information. Among participants living in the western United States, those who read that whites had lost their majority status in California were 11 points likelier than those not informed to say subsequently that they favored the Republican Party.

In another study, Craig and Richeson provided one group of white participants with a press release explaining that racial minorities will likely make up a majority of the U.S. populace by the year 2042. The other group of white participants received a race-neutral press release about geographic mobility. The group that read about the looming majority-minority shift subsequently reported more conservative responses on a range of issues, compared to those who received the race-neutral information. The first group reported greater concern about immigration and more skepticism about affirmative action. Interestingly, they also shifted in a conservative direction for issues that ostensibly had nothing to do with race, like defense spending and health care reform.

In an ingenious experiment carried out in the real world, the political scientist Ryan Enos sent Spanish speakers to randomly selected train stations in the white suburbs of Boston. The Latino men and women were instructed simply to catch trains and ride like any other passengers. The point of the subtle manipulation was to give the impression that the Latino population in these suburbs was increasing. In the days before and the days after sending the Latinos, Enos surveyed white passengers at the stations about their attitudes toward immigration. Before the Spanish-speaking visitors arrived, the mainly Democratic white respondents in these Boston suburbs provided responses that were generally welcoming of immigrants. After just three days of seeing Latinos at their train stations, however, the white respondents began to sound like Donald Trump, even to the point of endorsing policies to deport the children of undocumented immigrants.

The findings from Enos's study match results from the 2016 election. The biggest gains that Trump made over Mitt Romney, the 2012 Republican nominee for president, were in geographic areas where the Latino population had grown most quickly. One of these is Luzerne County, adjacent to Scranton, Pennsylvania, where the Latino population increased 6-fold between 2000 and 2014. Traditionally a Democratic bastion, the county went solidly for Trump in 2016.

As white Americans perceive their decline in relative numbers and power, they begin to look upon themselves as a besieged minority group. Whereas ethnic minority groups, like African Americans, have traditionally experienced significant discrimination in American society, typically at the hands of the white majority, white Americans are beginning to believe that they now are the ones who are the main targets of discrimination. In a 2011 study conducted by social psychologists Michael Norton and Samuel Sommers, more than half of white Americans surveyed said that they believed whites have replaced blacks as "the primary victims of discrimination" today.

What does this all add up to? White Americans with especially strong authoritarian tendencies form the rock solid base of Trump's political support. While only a small percentage would consider themselves white nationalists, they nonetheless perceive that the influence and power of traditional white culture have begun to wane in the past couple of decades. Even those whites who show relatively tolerant attitudes towards immigrants, Muslims, African Americans, and other out-groups are likely to experience some measure of anxiety and a heightened sense of in-group identification when they sense that their privileged status is now threatened. Whereas being "white" has always been the default identity in American society, by virtue of its overwhelming majority, as white people sense a decline in numbers and power, they may begin to see themselves as akin to a minority group. As such, the identity of "whiteness" may become a more salient category in their thinking, perhaps replacing ethnic identity labels like "German," "Dutch," and "Irish." The us becomes white people; the them becomes those many alien groups who threaten the security and privilege of being white.

The African American writer Ta-Nehisi Coates has labeled Donald Trump America's "first white president." What he means, in part, is that Trump is the first president who perceives his core constituency to be white people and only white people. The 43 white presidents who preceded Trump, as well as the one black president, each viewed himself as representing all Americans, regardless of race or ethnicity, and each was generally perceived as such by the American people, even among detractors. No doubt, all of these presidents harbored prejudices of various kinds. Previous white presidents explicitly or implicitly supported slavery before the Civil War and Jim Crow policies in the 20th century. Still, each likely viewed himself, and was viewed by Americans more generally, as the leader of all Americans.

But Trump is different—and remarkably strange by presidential standards. His overt orientation is strongly toward white Americans and white Americans only, over and against other ethnic/racial groups in the United States. And he does not try to hide it. In July 2019, Trump unleashed a torrent of incendiary, racist tweets aimed at four Democratic representatives, all women of color. He told them to get out of the United States and "go back" to their home countries, even though all four are American citizens and three of the four were born in the United States. (The fourth, Representative Ilhan Omar, from Minnesota, is a refugee from Somalia.)

As the leader of a white "us," Trump seems incapable of even faking a concern for the "them." There is no dignified Dr. Jekyll rising above it all, ecumenical and magnanimous, pledging adherence to the American creed of *e pluribus unum* (out of many, one), seeking to repress the racist Hyde inside. There is only the unadulterated Mr. Hyde, unapologetically fighting to make America white again. Trump is the arch champion of a declining majority in its waning years of hegemony. He is "the glorious leader" of a fading majority, who will soon be a minority. Many of those Americans who most strongly and blindly identify themselves with the besieged *us* of white people perceive him as their savior.

***

One of the strangest political alliances in the history of American politics is that between President Trump and white Christian evangelicals. They support him as strongly as they have ever supported any U.S. president. Approximately 80% of them voted for Trump in 2016, and two years into his presidency, his approval rating among them was over 75% (compared to about 40% nationwide). Yet Trump would seem to represent so much that is in opposition to the central messages of Christianity as well as traditional norms and customs associated with people of faith. Trump has been married three times and has admitted to many sexual affairs. He has been seen on tape boasting about groping women. In a public display of cruelty, he once shamelessly mocked a disabled journalist. He curses like a sailor. Jesus is reported to have said that it is more difficult for a camel to go through the eye of a needle than for a rich man to enter the Kingdom of God. Perhaps Jesus was exaggerating, but the Christian message has always aimed to uplift the poor and downtrodden, while casting some suspicion on excessive material wealth. And yet Trump has unashamedly sought to enrich himself his entire life, and has shown virtually no interest in nonmaterial concerns, such as matters of spirituality. He virtually never goes to church. He seems to know almost nothing about Christianity, or any other religion for that matter.

In early December 2018, the National Cathedral in Washington, DC, was the setting for a grand memorial service held for the 41st president of the United States, George Bush, Senior. Sitting in the front row of the church were the five living former and current presidents and their wives: President Jimmy Carter and Rosalynn Carter, President Bill Clinton and Hillary Clinton, President George W. Bush and Laura Bush, President Barack Obama and Michelle Obama, and President Donald Trump and Melania Trump. At the designated point in the long liturgy, the assembled crowd recited the Apostle's Creed, printed in the service folder: "I believe in God, the Father Almighty, creator of heaven and earth; I believe in Jesus Christ, his only Son, our Lord, who was conceived by the Holy Spirit . . ." As the four former presidents and their wives recited the creed, some by memory and some by reading the printed words, Donald and Melania Trump never moved their lips and never looked at their service folders. As the congregation sang hymns, Trump stared straight ahead, glowering.

Donald Trump was certainly not the first choice of white Christian evangelicals in the 2016 Republican primaries. His selection of the religiously pious Mike Pence to be his running mate, however, garnered approval from many evangelicals. His conversion to an ardently pro-life, anti-abortion position won him support too, as did his promise to appoint conservative judges who would defend religious liberties and potentially strike down *Roe v. Wade*. He won endorsements from influential evangelical pastors, including Reverend Jerry Falwell Jr., the president of Liberty University.

Once in office, President Trump filled his cabinet with people of strong and very conservative Christian faith, like Ben Carson (secretary of housing and urban development), a Seventh-Day Adventist, and Betsy DeVos (secretary of education), who was raised in the Calvinist tradition. Attorney General Jeff Sessions, a devout Methodist, questioned the wisdom of separating church and state. Tom Price (secretary of health and human services) once led an effort to repeal the federal mandate that insurers cover birth control on the grounds of religious freedom. Andrew Puzder (secretary of labor) worked to pass laws asserting that human life begins at conception. Vice President Pence and Kellyanne Conway, the counselor to the president, were well known in evangelical circles for their staunch opposition to abortion and for their firmly conservative Christian stances on other hot-button issues in the long-running culture wars.

In addition, President Trump showed an unprecedented receptivity to advice and counsel offered by evangelicals, like James Dobson (the founder of Focus on the Family), Tony Perkins (the president of the Family Research Council), and James Robison (a well-known Christian television preacher). He encouraged them all, and many others, to call him in the White House when they had concerns they wished to voice, and he accepted their calls. Trump invited scores of prominent Christian evangelical leaders to his inauguration events, and over the course of his first year in office, he gave numerous interviews with the Christian Broadcasting Network.

While Trump has never pretended to be a devout Christian himself, he showed respect for the opinions and viewpoints of evangelical Christian leaders. After winning their votes, he did not hold them at arm's length, as other Republican presidents have done. He did not condescend to them. He made good on his promise to appoint conservative judges who are likely to support religious freedom. Supreme Court justices Neil Gorsuch and Brett Kavanaugh won rave reviews from the evangelical community. So thrilled was Pastor Robison with Trump's support of a conservative Christian agenda that he proclaimed, "You [Mr. Trump] are, in fact, an answer to prayer. . . . I think you have been designed and gifted by God."

The alliance between Donald Trump and the Christian right may, therefore, have been fostered in an environment of common cause and mutual respect, but it may also reveal a deeper, emotional resonance. Trump may not believe that Jesus died for the sins of the world, but he nonetheless shares a world view with many evangelicals. It is the view captured in Romans 3:23, which was the first Bible verse I learned in Sunday School at Glen Park Baptist Church: "For all have sinned and come short of the glory of God." The human heart is riddled with sin, infected by malice, hatred, envy, greed, and pettiness. As a result, we live in a fallen world—a dangerous world filled with vicious people. Trump accepts the starting point of Christianity, even if he rejects the solution. He does not seek Christ's deliverance from sin. He has no conscious desire to be saved from it all. But he knows deep in his heart, as evangelical Christians know, too, that we are threatened from every direction, from others who seek to kill us or rape us or take advantage of us in some way, and from within, because human beings are sinners before they are anything else. "Man is the most vicious of all animals," Trump famously proclaimed, when an interviewer asked him to recite his philosophy of life. "And life is as series of battles ending in victory or defeat."

Ever since St. Augustine developed the idea in the 4th century BCE, Christians have accepted the doctrine of original sin. Christians agree that human beings are deeply flawed by their very nature and in need of some sort of correction. In his *Varieties of Religious Experience*, published in 1902, the eminent psychologist William James observed that all of the world's great religions begin with the idea that human beings are broken. Call it universal suffering or moral depravity or an unenlightened state, but there is something deeply wrong about us, as we naturally exist in the world. Through a variety of religious practices or mind activities, from ritual sacrifices to meditation, religions hold out the possibility of an ultimate deliverance from the wrongness. Christians call it redemption.

It is one thing to accept the idea that human beings are fundamentally flawed, as an abstract proposition. It is quite another to *feel* it in a direct and visceral way. In the United States, fundamentalist and evangelical Protestants, along with conservative Catholics, have tended to express a stronger sentiment regarding the fundamental brokenness of human beings—original sin, human evil, the fallen nature of humankind—than have other Christian groups. Self-proclaimed "progressive" Christians, including some mainstream Protestants (e.g., Episcopalians, Methodists, certain Lutherans) and liberal Catholics, have tended to soften the Christian message by placing more emphasis on the inherently positive features of human nature. We are sinners, but we are good, too, or hold out the potential for good. As such, progressive and liberal Christians tend to experience their faith from a somewhat more humanistic perspective.

These are gross generalizations, I realize. Every religious person's experience with faith is unique. It is no doubt true that some evangelicals are very progressive in their faith whereas some members of mainstream Protestant denominations are conservative and traditional. Nonetheless, social science research reveals general statistical trends that have held true for a long time. Fundamentalist and evangelical Christians, along with conservative Catholics, tend to report a stronger sentiment regarding human evil, compared to those with a more liberal or progressive faith stance. They apprehend sin in a more direct way. They feel it in themselves, and they see it in others. They worry about it. They seek deliverance from it. Yes, Mr. Trump, you got it right on this point: "Man *is* the most vicious of all animals."

Research also documents a strong connection between fundamentalist and evangelical Christianity on the one hand and right-wing authoritarianism on the other. Among white religious Americans, scores on RWA are strongly and positively associated with fundamentalist and evangelical Christianity, which itself trends in the direction of conservative politics. The research is clear: the Christian right tends toward authoritarianism. More than adherents of other religious traditions in the United States, fundamentalist and evangelical Christians report greater allegiance to their respective religious in-group and greater wariness of out-groups. Because they feel that the world is an especially dangerous place, they value loyalty to the in-group, which is designed to shelter them from the world's dangers, and from the evils that originate in the human heart. Besieged by the forces of sin and threatened by other sinners, the most dangerous of whom populate rival out-groups, Christian fundamentalists desire to be *saved*.

Over a decade ago, my students and I conducted a series of studies exploring the dynamics of authoritarianism among American Christians. Sampling from a range of Christian congregations in the Chicago area, we gathered together approximately 130 devout Christians, including Protestants and Catholics, ranging from fundamentalist/conservative to liberal/progressive in their theological (and political) views. Each participant completed a series of written questionnaires and engaged in a lengthy life-story interview. In one part of that interview, we asked each participant to imagine what his or her life would be like, and what the world would be like, if there were no Christian faith. If you had no Christian faith, what would your life be like? If there were no Christian faith worldwide, what would the world be like? The questions boiled down to what the devout Christians perceived as a troubling hypothetical: *What if there were no God?*

Nearly every respondent viewed the hypothetical scenario in a very negative light. If there were no God, my life would lack meaning. I would be very, very unhappy. The world would be in even worse shape than it is now. People would suffer greatly, even more than they do now. It was all bad—but different kinds of bad for different people. Christians scoring relatively high on RWA tended to imagine a chaotic world filled with ruined lives. Without God, they imagined, aggressive human impulses would no longer be held in check. Families would fall apart because husbands and wives would no longer remain sexually faithful to each other. Murder rates would climb. Drug abuse would be rampant. Their own lives would be ravaged, too. They often admitted that without God their own demons would be unleashed. They would not be able to control the world, nor regulate themselves, if it were not for God. The conservative celebrity pundit Glenn Beck is an evangelical Christian. When he was once asked about the importance of Christian faith in his life, he said that finding God, along with finding a wife, helped him immeasurably with the challenge of what he called "self-regulation." "If it weren't for my wife and my faith," he said, "I don't know if I would be alive today."

Devout Christians scoring *low* on RWA imagined their own brand of misery. But it wasn't so much about chaos and rampant sin. It was, instead, emptiness. Without God, the world would lack color and form. There would be no reason to get up in the morning. People would feel a deep hunger that could not be satisfied, a debilitating thirst that could never be quenched. Whereas conservative Christians with strong authoritarian tendencies imagined a fiery hell, their liberal and less authoritarian counterparts, equally devout in their faith, imagined something like the barren surface of the moon. Whereas those high on RWA seemed to view their faith as protecting them from the chaos of human nature, those low on RWA viewed their faith as providing them with nourishment, as if God were like a mother feeding them from Her breast. Both responses are evocative and primal. A strong God protects me from a dangerous world so I will remain safe; a nurturant God provides me with nutrition so I will grow. Of course, human beings need both: Security to live, and the bread of life.

Trump promises security rather than nourishment. His primal nature is strength and power. There is no nurturance there. Americans with strong authoritarian inclinations, including many conservative and evangelical Christians, are drawn to his message. And they are drawn to *him* as a personification of primal power. God saves them from sin. In a world of carnage and mayhem, like the world as Donald Trump has always imagined it (and the image of America he projected in his inaugural address), God shields them and keeps them safe.

Donald Trump may or may not be a Christian, but he feels the world the way some evangelical Christians feel it.

Moreover, he exudes power, as the Christian God does in the minds of highly authoritarian Christians. Trump promises to protect. When, in April 2018, a journalist asked her how she could vote for a man who has repeatedly cheated on his wife, Peggy Young Nance, an evangelical Christian who is president of Concerned Women for America, had a ready retort: "We weren't looking for a husband," she said. "We were looking for a bodyguard." Evangelical Christians often feel attacked and on the defensive in an increasingly secular world. They feel that they are at war. Trump promises to fight the evil foe, whether that foe is radical Islamic terrorism or Godless political liberals. He is a warrior for *us*, and authoritarian Christians respect warriors, and they understand the need for warriors in times of war. Trump channels the sentiment expressed in the Christian hymn that was a favorite in the Baptist church of my childhood:

> Onward Christian soldiers,
> marching as to war,
> with the cross of Jesus
> going on before.
> Christ the royal master
> leads against the foe;
> forward into battle
> see his banners go!

"Now we have a warrior at the helm who is willing to stand up and fight," remarked one minister at a meeting with President Trump and evangelical leaders in August 2018. He turned to Trump and said, "Sir, I commend you for your courage."

***

Donald Trump won the American presidency during a time when nationalist authoritarian movements threaten democratic traditions in many countries around the world, especially in Europe. Since the 2008 economic recession, xenophobic nationalist parties have gained increasing numbers of supporters in Britain, France, Spain, Greece, Italy, Austria, and the Scandinavian countries. A major force behind their rise in popularity has been the influx of immigrants and refugees from the Middle East and Africa. Nationalist political parties have rallied Europeans around the fear of immigrant out-groups, viewed as threats to economic prosperity and to Euro-Christian cultural values. They have also taken aim at the aspirations for a cohesive and integrated European Union. In

2016, a majority of voters in Great Britain chose the "yes" option for leaving the European Union. The "Brexit" vote was widely viewed as another indication of a broad movement toward nationalism and away from globalism. It also anticipated President Trump's "America First" philosophy. "From now on, it's going to be America first," Trump declared, shortly after he was elected. "There is no such thing as a global anthem, a global currency, a global flag." "We salute one flag, and that is the American flag." It all adds up to more focus on the *us*, and greater suspicion of the *them*.

Poland's Law and Justice Party came to power in 2015. The right-wing populist organization, headed by Jaroslaw Kaczynski, pushed a strong nationalist agenda. The party purged dissenters from civil service positions, exerted heavy-handed control over the state-sponsored media, and neutered many democratic institutions. In Hungary, Prime Minister Viktor Orban and his far-right nationalist party, Fidesz, won a third consecutive term in 2018. Orban's winning message was that Hungary is in mortal peril, threatened by hordes of Middle East immigrants ready to invade and an international order that aims to strip the small nation of its sovereignty. He contended that it was Hungary's "moral duty" *not* to take in foreign refugees or asylum seekers, as it has been urged to do by the European Union. Hungary is for native-born, Christian Hungarians only, Orban insisted. "The era of liberal democracy is over," Orban proclaimed, in a 2018 address to the Hungarian parliament.

This strange phenomenon that goes by the title of *President* Donald J. Trump is the result of a perfect storm. A peculiar set of historical conditions came into dynamic contact with an even more peculiar human being. The moment met the man. The result was a political hurricane—like one of those "thousand-year storms" that climate scientists warn will become more common as the planet heats up. Whether or not the world's political climate is heating up in a similarly dangerous way is a pressing question.

Political scientists, economists, and sociologists are better equipped than I am to explain the moment. Their analyses might begin by identifying worldwide discontent with, and even fear of, globalism as a signature feature of the current scene. As cultures mix in unpredictable ways and waves of migrants move across borders, tight-knit and traditional communities feel that their very identities are under siege. The *us* pushes back against the *them*, boosting nationalism and tribalism. Global trade and open markets have provided massive economic benefits for many Americans and have helped raise hundreds of millions of people in China, India, and other developing countries out of the depths of poverty. But the benefits have been uneven, and millions of working-class Americans feel that they have been left behind. As an upwardly mobile collection of highly skilled information experts and entrepreneurs achieves obscene levels of wealth in the United States, the rest of the country stagnates. Income inequality in America is higher than it has been for a century. The middle class is hollowing out.

On the political front, the response to these massive economic and cultural shifts has been polarization and paralysis. A year after Barack Obama assumed the presidency in 2009, the leader of Senate Republicans, Mitch McConnell, announced that his number one policy initiative was to assure that President Obama would be a one-term president. Not a single Republican supported passage of the Affordable Care Act in 2010, even though conservative Republicans developed the market-based contours of the program just a few years before. Republicans said that the Democrats froze them out of the conversations. In the last year of Obama's presidency, the Republican Senate refused even to grant a hearing for Obama's Supreme Court nominee, Merrick Garland. As the Democratic party moved to the left and the Republicans to the right, legislators aiming to find common political ground in the middle became a dying breed. The two parties dug in during the Obama years, refusing to work with each other to address the daunting policy problems facing the country. The ongoing stalemate frustrated many Americans, and undermined the vanishingly little faith in government they had in the first place.

As a fabulously wealthy businessman and celebrity, Donald Trump promised to rise above the fray and fix it all. With no political ideology to speak of, Trump seemed poised to transcend the liberal/conservative divide, to bring Republicans and Democrats together in order to make good deals for America, deals that would bring back jobs for coal miners and millwrights, while restoring America's status as the pre-eminent power in the world. He promised to fight for the forgotten American people—especially working-class white men emasculated by globalism—against the elites within the United States and against our enemies abroad. America First. America as it used to be—back before the concept of "globalism" had even been invented, when America stood tall to dominate the globe.

There is a paradox here. On the one hand, Trump presented himself in 2016 as a strikingly nonideological candidate who offered pragmatic solutions to America's problems. He would transcend the partisan divide to make good deals and to fix things. On the other hand, he was nakedly partisan in excoriating anybody who disagreed with him, even those within the Republican party, and in reinforcing the walls that American tribes had already built to separate themselves from each other—walls dividing liberals from conservatives, women from men, blacks from whites, urban from rural, them from us. Still, Trump believed that he could unite all Americans in one primal way—by winning. Americans will win again, Trump promised. And when everybody is winning, everybody is happy. It is like a professional baseball team filled with high-priced free agents. The players don't especially like each other. But if the team wins the championship, they are suddenly best friends—for a while at least. Winning may not heal all wounds, but it hides them for the time being, for the moment. In life and in politics, Trump has always been about winning the moment.

In Donald Trump's mind, *them* were consistently defeating *us* until that magic day in January 2017, when he was sworn into office. From that point onward, *us* has been winning. Still, every day is a battle, Trump contends—indeed every day *must* be a battle if the winning is to continue. To create the psychological conditions of constant warfare, Trump creates chaos on nearly a daily basis, and revels in the chaos he has created. When the world seems to be spinning out of control, we imagine ominous forces lurking outside our awareness, working in concert to upend the expected order of things. We imagine a diabolical host of *them* threatening the well-being of *us*. Amidst the disruption, our senses are sharpened, our attention held hostage. On edge, we keenly monitor the upheaval, trying to make sense of it.

As Trump continues to create chaos, we find it impossible not to watch. Tim Wu, a professor of law at Columbia University, has written about how the riotous confusion that President Trump creates through his outlandish behaviors, his incinerating tweets, and his blatant violation of norms captures the "mindshare" of the American people. Wu writes: "Every day of the Trump administration seemingly brings another plot twist, a new initiative, outlandish attack or bizarre reversal. Not since wartime has news been so riveting—and with the president fighting so many 'enemies,' it is actually not unlike war coverage."

By creating chaos in the moment, Trump establishes the conditions of warfare in which a strongman is expected to rise. With evil enemies threatening us from every direction and with chaos engulfing our lives, we look to the glorious leader for protection, and for the victory we deserve. Fear and chaos work in Trump's favor. They are his best friends for sustaining the authoritarian dynamic. Conveniently for him, fear and chaos capture well how Donald Trump has always experienced the world. This is how he has always lived. And now we are living it, along with him.

Donald Trump strives to win every battle, but even when he loses, he can still win. Wu writes: "While he may prefer winning to losing, he can still win *by* losing. For what really matters are the contests themselves—the creation of an absorbing spectacle that dominates headlines, grabs audiences and creates a world in which every conversation revolves around Mr. Trump and his doings. By this standard, Mr. Trump is not just winning, but crushing it." In the words of George Orwell, "The war is not [necessarily] meant to be won, it is meant to be continuous." For the autocratic regime that Orwell made famous in *1984*, continuous warfare feeds the authoritarian dynamic.

The man meets the moment. Basking and raging in the disorder he creates, this strangely antagonistic human being seems perfectly made for the strangely authoritarian times in which America and the world find themselves. He is the episodic hero who has never been able to create a full-bodied story to make moral sense of his own life, let alone the life of his nation—nothing, that is, beyond "we win, and they lose." And for some strange reason, that message seems to work today. It is a message that gets noticed. It monopolizes mindshare. He is the self-obsessed strongman who has always wanted to win your attention right here and right now, in the here-and-now moment, even if you despise him now and forever, even if you are one of *them*.

Primate

From early 1974 through the bulk of 1976, a male chimp named Yeroen held the position of alpha leader in the large, open-air chimpanzee colony at Burgers Zoo in Arnhem, the Netherlands. His reign was roughly coterminous with the administration of President Gerald R. Ford in the United States.

Yeroen became famous (among *Homo sapiens*) when the Dutch primatologist Frans de Waal showcased his leadership style in a classic book entitled *Chimpanzee Politics*. Based on countless hours of observing the interpersonal dynamics of chimpanzee groups, de Waal concluded that "the social organization of chimpanzees is almost too human to be true." Like human beings, chimps organize themselves into status hierarchies. They adopt different roles in their respective groups, and they move flexibly from one role to the next when the situation demands it. They develop social reputations in their groups. They jockey for power, cut deals, and form coalitions and alliances in ways that are remarkably human. They are intensely political. "Entire passages of Machiavelli seem to be directly applicable to chimpanzee behavior," de Waal wrote.

When the first edition of *Chimpanzee Politics* appeared in 1982, readers were shocked by how much chimps turn out to be like humans. But the strange case of Donald Trump shows how much humans turn out to be like chimps.

There are anywhere from 200 to 350 different species of primates on the planet today. Among the most well-known are chimpanzees, monkeys, apes, gorillas, orangutans, baboons, and humans. In everyday talk, attributing characteristics from our primate cousins to other human beings is usually the stuff of insult or humor. For example, to "ape" someone is to imitate them in a mocking way, as if a real ape were trying to act like a human being. To say that somebody resembles an ape or a monkey is to suggest that they are primitive, crude, or destructive. In *The Strange Case of Dr. Jekyll and Mr. Hyde*, Jekyll was mortified when Hyde played "ape-like tricks" on him, "scrawling in my own hand blasphemies in the pages of my books, burning letters and destroying the portrait of my father." Hyde exuded primal force. He was the uncivilized primate hovering just beneath the surface of Jekyll's refined persona.

It has been reported that when he served as White House counsel, Don McGahn nicknamed President Trump "King Kong." Since he first appeared in a 1933 movie, King Kong has represented the paradigmatic giant gorilla, posing

The Strange Case of Donald J. Trump. Dan P. McAdams, Oxford University Press (2020). © Oxford University Press.
DOI: 10.1093/oso/9780197507445.001.0001

a threat to humankind. McGahn used the name behind Trump's back. Yeroen would have destroyed a beta male who insulted him face to face.

Appearing on the *Tonight Show* in January 2013, comedian Bill Maher offered Donald Trump $5 million if he could prove that he was *not* the biological product of the union between a human mother and orangutan father. Maher was joking, of course. In response, Donald Trump sent Maher a copy of his birth certificate, apparently without irony. He then requested the $5 million reward. When Maher refused to pay up, Trump sued him.

Would anybody else in the world have responded to Maher in that way? I *told* you Trump was *strange!*

Strange, but also deeply familiar. Familiar in a primal way. And in a way that frightens, even as it fascinates.

In an interview with Bob Woodward and Robert Costa on March 31, 2016, Donald Trump said this: "Real power is—I don't even want to use the word—fear." I want to say that Trump was channeling his inner Yeroen when he made that statement to Woodward and Costa. But saying that would not be quite right, because there is very little by way of "inner" when it comes to Donald Trump. He is not Jekyll with an inner Hyde. He is, instead, all Hyde. And like Hyde, Trump projects an awesomely primal appeal. We recognize it because we are primates, too.

***

Evolution has taught us to recognize two forms of leadership in human groups. There is leadership by *prestige*, and there is leadership by *dominance*.

Prestige is the newer form, tracing back one million years or so. Dominance is much older.

When Donald Trump published *The Art of the Deal* in the mid-1980s, he burst onto the national scene in the would-be guise of a prestige leader. Prestige comes from expertise. According to the hype, Trump's book was a product of expertise, containing invaluable knowledge about how to make deals and how to get rich in America. Trump presented himself as a cultural expert. He had honed a set of special skills, prospective readers assumed, that were greatly valued by his society. Through his book, he was promising to share those skills with a grateful audience. By doing so, he would presumably obtain prestige and win admiration from others in his society.

The importance of prestige derives from the critical role of *culture* in human evolution. By culture, I mean the things and ideas—artifacts, practices, beliefs, customs, stories, and so on—that humans create in their groups and pass down to future generations. Culture is cumulative. Each new generation gets a head start, as it were, on adaptation to the environment by having at its disposal the accumulated knowledge of previous generations. For example, once our evolutionary forebears learned to cook with fire, they taught the skill to others, such that subsequent generations did not need to re-invent the practice all over again. Each generation, then, starts with a baseline of culture and then builds on that, adding to culture and changing culture over time. Donald Trump and I were born into a culture in which the automobile and pizza had already been invented, Christianity enjoyed widespread currency, educated people read Shakespeare in college, unwed motherhood was considered a disgrace, businessmen smoked and drank martinis at lunch, and democracy had recently triumphed over tyranny in a world war. My grandson was born into a much different cultural milieu.

The evolutionary anthropologist Joseph Henrich has argued that around one million years ago the forerunners to *Homo sapiens* began to live as cultural animals. Our evolutionary ancestors developed hunting skills, basic tools, knowledge about edible plants, and other critical inventions (in their minds and in the world), and they passed those ideas and things down to subsequent generations. The spread of culture, however, was uneven. Whereas some group members might develop valued cultural skills, others might lag behind. Culture began to distribute itself across different individuals. One member of a group might develop skills in hunting, whereas another might cultivate knowledge in the area of childrearing, or cooking, or resolving disputes between group members. Those with valued expertise enjoyed high prestige in their respective groups. Individuals who sought to learn those skills—children, novices, those who did not have the skills but wanted them—sought out the experts for guidance. As cultural expertise became more and more valued, the prestige of experts increased, giving them greater status in human groups. Experts were elevated to positions of leadership in groups. It was no longer enough for a leader to be strong. He or she needed to be smart, too—smart in a cultural way, possessing and expressing expertise that other group members valued highly, admired for that expertise, given honor and prestige.

Culture began to shape evolution, which began *to change human nature.* We usually think of human nature as causing culture, but Henrich turns the assumption around. As culture changed, new forms of adaptation became valued. Those individuals who learned and embodied those new forms garnered advantages over others in the group, by virtue of their heightened status. Those advantages ultimately translated into greater access to limited resources in the group, which promoted the survival and reproductive success of those who were advantaged. In the never-ending contest that we call "evolution," the "winners" pass more of their genes down to subsequent generations than do the "losers." As what it means to be a winner changes, those genes associated with the new forms of winning come to predominate. The very nature of the species changes.

The process I am describing is called *culture–gene co-evolution*. As human groups became more cultural, natural selection began to favor those group members who possessed cultural expertise, and to favor those group members who had the skills to learn that expertise from experts. As human groups began to confer prestige on experts, those experts began to enjoy higher status in groups, giving them an advantage in obtaining the resources needed to reproduce and pass their genes down to future generations. In simple terms, having cultural knowledge became an asset in the mating game. Although language had not yet entered the scene, if our million-year forerunners could speak, they might have begun to say this kind of thing for the first time: "It's not just your body—I love you for your brain, too!" More generally, cultural expertise became a ticket to a good reputation in the group, which conferred many advantages, short-term and long-term, including those that led to greater reproductive success, all other things being equal.

As experts became the winners (in love and in life), subsequent generations ended up containing more and more experts-in-waiting—that is, individuals with the biological potential to be especially good with and at culture. And this had the downstream effect of advancing or enriching or enlarging culture further, leading to the development and proliferation of further cultural knowledge over time. Henrich argues that culture–gene co-evolution gradually resulted in the self-domestication of our species. *We literally domesticated ourselves.* We invested our minds and bodies into garnering cultural expertise, which, in turn, enriched our groups, enlarging them and giving them more complexity, from one generation to the next. As social life became richer and more complex, norms were established for how to live successfully in the group. Those who followed the norms were favored in the group, attaining a kind of social expertise in that manner, which redounded to a good social reputation. Prestige leadership combines with strong group norms to enhance cooperation among group members and to favor that group, in broad terms, over rival, less domesticated groups. All other things being equal, cooperative groups (valuing expertise, prestige leadership, and intricate collaboration within the group) win out over groups that are riven by internal discord.

Within hunting and gathering bands of *Homo sapiens*, prestige was (and is today) the main ticket to social status. Anthropologists generally believe that human hunters and foragers typically formed relatively egalitarian communities that distributed power across a range of cultural experts. Of course, no human group is ever devoid of hierarchy, but the mobile human bands that prevailed on the planet 200,000 years ago, and probably much earlier, developed cultural practices and social norms that aimed to spread power around, working against the accumulation of immense power by despots. In the words of the evolutionary anthropologist Christopher Boehm, early humans "lived in what might be called societies of equals, with minimal political centralization and no social classes. Everyone participated in group decisions, and outside the family there were no dominators." In these "moral communities," social rank was a function of prestige, which itself stemmed from expertise in specific cultural domains such as hunting, healing, cooking, caregiving, and the arts of defense.

Consistent with our evolutionary lineage, then, the human mind is well prepared to appreciate the intricacies of a *prestige psychology*. Prestigious people are freely admired and emulated; they do not need to coerce others to obtain support. As leaders, prestigious people are expected to call upon the advice of other experts and to encourage collaboration among subordinates in order to solve group problems. They are expected to adhere to group norms and work within established institutions. In so doing, they are expected to demonstrate some degree of magnanimity, generosity, forbearance, and dignity in their leadership roles. They are expected to commit themselves to the welfare of the group, rather than to self-aggrandizement. Observing hunter-gatherers on the remote Adaman Islands over 100 years ago, the renowned British anthropologist A. R. Radcliffe Brown wrote:

> Besides the respect for seniority, there is another important factor in the regulation of social life, namely the respect for certain personal qualities. These qualities are skill in hunting and warfare, generosity and kindness, and freedom from bad temper. A man possessing them inevitably acquires a position of influence in the community. His opinion on any subject carries more weight than that of another.

Social psychologist Jon Maner and his colleagues have conducted empirical studies of modern-day business teams to flesh out the psychology of prestige. They find that when leadership is framed in prestige terms, rather than in terms of sheer dominance or coercion, team members enjoy their interactions more and develop more creative solutions to problems. Prestige-oriented leaders tend to be especially encouraging of other talented group members, viewing them as allies rather than rivals. Compared to leaders who focus more on dominance, prestige leaders tend to share information freely with other group members. They are especially adept at matching subordinates to the appropriate tasks wherein their respective skill sets can be best utilized. On the down side, however, prestige leaders sometimes give too much credence to the many different views of group members to win their admiration. Sometimes prestige leaders worry too much about being liked and respected, and that may result in slower decision-making and a failure to achieve group goals in an efficient manner.

If one knew nothing else about Donald Trump beyond the fact that he once published a book sharing culturally valued expertise in the real estate industry, one might expect that his own approach to leadership would follow the paradigm of prestige. But, in fact, nothing could be further from the truth, as even Trump's most ardent admirers would acknowledge. Even a casual reading of *The Art of the Deal* reveals that the cultural knowledge Donald Trump aims to transmit is not so much a specialized portfolio formulated to address a specific problem in culture but rather a more general set of strategies aimed at achieving social *dominance*—dominance in virtually any context in which "deals" are to be made, from real estate to politics to interpersonal relationships. "Think big," Trump counsels in his book. "Fight back. . . . Use your leverage. . . . The best thing you can do is deal from strength." And "sometimes, part of making a deal is denigrating your competition."

Donald Trump completely disavows the psychology of prestige. He renounces this feature of human nature as strongly as he renounces anything. In its place, Trump harkens back to an evolutionarily older paradigm for achieving status in primate groups. It is the paradigm of brute dominance, an atavistic proclivity whose primal appeal never seems to fade.

***

My favorite model of dominance leadership is Yeroen. Alpha chimps like Yeroen achieve their exalted status in their groups not through prestige, but through repeated displays of dominance. In *Chimpanzee Politics*, Frans de Waal provided a vivid description of Yeroen's leadership style:

> A heavy steam engine, an advancing tank, an attacking rhinoceros; all are images of contained power ready to ride roughshod over everything in its path. So it was with Yeroen during a charging display. In his heyday he would charge straight at a dozen apes, his hair on end, and scatter them in all directions. None of the apes dared to remain seated when Yeroen approached, stamping his feet rhythmically. Long before he reached them they would be up, the mothers with their children on their backs or under their bellies, ready to make a quick getaway. Then the air would be filled with the sound of screaming and barking as the apes fled in panic. Sometimes this would be accompanied by blows. Then, as suddenly as the din had begun, peace would return. Yeroen would seat himself, and the other apes would hasten to pay their respects to him. Like a king he accepted this mass homage as his due.

Both in the wild and in captivity, chimpanzees organize themselves into strict hierarchies. The top chimp achieves his standing through aggression, intimidation, and threat. Prerequisites for the top post include being large and being strong. Indeed, alpha chimps regularly exhibit *piloerection*—their hair stands on end, as with Yeroen in the charging display—which makes them appear even larger than they really are. In addition, they must be endowed with the kinds of temperament traits that drive social dominance (introversion and high agreeableness are disqualifiers). And they must be amenable to forging coalitions with other high-status chimps in the group, lest their subordinates plot to overthrow them. In *Chimpanzee Politics*, de Waal famously described these coalitions as short-term Machiavellian projects of surprising intricacy. Utterly pragmatic, rival chimps may severely injure each other in a battle for dominance and then engage in mutual grooming and other friendly behaviors to consolidate rank order once the battle is over. When (after a 72-day uprising) Luit finally overthrew Yeroen to achieve top status in 1976, Yeroen angled to become his closest ally.

The human and chimpanzee lineages split off from their common ancestor five to seven million years ago. What both lines took with them was an abiding proclivity for social hierarchy and a corresponding psychology of dominance. Therefore, the human expectation that social status can be seized through brute force and intimidation, that the strongest and the biggest and boldest will lord it over the rank and file, is very old, awesomely intuitive, and deeply ingrained. Its younger rival—prestige—was never able to dislodge dominance from the human mind, even during the long and relatively egalitarian epoch—hundreds of thousands of years—when hunter-gatherer bands and tribes crisscrossed the African continent. Indeed, dominance got its second wind with the advent of agriculture, around 12,000 years ago, and the rise of kingdoms and city-states. Ancient kingdoms were brutally hierarchical, with monarchs at the top and slaves at the bottom.

Flashing forward to the 21st century, prestige and dominance compete with each other as two evolutionarily grounded strategies for attaining status in human groups, contoured by wide variations across the globe in political structures, religions, economies, and wealth. Barack Obama was all about prestige; Trump is all about dominance.

Consider the similarities between President Trump and Yeroen when Yeroen was at the height of his powers. Trump is physically big and dynamic. He gives the impression of a volcano about to explode. When I watched him in the Republican debates and during his debates with Hillary Clinton, I could not keep my eyes off of him, even when others were speaking. He is more overtly aggressive than any political figure in the United States today, so aggressive, so insulting, so egregiously self-promoting that you think he might be bluffing—but is he? What if he isn't? Bluffing, it should be noted, is a cardinal strategy in the alpha chimp repertoire. It is also prevalent in those agonistic life contexts Donald Trump knows so well—the Manhattan real estate market, for example, the world of professional wrestling, and the cut-throat ethos of his reality show, *The Apprentice*.

On Twitter, Trump's incendiary tweets are like Yeroen's charging displays. In chimp colonies, the alpha male occasionally goes berserk and starts screaming, hooting, and gesticulating wildly as he charges toward other males nearby. Pandemonium ensues as rival males cower in fear and females grab their little ones and run for cover. Once the chaos ends, there is a period of peace and order, wherein rival males pay homage to the alpha, visiting him, grooming him, and expressing various forms of submission. In Trump's case, his tweets are designed to intimidate his foes and rally his submissive base. When he wants to be especially aggressive, he will tweet in capital letters. These verbal outbursts reinforce the president's dominance by reminding everybody of his wrath and his force. When the alpha chimp charges, you cannot help but take note. Teddy Roosevelt believed that a leader should "talk softly, but carry a big stick." Trump yells loudly; indeed, he hoots, screams, and screeches—mainly to vent his anger and to invoke fear. And now that he is president, he also carries the big stick.

One of the most bizarre (and psychologically telling) events during Trump's first year in office was his first full cabinet meeting, held on June 12, 2017. With the cameras rolling, each cabinet official in turn proclaimed how honored or blessed he (or she) was to serve the primal leader. The vice president, Mike Pence, began the submission fest with these words: "Thank you, Mr. President, and this is the greatest privilege of my life, to serve as vice president to a president who is keeping his word to the American people and assembling a team that is bringing real change, real prosperity, and real strength back to our nation." And on it went, around the room, one obsequious gesture after another. In a parallel fashion, chimps show a wide range of deference displays in the presence of the alpha, including grooming, stroking, bowing, and other variations on the theme of sucking up.

It should be noted that subsequent cabinet meetings in the Trump administration have generally followed the same pattern. When Trump convened his first cabinet meeting of 2019, he called on select cabinet members to talk about their contributions to securing the nation's borders. One by one, they responded by praising Mr. Trump. Kirstjen Nielsen, the homeland security secretary (later fired by Trump because she was not tough enough on immigration), applauded the president's leadership on border security. Matthew Whitaker, the acting attorney general, followed her by saluting the president for staying in the White House during the Christmas and New Year's holidays "while some members of Congress went on vacation." Rick Perry, the energy secretary, also praised the president for "standing up and saying don't come" to those who are trying to enter the United States illegally. Always ready to applaud his master, the beta chimp-in-chief, Vice President Pence, summed up the sentiment of the adoring group: "I want to thank you [Mr. President] for the strong stand you have taken on border security." The entire submission display was televised.

In the prestige paradigm of leadership, the president's cabinet would never be chosen for the prime purpose of fawning admiration. Instead, it would be viewed as a body of experts charged with running government agencies and providing the president with critical advice. While some deference to the chief executive has always been expected, presidents of the United States have historically relied on their cabinet officers for critical input, typically behind closed doors. From Teddy Roosevelt to Barack Obama, this was generally how cabinet meetings went.

The role of fear is central to a dominance psychology. The alpha male cannot sustain the dominant position unless others in the group fear him. Accordingly, President Trump has suggested that the use of fear may pay big dividends in his administration. For example, elected officials may go along with certain proposals they would typically oppose out of fear of offending Trump's rabid political base. Business leaders may fear retaliation from Trump, in the form of steep import taxes, if they decide to move their operations out of the country.

For an American president beholden to the principles of dominance, fear may also prove useful in international relations. Shortly before Trump assumed the presidency, Mark Moyar, the director of the Center for Military and Diplomatic History, wrote an influential op-ed asserting that it is a good thing for foreign leaders to fear the president of the United States. It is good in the case of the nation's enemies, in that they may think twice about challenging American power, Moyar asserted. It is also good in the case of the nation's allies who "must know that the world's most powerful nation is prepared to practice tough love if they take actions inconsistent with the strength of the United States or the stability of the international system."

Trump is more than eager to provoke fear—at home and abroad. "Sometime you have to be a little wild," he wrote in *The Art of the Deal*. The sentiment channels what Richard M. Nixon once termed the "madman theory of leadership." The president should be a little unpredictable and reckless, Nixon believed, to convince America's enemies, and maybe even its friends, that he might just do something really crazy—so watch out!

While the dominance-oriented leader relies on fear and intimidation to remain on top, he is also eager to create short-term coalitions to accomplish leadership goals. Trump has always been a pragmatic dealmaker, willing to form expedient working relationships with former opponents and enemies. These deals resemble the short-term, opportunistic collaborations that chimpanzees develop, as described by de Waal. "I don't hold it against people that they opposed me," Trump wrote in *The Art of the Deal*. Former targets of his wrath have become business associates and members of his cabinet. On the one hand, Trump has shown he can forgive and forget to promote his agenda. On the other, he will quickly fire an associate, or terminate a friendship, when the relationship no longer serves his immediate interests.

Early in the Trump administration, this kind of contractual, short-term approach to leadership manifested itself in especially jarring ways in the realm of international diplomacy. Diplomats aim to build trust and loyalty among allies and long-term bonds of commitment between nation-states. Trump's first meetings and phone calls with heads of state of Mexico, Australia, the United Kingdom, and Germany were fraught with awkwardness and high levels of conflict, even though these four nations have been good friends of the United States for more than half a century. When President Trump accused America's closest ally—the United Kingdom—of colluding with former President Obama to wiretap Trump Tower, the diplomatic community was aghast.

Jeremy Shapiro, a former State Department official and research director at the European Council on Foreign Relations in London, remarked that it is very easy in the beginning to have a good and pleasant relationship with President Trump. But Trump cannot be trusted in the long run, for he seems to move from the exigencies of one contractual moment to the next. Trump focuses unswervingly on what will work in the immediate situation rather than on long-term consequences. If you make an agreement on Monday, he may no longer recall it on Wednesday, if indeed Wednesday raises new contingencies. Mr. Trump is "very pleasant in person," Shapiro told journalists in the spring of 2017. "He'll promise you the world. And 48 hours later, he'll betray you without a thought. He won't even know that he'll be betraying you."

Laboratory research conducted by social psychologists shows that dominance can sometimes work well in groups facing short deadlines or harsh circumstances. It remains a viable leadership strategy, as it has for over five million years. Dominance-oriented leaders tend to achieve solutions more quickly than do prestige-oriented leaders. When dominance-oriented leaders feel that their authority is threatened, however, they may withhold information from group members, monitor their actions closely, discourage collaborations, and actively undermine the development of talented subordinates—all with the aim of retaining their own powerful status.

Rather than praise group members, dominant leaders may take all the credit for the group's success, basking in what the psychologists Jessica Tracy and Rick Robins call *hubristic pride*. They consider hubristic pride to be the human analogue of the ostentatious bluff displays that dominant chimps express. It is as if the dominance leader, like King Kong, is beating his mighty chest. What Tracy and Robins call *authentic pride* is subtler and based more on achievement, as in the quiet pride experienced in a job well done. Many expressions of authentic pride signal the success that comes from hard work, careful study, long-term commitment, and the creative or judicious application of human ingenuity. By contrast, the preening expression of hubristic pride typically celebrates *the self*— the pride I may feel for simply being the great (brilliant, powerful) person that I happen to be. Authentic pride celebrates what I have done, whereas hubristic pride celebrates who I am.

The contrast between hubristic and authentic pride points to a key difference between how dominance and prestige leaders *think* about themselves and the groups they lead. The distinction tracks the dichotomy articulated by the social psychologist Carol Dweck between *fixed* and *growth* mindsets. A person with a fixed mindset tends to believe that people have essential and unchanging characteristics. For example, from a fixed or essentialist point of view, I may conclude that I am smart or I am dumb and that my standing on that dimension (let us call it intelligence) is not going to change. By contrast, a person with a growth mindset tends to believe that people's characteristics can change, grow and improve (or decline) as a function of experience: I flunked that test, but if I study harder next time, I will do better; I used to be a terrible golfer, but I have improved with practice.

For as long as he has been in the public eye, Donald Trump has bragged about his general intelligence. On the campaign trail, Trump repeatedly claimed that he was smarter than all of the generals in the military and, therefore, did not need their counsel. As president-elect, he claimed that he would not need to receive daily intelligence briefings once in office because he was smart enough to figure out what needed to be done on his own. He has also projected the general trait of intelligence onto others when it reflects well on him. For example, the day before he was inaugurated Trump announced, "We have by far the highest IQ of any cabinet ever assembled." He tweeted admiration for Vladimir Putin's intelligence: "Great move . . . [by V. Putin]—I always knew he was very smart!" Trump attributes his own intelligence to a "gift" from his father. In a weirdly sentimental passage from his campaign manifesto, *Crippled America*, Trump thanked his father for the gift:

> When my father passed away at the age of 93, he left his estate to his children. . . . What he left me, much more importantly, were the best "genes" that anybody could get. He was a special man and father.

Trump's repeated invocation of the broad trait of intelligence reveals a fixed mindset that, in its deep logic, celebrates dominance and impugns prestige. Trump views intelligence as a fixed entity in a person, an essence that is impervious to change. It comes from your genes, Trump asserts, as he thanks his father for the wonderful genetic gift. Intelligence is broad and multipurposed. *And so is dominance.* If you are smart, you can figure out anything, and you don't need experts to help you out. If you are supremely dominant, like Yeroen, others' expertise is moot.

Whether we are talking about chimpanzees or human beings, the dominance leader possesses a general, all-purpose asset—that is, dominance. He is the "killer" and the "king"—two of his father's favorite appellations for the young Donald, who thrilled to be described as such. The psychology of prestige, by contrast, rejects the idea that any single individual can do (or know) it all. Culture builds from one generation to the next, and the critical knowledge that pushes culture forward resides in the minds of many different experts, who garner prestige because of their expertise. Whereas dominance, then, is akin to a general essence (parallel to Trump's lay conception of inherited intelligence), expertise is domain-specific (instantiated within particular fields or domains, such as economics, chess, cooking, and poetry), something learned within a given tradition of inquiry and skill. In the prestige model, leadership itself is a kind of expertise, and good leaders call upon the expertise of others. From the standpoint of a prestige psychology, we do not expect the president of the United States to know more about military strategy than his generals, any more than we would expect him to be a better physicist than Stephen Hawking or a better novelist than Toni Morrison.

A man who does not read books and shows virtually no curiosity regarding human achievements in the arts, humanities, and sciences, Donald Trump has little appreciation for experts of any kind, writing them off as elitists. Although he has pledged to create millions of high-paying jobs for Americans, Trump has effectively rejected any advice from mainstream economists, even those who have traditionally lined up with conservative presidents. During the first two years of his presidency, he left many expertise positions vacant in the U.S. government, failing to appoint officials to fulfill vital government roles. He has completely ignored the expert advice of government and private scientists on the topic of climate change, stating that he simply does not believe what 99% of the scientific establishment says is fact. As a result, he has withdrawn American support from the Paris climate accord. He has ignored experts in history and political science by calling into question the international alliances and institutions that have worked to promote democracy and guarantee international order and peace since the end of World War II.

Consider this contrast: Barack Obama appointed a Nobel prize–winning scientist to be his first Secretary of Energy. Donald Trump appointed a former governor who did not even know that the Department of Energy had purview over nuclear weapons.

In derogating experts and ignoring the prestige that they have traditionally earned, Trump has effectively channeled a rising populist suspicion of intellectuals and other elite professionals. This dominance strategy has won him many supporters among poorly educated white Americans. Not surprisingly, it has become a source of alarm among experts themselves. Less than a week after Donald Trump was sworn in as president, the *Bulletin of Atomic Scientists* moved its famous Doomsday Clock forward by 30 seconds (2½ minutes before midnight), to indicate how close the scientists involved feel the earth is to an imminent disaster. The clock had not been this close to midnight since 1953, the year the United States and the Soviet Union conducted competing tests of the hydrogen bomb. In explaining the rationale for the move, the executive director Rachel Bronson said: "We're so concerned about the rhetoric [of Donald Trump], and the lack of respect for *expertise.*" Responding in 2017 to President Trump's refusal to appoint officials to important science jobs in the federal government, Phil Larson, a former science and technology advisor to President Obama, told journalists: "We are all sitting on the edge of our seats hoping nothing catastrophic happens in the world. But if it does, who is going to be advising him?"

***

Whenever (nearly always) and wherever (nearly everywhere) human beings organize themselves into groups, they run into the challenge of leadership. Who should lead? And how? For chimpanzees, these two questions are easily answered. The most dominant chimp will always lead. He will lead by following the ancient rules of primate dominance. But humans have a choice. Dominance or prestige? It is important to note that both of these paradigms are deeply ingrained in human nature. Whereas the first traces back millions of years to our primate heritage, the latter reflects our evolution as a hunting-and-gathering species, going back at least one million years. As members of *Homo sapiens*, we have evolved to favor both of them, leaving us conflicted at our social core. The choice between dominance and prestige was especially stark in the 2016 American presidential election. Stripped to the dynamics of adolescent stereotypes, it was as if the school bully (dominance) ran against the smartest girl in the class (prestige). And this time, he won.

Research suggests that, when it comes to leadership in the work place, more people prefer the prestige model to the dominance model. This finding is especially true among women. It is more pleasant to work under a prestige leader who values expertise and seeks your admiration than under a dominant leader who poses a constant threat. Dominance, nonetheless, consistently wins respect in contexts that seem to call out for strength, courage, and firmness—in professional football and some other sports, for example, as well as in the military, certain corporate milieus, and organized crime. The Mafia runs by dominance.

When it comes to national governments, different countries have different norms regarding who should lead and how. Dominance seems to have been the favored strategy in Russia since the time of the czars. The European Union, by contrast, values the prestige model. The fact that American citizens elected both Barack Obama and Donald Trump as presidents suggests that either prestige or dominance can be a winning formula in the United States. Most Americans would probably say that the ideal leader should be able to combine both prestige and dominance in an effective way, for there would seem to be merits in both.

The psychology of dominance regularly competes with the psychology of prestige—in human groups and in human minds. Let me end this chapter by pitting the two against each other one last time in a side-by-side comparison, with special attention paid to the strange case of Donald J. Trump. Five points of comparison deserve our attention.

Point #1: Dominance is vertical; prestige is horizontal

The dominance paradigm for leadership works best within a strictly vertical hierarchy, where there is a grand pecking order, running from top dog to the bottom dwellers. Kiss up, and kick down. By contrast, the prestige model works best within a more horizontal context, where power is distributed across different agents and institutions, and there are checks and balances. Of course, some hierarchy is always needed, but the prestige model seeks to flatten things out somewhat, as was (and continues to be) the status arrangement in human hunting-and-gathering groups, as well as in certain modern bureaucracies.

Dominance is the primal psychology that undergirds modern authoritarian states, paving the way for the authoritarian dynamic that connects the glorious leader to those under his rule. By contrast, prestige psychology would seem to provide the psychological infrastructure that makes liberal democracy possible. Under the aegis of dominance, loyalty to the leader is greatly prized in the authoritarian dynamic. Indeed, the leader becomes the personification of the in-group, and those who question the norms of the in-group are strongly sanctioned, or ostracized. Out-groups are never trusted and are often vilified.

Within the dominance framework, the idea of hierarchy may transcend the group structure itself to apply to the imagined pecking order of rival groups. The glorious leader may convince members of the in-group that they are superior to all other groups. Donald Trump is psychologically well equipped to carry out this kind of program. With his belief in his own inherent superiority and that of people like him, Trump expresses a cluster of personal values and beliefs that social psychologists call *social dominance orientation* (SDO). Individuals with high scores on SDO tend to believe that their group (e.g., race, ethnicity, nation, religion) is innately better than all other groups and will, therefore, prevail in the end.

People who score high on measures of SDO tend to take an especially hard-edged approach to intergroup competition. They readily justify aggressive actions against other groups, up to and including physical attacks and warfare. They tend to see the world as a zero-sum jungle, group against group in a brutal and endless struggle. The strongest will survive. High scores on SDO are also regularly associated with low scores on empathy, kindness, modesty, and other aspects of the broad trait of agreeableness, and with high scores on extraversion. Low agreeableness and high extraversion constitute Trump's signature trait profile as a social actor. In the spirit of SDO, Trump aims to convince Americans—or to remind them again—that they are the superior people on the planet. We will make America great again, Trump promises. We will win, and others will lose. We are winners. They are losers.

Point #2: Dominance uses aggression to induce fear; prestige uses expertise to induce admiration

One of Donald Trump's biggest fans is Newt Gingrich, the former congressman and Speaker of the House, from Georgia. Gingrich sees Trump as a dominant force, dynamic and strong, brimming with "total energy" as he vanquishes all foes standing in his way. "Donald Trump is the grizzly bear in [the movie] *The Revenant*," Gingrich proclaimed during a 2016 speech on "The Principles of Trumpism." "If you get his attention, he will awake. . . . He will walk over, bite your face off, and sit on you."

With due respect to Gingrich, the better analogy from the world of mammals is Yeroen. When the alpha chimp stirs up mayhem in the charging display, you do not look him in the eye. But you never lose sight of him. You keep him in your peripheral vision. Fearing for your status in the group, if not your life, you continue to monitor the alpha chimp, but out of the sides of your eyes, and with your ears and nose and other less obtrusive senses. You must never forget where he is and what he is doing, for he is a constant threat. And he will never let you forget that he should be a dominant presence in your attention. He will continue to stir up chaos—in the news every day, CNN and Fox, by charging or tweeting, by continuing to engage in the most outlandish and attention-getting antics—so that you cannot help but take note. There is no way to blot him out. He is always in your consciousness, if not in your line of vision. Nonetheless, if you keep your attention on what he does and how he looks without directly challenging his hegemony, and if you offer the appropriate displays of deference, you may be okay. You may be able to go about your daily business. You may be able to keep your place in the hierarchy, more-or-less secure within a more-or-less stable, but tense, group context. This is what it is like to live in a chimpanzee colony and in certain authoritarian states.

In the prestige paradigm, by contrast, leaders aim to instill admiration in others by demonstrating their skill and efficacy. They like to show off, but not through brute force. Instead, they show off their expertise. They want you to admire them for what they have accomplished in their lives. They want to be a role model for you. They want you to look them in the eye and say, "I want to be like you when I grow up." Or, "I wish I were like you." Or, "In the perfect world, I would be like you." They do *not* want to be feared. They want to be liked and respected. They would like you to say, "I want to be your friend." They want to be your friend, too. They want to empower you, to make you feel better about yourself, to give you a stake in the group's ongoing regime of authority and esteem.

Going back as far as his high school days at the New York Military Academy, Donald Trump has consistently rejected the logic of prestige psychology, in favor of dominance. To the extent he wants to be liked, Donald Trump wants you to like him the way your pet likes you. His many acquaintances and wannabe friends are always subordinate to him, dependent on his largesse. They orbit around him, like planets around a star. If they get too close, they will burn up. If they stare straight into his brilliant countenance, they will be blinded. The author of an extensive biography of Trump, Michael D'Antonio insists that Donald Trump has no true friends in the world, even though people constantly surround him. The indictment seems harsh. Trump does certainly confide in many people, including the women who have served as his wives and mistresses. But these interactions rarely seem to be reciprocal. In the highest forms of intimacy between friends, people open up to each other and show mutual regard and concern. Friends are nearly as interested in each other as they are in themselves. With that as the criterion for true friendship, D'Antonio may be right.

Speaking of friendship, what do friends do when they get together? One of the things they often do, in my experience at least, is *laugh*. Friends enjoy being with each other. They have fun together. One of the manifestations of enjoyment and fun is laughter.

I ask you: Have you ever seen Donald Trump laugh? The answer is *no*. Scour your memory. Think back on all of the times you recall watching Donald Trump on television. Do a Google search. I conducted just such a search back in 2016. In his book, *A Higher Loyalty*, the former head of the Federal Bureau of Investigation, James Comey, claimed he also conducted a search. Both Comey and I found the same result—that is, almost nothing. Donald Trump will smile. He can be very funny. He can make others laugh. But there is virtually no evidence to be found in the public sphere showing Trump laughing. Comey and I did find one example, though. At a campaign rally in New Hampshire in early 2016, Trump heard what he thought was a dog barking in the distance. He asked the crowd if that was a dog. Somebody yelled out, "It's Hillary!" Trump exploded in laughter. It was a strange thing to see.

Why does Donald Trump never laugh? Perhaps because laughter signals a temporary suspension of dominance. To laugh is to lose control for a second, to let your guard down, to admit, even for just a moment, that you are not the funniest and most dominant person in the room. If you laugh at somebody else's joke, you are acknowledging the momentary dominance of the person telling the joke. You are stepping away from the alpha position. Trump virtually never does that. Moreover, pay attention to the one instance when he *did* laugh. What does it say? The man who has often used the word "dog" to describe women he does not like found it hilarious when a crowd member compared Hillary Clinton to a dog. The "joke" is juvenile, misogynist, and cruel. And, it is, well, *not* very funny! There are so many really funny jokes in the world. It is so strange to pick that one as the funniest.

Point #3: Dominance leaders take decisive action under conditions of threat; prestige leaders take deliberative action under conditions of hope

Twice a year, the Kellogg School of Management at Northwestern University holds a weeklong workshop on leadership. Organized by Robert S. Hughes, a former military officer and an expert on leadership in the workplace, the program enrolls prospective leaders in business, academia, government, and other domains. A team of professors teaches the individual courses that make up the program. My role is to lead one 3-hour seminar at the beginning of the week on the psychology of leadership. I begin the class by making the distinction between dominance and prestige leadership. But nearly all of the discussion that follows is framed within the prestige paradigm. The same is true, I think, for the other courses. The overall aims of the program at Kellogg are (i) to acquaint prospective leaders with their own strengths and expertise, while also identifying weaknesses, and (ii) to build a leadership identity that will promote success in the workplace. The overall philosophy views leadership as collaborative, deliberative, and oriented toward growth.

Kellogg's program mirrors, I suspect, the academic ethos of many top business schools in the United States today. In the for-profit sphere, it is generally assumed, capitalism flourishes in an atmosphere of hope and potential fulfillment. Businesses grow, wealth increases, and people work together to maximize profits, which ideally enhances the American pursuit of happiness. In the not-for-profit sphere, organizations work to improve the lives of people or to solve important social problems, under the hopeful assumption that such work is meaningful and important. Whether we are talking about multinational corporations or a local food pantry, people work in teams, optimistically striving to make a positive difference—smiles all around and earnestness. Ideally, managers and leaders make thoughtful decisions based on reason and evidence. They are willing to take risks in a world that rewards vision and expertise. They are hopeful about the risks they take.

The dominance-oriented leader does not feel comfortable in the world I just described. He would hate the seminar I teach. Too much navel gazing, he would say. Too much deliberation and teamwork. It is all maddeningly inefficient, from the standpoint of the dominance leader. Sort of like democracy. Moreover, the entire regime is based on a misunderstanding of the world, he would say. The world rarely gives us conditions of hope and happy growth. Instead, the world is a menacing place. Chaos reigns. Under conditions of threat, dominance leaders are the only leaders who will win the day. When things are spinning out of control, what good does it do you to articulate a leadership identity? Good luck with all that hopey/changey stuff you learn in those seminars. None of it will help you win the war. The namby-pamby workshop at Kellogg is for losers and sissies.

Research documents a link between the perception of threat and an affinity for dominance. In a recent study, two social scientists surveyed 140,000 participants living in 69 different countries and spanning the past two decades. They found that "under a situational threat of economic uncertainty (as exemplified by the poverty rate, the housing vacancy rate, and the unemployment rate) people escalate their support for dominant leaders." In other words, when people begin to lose hope in their economic prospects, they look to dominant political leaders for help. The researchers identified the "psychological sense of a lack of personal control" to be the key variable behind the relationship. As economic prospects decline, people begin to feel that they are losing control of their lives, which in turn motivates them to favor strong leaders who display dominance over prestige. What they want is decisive action. In an emergency, there is no time for the cautious deliberation of experts, no time for group projects and happy collaborations. Instead, people who feel threatened look for deliverance in a strong leader who will vanquish the foes, even if it is not clear who the foes really are, or how real the perceived threats may indeed be.

Point #4: Dominance promotes short-term contractual relationships; prestige promotes long-term collaborations based on trust

Yeroen did well to stay in power for nearly as long as President Gerald Ford did, in 1974–1976. When Ford assumed the office of president after the resignation of Richard Nixon, Article II of the U.S. Constitution guaranteed that he would ride out the rest of Nixon's term, barring impeachment or death. The chimpanzee colony at Burgers Zoo provided no such guarantee for Yeroen. Instead, the alpha chimp has to prove his dominance day after day, over and over. To make a very difficult challenge somewhat easier, he will develop alliances with other chimps, trading favors and establishing implicit agreements that are negotiated through grunts and body language, rather than through the language of lawyers and diplomats. But these alliances are always short-term. They are temporary contracts, provisional deals that are readily broken when circumstances change. Monday's deal may give way by Wednesday.

Contractual deals, short-term and utterly pragmatic, are the lingua franca for dominance leadership in *Homo sapiens*. The strongman stays strong by negotiating favorable agreements with allies and adversaries. He employs leverage to hammer out agreements that maximally benefit him while minimizing his cost. As Donald Trump instructed in *The Art of the Deal*, the dominance leader will always try to negotiate from a position of overwhelming strength and superiority. He will drive the hardest possible bargain, maximizing the advantages he enjoys from his position on top. He may not be on top for long, however. He knows that the world is chaotic and that inimical forces lie in wait everywhere. He senses that rivals would probably not hesitate for a second before seeking to upend his reign, should the opportunity arise. So, he focuses on the short-term battle. Eat, drink, and win today, for tomorrow . . .

By contrast, prestige leadership aims to develop long-term agreements based on trust and social norms. Prestige leaders aim to work within broad frameworks of law and convention. They are reluctant to tear up long-term agreements, like treaties and international accords, to obtain short-term gains. Their response to pending danger and unpredictability in the world is to establish systems that reduce uncertainty in the long run. If they make a deal on Monday, they honor the deal on Wednesday. Not do so would undermine trust. And without trust, social life devolves into a Hobbesian world of all against all, the kind of world that undermines prestige and cries out for dominance.

Whether we are talking about real estate deals, reality television, branding opportunities, presidential policy, or his three marriages, Donald Trump has always been in it for *the short-run*. He is a sprinter rather than a marathon runner. He goes flat out every day. He strives to win today's battle, without too much thought given to what happened yesterday or what may happen tomorrow. He is all tactics, no strategy. President Trump, therefore, is not psychologically capable of committing to long-term aims that would compromise short-term gains. He might be the last head of state on the planet to agree to a long-term strategy requiring trust and cooperation with rival countries, even one to save the planet from extinction. Jeremy Shapiro had it right when he said that Trump "will promise you the world" and then "48 hours later he'll betray you without a thought." For the dominance leader who lives to win the moment, an awful lot can change in the span of 48 hours.

Point #5: Dominance leaders project strength; prestige leaders project stories

Leaders create strong bonds with those whom they lead. For dominance leaders, the bond is cemented by power. Their followers, and those who might defy them but must follow, at least for the time being, remain tied to the leaders by the perception of power. The dominance leader inspires fear and awe. People respect him because he projects strength. As a presidential candidate, Donald Trump once admitted that many of his opponents "are very fine people." "But they are weak," he immediately added. In the psychology of dominance, the worst thing you can say about a potential leader is that he or she is weak. Within the dominance paradigm, then, a leader holds legitimacy only to the extent that the leader can project strength. As Machiavelli counseled centuries ago, the dominance leader does not have to be strong *in reality*. But he must be *perceived* to be strong. Once that perception fades, the emperor truly has lost his clothes.

The prestige leader relies on admiration, grounded in the perception of expertise. People value the expertise that they attribute to the prestige leader, and they perceive the prestige leader as somebody worthy of emulation. They look to the prestige leader for inspiration. They search the prestige leader's life and personality for qualities to be admired. They may even seek to imitate those qualities. They want to know everything they can know about the prestige leader. What is the prestige leader really like? How did the prestige leader come to be who he or she is? How might I model my life after that of the prestige leader? How might my children model their lives in the same way?

In turn, prestige leaders are often aware of how others perceive them. As such, they seek to manage those perceptions. They selectively disclose features of themselves that they hope will be admired. They try to burnish their most admirable traits. They share anecdotes about their lives. In contemporary politics and in other realms where prestige leaders hold sway, they often aim to project inspiring *narratives* about their own lives. John F. Kennedy wrote a book about his experiences in World War II. Ronald Reagan told powerful stories about growing up with an alcoholic father and overcoming other daunting challenges he faced early on. George W. Bush narrated his own developmental journey from favored son to drunken derelict to born-again man of God. Barack Obama, born to a white mother and black father, spoke and wrote eloquently about his struggles to find an authentic American identity. The respective millions who admired Kennedy, Reagan, Bush, and Obama knew those stories, or knew about them. In many instances, they found inspiration in those stories. They were able to relate those life stories to their own. They might even see parallels between those admired stories and their own understanding of the story of America.

It should be noted that there is nothing to keep a dominance-oriented leader from projecting a life story, too. In our media-saturated age, dominance leaders who are media savvy may reinforce their bonds with followers by sharing interesting details of their own lives. But within the dominance paradigm, the personal narrative is still secondary. Displaying strength remains paramount.

In the case of Donald Trump, it is pure dominance from beginning to end. He does not even dabble in the prestige game, not for a second. When it comes to a life story, he has almost nothing to offer—no narrative in his head to help him make sense of his own life in the long run, and no story that he can project to help his followers (and anybody else, for that matter) to make narrative sense of him. Again and again in this book, I have returned to the idea that Trump is the episodic man. Moment by moment, deal by deal, battle by battle, day by day—he confronts each episode on its own terms, with the short-term always in mind, striving to win each episode, one by one. Nothing adds up. There is no long-term story to tell, no narrative arc to his life or to his presidency. It is just a series of instances, random and chaotic. For the pure dominance leader, the more chaotic, the better. He can continue to display his prowess in every contentious moment. As danger seems to mount and chaos runs wild, he can continue to promise that he will prevail against the evil foes. He will win because he is the strongest. We will win because he is the strongest.

When you have always been the strongest, in your own mind; when you have always been the winner and never ever lost; when you have always had the largest brain in the world; when you are the world's most stable genius, and have always been; when you have all the right stuff to prevail at all times and in all places as the supremely dominant force—when you have all of that and have always had all of that, then there is no story to tell. There is no adversity to overcome. There is no trouble to complicate the plot. There is no narrative build-up and release. There is no uncertainty to keep the reader in suspense.

The pure dominance leader, with no human story to project to his human followers, sees himself to be the embodiment of an unchanging essence. He does not grow and change. He just is. You cannot tell a story about something that simply "is." Donald Trump is power personified, moment to moment. In that sense, he is very much like Yeroen and all the other alphas who have ever lorded it over chimpanzee colonies for the past five million years. When it comes to leadership, he is much more like Yeroen than he is like any other American president.

Redemption

My analysis of the strange case is coming to its conclusion. We began with Dr. Jekyll and Mr. Hyde. We ended with Yeroen, the alpha chimp. From beginning to end, my animating thesis has been that Donald Trump does not know himself in terms of narrative beginnings and endings. He has no story in his mind about who he really is and how he came to be. Donald Trump is instead *the episodic man.* He immerses himself in each life episode. He lives to win each episode.

In this final chapter, I will recap the main argument as it has developed over the course of the book, and then I will consider one broad implication of my thesis for our nation as a whole. Leaders project stories for the people they lead, defining their group's identity and mission. We expect the leader of a nation to tell a story that showcases the nation's values while charting where the nation has been and where it is going. In the United States, we have traditionally expected our leaders to project a *redemptive story* for America, a story about overcoming suffering and adversity and fulfilling an exalted destiny. But Trump refuses to do this. His refusal is psychologically rooted in the fact that he has never composed a redemptive story for his own life. Indeed, he has never formulated a personal life story of any kind—or, at most, it is a severely depleted story, barely a story at all. What does Trump's stark departure from the norms of personal and national sense-making mean for how we Americans now think about ourselves and about our nation?

Let me review my central argument through the lens of personality development. Over the human life course, personality develops along three lines.

The first line of personality development begins at birth or shortly thereafter, when human infants start to display consistent differences in temperament. Every parent who has had more than one child knows that different babies start off in very different ways. Characteristic variations in attention, emotion, and social behavior reveal that infants are born with markedly different styles of performance. As their genetic endowments and the environments they experience continue to shape their performances over time, infants grow up to become unique *social actors.* Upon reaching adulthood, they exhibit differences from each other on the Big Five traits of extraversion, neuroticism, openness, conscientiousness, and agreeableness. In that human beings evolved to live in groups, a

The Strange Case of Donald J. Trump. Dan P. McAdams, Oxford University Press (2020). © Oxford University Press.
DOI: 10.1093/oso/9780197507445.001.0001

person's characteristic way of being a social actor—the manner in which a particular person performs social roles and displays emotion to others—becomes the most recognizable feature of personality.

The second line of personality development begins in the preschool years. Around age 4, children develop a simple theory of the human mind. They come to understand that people, themselves included, have desires and beliefs in their minds, which motivate goal-directed behavior. As *motivated agents*, children seek to accomplish valued goals, developing plans to guide their behavior and shape the decisions they make. In adulthood, a person's motivational agenda includes life goals, long-term plans and projects, religious and political values, ethical beliefs, ideologies, and an elaborate cognitive infrastructure designed to support a person's program for achieving desired ends. The motivational agenda continues to develop over time, as does the person's characteristic profile of dispositional traits. Within the same person, then, the motivated agent develops alongside the social actor.

For most people, adolescence introduces a third line of personality development. To the team of social actor and motivated agent we add the *autobiographical author*. Beginning in adolescence or young adulthood, human beings construct stories to make sense of the past, present, and anticipated future. They begin to imagine their lives as extended narratives in time. They create in their minds *narrative identities* (life stories) to integrate the reconstructed past with the anticipated future. Each person's narrative identity explains, in story terms, how that person came to be the person he or she is becoming. The story is a myth, because human beings do not really know how they came to be or where their lives are going. The myth oversimplifies life, too, leaving out many details to reveal a general through-line. Nonetheless, a person's internalized narrative of the self provides life with meaning and purpose. Moreover, narrative identities situate a life in a moral universe. By framing the social actor's traits and the motivated agent's goals and values into a broad story for life, the autobiographical author confers a distinctive moral meaning upon a life. In sum, our traits determine how we typically act and feel; our motivational agendas specify what we want in life and how we plan to get it; our life stories convey who we believe we truly are.

Actor, agent, author—together, they comprise the psychological trinity of human personhood. We begin life as actors only; by middle childhood, we are actors and agents together; by adolescence or young adulthood, we live life fully and complexly as social actors and motivated agents and autobiographical authors—performing, striving, and making sense. As adults, we display our developing traits in a range of social roles, we strive to accomplish our most cherished goals and values, and we endeavor to make moral sense of it all through narratives. Or at least most of us do.

But not Donald Trump. The central thesis of this book is that Donald Trump never embraced the third figure in the psychological trinity of personhood. He never became the author. He never created a story for his life. Instead, Donald Trump, even as president, moves through life as the episodic man, displaying traits and pursuing goals but never understanding why he is doing what he does—except to tell himself, "I must win." He is a dynamic actor on the world stage. He is a powerful agent who strives to win and win and win. But when it comes to finding a broader and deeper meaning to life, Donald Trump doesn't have a narrative clue. The man who can spin stories about Mexican rapists and the evil media for his adoring audiences has no integrative story to tell for his own life. He can act, and he can strive. But he cannot narrate, because he does not go back in time or forward; he does not make retrospective sense of the past or prospective sense of the future. He is psychologically incapable of escaping the moment. He simply *is*, in the here and now, like Hyde without his Jekyll. There will always be something missing in the strange case of Donald Trump. It is the missing story.

In this book's first chapter, "Story," I describe how Donald Trump has stead-fastly and forever resisted the urge to make narrative sense of his own life. He has always had at his disposal a handful of anecdotes that he repeats again and again, like his punching out his second-grade music teacher or his walking with his father through tough New York neighborhoods to collect overdue rents. But these recollected episodes are never collected together in his mind to create a meaningful narrative arc. They are little stories, but they do not add up to a big story. By young adulthood, most people use autobiographical reasoning to draw conclusions about their lives. They analyze sequences of episodes in their remembered past and make narrative sense of them. Donald Trump does not do this.

To the frustration and occasional amazement of biographers and many others who have sought to understand Trump over the years, he is not introspective, ret-rospective, or prospective. He does not go deep into his mind; he does not travel back to the past; he does not project far into the future. He is always on the sur-face, always right now. *In his own mind*, he is more like a persona than a person, more like a primal force or superhero, rather than a fully realized human being. Even at the Republican National Convention in the summer of 2016, when the presidential nominee was expected to appeal to the American public by telling his own story, Trump refused to humanize himself. He passed up the golden op-portunity to convey who he is, who he was, and how he came to be.

Donald Trump is never able, or willing, to step back from the moment, be-cause every moment comes to him as a battle to be fought and won. Almost 40 years ago, he set forth his philosophy of life: "Man is the most vicious of all animals, and life is a series of battles ending in victory or defeat." Trump is always fighting, in the moment. The unexpected result of this is that Donald Trump comes across as extraordinarily *authentic* in the eyes of many people who watch the fighting. There is something extremely real and primal about him. And yet as a consummate social actor, he is always playing a role, as if he were on the set for *The Apprentice*. For Trump, there is no difference between acting on reality TV and acting in reality. Whereas most of us, as social actors, see a difference between being fake and being real, Trump sees no difference in his own life. He is always Donald Trump playing Donald Trump. He is a *fake*. Right? But wait! Isn't there a real Donald Trump behind it all? No! He is only what you see. The strangeness of it all is that he is a truly authentic fake, as only a man without a story can be.

For the author of *The Art of the Deal*, making a deal is the same thing as fighting a battle. For Trump, deal-making is not so much about the arts of nego-tiation and compromise. It is instead about wielding power in the ever-present moment, without considering long-term consequences. In the chapter "Deal," I describe five fundamental principles of Trumpian deal making, applicable to real estate deals and to dealing with the leader of North Korea, as President Trump did in the summer of 2018. You must (i) fill a need; (ii) bend the rules; (iii) put on a show; (iv) exert maximal pressure; and (v) always win. The last one is the most important. You must frame every deal, and every battle, as a victory, no matter what really happened. And then, you must move on, to the next deal, the next battle, the next moment in your life. There is no long-term narrative arc to the deal, in Trump's mind. It is here today and gone tomorrow—like each self-contained scene in his episodic life.

Human beings evolved to live in complex social groups, striving to get along and get ahead. As social actors, we develop social reputations in our groups. These reputations come from the repeated observation of our emotional displays and our behavior. Other group members observe us; we observe ourselves; we observe others observing us; we hear how others talk about us; we talk about ourselves to others. Through all the back and forth, from one performance to the next, our social reputations gradually take form, as dispositional attributions of personality traits. From the perspective of the social actor, two broad traits capture Trump's inimitable style: sky-high *extraversion* and rock-bottom *agreeableness*.

In the chapter "Reward," I trace Donald Trump's extraordinary extraversion back to his earliest years. As far back as preschool, Donald Trump was viewed by others to be highly enthusiastic, energetic, gregarious, dominant, and reward-seeking. Extraversion is fundamentally about the vigorous pursuit of social re-ward, more about the pursuit than the actual enjoyment of attaining the reward itself. It is about the chase, and Donald Trump has always loved the chase. Highly extraverted people draw upon the positive emotions of excitement and joy to fuel their energetic forays into the world. They may also draw upon the emotional resource of anger, as Trump masterfully does. Donald Trump's highly extraverted temperament is arguably his greatest psychological asset. It gives him the charisma that many of his supporters find so appealing. It enables him to inject tremendous social energy into each moment, moment by moment, inspiring the millions who find thrilling his dominance and his force.

In the chapter "Venom," I consider Trump's remarkably *low* standing on what is probably the most valued personality trait in the world. Agreeableness is more than being nice, although being nice is at the heart of it. It is also about humility, sincerity, caring for other people, expressing empathy, cooperating with others, following social norms, and expressing a range of admirable dispositions distilled from the milk of human kindness. As a social actor, Trump is the antithesis of agreeableness—even his friends and family members concede this indisputable reputational fact.

Why is Donald Trump so mean? Where does the venom come from? There are a number of plausible developmental explanations, I believe. For one, he was likely born with a highly aggressive temperament and with deficits in effortful control. His aggressive tendencies, which he has never been able to suppress for long, shaped the environments that, in turn, shaped him, revealing a kind of unwitting conspiracy between nature and nurture. His father groomed him to be a "killer" and a "king" early on. He came to identify strongly with tough guys, like the gangster-lawyer Roy Cohn, and to reject any association with weaklings, like his gentle but tragically flawed older brother, Freddy. And Donald Trump never transported himself away from the bellicose world he created through reading stories or other exercises in imagination. Research shows that reading good fiction exposes us to the perspectives of others while nurturing empathy and psychological understanding. Stories get us out of the here-and-now moment. They provide a welcomed escape route from the ugliness of daily life, enabling us to return to our respective, real-world lives enriched and refreshed. Trump has never been able to escape the angry moment, or else he has never wanted to. In the Hobbesian world Trump has created in his mind, and projected onto America, there is no time for gentleness and kindness, no time for reading stories or enjoying the diversions of art and literature. No time to be fully human.

People who score extremely low on measures of agreeableness also tend to be seen by others as lacking in honesty and trustworthiness. What Donald Trump famously characterized as "truthful hyperbole" in *The Art of the Deal* is the least of it. Most presidents exaggerate to make themselves look good, and most have surely been guilty of concealing the truth at one time or another. But Donald Trump has set new standards for making unsubstantiated claims, spreading false stories, and concocting outrageous lies that are so blatantly false that almost nobody truly believes them. He is especially prone to making false claims that are designed to hurt other people.

Why does he do this? In the chapter "Truth," I argue that part of the reason behind Trump's incessant descent into untruth stems from his being the episodic man, for whom truth equates at the moment to whatever he might say to win the moment, to prevail in the episode at hand. Mr. Trump has always aimed to surround himself with people who share his disregard for the truth and are willing to parrot him, "even if it's a lie, even if they know it's a lie, and even if he said the opposite the day before," said Gwenda Blair, a Trump biographer, in late 2018. They must be "loyal to what he is saying *right now*," she said, or he sees them as "a traitor."

Why do Trump's supporters put up with his lies? Even when they concede that a Trump statement is inaccurate or even a bald-faced lie, many Americans nonetheless believe that what he says conveys a deeper truth, or else could be true. Others revel in his lying because they believe it helps him win, and they believe he is fighting to win for them. Finally, many Americans hold Trump to a different standard of truthfulness than they apply to nearly anybody else. He is a different kind of being, they believe. They project onto him superhuman powers and inclinations, even as they know that he is a flesh-and-blood man. The rules of conventional morality do not always apply to those men and women who are more like gods and mythic forces than they are like regular humans. These kinds of beings are qualitatively different from the rest of us, more than human, but less than human, too. To a certain extent, Trump shares this view with his fans. Like them, he truly believes that he is fundamentally different from the rest of humankind.

Still, even the most dishonest and disagreeable social actors are, in principle, capable of human love. This is because all human beings experience a more-or-less loving attachment bond with their primary caregivers in the first couple years of life. The chapter, "Love," is something of an interlude, poised between our consideration of Trump as a social actor and Trump as a motivated agent, wherein I examine his relationships with wives and lovers. Ivana, Marla, and Melania each personified a different kind of love object for Donald Trump, with Melania coming closest to re-enacting the emotional dynamic that Trump may have experienced with his own mother, Mary MacLeod Trump. Yet, Trump's relationship with his mother is mainly shrouded in mystery, and the shroud extends to his wives, as well, by virtue of the nondisclosure agreements he has forced them to sign. As of this writing, at least 22 women have publicly accused Donald Trump of sexual harassment or worse. Whatever the status of those claims, it is clear that Trump has always objectified women, viewing them as things rather than people, the value of which derives from appearance and utility. Interestingly, he applies the same kind of dehumanizing objectification *to himself*. He is himself his most desired love object—loved in the manner one loves a *thing* rather than in the manner one typically loves a person. Donald Trump loves himself the way I love my new car.

The topic of self-love is central to the chapter "Me," which plumbs the depths of human narcissism. In the ancient Greek story, the young boy Narcissus falls so hopelessly in love with the beautiful image of himself reflected in a pool that he ultimately melts away and dies. As a motivated agent, Trump is a narcissist for the ages. Beneath his dispositional traits of high extraversion and low agreeableness lies the realm of Trumpian desire, which is all about the desire to love himself as the beautiful and omnipotent object he has always been. Trump's motivational agenda—the complex organization of goals, values, and supporting beliefs that organize his life strivings—is devoted to defending and promoting the self, and nothing else.

While a full developmental explanation for Trump's overmastering narcissism may never be known, we can nonetheless follow Trump's 70-year career in narcissism. It begins with his parents repeatedly telling him he is the favored son even if they do not fully express the same message on an emotional level. It runs through the development of a me-focused agenda in grade school, strongly reinforced in his teenage years at the New York Military Academy. Through his adult years, Trump stocks his mind with glorious images of himself. Again and again, he pulls an image up to gaze upon it, like Narcissus gazing into the pool. Three of Trump's favorite images are set as action tableaus, each tagged to a period in his adult life. The first portrays the 30-something lady's man, swashbuckling and impossibly rich, strolling down a Manhattan street with a beautiful woman on each arm. The second is the midlife plutocrat sitting majestically on the set of *The Apprentice* as he decisively utters those famous words, "You're fired!" The third reflects his present situation. It is what has now become an iconic tableau of the awe-inspiring presidential candidate—and now the president himself—standing triumphantly in front of a frenzied crowd at a small-town political rally. We will build a great wall, he tells the audience. We will make America great again.

Pursuing a motivational agenda of pure narcissism is hard work. Most people would grow tired of it. But for the episodic man frozen in each moment, moment by moment, the beautiful self-image, the gorgeous and inspiring tableau, the day-in and day-out magnification of the self on television screens around the world—all of this and more, always about me and me and me, well, it never ever gets old. Narcissism is refreshed with each click of the moment. And if a moment should go by without the reflection of a glorious me, an aching longing for the *me* sets in, like the overpowering need an addict feels without the fix. It is as if Trump is addicted to *me*.

Trump's obsession with himself—his devotion to *me* and only *me*—strikes many people as pathological. Psychiatrists and other mental health professionals

238 THE STRANGE CASE OF DONALD J. TRUMP

have often invoked the language of mental illness to depict Trump's psychological state. He suffers from a *narcissistic personality disorder*, many have said. He is a *psychopath*, too. He is dangerously unstable and *mentally unfit* to hold office. In the chapter "Goldwater," a short and technical interlude, I cast some doubt upon the utility of these claims. The so-called Goldwater Rule prohibits psychiatrists from diagnosing psychiatric illnesses in public officials. The rule is controversial, and I admit to my own ambivalence about it. Nonetheless, I do not find the medical language of diagnosis and illness to be especially useful for understanding the strange case of Donald Trump. Diagnostic labels do not explain much, in my view. Is he crazy? Maybe. But he is much stranger than that.

Like Andrew Jackson in the 1820s and 1830s, Donald Trump ran as a populist presidential candidate in 2016, railing against the elites. As with Jackson, Trump's opponents feared that the authoritarian dynamic created between the glorious leader and his devoted followers might undermine the institutions of good government. As a motivational agenda, authoritarianism pits the good *us* against the evil *them*. The authoritarian leader protects and glorifies the in-group, derogates threatening out-groups, and promulgates a doctrine that aims to purify the in-group of all dissent. Authoritarianism is, in a sense, a feature of Trump's own value system, as a motivated agent. But more than that, authoritarianism applies to Trump's relationship with the American people, especially those who look to him for salvation. In other words, authoritarianism happens in the space between the leader of a group and his followers.

In the chapter "Us," I examine Trump's authoritarian dynamic from many different perspectives, including race relations and the emergence of the alt-right, the changing demographics of the United States, and Trump's appeal to evangelical Christians. For Trump and his most loyal supporters, the *us* includes those white Americans, trending male and older and less educated, who feel dispossessed and disenfranchised in 21st-century America. The *them* includes societal elites of various kinds, such as Washington insiders, the mainstream media, the scientific establishment, the educational establishment, the legal establishment, Hollywood, Silicon Valley, Democrats, people of color, and nearly any other group or constituency that questions Mr. Trump's hegemony. Importantly, *them* also includes Muslims and other groups who are perceived to threaten America's Christian heritage. And, most important, the *them* is immigrants. Trump imagines hordes of immigrants invading America at the southern border. They are criminals, rapists, drug dealers, and terrorists. From late 2018 to early 2019, Trump shut down the federal government for 35 days because Congress refused to authorize funding to begin construction of a wall on the Mexican border. The president desperately wants to make good on the campaign promise that, more than any other, got him elected—to build the great wall that will protect *us* from *them*.

Authoritarianism is a modern phenomenon, but its psychological roots may be traced back millions of years. Human beings and our chimpanzee cousins descended from a common evolutionary ancestor between five and seven million years ago. Both lines took with them an affinity for social dominance. The evolutionary line that led to present-day humans eventually developed a second, rival sensibility for group status—an affinity for prestige, through which individuals garner status by displaying cultural expertise. In the chapter "Primate," I contrast leadership by dominance (think: alpha chimps) with leadership by prestige (think: President Obama). More than any president in American history, Donald Trump displays leadership by dominance, through distinctively human manifestations of brute force, bluffing, and intimidation.

Social-psychological research on leadership shows that people prefer to work under conditions that resemble prestige leadership, but dominance leadership still often prevails. Dominance relies on fear; prestige relies on admiration. Dominance leaders typically take decisive action under conditions of threat; prestige leaders typically take deliberative action under conditions of hope. Dominance leaders project strength; prestige leaders project a *story*. In *Leading Minds: An Anatomy of Leadership*, the eminent developmental psychologist Howard Gardner wrote: "The artful creation and articulation of stories constitutes a fundamental part of the leadership vocation." Prestige leaders express stories in the way they live their lives, and they aim to evoke stories in the lives of those they lead. Rather than scare their subordinates into compliance, prestige leaders rally people around shared narratives that define the mission of their respective organization, group, or nation.

***

Americans love stories of *redemption*—and so do our leaders. In a redemptive story, characters endure suffering early on but they are eventually delivered from their pain to a better status or state. The plot may move from sin to salvation, for example, or from slavery to freedom, sickness to health, shame to celebration, or rags to riches. The story's protagonist strives to overcome adversity. While the story does not need to end with everybody's living happily ever after, there still must be a movement from negativity toward fulfillment, growth, or gratification. Redemption is the narrative arc for many of our favorite Hollywood movies. It is the stuff of Sunday sermons, commencement speeches, self-help books, and the applicant essays typically preferred by college admissions committees. It is captured in countless well-worn clichés, like "No pain, no gain" and "It's always darkest before the dawn." It is the kind of story that President Ronald Reagan projected when he proclaimed, at the end of his first term, "It's morning again in America." It's the story that the presidential candidate Bill Clinton invoked when he called himself "the comeback kid." It is the story that George W. Bush lived and told, the born-again sinner who left drinking behind. It is Barack Obama's story of America's progress toward a more just society for all.

In the psychological literature on narrative identity, redemption is a favored story form. My students and I have been coding life-story interviews for themes of redemption for over two decades, publishing our results in scientific journals. Other labs in personality and developmental psychology have conducted similar research. The empirical findings consistently show that people who narrate their lives in redemptive terms tend to enjoy better mental health and higher levels of happiness, compared to people whose life stories show fewer themes of redemption.

An important line of research has documented strong associations between redemptive life stories and the experience of *generativity*. Generativity is an adult's concern for and commitment to promoting the well-being of future generations. Generativity may be expressed through parenting, teaching, mentoring, leadership, and engaging in a range of activities aimed at making the world a better place for generations to come. In terms of personality development, generativity becomes an especially important part of people's motivational agendas as they move into and through midlife. And yet midlife adults differ substantially in their desire to be generative and in their commitments to working for the good of future generations. Research shows that those American women and men with the most sterling records of working hard to promote future generations—in their family life, through their jobs, in the community—tend also to construct highly redemptive stories to make sense of their own lives. The redemptive stories they have created for narrative identity help to sustain their generative commitments in the world. Their redemptive stories give them strength and confidence that they can meet the daunting challenges of generativity. If you are going to try to make the world a better place, a redemptive story is an invaluable asset to own.

One of the reasons that personal stories of redemption link up with psychological well-being and positive adjustment in American lives is that they conform to what the psychologists Phillip Hammack, Kate McLean, and Moin Syed call a *master narrative* of American culture. Master narratives are broad stories that prevail in a given society or group regarding how to live a good life. They may be reflected in a group's perceived history and heritage, in art and folk wisdom, in religious traditions and parenting practices, and in the idioms of everyday talk. People in a given cultural context may take master narratives for granted. Accordingly, they may assume that these stories are actually more than mere stories, that they are instead the way things really and naturally *are*. Master narratives are so pervasive as to be almost invisible, as water is to fish. People know the stories even if they don't realize they know them. Their implicit, nearly unconscious, apprehension of the story may become explicitly conscious to them only when a given master narrative is challenged in some way, or when a person from outside the culture recognizes the master narrative and points it out, or critiques it, or offers a compelling alternative.

In it broadest outline, the master redemptive narrative of American culture tells the story of a chosen people who journey forth in a dangerous world and who, bolstered by their deep and abiding beliefs about what is good and true, overcome daunting obstacles to build a better and happy future. Rooted in 18th-century Christianity and the principles of the European Enlightenment, the master narrative of redemption in American culture is captured in the iconic image of a shining city on a hill and in the idea of American exceptionalism. There are many versions of the story, but they tend to have in common the broad notion that Americans are different from the rest of the world and destined to transform themselves and the world into something better.

As such, the master cultural narrative of American redemption is a myth. History is much too complicated and fraught to be captured accurately and fully in such a simple, feel-good story. But that can be okay, as long as the myth motivates positive behavior. In a parallel way, a human life is more complex than any story a person can tell about it. The narrative identity that an autobiographical author constructs to create meaning and purpose in his or her life is, therefore, a myth, too. But it can be a very useful myth, psychologically speaking, especially when it lines up with a broader myth about American culture. There are advantages to making your story look and sound like one of the favored narratives of your culture. People who implicitly ascribe to the same cultural myth are likely to affirm your story, to encourage you to pursue a life that is consonant with the story, to praise you when you are successful in doing so. Yes, we love stories of redemption in America, whether they are about our nation as a whole or about individual American lives.

We have four favorites.

The first and oldest is the redemptive narrative of *atonement*, imported to the New World by the New England Puritans in the 17th century. Atonement tracks the move from sin to salvation. Couched in the language of American Christianity, atonement can encompass a wide variety of perceived transformations in human life. These include personal religious conversions of the kind celebrated by millions of American evangelicals. But there are many other forms as well, including nonreligious stories through which a person (or a people) comes to terms with or makes amends for transgressions, which leads to an improvement or advance in life.

In shaping his own narrative identity, George W. Bush drew deeply from the mythic reservoir of atonement. By the time he ran for public office, Bush had crafted a compelling and authentic story of atonement for his own life. The story told how he had lived a good and wholesome life growing up in Midland, Texas, but gave it all up when he descended into alcoholism. The story tracks his re-demption in three steps: (i) He married a good woman at the age of 31, (ii) he accepted Jesus Christ as his personal savior around age 38, and (iii) he had his last drink on his 40th birthday. From that point on, the story says, he committed himself to positive generative goals, an abject sinner who repented and was now saved, the prodigal son who came back to his God.

The second form of American redemption traces back at least as far as Benjamin Franklin's iconic autobiography, wherein he effectively invented the American Dream. At the beginning of the tale, Ben Franklin is a hungry teen-ager with nothing more than two coins in his pocket. By the end he is a great statesman, scientist, and founding father of the American republic. This is the rags-to-riches narrative of *upward social mobility*, celebrated in Horatio Alger stories and countless tales of moving up from poverty and making it big—or at least making it—in American society. It was Friedrich Trump's dream when he boarded a steamer in 1885 to come to America. It is the aspiration of many immigrants.

The third redemptive variation on the master cultural form is the narrative of *liberation*. It tracks the move from slavery (or oppression) to freedom. In the first half of the 19th century, a few of the slaves who escaped to the north wrote gripping accounts of their travails, like *Narrative of the Life of Frederick Douglass, an American Slave, Written by Himself.* Their accounts were published as slave narratives, establishing an influential literary tradition for African Americans and other oppressed minorities, and for the white majority, too. For African Americans since the end of the American Civil War, there has always been the promise, more often betrayed than upheld, that a people once enslaved and still marginalized will someday enjoy full standing as free agents in the American community. The same narrative tropes have inspired other liberation movements in American history, such as women's liberation, campaigns for disability rights, and the recent movement toward granting full freedoms, including the freedom to marry for gays, lesbians, and other sexual minorities.

In his book, *Dreams from My Father*, Barack Obama recounted how he came to appropriate the grand cultural narrative of liberation for his own life. From about the age of 30, he began to see himself as following in the steps of that story's greatest heroes, like Martin Luther King Jr. While Obama himself never ex-perienced the travails of the slaves, or even the rank discrimination of the Jim Crow era in the South, he nonetheless identified himself with the great story of American liberation. A master narrative of American culture became his own.

The fourth canonical story form for American redemption is the narrative of *recovery*. In this kind of redemptive story, a person or a group aims to recover something good that has been lost. The most common venue for a recovery story is medicine, through which a person who is sick regains health. But from a psychological and cultural standpoint, the most influential stories of recovery today pertain to the loss of control, or the loss of innocence, or the loss of some form of inherent goodness, and the long-term effort to regain what has been lost. We think of recovering alcoholics and others who ascribe to 12-step programs. We think of recovery from abuse or neglect. We think of recovering a lost self that has been damaged or compromised in some way.

In the first half of the 19th century, the philosopher and theologian Ralph Waldo Emerson traveled from one small town in America to the next proclaiming the power of recovery. He urged Americans to reject social conventions and to recommit themselves to the intuitive truths that lay in their individual hearts. Oprah Winfrey is Emerson's heir apparent. Over the past three decades, she has been the most influential purveyor of recovery stories in the world. An extraordinarily generative woman by anybody's measure, Oprah has lived a life that followed a dramatic recovery path. Sexually abused as a child and beaten down by poverty and prejudice, Oprah eventually recovered her original goodness and strength to become an American icon—rich, influential, and inspirational. Along the way, she taught people how to see their own lives in similar terms. Through her long-running television show, her book club, her magazines, and her extensive program of philanthropy, Oprah taught Americans—women and men, black and white—how to recover the lost kernels of goodness in their lives and how to move forward courageously to fulfill the vast potential of the good, true, and beautiful inner self. She is a teller and a teacher of redemptive stories.

In his own way, Donald Trump inspires stories of redemption, too, at least on the national level. These stories resemble recovery narratives. The genre is Make America Great Again (MAGA). The three-step logic behind the story goes like this: (i) Once upon a time America was a great and powerful nation; (ii) it no longer is great and powerful; (iii) Donald Trump will make America great and powerful again. The story promises to recover a golden age, to restore America's rightful place in the world as the greatest. What has been lost or taken away will be recovered.

It must be noted that President Trump has never filled in the details of MAGA. He has never identified, for example, the precise era in which America experienced the apogee of greatness. Mr. Trump has a very poor sense of history, and he rarely refers to specific events from the distant past. Many people assume, however, that MAGA implicitly references the years immediately following World War II. The 1950s may indeed be the golden era in Trump's mind. Having emerged from the war as the most powerful democratic nation in the world, the United States enjoyed the status of a superpower in the postwar years, although it shared that status with its Cold War rival, the Soviet Union. Heavy industry reached its zenith in America, and good union jobs in the mills, mines, and factories brought prosperity to the masses, lifting many families into the middle class. The building trades were booming through much of the postwar era, which greatly enriched Fred and Mary Trump's family.

If the 1950s were the greatest, how did America lose its greatness? Trump has never provided specific details for this part of the story, either. We might assume, however, that Trump aligns himself with many observers of recent American history in pointing to the failed involvement in the Vietnam War as a turning point. Political leaders lied to the American public about the war, and worse (from Trump's standpoint), we lost the war. And then there was Watergate, which may have further eroded Americans' trust in their government. Beginning in the 1970s and continuing to the present day, heavy manufacturing jobs declined in the United States, due to automation and increasing competition from other countries. Trump might also point to cultural changes in the United States that may be construed, from the points of view held by many of his supporters, as undermining American greatness. The women's movement and the civil rights movement cut into the power of the white patriarchy, which had reigned supreme in the 1950s. Moreover, galloping consumerism, increased secularization, the sexual revolution, the hippies and the counterculture, political correctness run amok, and a range of other factors seemed to threaten traditional family values, beginning in the 1960s. It is not clear that Donald Trump ever embraced traditional family values, but they are cherished by some of his most ardent supporters.

The details may not matter, however. Many people in the United States feel that things were better in "the old days"—or at least, *some* things were better. Nostalgia is a powerful narrative force, with endless possibilities. Building on nostalgia, MAGA promises that Donald Trump will bring back the greatness that has been lost.

Is MAGA a *good story* for America? Does MAGA function as a good story for Donald Trump?

Not so much, I would say. As a master narrative, MAGA is severely compromised by its lack of a moral framing. Master narratives of culture always uphold social values that are infused with moral meaning. They inspire people to live good lives. They inspire societies to strive for noble ends. Narratives of atonement urge people to put away evil or selfish proclivities and embrace higher aspirations or states of being, like a life of service, the pursuit of ethical virtues, or the experience of salvation through God's grace. Redemptive stories of upward mobility affirm the values of hard work, thrift, prudence, and honesty. Liberation narratives celebrate freedom and fairness, and they abhor oppression. Recovery narratives suggest that there is something *good*—morally good or virtuous or ethically noteworthy—in a person or in a society, a goodness that has been lost and that we now aim to restore or recover.

By contrast, making something *great* again does not specify a moral end. Bringing the greatness back is good in an instrumental way, but it has no specific moral meaning. It is like winning. We would all rather win than lose. But winning in and of itself confers no moral value. When the Cubs won the World Series in 2016, five days before Trump's election, the city of Chicago celebrated as it had never celebrated before. Deliriously happy Cubs fans, like myself, rejoiced in the victory. We were now the best! After 108 years of frustration, Chicago's favorite team had made itself great again—MCGA! I still get chills when I recall the final play of the final game, as Kris Bryant threw the ball across the diamond to Anthony Rizzo. But there is nothing "moral" about the event. There is no ethical dimension. Sure, the Cubs' players worked hard to win, showcasing the values of hard work and team work. But all the teams worked hard. For fans the world over, sports convey "the thrill of victory and the agony of defeat," to quote the memorable catchphrase from a 1960s American sports show. But it is all a game.

For Trump, life is all about winning for winning's sake—as if it were a game. After each game, and after each season, the team goes home and then starts all over again, trying to win again—game after game, season by season. Trump sees life the same way, even as it applies to the life of a nation. MAGA is the perfect story for this kind of worldview. In MAGA, the story looks to restore greatness for the mere sake of greatness. MAGA wants the United States to be the greatest team again—the team that wins the most often. We can be like the New York Yankees in baseball or the New England Patriots in football. This may be a great aspiration for sports, but it is not an expressly moral aspiration.

One of the most shocking and unprecedented features of the Trump presidency is Trump's refusal to adopt a moral language for leadership. "The presidency is a center of moral authority in this country," said the historian Robert Dallek in a 2017 interview. "Every president before Trump thought of it in this way." In his second inaugural address, Abraham Lincoln called on Americans to bind up their wounds from the Civil War "with malice toward none; with charity for all; with firmness in the right." Woodrow Wilson prayed that World War I would be a war to end all wars, and he envisioned a postwar League of Nations as a great moral project for humankind. Barack Obama sang the opening refrain of *Amazing Grace*, on June 26, 2015, when he eulogized Reverend Clementa C. Pinckney, killed by a white supremacist. Invoking religious imagery and appealing to the better angels of America's nature, Obama spoke of the United States as "a constant work in progress," a never-ending moral experiment. He characterized history as a manual to "avoid repeating the mistakes of the past" while building a "roadway to a better world." Obama was fond of quoting Martin Luther King Jr., who quoted the words of the 19th-century minister Theodore Parker: "The arc of the moral universe is long, but it bends towards justice."

President Trump sees the United States as a force in the world, but *not* a *moral* force. Unlike any U.S. president for the past 100 years, Trump does not even feign interest in championing such hallowed American values as respect for human rights or opposition to tyranny. He is purely transactional, aiming to make good deals for Americans and to put America first. When white supremacists marched in Charlottesville in August 2017, one of Trump's closest aides urged him to be "a redeemer" and speak out against racial hatred. Instead, Trump said, "I'm not putting anybody on a moral plane." When operatives for the Saudi crown prince killed and dismembered the dissident (and *Washington Post* columnist) Jamal Khashoggi, in October 2018, President Trump refused to sanction Saudi Arabia or even to acknowledge that the crown prince was involved in the horrific act. Amidst international outrage, Trump insisted that the murder was irrelevant, given the huge quantities of oil we buy from the Saudis and the millions of dollars in military equipment we sell them.

Beyond the absence of a moral meaning, there is a second problem with MAGA as it applies to Donald Trump: *MAGA is not Trump's story.* The cultural myth it suggests does not correspond in any way to Donald Trump's personal story or to his life more generally. To be fair, there is no psychological rule that says that the president of the United States must promote a story for America that reflects his own personal narrative. But it can help. George W. Bush's commitment to compassionate conservatism and his belief in the fundamental goodness of the United States were partly rooted, I believe, in his redemptive narrative of atonement. In a parallel manner, Barack Obama identified his own quest for personal identity with America's broader redemptive narrative of liberation and progress. In both cases, these leaders developed a passionate sensibility about America that derived, in part, from the stories they had crafted for their own lives.

But President Donald Trump is strangely different. MAGA does not apply to Trump's personal life story because Trump *does not have* a personal life story. We can never forget that he is the episodic man, bereft of an internalized narrative identity. Beyond that, MAGA does not really connect to Trump's life in an objective sense either. What I mean is that Trump's life, as it has played out over the past seven decades, is not in any way about restoring something that has been lost. If you were to script a movie version of his life, you would not entitle it, "Making Donald Trump Great Again." In terms of the real things that have happened in Donald Trump's real life, there is no golden age that he lost once upon a time and then sought to recover. To the extent his life, as we objectively view it, conforms to any recognizably redemptive story arc, it vaguely resembles the upward social mobility narrative. Not "rags to riches," though. More like "rich to richer."

***

I had lost my identity beyond redemption. (Dr. Jekyll, in *The Strange Case of Dr. Jekyll and Mr. Hyde*)

There is no redemption in Trump World. There is only the vortex. (Roger Cohen, in *The New York Times*, February 23, 2018)

About a week after Donald Trump won the vote in 2016, an Israeli friend and I were discussing the election. My friend said that he was not completely surprised by Trump's victory. His theory was that many Americans had grown tired of all the lofty rhetoric coming from their politicians, especially from Obama. Coming from another culture, my friend had always found the earnest idealism and hopefulness of Americans to be charming, even inspiring—but not very realistic. Americans are waking up to the fact that it is a really tough world out there, he said. Lofty sentiments about democracy and progress sound good, but the gap between rhetoric and the everyday realities of American lives may be too large to sustain America's noblest ideals. The belief in redemption may be naïve, he was suggesting. In 2016, Americans suspended their idealism and voted for a straight-talking tough guy who could go out into the world and kick ass.

My good friend may have been right for 2016. But is he right for the long term? Have Americans lost their faith in redemptive stories?

Let me concede here that redemptive life stories can be problematic, at the level of the individual and the level of the group. As narrative identities, redemptive stories are positively associated with happiness and generativity in individual American lives. But the statistical trend from the research findings hides exceptions to the rule. We all know cases of highly generative adults who are so self-righteous about their mission to change the world as to be insufferable. The belief in redemption can also be naïve. No rule of the universe says suffering will always lead to enhancement. Good things do not invariably follow from bad things. Sometimes there is pain and no gain. Sometimes horrible things happen, and there is absolutely no upside to follow—no long-term reward, no growth, no meaning. Think of the death of a child. Think of the Holocaust. The urge to redeem negative events does not always work, or it can be taken too far. For some redemptive life stories, the narrator may be nearly delusional, and dangerously divorced from reality.

National stories of American exceptionalism can be dangerous, too. In his 1968 book *Redeemer Nation*, the historian Ernest Lee Tuveson described America's self-proclaimed redemptive mission: "Providence, or history, has put a special responsibility on the American people to spread the blessing of liberty, democracy, and equality to others throughout the earth, and to defeat, if necessary by force, the sinister powers of darkness." The sentiment is as arrogant and imperialistic as it is idealistic. It puts America on a higher moral plane than everybody else.

Under the banner of manifest destiny, the United States effectively appropriated territory from rival nations in the 19th century and dispossessed indigenous peoples. Historian Richard Slotkin analyzed how white Americans, between 1600 and 1860, came to understand their own relentless and ultimately successful campaigns to tame the wilderness, defeat the Indians, and expand their domain to encompass the vast land that is now the United States. He argued that Americans of European descent justified these acts of violence in terms of *regeneration*. To generate something new and good, we needed to destroy the old. We purged the land of its original inhabitants. We stole the land from others who claimed it was theirs. We glorified the violent heroes who were so instrumental in helping us win this ongoing war—the hunters, pioneers, and Indian fighters. In Slotkin's view, the organizing theme of American history is *redemptive violence*. In the name of regeneration and redemption, Americans have always aimed to wipe out the old in order to start fresh anew. In a related sense, Americans have also sought to reform and remake the lives of others who are not like us, to rescue *them* from their own badness, to redeem them and to make them *good* like *us*.

Donald Trump rejects the concept of America as a redeemer nation. He has absolutely no interest in transforming the world into America's image. He has no designs on foreign territories. He does not want to expand America's frontiers. He is not concerned about promoting democracy abroad. Rather than expand, President Trump wants to contract. His philosophy of America First aims to disentangle the United States from international involvements, like multilateral trade pacts and long-term alliances. He withdrew American support for the Trans-Pacific Partnership on trade, the Paris climate accord, and the Iran nuclear deal. He renegotiated NAFTA. He has threatened to leave NATO. He has threatened to pull back military forces in the Pacific. In December 2018, he announced that all American troops will soon leave Syria, blind-siding our allies and overriding the strong recommendations of his Secretary of Defense and military officials. He has shown nothing but scorn for the United Nations. In Trump's vision, America will be great again when America stands alone.

In an interview in late 2018, the conservative policy expert Robert Kagan strongly condemned Trump's go-it-alone approach: "We are moving back to an earlier conception of America's role in the world, looking out for ourselves, hoping the two oceans protect us, and when necessary saying the rest of the world is full of freeloaders who can go to hell if they don't get on board." He added: "It may be an era more destructive of the world order than in the 1930s. Back then, at least, Britain and France were responsible for keeping part of the order. Now we are the responsible world power—and we are undermining it."

As a leading neoconservative voice in the early years of the George W. Bush administration, Kagan advocated strongly for an American invasion of Iraq. Like Paul Wolfowitz, Condoleezza Rice, and a number of other advisors to President Bush in 2003, Kagan believed that American military force could be deployed to spread democracy in the Middle East. It was never just about finding the weapons of mass destruction. Deposing the Iraqi dictator Saddam Hussein was also very much in keeping with the old idea of America as a redeemer nation. Bush's own redemptive story, in my opinion, helped convince him that the bold initiative to invade Iraq was right and sure to succeed. In his own life, he had overthrown personal demons with the help of God and restored the goodness of self he had known growing up in small-town Texas. So too, Bush's story told him, might God's favored nation oust the demonic tyrant in Iraq and restore to the Iraqi citizens their God-given rights of freedom and self-determination. As we know, things did not quite work out that way in Iraq. Donald Trump knows it, too.

The terrorist attacks on 9/11, the disastrous war in Iraq, the devastating recession of 2008, and the endless quagmire in Afghanistan are four prodigiously negative events of the early 21st century that may have worked to undermine America's collective confidence. Whether we are talking about military power, economic strength, or political and cultural influence, many Americans today may believe that their country is no longer capable of being a force for good in the world. We have too many problems at home to worry about anybody else. Donald Trump's life dictum, moreover, may be correct: Man *may* be the most vicious of all animals, and perhaps life *is* indeed a series of battles ending in victory or defeat. There is trouble all around—enemies from abroad and enemies from within. It is *us* against *them*. Under such dire conditions, redemptive stories about progress, the advance of human rights, and other idealistic quests are a superfluous luxury. Stories of atonement, upward mobility, liberation, and recovery cannot even be told when we are fighting for our very survival. As one delegate at the 2016 Republican National Convention put it, "Our city on a hill is now a city under siege. . . . It's time to take back our country."

Every large collective of human beings carries with it many different stories about how the world works and how to live well in the world. At the level of the nation state, conflicting cultural narratives compete with each other for the people's attention and allegiance. Redemptive stories have long inspired Americans' aspirations for themselves and their nation, for better and for worse. But many other stories have also proliferated, including those that resemble MAGA. The election of Donald Trump may mark a dramatic turning point in how Americans think of themselves and narrate their place in the world. As much a true believer in American progress as anybody on the planet, Barack Obama came to question his faith in American redemption when the American voters chose Donald

Trump to be his successor. "What if we were wrong?" Obama asked aides, as they were riding in a limousine in Lima, Peru, shortly after Trump's election. "Maybe we pushed too far," he said. "Maybe people just want to fall back into their tribe."

The belief in American exceptionalism may be on the wane. In an op-ed entitled "We Will Never Be the Same," a European scholar and expert on international relations wrote, "The world will not boomerang back to where it was" once Trump leaves office. Ivan Krastev argued that the Trump presidency ushered in what will be a permanent change in the American mythos. He wrote: "Americans have lost confidence in their exceptionalism. It's not just the president but also the millennials (who predominantly oppose him) who no longer share the belief that America is an 'indispensable nation' with a moral obligation to make the world safe for democracy." Young Americans no longer believe that the United States is morally or institutionally "better" than other countries, Krastev argued. Trump thinks the same, but he insists that the United States can still be the strongest if it is also "nastier than others."

Krastev is right about Trump, but he may be selling millennials (and other Americans) short. American exceptionalism may take milder forms. One does not need to believe in manifest destiny or the inherent superiority of the United States to take pride in American values and institutions. When it comes to cultural narratives, citizens may not need to harbor triumphalist theories about America to believe that economic, political, cultural, and moral progress may still be possible. The American experiment is ongoing. The long-term results are yet to be known.

The journalist James Fallows and his wife Deborah Fallows spent five years piloting their private plane to dozens of American cities and towns, from Eastport, Maine, to Redlands, California. Amidst the political polarization in Washington, DC, the Fallowses wanted to see whether and how local political bodies were solving local problems. Their 2018 book, *Our Towns*, provided a group portrait of 42 success stories. Writing about the book in the *New York Times*, the columnist David Brooks observed that "most of the cities tell a redemption story about themselves." In many cases, a city once had a "booming industry," but it collapsed, and now the citizens "are rebuilding with new industries and new wealth." In many of the cities, generative business leaders bring the spirit and skills of entrepreneurship to the task of redeeming and rebuilding their cities, while committing themselves to the common civic good. Brooks wrote: "The cities have strong civic stories and clear narratives about where they've been, where they are going and what makes them distinctive." Americans need to ramp up these kinds of collective narratives and nationalize them. As Brooks sees it, the best stories for America can still be redemptive. But redemptive American stories for the 21st century may need to be humbler and more oriented toward community than they have been in the past.

Nobody knows what kinds of stories Americans will tell about themselves in the future. Nobody knows how Americans will narrate their history as a nation—what kinds of stories they will tell about who they were once upon a time, who they are now, and who they will become in the future. The Trump presidency may change American narrative identity forever. Or it may not. People may look back decades from now and wonder why everybody seemed to be so worked up when Donald Trump was the president of the United States. From their perspective in the distant future, it may all have been nothing more than a momentary blip. I cannot say if MAGA will become a long-term American idea, a master narrative for the 21st century. Perhaps it will. Perhaps it will mutate into a more explicitly redemptive form. Or maybe it will die.

Still, I believe in the power of redemption. For all their limitations, redemptive stories affirm hope and the expectation of human progress over time. They suggest that human lives and the lives of collectives can, in principle, overcome fearsome obstacles and develop toward positive ends. Hope for the future and the belief in progress may be naïve, but I cannot help but embrace them. Perhaps I am too American.

The columnist Roger Cohen may have been channeling a similar sentiment when he wrote: "There is no redemption in Trump World. There is only the vortex."

The "vortex" is an apt metaphor to invoke as I come to the end of this strange case. A vortex is like a whirlpool or whirlwind. Things spin around an empty center. Around and around and around. When the vortex is strong, there is no way to escape the centripetal power. There is no way to break away and move forward.

Applied to America today, it is as if we are all spinning around Donald Trump. He is the emptiness at the center, and we cannot escape him. Extending the metaphor further, we may imagine that Trump is like a black hole in the universe. Millions of stars swirl round it. In a sense, a black hole is the opposite of a nothing. It is so dense, so packed with the stuff of matter and energy, that not even light can escape—which is why we cannot see it. In the long run, it swallows everything up.

Writ small and psychological, the vortex is also Donald Trump himself. He is a vortex in a vortex. At the strange and innermost center is a narrative vacuum. The episodic man has no life story. Orbiting around the void are all the psychological characteristics I have described in this book—his dispositional personality traits, his characteristic beliefs and attitudes, his deal-making skills, his orientation to love, his proclivity for untruth, his narcissistic goal agenda, his authoritarian sentiments, his manifestation as the alpha chimp. These features of his strange personality can be fully appreciated and understood only if we realize that they revolve around the empty narrative core, the hollow inner space where the story should be, but never was.

Think of the vortex as a void, or think of it as a black hole. Either way, there is no way out. In the first instance, we go round and round forever. In the second, we are sucked inexorably into oblivion.

Notes

Prologue

Page 1 Regarding the reaction to the great reveal in *The Strange Case of Dr. Jekyll and Mr. Hyde*, Jefferson Singer writes that "the contemporary reader can no longer imagine what sheer icy astonishment must have hit an unsuspecting audience of Stevenson's time in response to Lanyon's discovery." Singer, J. A. (2017). *The proper pirate: Robert Louis Stevenson's quest for identity*. New York: Oxford University Press, p. 14.

Page 1 Stevenson, R. L. (2003). *The strange case of Dr. Jekyll and Mr. Hyde, and other stories: With an introduction and notes by Jenny Davidson*. New York: Barnes and Noble Classics, p. 60. (The novel was originally published in 1886).

Page 1 Decker, C. (2018, May 6). Trump assails foes as friend probed. *Chicago Tribune*.

Page 2 Kessler, R. (2018). *The Trump White House: Changing the rules of the game*. New York: Crown Forum, p. 10.

Page 2 Mayer, J. (2016, July 25). Donald Trump's ghostwriter tells all. *The New Yorker*.

Page 2 Dowd, M. (2018, April 29). Trump: Our cartoon Nobel laureate. *New York Times*.

Page 2 D'Antonio, M. (2015). *Never enough: Donald Trump and the pursuit of success*. New York: St. Martin's Press, p. 335.

Page 3 Singer, M. (2011, April 26). Best wishes, Donald. *The New Yorker*.

Page 3 On the idea that people have life stories, and the stories organize their different selves or characters: McAdams, D. P. (1993). *The stories we live by*. New York: Guilford Press. See also: McAdams, D. P., and Manczak, E. (2015). Personality and the life story. In M. Mikulincer and P. R. Shaver (Eds.), *APA handbook of personality and social psychology*. Vol. 4, *Personality processes and individual differences* (pp. 425–446). Washington, DC: American Psychological Association Press.

Page 5 Stevenson, *The Strange Case of Dr. Jekyll*, pp. 64, 77.

Page 5 Books and articles on Bush and Obama, written by Dan P. McAdams: McAdams, D. P. (2011). *George W. Bush and the redemptive dream: A psychological portrait*. New York: Oxford University Press; McAdams, D. P. (2013). *The redemptive self: Stories Americans live by* (Rev. and exp. ed.). Obama versus Bush: Competing Stories of Redemption (Chapter 10). New York: Oxford University Press.; McAdams, D. P. (2013). Life authorship: A psychological challenge for emerging adulthood, as illustrated in two notable case studies. *Emerging Adulthood*, *1*, 151–158.; McAdams, D. P. (2015). Leaders and their life stories: Obama, Bush, and narratives of redemption. In G. R. Goethals, S. T. Allison, R. M. Kramer, and D. M. Messick (Eds.), *Contemporary conceptions of leadership* (pp. 147–165). New York: Palgrave Macmillan.

Page 5–6 McAdams, D. P. (2016, June). The mind of Donald Trump. *The Atlantic*, pp. 76–90.

Story

Page 8 Biographical material on Donald Trump for this chapter comes mainly from the following sources: D'Antonio, *Never Enough*. Blair, G. (2000). *The Trumps: Three generations of builders and a presidential candidate*. New York: Simon & Schuster.; Kranish, M., and Fisher, M. (2016). *Trump revealed: The definitive biography of the 45th president*. New York: Simon & Schuster.; O'Brien, T. L. (2005). *TrumpNation: The art of being the Donald*. New York: Warner Business Books.; Trump, D. J., with T. Schwartz. (1987). *The art of the deal*. New York: Ballantine Books.; Trump, D. J. (2015). *Crippled America: How to make America great again*. New York: Simon & Schuster.

Page 8 On Saturday morning, "'the telephone was always ringing,' recalled Jan von Heinigen, one of Fred Jr's classmates. 'It was always for Fred's father, and it was always about business. My impression was that this was normal—you know, doesn't everyone do this, we're awake so we must be working.'" Blair, *The Trumps*, p. 226.

Page 8 Trump, *Crippled America*, p. 128.

Page 9 Blair, *The Trumps*, p. 231.

Page 9 Trump, *Crippled America*, p. 129.

Page 9 Trump and Schwartz, *The Art of the Deal*, p. 71.

Page 10 Trump, *Crippled America*, p. 51.

Page 10 O'Brien, *TrumpNation*, p. 50.

Page 10 Trump and Schwartz, *The Art of the Deal*, pp. 73–74.

Page 10 D'Antonio, *Never Enough*, p. 107.

Page 11 Ibid., p. 78.

Page 11 Klemesrud, J. (1976, November 1). Donald Trump, real estate promoter, builds image as he buys buildings. *New York Times*.

Page 12 Mayer, "Donald Trump's Ghostwriter."

Page 13 Fivush, R. (2011). The development of autobiographical memory. In S. T. Fiske, D. L. Schacter, and S. E. Taylor (Eds.), *Annual review of psychology* (Vol. 62, pp. 550–582). Palo Alto, CA: Annual Reviews.

Page 13–14 Mandler, J. (1984). *Stories, scripts, and scenes: Aspects of schema theory*. Hillsdale, NJ: Lawrence Erlbaum.

Page 14 McAdams, "Life Authorship"; McAdams and Manczak, "Personality." See also McAdams, D. P. (2013). The psychological self as actor, agent, and author. *Perspectives on Psychological Science, 8*, 272–295.; McAdams, D. P., and McLean, K. C. (2013). Narrative identity. *Current Directions in Psychological Science, 22*, 233–238.; McLean, K. C, Pasupathi, M., and Pals, J. L. (2007). Selves creating stories creating selves: A process model of self-development. *Personality and Social Psychology Review, 11*, 262–278. The concept of narrative identity made its debut in personality and developmental psychology in the mid-1980s, initially described as "the life story model of identity": McAdams, D. P. (1985). *Power, intimacy, and the life story: Personological inquiries into identity.* Homewood, IL: Dorsey Press. See also McAdams, D. P. (1990). Unity and purpose in human lives: The emergence of identity as a life story. In A. I. Rabin, R. A. Zucker, R. A. Emmons, and S. Frank (Eds.), *Studying persons and lives* (pp. 148–200). New York: Springer.

Page 14   Thomsen, D. K., and Bernsten, D. (2008). The cultural life script and life story chapters contribute to the reminiscence bump. *Memory, 16,* 420–435.

Page 15   Habermas, T., and Bluck, S. (2000). Getting a life: The emergence of the life story in adolescence. *Psychological Bulletin, 126,* 748–769.; Pasupathi, M., and Mansour, E. (2006). Adult age differences in autobiographical reasoning in narratives. *Developmental Psychology, 42,* 798–808.

Page 15–16   Obama, B. (1995). *Dreams from my father.* New York: Three Rivers Press. See also McAdams. "Life Authorship" and McAdams, "Leaders."

Page 17   McAdams, *George W. Bush.* See also McAdams, "Life Authorship" and McAdams, "Leaders."

Page 16   Andersen, C. (2002). *George and Laura: Portrait of an American marriage.* New York: William Morrow, p. 105.

Page 16   Bush, G. W. (1999). *A charge to keep: My journey to the White House.* New York: Harper, p. 79.

Page 17   Barbaro, M. (2016, July 22). Escape his caricature? Donald Trump passes up the chance. *The New York Times.*

Page 17   D'Antonio, *Never Enough,* p. 211.

Page 18   Ibid., p. 306.

Page 19   Ibid., p. 268.

Page 19   Gabriel, S., Paravati, E., Green, M. C., and Flomsbee, J. (2018). From *Apprentice* to president: The role of parasocial connection in the election of Donald Trump. *Social Psychological and Personality Science, 9,* 299–307.

Page 20   D'Antonio, *Never Enough,* p. 154.

Page 21   Burns, A. (2016, November 30). Trump, a free-form leader, experiments and invites drama. *The New York Times.*

Page 21   Kessler, *The Trump White House,* p. 23.

Page 21   Brooks, D. (2017, January 3). The Snapchat presidency of Donald Trump. *The New York Times.*

Page 22   Schwartz, T. (2017, May 16). I wrote "The Art of the Deal" with Trump: His self-sabotage is rooted in his past. *The Washington Post.*

Page 23   Meacham, J. (December 29, 2017). Donald Trump and the limits of the reality TV presidency. *The New York Times.*

Page 23   Trump, *Crippled America,* p. 31.

Deal

Page 25 O'Brien, *TrumpNation*, p. 204. From interview with Nancy Collins on ABC *Primetime Live*, March 10, 1994. The context was a discussion of Trump's relationship with Marla Maples.

Page 25 Trump and Schwartz, *The Art of the Deal*, p. 1.

Page 25 Blair, *The Trumps*. See also D'Antonio, *Never enough*; Kranish and Fisher, *Trump Revealed*.

Page 26 Blair, *The Trumps*, p. 86. Originally from *Yukon Sun*, April 17, 1900. Retrieved from https://news.google.com/newspapers?nid=3fE2CSJIrl8C&dat=19000417&printsec=frontpage&hl=en

Page 27 D'Antonio, *Never Enough*, p. 24. See also Blair, *The Trumps*; D'Antonio, *Never Enough*; Kranish and Fisher, *Trump Revealed*; O'Brien, *TrumpNation*.

Page 28 D'Antonio *Never Enough*, pp. 15–19.

Page 29 Ibid., p. 19.

Page 30 Freud, S. (1900/1953). *The interpretation of dreams.* In J. Strachey (Ed.), *The standard edition of the complete psychological works of Sigmund Freud* (Vols. 4–5). London: Hogarth.

Page 30 Trump and Schwartz, *The Art of the Deal*, p. 102.

Page 31 Ibid., pp. 52–53.

Page 31 Ibid., p. 58.

Page 31 Dowd, M. (2016, March 6). Chickens, home to roost. *New York Times.* See also: Konnikova, M. (2016). *The confidence game: Why we fall for it every time.* New York: Penguin Books.

Page 31–32 Genesis 25: 27–33.

Page 32 Trump and Schwartz, *The Art of the Deal*, p. 58.

Page 32 Ibid., p. 58.

Page 32 Ibid., pp. 214–215.

Page 33 Ibid., p. 215.

Page 32 O'Brien, *TrumpNation*, pp. 119–122.

Page 33 Blair, *The Trumps*, p. 351.

Page 33–34 Barstow, D., Craig, S., and Buettner, R. (2018, October 2). Special investigation: Trump engaged in suspect tax schemes as he reaped riches from his father. *New York Times.*

Page 34 Buettner, R., Craig, S., and Barstow, D. (2018, October 2). 11 takeaways from the *Times's* investigation into Trump's wealth. *New York Times.*

Page 34 Kranish and Fisher, *Trump Revealed*, p. 30.

Page 34 On Aaron Burr's desire to make deals in "the room where it happens," see Miranda, L-M., and McCarter, J. (2016). *Hamilton: The revolution.* New York: Grand Central.

Page 35 Trump and Schwartz, *The Art of the Deal*, p. 65.

Page 35   Ibid., p. 80.

Page 35   Ibid., p. 77.

Page 35   Ibid., p. 56.

Page 35   Ibid., p. 56.

Page 35   Ibid., p. 57.

Page 36   Ibid., p. 45.

Page 36   Ibid., p. 45.

Page 36   Ibid., p. 53. "Use Your Leverage" is the fifth element of the deal in Trump's list (see pp. 53–54).

Page 36   Ibid., p. 58. "Fight Back" is the eighth element of the deal in Trump's list (see pp. 58–59).

Page 36   Ibid., p. 46. "Think Big" is the first element of the deal in Trump's list (see pp. 46–48).

Page 36   Ibid., p. 53.

Page 36   Ibid., p. 53.

Page 36   Ibid., p. 53.

Page 36   Ibid., pp. 46–47.

Page 37   Ibid., p. 108.

Page 36   Ibid., pp. 58–59.

Page 36–37   D'Antonio, *Never Enough*, pp. 297–313.

Page 37   Trump and Schwartz, *The Art of the Deal*, p. 113.

Page 37   Baxter, A. (Dir.). (2011). *You've been Trumped* [Documentary] (R. Phinney, Prod.). New York: New Video.

Page 37   Trump and Schwartz, *The Art of the Deal*, p. 45.

Page 37   Ibid., p. 47.

Page 37–38   Ibid., p. 48.

Page 38   O'Brien, *TrumpNation*, p. 4.

Page 38   For the exposé regarding Trump's business losses between 1985 and 1994, see Buettner, R., and Craig, S. (2019, May 8). Trump tax figures show a decade of huge losses. *New York Times*.

Page 38   Blair, *The Trumps*; O'Brien, *TrumpNation*.

Page 38   Blair, *The Trumps*, p. 409.

Page 38   O'Brien, *TrumpNation*, pp. 137–138.

Page 39   D'Antonio, *Never Enough*, p. 201.

Page 40   Sanger, D. E. (March 10, 2018). After talks, verification. *New York Times*. Also see Perlez, J. (2018, March 10). Pomp and fizzle: Negotiating with a North Korean leader in 2000. *New York Times*.

Page 40   Sang-Hun, C. (2018, April 28). Two Koreas unite in goal to banish nuclear weapons: Kim and Moon vow to forge official end to the war. *New York Times*.

Page 40 Sanger, D. E., and Sang-Hun, C. (2018, June 11). News analysis: Murky path to a deal for erratic leaders. *New York Times.*

Page 40 Sanger, "After Talks." Also see Landler, M., and Sanger, D. E. (March 7, 2018). Trump is in same spot as his predecessors. *New York Times*; Landler, M. (2018, March 9). Trump agrees to talk to Kim within weeks. *New York Times*; and Baker, P., and Sang-Hun, C. (2018, March 11). With a snap "yes," Trump rolls dice on North Korea. *New York Times.*

Page 41 Bierman, N. (2017, August 8). Trump warns North Korea of "fire and fury." *Los Angeles Times.*

Page 41 Landler, M. (2018, June 12). Taunts put aside as Trump and Kim meet to end crisis. *New York Times.* Also see Perlez, J., and Sang-Hun, C. (2018, June 15). Pompeo renews demands for "complete denuclearization." *New York Times.*

Page 41 Landler, M. (2018, June 13). For Trump, power and values matter less than dollars and cents. *New York Times.*

Page 42 Sanger, D. E. (2018, May 25). President's gamble hits a reality check. *New York Times.*

Page 42 Sanger and Sang-Hun, "News Analysis."

Page 42 Ibid.

Page 42 de Callieries, F. (1983). *The art of diplomacy* (H. M. A. Keens-Soper and K, W. Schweizer, Eds.). London: Leicester University Press. (Originally published in 1716 as *De la maniere de negocier avec les souverains*)

Page 42 Sanger, D. E. (2018, May 20). Trump grappling with risks of proceeding with North Korea meeting. *New York Times.*

Page 43 For list of the key issues that need to be resolved for full denuclearization of North Korea, see Broad, W. U., Sanger, D. E., and Griggs, T. (2018, June 12). The nine steps required to really disarm North Korea. *New York Times.* See also Kristof, N. (2018, June 12). Trump was outfoxed in Singapore. *New York Times.*

Page 43 Sanger, D. E. (2018, July 5). News analysis: Trump eases hostile tone toward Kim. *New York Times.*

Page 43 Banres, J. E., and Schmitt, E. (2018, August 1). North Korea keeps building missiles despite U. S. overtures. *New York Times.*

Page 43 Sanger, D. E. (2019, January 1). Kim and Trump back to Square 1: If U. S. keeps sanctions, North Korea will keep nuclear program. *New York Times.*

Page 43 Sanger, "Trump Grappling."

Page 43 Landler, "Taunts Put Aside."

Page 43 Sanger, D. E., and Sang-Hun, C. (2018, April 27). Leaders of two Koreas meet. *New York Times.*

Page 43–44 Cochrane, E. (2018, May 10). Forged nominations aside, a Nobel for Trump is not so far-fetched. *New York Times.* See also Baker, P., Davis, J-H., and Sang-Hun, C. (2018, May 10). Releasing three, North Koreans signal openness. *New York Times.*

Page 44 Mullany, G. (2018, May 23). Any meeting is uncertain, but U.S. has minted coins. *New York Times.*

Page 44 Sanger, D. E. (2018, April 28). News analysis: Parameters are set for Trump meeting. *New York Times.*

Page 44 Gambino, L. (2018, January). Donald Trump boasts that his nuclear button is bigger than Kim Jong-un's. *The Guardian.*

Page 44–45 Baker, P. (2018, June 10). Escalating clash with Canada, Trump is isolated before North Korea meeting. *New York Times.*

Page 45 Landler, M. (2018, May 23). Trump backs off demand that Kim give up weapons. *New York Times.*

Page 45 Kristof, "Trump Was Outfoxed."

Page 45 Rich, M. (2018, May 23). If the North keeps nuclear arms, could Trump still claim success? *New York Times.*

Page 45 Baker, P. (2018, June 2). Trump says nuclear talks with Kim are on after all. *New York Times.*

Page 45 Landler, "Taunts Put Aside."

Page 45 Perez and Sang-Hun, "Pompeo Renews Demands."

Page 46 Sanger, D. E. (2018, July 5). News analysis: Trump eases hostile tone toward Kim. *New York Times.*

Page 46 Mandler, *Stories, Scripts.*

Page 48 Baker, P. (2018, June 22). President Trump, deal maker? Not so fast. *New York Times.*

Reward

Page 51 For accounts of human prehistory as it relates to brainy sociality, see McAdams, D. P. (2015). *The art and science of personality development.* New York: Guilford Press, Chapter 1. See also Wilson, E. O. (2012). *The social conquest of earth.* New York: Liveright.

Page 51 On the importance of taming fire and developing cooking for human evolution, see Wrangham, R. (2009). *Catching fire: How cooking made us human.* New York: Basic Books.

Page 51–52 On the importance of developing weapons (and warfare) in human evolution and in shaping human nature, see Turchin, P. (2016). *Ultrasociety: How 10,000 years of war made humans the greatest cooperators on earth.* Chaplin, CT: Beresta Books.

Page 53 A strong line of theorizing in evolutionary biology suggests that increasing brain size in humans evolved to cope with the increasing complexity of social life. Nonetheless, this idea remains controversial, and some scholars link increased brain size to ingenuity, advancing information processing skills, and other processes that are not explicitly social in nature. See Dunbar, R., and Sutcliffe, A. G. (2012). Social complexity and intelligence. In J. Vonk and T. K. Shackelford (Eds.), *The Oxford handbook of comparative evolutionary psychology* (pp. 102–117). New York: Oxford University Press.

Page 53 The eminent personality psychologist Robert Hogan was the first to identify "getting along" and "getting ahead" as the two great motivations for human beings, as brainy, ultrasocial animals. See Hogan, R. (1982). A socioanalytic theory of personality. In M. Page (Ed.), *Nebraska symposium on motivation* (Vol. 29, pp. 55–89). Lincoln: University of Nebraska Press.

Page 54 McAdams, *The Art and Science*, Chapters 1 and 2.

Page 54 Scholars who study this sort of thing do not know for sure when language emerged as a human adaptation. But nearly all agree that it is a relatively recent emergence, probably within the last 100,000 to 50,00 years of human history. See Dor, D. (2015). *The instruction of imagination: Language as a social communication technology*. New York: Oxford University Press.

Page 54 Goldberg, L. R. (1981). Language and individual differences: The search for universals in personality lexicons. In L. Wheeler (Ed.), *Review of personality and social psychology* (Vol. 2, pp. 141–166). Beverly Hills, CA: Sage.

Page 54 Ashton, M. C., Lee, K., and Paunonen, S. (2002). What is the central feature of extraversion? Social attention versus reward sensitivity. *Journal of Personality and Social Psychology, 83*, 245–252.

Page 54–55 Funder, D. C. (1995). On the accuracy of personality judgment: A realistic approach. *Psychological Review, 102*, 652–670. The agreement, however, is not perfect, and it can vary from one trait to the next and as a function of how well people know the person being rated; see Vazire, S. (2010). Who knows what about a person? The self-other knowledge asymmetry (SOKA) model. *Journal of Personality and Social Psychology, 98*, 281–300.

Page 55 Klemesrud, "Donald Trump."

Page 56 O'Brien, *TrumpNation*, pp. 61–62.

Page 56 Trump and Schwartz, *The Art of the Deal*, p. 2.

Page 56 Egan, T. (2016, February 26). A unified theory of Trump. *New York Times*.

Page 56 Three tweets from April 2016: Gathered by the staff of *The Atlantic*, in McAdams, "The Mind of Donald Trump," p. 79.

Page 56 Ehrenfreund, M. (2015, October 15). I asked psychologists to analyze Trump supporters. This is what I learned. *Washington Post*.

Page 57 Stevenson, *The strange case of Dr. Jekyll*, p. 64.

Page 57 McAdams, *The Art and Science*, Chapter 2. See also Smillie, L. D., Cooper, A. J., Wilt, J., and Revelle, W. (2012). Do extraverts get more bang for the buck? Refining the affective-reactivity hypothesis of extraversion. *Journal of Personality and Social Psychology, 103*, 306–326.

Page 57–58 D'Antonio, *Never Enough*, p. 185.

Page 57 O'Brien, *TrumpNation*, p. 6.

Page 57 The empirical evidence for a positive correlation between extraversion and self-reported happiness is everywhere in the personality psychology literature. For example, see Costa, P. T., Jr., and McCrae, R. R. (1980). Influence of extraversion and neuroticism on subjective well-being: Happy and unhappy people. *Journal of Personality and Social Psychology, 38*, 668–678.; Lucas, R. E., Le, K., and Dyrenforth, P. S. (2008). Explaining the extraversion/positive affect relation: Sociability cannot account for extraverts' greater happiness. *Journal of Personality and Social Psychology, 76*, 385–414.

Page 58 I am happy you looked this up! Here is the citation for the study showing that extraverts can experience more enjoyment than introverts even in pleasant nonsocial situations: Lucas, R. E., and Diener, E. (2001). Understanding extraverts' enjoyment of social situations: The importance of pleasantness. *Journal of Personality and Social Psychology, 81*, 343–356.

Page 57 O'Brien, *TrumpNation*, p. 159.

Page 58 Ibid., p. 49.

Page 58 Peale, N. V. (1952). *The power of positive thinking*. New York: Prentice-Hall.

Page 58 D'Antonio, *Never Enough*, p. 53.

Page 59 O'Brien, *TrumpNation*.

Page 59 Eysenck, H. J. (1973). *Eysenck on extraversion*. New York: Wiley.

Page 59 Trump and Schwartz, *The Art of the Deal*, p. 5.

Page 59 Blair, *The Trumps*, pp. 232–233.

Page 59 O'Brien, *TrumpNation*, p. 83.

Page 60 Carver, C. S. (2004). Negative affects derived from the Behavioral Approach System. *Emotion, 3*, 3–22. See also Harmon-Jones, E., and Allen, J. J. B. (1998). Anger and frontal brain activity: EEG asymmetry consistent with approach motivation despite negative affective valence. *Journal of Personality and Social Psychology, 74*, 1310–1316.

Page 60 Pilkington, E. (2015, December 8). How does Trump do it? Understanding the psychology of a demagogue's rally. *The Guardian*. See also Irwin, J. (2016, February 4). Trump schools us on the psychology of insults. *The Star-Telegram*.

Page 60 The psychiatrist John Gartner has argued that Trump's central psychological characteristic is hypomania, a temperament he shares with Bill Clinton. Gartner writes that hypomanic people are "restless, impatient, and easily bored, needing constant stimulation. They can be exuberant, charming, witty, gregarious, but also arrogant. They are impulsive in ways that show poor judgment. They are risk takers. All their appetites are heightened." Gartner has grouped together a hodgepodge of characteristics, many of which are aspects of extraversion, and shaped them into a configuration that sounds a lot like Donald Trump. In so doing, he has drawn from other personality traits that are independent of extraversion, like (low) conscientiousness and (high) neuroticism. The research literature is not clear, however, on what the status of "hypomania" really is, beyond exaggerated extraversion. In any case, I am not especially keen on the utility of clinical labels for describing personality, as I describe in this volume's chapter, "Goldwater." See Gartner, J. (August 25, 2015). Donald Trump and Bill Clinton have the same secret weapon. *The New Republic*.

Page 61 For a concise summary of the main behavioral correlates of extraversion, see McAdams, *The Art and Science*, Chapter 2, especially Table 2.1, p. 55.

Page 61 Paunonen, S. V. (2003). Big Five factors of personality and replicated predictions of behavior. *Journal of Personality and Social Psychology, 84*, 411–422. See also Krueger R. F., Caspi, A., Moffitt, T. E., Silva, P. A., and McGee, R. (1996). Personality traits are differentially linked to mental disorders: A multitrait-multidiagnosis study of an adolescent birth cohort. *Journal of Abnormal Psychology, 105*, 299–312.

Page 61 Dunbar, R. (2004). Gossip in evolutionary perspective. *Review of General Psychology*, 8, 100–110.

Page 61 The story of how psychologists began with the English lexicon and eventually derived the Big Five traits is told in many places. See John, O. P. (1990). The "Big Five" factor taxonomy: Dimensions of personality in the natural language and in questionnaires. In L. Pervin (Ed.), *Handbook of personality: Theory and research* (pp. 66–100). New York: Guilford Press.

Page 62 I am adopting McCrae and Costa's terms for labeling the Big Five. There are other terms used, but these are the most popular. See McCrae, R. R., and Costa, P. T., Jr. (2008). The five-factor theory of personality. In O. P. John, R. W. Robins, and L. A. Pervin (Eds.), *Handbook of personality theory and research* (3rd Ed., pp. 159–180). New York: Guilford Press.

Page 63 D'Antonio, *Never Enough*, p. 35.

Page 63 Roberts, B. W., and DelVecchio, W. (2000). The rank-order consistency of personality from childhood to old age: A quantitative review of longitudinal studies. *Psychological Bulletin*, 126, 3–25.

Krueger, R. F., and Johnson, W. (2008). Behavioral genetics and personality: A new look at the integration of nature and nurture. In O. P. John, R. W. Robin, and L. A. Pervin (Eds.), *Handbook of personality: Theory and research* (3rd. ed., pp. 287–310). New York: Guilford Press.

Specht, J., Bleidorn, W., Denissen, J. J. A., Hennecke, M., Hutteman, R., Kandler, C., Luhmann, M., Orth, U., Reitz, A. K., and Zimmerman, J. (2014). What drives adult personality development? A comparison of theoretical perspectives and empirical evidence. *European Journal of Personality*, 28, 216–230.

Page 63 For the study involving ranking U.S. presidents on each of the Big Five traits, see Rubenzer, S. J., and Faschingbauer, T. R. (2004). *Personality, character, and leadership in the White House: Psychologists assess the presidents*. Washington, DC: Brassey's. The rankings on extraversion appear on page 25.

Page 63 I make a strong case for George W. Bush's extraversion in McAdams, *George W. Bush*, Chapter 1. See also McAdams, *The Art and Science*, Chapter 2.

Page 64 The story about Calvin Coolidge and the woman at dinner comes from Rubenzer and Faschingbauer, *Personality, Character*, p. 63.

Page 65 For rankings of U.S. presidents on neuroticism, see Rubenzer and Faschingbauer *Personality, Character*, p. 23.

Page 63 On the psychology of neuroticism, see McAdams, *The Art and Science*, Chapter 2. See also Barlow, D. H., Ellard, K. K., Sauer-Zavala, S., Bullis, J. R., and Carl, J. R. (2014). The origins of neuroticism. *Perspectives on Psychological Science*, 9, 481–496.

Page 64 McCrae, R. R., and Costa, P. T., Jr. (1997). Conceptions and correlates of openness to experience. In R. Hogan, J. Johnson, and S. Briggs (Eds.), *Handbook of personality psychology* (pp. 825–847). San Diego, CA: Academic Press.

Page 64 McAdams, *George W. Bush*, Chapter 1. See also Simonton, D. K. (2006). Presidential IQ, openness, intellectual brilliance, and leadership: Estimates and correlations for 42 U.S. chief executives. *Political Psychology*, 27, 511–526.

Page 63–64 Sanger, D. E. (2001, July 25). On world stage, America's president wins mixed reviews. *New York Times.*

Page 65 Unger, C. (2007). *The fall of the house of Bush.* New York: Scribner, p. 198.

Page 65 Singer, P. (2004). *The president of good and evil: The ethics of George W. Bush.* New York: Dutton, p. 211.

Page 65 For rankings of U.S. presidents on openness, see Rubenzer and Faschingbauer, *Personality, Character,* p. 26.

Page 65 Crockett, E. (2016, March 30). Donald Trump: "There has to be some form of punishment" for women who have abortions. *Vox.*

Page 65 On the psychology of conscientiousness, see McAdams, *The art and science,* Chapter 3. On the relationship between conscientiousness and achievement/success, see Spengler, M., Brunner, M., Damian, R. I., Ludtke, O., Martin, R., and Roberts, B. W. (2015). Student characteristics and behaviors at age 12 predict occupational success 40 years later over and above childhood IQ and parental socioeconomic status. *Developmental Psychology, 51,* 1329–1340.

Page 66 For the original study linking conscientiousness at age 10 to mortality, see Friedman, H. S., Tucker, J. S., Tomlinson-Keasy, C., Schwartz, J. E., Wingard, D. L., and Criqui, M. H. (1993). Does childhood personality predict longevity? *Journal of Personality and Social Psychology, 65,* 176–185.

Page 66–67 For rankings of U.S. presidents on conscientiousness, see Rubenzer and Faschingbauer, *Personality, Character,* p. 28.

Venom

Page 68 Herbart, S. (2018, August 26). Tributes to a "true American patriot" John McCain cross political divide. *The Telegraph.*

Page 68 McFadden, R. D. (2018, August 26). A symbol of courage in half a century of battles. *New York Times.*

Page 68 Eder, S., and Philipps, D. (2016, August 1). Donald Trump's draft deferments: Four for college, and one for bad feet. *New York Times.* See also D'Antonio, *Never Enough.*

Page 69 Schreckinger, B. (2015, July 18). Trump attacks McCain: "I like people who weren't captured." *Politico.* Also see Trump on McCain: "He's a war hero because he was captured" [Reuters video]. *Chicago Tribune.*

Page 69 Trump slams McCain for opposing latest Republican attempt to overhaul health care (2017, September 23). *VOA News.*

Page 69 Davis, J. H. (2018, August 26). As a nation mourns McCain, Trump is conspicuously absent. *New York Times.*

Page 69 Pitzi, M. T., and Nowicki, D. (2018, August 24). Tweet by tweet: John McCain and Donald Trump feuded for years. *Arizona Republic.*

Page 69–70 Rogers, K., Fandos, N., and Haberman, M. (2018, August 28). Trump relents, offering praise for bitter rival. *New York Times.*

Page 70   Carmon, I. (2016, August 11). Donald Trump's worst offense? Mocking disabled reporter, poll finds. *NBCNews.com*.

Page 70   Newman, O. M. (2018). *Unhinged: An insider's account of the Trump White House.* New York: Simon and Schuster.

Page 70   Shear, M. D., and Sullivan, E. (2018, August 14). Trump calls Omarosa Manigault Newman "That Dog" in his latest insult. *New York Times*.

Page 70   D'Antonio, *Never Enough*, pp. 10–11.

Page 70   Ibid., p. 277.

Page 70   Shear and Sullivan, "Trump calls Omarosa."

Page 70   Reilly, K. (2016, September 23). 14 times Donald Trump and Ted Cruz insulted each other. *Time.com*.

Page 71   Barbaro, M., Haberman, M., and Rappeport, A. (2016, September 30). As America sleeps, Donald Trump seethes on Twitter. *New York Times*.

Page 71   Ibid.

Page 71   Schmidt, S. (2017, May 26). Breaking down Trump's "shove." *Washington Post*.

Page 71   Newman, "Unhinged," p. 251.

Page 71   Estepa, J., and Jackson, D. (2017, June 29). President Trump hurls crude new insults at "Morning Joe" hosts. *USA Today*.

Page 71   Davis, J. H., and Rogers, K. (2018, August 21). Trump attacks Democrats at rally, but mostly steers clear of scandals. *New York Times*.

Page 71   D'Antonio, *Never Enough*, p. 331.

Page 71   O'Brien, *TrumpNation*, p. 160.

Page 71   Vitali, A., Hunt, K., and Thorp, V. (2018, January 11). Trump referred to Haiti and African nations as "shithole" countries. *NBCNews.com*.

Page 72   Mark, M. (2017, December 23). Trump reportedly said Haitians "all have AIDS" during outburst on immigration. *Business Insider*.

Page 72   Time staff. (2015, June 16). Here's Donald Trump's presidential announcement speech. *Time.com*.

Page 72   Bierman, "Trump Warns."

Page 72   Bump, P. (July 30, 2016). Donald Trump responds to the Khan family: "Maybe she wasn't allowed to have anything to say." *Washington Post*. Also see Hattenstone, S. (2017, October 21). Khizr Khan: The patriotic American Muslim who called out Donald Trump. *The Guardian*.

Page 72   Gottlieb, J., and Maske, M. (2017; September 23). Roger Goodell responds to Trump's call to "fire" NFL players protesting during national anthem. *Washington Post*.

Page 72   Kranish and Fisher, *Trump Revealed*, pp. 41–42.

Page 72   Ibid., p. 34.

Page 73   Trump and Schwartz, *The Art of the Deal*, p. 71.

Page 73 Kranish and Fisher, *Trump Revealed*, p. 35.

Page 73 Ibid., p. 33.

Page 74 For a review of the scientific literature on agreeableness, see McAdams, *The Art and Science*, pp. 89–96.

Page 75 Roberts, B. W., Kuncel, N. R., Shiner, R. L., Caspi, A., and Goldberg, L. R. (2007). The power of personality: The comparative validity of personality traits, socioeconomic status, and cognitive ability for predicting important life outcomes. *Perspectives on Psychological Science, 2*, 313–345.

Page 75 Lodi-Smith, J., and Roberts, B. W. (2007). Social investment and personality: A meta-analysis of the relationship of personality traits to investment in work, family, religion, and volunteerism. *Personality and Social Psychology Review, 11*, 68–86.

Page 75 Belsky, J., Crnic, K., and Woodworth, S. (1995). Personality and parenting: Exploring the mediating role of transient mood and daily hassles. *Journal of Personality, 63*, 905–929.

Page 75 Asendorpf, J. B., and Wilpers, S. (1998). Personality effects on social relationships. *Journal of Personality and Social Psychology, 74*, 1531–1544.

Page 75 Lodi-Smith and Roberts, "Social Investment."

Page 75 Saroglou, V. (2010). Religiousness as a cultural adaptation to basic traits: A five-factor model perspective. *Personality and Social Psychology Review, 14*, 108–125.

Page 74 Hogan, R., Hogan, J., and Roberts, B. W. (1996). Personality measurement and employment decisions. *American Psychologist, 51*, 469–477.

Page 74 Judge, T. A., Livingston, B. A., and Hurst, C. (2012). Do nice guys—and gals—really finish last? The joint effects of sex and agreeableness on income. *Journal of Personality and Social Psychology, 102*, 390–407.

Page 74–76 For ratings of U. S. presidents on the trait of agreeableness, see Rubenzer and Faschingbauer, *Personality, Character*, p. 27.

Page 75 D'Antonio, *Never Enough*, p. 11.

Page 75 O'Brien, *TrumpNation*, p. 107.

Page 75 Stevenson, *The Strange Case of Dr. Jekyll*, p. 71.

Page 76 The story about Trump's offering Cindy McCain a position comes from Woodward, B. (2018). *Fear: Trump in the White House*. New York: Simon & Schuster, pp. 104–105.

Page 76 D'Antonio, *Never Enough*, p. 264.

Page 76 Kessler, *The Trump White House*, p. 11.

Page 77 Lee, J., and Quealy, K. (2016, October 24). All the people, places and things Donald Trump has insulted since declaring his candidacy for president. *New York Times*. And Lee, J., and Quealy, K. (2018, January 29). All the people, places and things Donald Trump has insulted since being elected president of the United States. *New York Times*.

Page 77 Shear, M. D. (2016, December 8). Trump as cyberbully in chief? Twitter attack on union boss draws fire. *New York Times*.

Page 77 O'Brien, *TrumpNation*, p. 30.

Page 77 Ibid., p. 190.

Page 78 Schriber, R. A., Chung, J. M., Sorenson, K. S., and Robins, R. W. (2017). Dispositional contempt: A first look at the contemptuous person. *Journal of Personality and Social Psychology*, *113*, 280–309.

Page 78 On the prevalence of violence and the lack of empathy at the low end of trait agreeableness: Muris, P., Merckelbach, H., Otgaar, H., and Meijer, E. (2017). The malevolent side of human nature: A meta-analysis and critical review of the literature on the dark triad (narcissism, Machiavellianism, and psychopathy). *Perspectives on Psychological Science*, *12*, 183–204.

Page 78 Trump and Schwartz, *The Art of the Deal*, p. 73.

Page 78 Trump, *Crippled America* (pp. 32, 51).

Page 78 Kranish and Fisher, *Trump Revealed*, pp. 260–262.

Page 78–79 Healy, P., and Haberman, M. (2015, December 5). 95,000 words, many of them ominous, from Donald Trump's tongue. *New York Times*. Also see The Editorial Board. (2018, August 29). After Trump, the deluge? *New York Times*.

Page 79 Corasaniti, N., and Haberman, M. (August 6, 2016). Donald Trump suggests "Second Amendment People" could act against Hillary Clinton. *New York Times*.

Page 79 Comey, J. (2018). *A higher loyalty: Truth, lies, and leadership*. New York: Flatiron Books, p. 240.

Page 79 Newman, "Unhinged," p. 144.

Page 79 Mayer, "Donald Trump's Ghostwriter,"

Page 80 Blair, *The Trumps*, p. 311.

Page 80 Davis, J. H. (2018, February 22). What do jotted talking points say about Trump's empathy? *New York Times*.

Page 80 For background on the concept of "temperament," see McAdams, *The Art and Science*, Chapters 2 and 3.

Page 81 Blair, *The Trumps*, p. 231.

Page 81 Trump and Schwartz, *Art of the Deal*, p. 71.

Page 81 Kranish and Fisher, *Trump Revealed*, p. 34.

Page 81 Ibid., p. 34.

Page 81 Ibid., p. 36.

Page 81 On the relationship between effortful control and the personality trait of agreeableness, see McAdams, *The Art and Science*, Chapters 3 and 4.

Page 82 For more information on effortful control, see Rueda, M. R. (2012). Effortful control. In M. Zentner and R. L. Shiner (Eds.), *Handbook of temperament* (pp. 145–167). New York: Guilford Press. See also Rothbart, M. K. (2007). Temperament, development, and personality. *Current Directions in Psychological Science*, *16*, 207–212.

Page 82 Else-Quest, N. M., Hyde, J. S., Goldsmith, H. H., and van Hulle, C. A. (2006). Gender differences in temperament: A meta-analysis. *Psychological Bulletin*, *132*, 33–72.

Page 83 Blair, *The Trumps*, pp. 225–231.

Page 83   Ibid., p. 228.

Page 83   Ibid., p. 230.

Page 83   Ibid., p. 227.

Page 84   D'Antonio, *Never Enough*, p. 39.

Page 84   Trump and Schwartz, *The Art of the Deal*, p. 65.

Page 84   Ibid., p. 70.

Page 84   Ibid., p. 65.

Page 84   Ibid., p. 71.

Page 84   Ibid., p. 72.

Page 84   Ibid., p. 73.

Page 84   D'Antonio, *Never Enough*, p. 40.

Page 84   Ibid., pp. 41–47. Also see Kranish and Fisher, *Trump Revealed*, pp. 38–45.

Page 84   Trump and Schwartz, *The Art of the Deal*, p. 73.

Page 85   D'Antonio, *Never Enough*, p. 43.

Page 85   McAdams, *The Art and Science*, pp. 111–117.

Page 86   Roberts, B. W., Wood, D., and Caspi, A. (2008). The development of personality traits in adulthood. In O. P. John, R. W. Robins, and L. A. Pervin (Eds.), *Handbook of personality: Theory and research* (3rd ed., pp. 375–398). New York: Guilford Press.

Page 87   Trump, *Crippled America*, p. 31.

Page 88   Erikson, E. H. (1963). *Childhood and society* (2nd ed.). New York: Norton. See also McAdams, D. P., and Zapata-Gietl, C. (2015). Three strands of identity development across the human life course: Reading Erik Erikson in full. In K. C. McLean and M. Syed (Eds.), *Oxford handbook of identity development* (pp. 81–94). New York: Oxford University Press.

Page 89   Blair, *The Trumps*, pp. 243–244.

Page 89   Ibid., p. 244.

Page 89   Ibid., p. 244.

Page 89   D'Antonio, *Never Enough*, pp. 154–155.

Page 89   Blair, *The Trumps*, p. 245.

Page 89   Ibid., p. 245.

Page 89   O'Brien, *TrumpNation*, p. 189.

Page 89   Trump and Schwartz, *The Art of the Deal*, p. 71.

Page 89   D'Antonio, *Never Enough*, p. 155.

Page 90   Kranish and Fisher, *Trump Revealed*, p. 63.

Page 90   Ibid., p. 64.

Page 90   On Roy Cohn, see Kranish and Fisher, *Trump Revealed*; D'Antonio, *Never enough*.

Page 90   Kranish and Fisher, *Trump Revealed*, p. 64.

Page 91   D'Antonio, *Never Enough*, p. 127.

Page 91   Ibid., p. 78.

Page 91   Kranish and Fisher, *Trump Revealed*, p. 111.

Page 92   The link between reading stories and the development of social cognition and empathy is discussed in Carroll, J. (2018). Minds and meaning in fictional narratives: An evolutionary perspective. *Review of General Psychology, 22,* 135–146. See also Mar, R. A., and Oatley, K. (2008). The function of fiction is the abstraction and simulation of social experience. *Perspectives on Psychological Science, 3,* 173–192.

Page 92   Mar, R. A. (2011). The neural basis of social cognition and story comprehension. In S. T. Fiske, D. L. Schacter, and S. E. Taylor (Eds.), *Annual Review of Psychology, 62,* 103–134. See also Jacobs, A. M., and Willems, R. M. (2018). The fictive brain: Neurocognitive correlates of engagement with literature. *Review of General Psychology, 22,* 147–160.

Page 92   Mar, R. A., Oatley, K., Hirsch, J., dela Paz, J., and Peterson, J. B. (2006). Bookworms versus nerds: Exposure to fiction versus non-fiction, divergent associations with social ability, and the simulation of fictional social worlds. *Journal of Research in Personality, 40,* 694–712.

Page 93   O'Brien, *TrumpNation*, p. 190.

Page 93   Mayer, "Donald Trump's Ghostwriter."

Page 93   Donald Trump quotes "Two Corinthians" in Liberty University speech. (2016, January 18). *Fox4News.com* .

Page 93–94   Eggers, D. (2018, June 30). The cultural vacuum in the White House. *New York Times.*

Page 94   Cillizza, C. (2018, August 31). The 43 most staggering lines from Donald Trump's Indiana speech. *CNN.com.* Also see Seggers, G. (2018, August 30). Trump rallies for Senate candidate Mike Braun in Indiana as it happened. *CBSNews.com.*

Page 94–95   Langhorne, T. B. (2018, August 31). Evansville Trump rally got Ford Center's largest-ever crowd. *Evansville Courier and Press.*

Truth

Page 97   The 40-day lying streak is documented in Leonhardt, D., and Thompson, S. A. (2017, June 25). Trump's lies. *New York Times.* The article lists all of the documented falsehoods uttered by President Trump during the first six months of his presidency. Following March 1, Trump publicly said something demonstrably untrue on at least 74 of the following 113 days.

Page 97   Shear, M. D., and Schmidt, M. S. (2017, March 4). Trump, offering no evidence, says Obama tapped his phone. *New York Times.*

Page 97–98   Li, D. K., and Frederick, B. (2016, May 3). Trump links Ted Cruz's dad to JFK assassination. *New York Post.*

Page 98   McAdams, "The Mind," p. 81.

Page 98   Wootson, C. R., Jr. (2016, November 27). Donald Trump: "I won the popular vote if you deduct the millions of people who voted illegally. *Washington Post.*

Page 98 Kakutani, M. (2018). *The death of truth: Notes on falsehood in the age of Trump.* New York: Crown.

Page 99 Cockburn, H. (2017, January 26). Donald Trump again claims to have largest presidential inauguration in history. *The Independent.*

Page 99 Kakutani, *The Death of Truth,* p. 21.

Page 99 Kessler, G., and Kelly, M. (2018, January 10). President Trump made 2,140 false or misleading claims in his first year. *Washington Post.*

Page 99–100 Cohen, R. (2018, August 10). Trump's nemesis in the age of Pinocchio. *New York Times.*

Page 100 Woodward, *Fear,* p. 16.

Page 100 Trump and Schwartz, *The Art of the Deal,* p. 58.

Page 100 *New York Times.* (February 16, 2017). [Full transcript and video: Trump's news conference]

Page 101 Davis, J. H., and Haberman, M. (2018, May 28). With "Spygate," Trump shows how he uses conspiracy theories to erode trust. *New York Times.*

Page 101 Detrow, S. (2016, September 16). After promoting birther movement, Trump admits Obama was born in U.S. *National Public Radio.*

Page 101 Baker, P., and Chan, S. (2017, February 20). From an anchor's lips to Trump's ears to Sweden's disbelief. *New York Times.*

Page 102 Woodward, *Fear,* p. 223.

Page 102 Ibid., p. 209.

Page 102 Ibid., pp. 354–357.

Page 102 Anonymous. (2018, September 5). I am part of the resistance inside the Trump administration. *New York Times.*

Page 103 Harris, G. (2018, May 16). In rebuke of Trump, Tillerson says lies are a threat to democracy. *New York Times.*

Page 103 Arendt, H. (1973). *The origins of totalitarianism.* New York: Harcourt, p. 474. See also Kakutani, *The Death of Truth,* pp. 11–20.

Page 104 On agreeableness and honesty, a rival taxonomy to the Big Five—the HEXACO—posits six basic traits, five of which are quite similar to the five I have described with an added sixth designating a dimension of honesty/humility. According to this perspective, truthfulness may be rather more independent of agreeableness than the Big Five enthusiasts claim. I don't have a dog in this fight. See Ashton, M. C., Lee, K., Perguini, M., Szarota, P., de Vries, R. E., Di Blias, L., . . . De Raad, B. (2004). A six-factor structure of personality descriptive adjectives: Solutions from psycholexical studies in seven languages. *Journal of Personality and Social Psychology, 86,* 356–366.

Page 104 DePaulo, B. (2017, December 8). I study liars. I've never seen one like President Trump. *Washington Post.*

Page 105 Klemesrud, "Donald Trump."

Page 106 Singer, M. (May 19, 1997). Trump solo. *The New Yorker.*

Page 106 O'Brien, *TrumpNation*, p. 124.

Page 106 Mayer, "Donald Trump's Ghostwriter."

Page 106 Trump, D. J., and Zanker, B. (2009). *Think big.* New York: Harper Collins, pp. 174–175.

Page 106–107 Singer, M. (May 19, 1997). Trump solo. *The New Yorker.*

Page 107 Estepa, J. (2017, May 1). Note to President Trump: Andrew Jackson was not alive for the Civil War. *USA Today.*

Page 107 Wootson, C. R. (2017, February 2). Trump implied Frederick Douglass was alive. The abolitionist's family offered a history lesson. *Washington Post.*

Page 107 Woodward, *Fear*, p. 291.

Page 107 Trump, *Crippled America*, p. 32.

Page 108 Robles, F. (2018, September 11). Trump calls storm response in Puerto Rico, where 3,000 died, "one of the best." *New York Times.* See also Knowles, S. G. (2018, September 13). What Trump doesn't get about disasters. *New York Times.*

Page 108 Knowles, "What Trump Doesn't Get."

Page 108 Ibid.

Page 108 Robles, "Trump Calls Storm Response."

Page 108 Egan, T. (2018, September 14). The secret to cracking Trump's base. *New York Times.*

Page 109 From interview with Brian Stelter, CNN (2017, July 24).

Page 110 Kakutani, *The Death of Truth*, p. 60.

Page 110 Trump and Schwartz, *The Art of the Deal*, p. 58.

Page 111 Effron, D. A. (2018). It could have been true: How counterfactual thoughts reduce condemnation of falsehoods and increase political polarization. *Personality and Social Psychology Bulletin, 44,* 729–745.

Page 111 Effron, D. A. (2018, April 29). Why Trump supporters don't mind his lies. *New York Times.*

Page 112 Trump and Schwartz, *The Art of the Deal*, p. 58.

Page 114 Ogden, E. (2018, August 5). Donald Trump, mesmerist. *New York Times.*

Page 114 Diamond, J. (2016, January 24). Trump: I could "shoot somebody and I wouldn't lose votes." *CNN.com.*

Page 114 Kessler, *The Trump White House*, p. 10.

Page 115 Brooks, D. (2016, February 26). The governing cancer of our time. *New York Times.*

Page 115 Bailey, K. G. (2015, August 21). Donald Trump: Warrior male extraordinaire. *www.wind.com.*

Page 116 Gabriel, T. (2016, February 27). Donald Trump, despite impieties, wins hearts of evangelical voters. *New York Times.*

Page 117   Woodward, *Fear*, pp. 214–215.

Page 117   D'Antonio, *Never Enough*, p. 191.

Page 117–118   Ibid., p. 335.

Page 118   Singer, M. (May 19, 1997). Trump solo. *The New Yorker*.

Page 118   D'Antonio, *Never Enough*, p. 191.

Page 118   Singer, M. (May 19, 1997). Trump solo. *The New Yorker*.

Page 118   Schmidt, M. (2017, December 28). Excerpts from Trump's interview with *The Times*. *New York Times*.

Love

Page 119   Research on the interpersonal correlates of the Big Five traits is reviewed in McAdams, *The Art and Science*, Chapters 2–4. See also McAdams, D. P., Shiner, R. L., and Tackett, J. L. (Eds.). (2019). *The handbook of personality development*. New York: Guilford Press.

Page 120   Freud, S. (1916/1961). Introductory lectures on psychoanalysis. In J. Strachey (Ed.), *The standard edition of the complete psychological works of Sigmund Freud* (Vols. 4–5) London: Hogarth, p. 314.

Page 120   Bowlby, J. (1969). *Attachment and loss*. Vol. 1, *Attachment*. New York: Basic Books. Bowlby's book is one of the greatest psychological works of the 20th century. See also Ainsworth, M. D. S. (1969). Object relations, dependency, and attachment: A theoretical review of the mother-infant relationship. *Child Development, 40*, 96901025; Ainsworth, M. D. S., and Bowlby, J. (1991). An ethological approach to personality development. *American Psychologist, 46*, 333–341. A good source on contemporary theory and research on mother-infant attachment is Simpson, J. A., and Jones, R. E. (2019). Attachment and social development within a life-history perspective. In D. P. McAdams, R. Shiner, and J. Tackett (Eds.), *Handbook of personality development* (pp. 257–275). New York: Guilford Press.

Page 121   Blair, *The Trumps*; D'Antonio, *Never Enough*. Also see Kruse, M. (2017, November/December). The mystery of Mary Trump. *Politico*. Also see Burleigh, N. (2018). *Golden handcuffs: The secret history of Trump's women*. New York: Gallery Books.

Page 122   Kruse, "The Mystery."

Page 123   Blair, "The Trumps," p. 229.

Page 123   O'Brien, TrumpNation, p. 190 (emphasis added).

Page 123   Kruse, "The Mystery."

Page 123   Ibid.

Page 124   Critical response to my June 2016 article in *The Atlantic*, published in *The Atlantic* (2016, September), p. 12.

Page 124   Kruse, "The Mystery."

Page 126   Hurt, Harry, III (1993). *Lost tycoon: The many lives of Donald J. Trump*. New York: W. W. Norton, p. 78.

Page 126 Kranish and Fisher, *Trump Revealed*, p. 49.

Page 126 Ibid., p. 49.

Page 126 Klemesrud, "Donald Trump."

Page 126 O'Brien, *TrumpNation*, p. 53.

Page 127 Trump, I. (2017). *Raising Trump*. New York: Simon & Schuster, p. 41.

Page 127 Ibid., p. 40.

Page 127 Kranish and Fisher, *Trump Revealed*, p. 79.

Page 127 Ibid., p. 79.

Page 128 Trump, *Raising Trump*, p. 63.

Page 128 Fox, E. J. (2018). *Born Trump: Inside America's first family*. New York: HarperCollins. Fox writes: "Workaholics and social climbers, they [Ivana and Donald] left it mostly to two dedicated nannies, bodyguards, drivers, hotel workers, club employees, and caretakers on various properties to look after Eric and the other children Trump, whether it was their official job or simply a role they took on out of necessity or the goodness of their hearts. 'My father, I love and appreciate, but he always worked 24 hours a day,' Eric told the *New York Times*. Bridget and Dorothy, the family's nannies, doted on the kids, as did Ivana's parents, Dedo and Babi" (pp. 283–284). See also Trump, *Raising Trump*.

Page 128 Kranish and Fisher, *Trump Revealed*, p. 82.

Page 128 Ibid., p. 82.

Page 128–129 Trump, *Raising Trump*, pp. 169–170.

Page 128 Kranish and Fisher, *Trump Revealed*, pp. 82–83.

Page 129 Blair, *The Trumps*, p. 299.

Page 129 Hurt, *Lost Tycoon*, p. 187.

Page 129 Ibid., p. 188.

Page 130 Sternberg, R. J. (1998). *Love is a story: A new theory of relationships*. New York: Oxford University Press, p. 152.

Page 130 Sternberg, *Love Is a Story*, p. 157.

Page 130 Trump, D. J., with K. Bohner. (1997). *Trump: The art of the comeback*. New York: Random House, pp. 137–138.

Page 130 Trump, *Raising Trump*, p. 178.

Page 131 Hurt, *Lost Tycoon*, p. 15.

Page 131 Ibid., p. 56.

Page 131 Ibid.

Page 132 Ibid., p. 54.

Page 132 Ibid., p. 55.

Page 132 Ibid.

Page 133 Ibid., p. 255.

Page 133 Ibid., p. 255.

Page 133 Ibid., p. 255.

Page 133 Fox, *Born Trump*, pp. 109–110. See also O'Brien, *TrumpNation*, p. 134; Hurt, *Lost Tycoon*, pp. 253–256; Trump, *Raising Trump*, pp. 163–164.

Page 133 Trump, *Raising Trump*, p. 164.

Page 134 Fox, *Born Trump*, p. 131.

Page 134 Kranish and Fisher, *Trump Revealed*, p. 170.

Page 135 Hurt, *Lost Tycoon*, p. 309.

Page 135 D'Antonio, *Never Enough*, p. 215.

Page 135 Hurt, *Lost Tycoon*, p. 292; originally from an interview in *New York* magazine.

Page 135 O'Brien, *TrumpNation*, pp. 132–133.

Page 136 Hurt, *Lost Tycoon*, p. 195.

Page 136 Ibid., p. 196.

Page 136 Ibid., p. 197.

Page 136 D'Antonio, *Never Enough*, p. 216.

Page 136 Ibid., p. 216.

Page 137 Fox, *Born Trump*, p. 140.

Page 137 Blair, *The Trumps*, p. 420.

Page 137 O'Brien, *TrumpNation*, pp. 202–203.

Page 137 Blair, *The Trumps*, p. 420.

Page 137 Kranish and Fisher, *Trump Revealed*, p. 159.

Page 137 Ibid., p. 159.

Page 137 Sternberg, *Love Is a Story*, pp. 127–134.

Page 137–138 Kranish and Fisher, *Trump Revealed*, p. 160.

Page 138 Sternberg, *Love Is a Story*, pp. 109–115.

Page 138 Kranish and Fisher, *Trump Revealed*, pp. 267–268.

Page 138 Kessler, *The Trump White House*, pp. 73–74.

Page 139 Ibid., p. 78.

Page 139 On Melania's "Be Best" program, see Rogers, K. (2018, May 7). Melania Trump rolls out "Be Best," a children's agenda with a focus on social media. *New York Times*. Also see Rogers, K. (2018, May 8). As Melania Trump faces plagiarism claims, her staff lashes out at news media. *New York Times*; Rogers, K., Davis, J. H., and Haberman, M. (2018, August 17). Melania Trump, a mysterious first lady, weathers a chaotic White House. *New York Times*.

Page 139 Kranish and Fisher, *Trump Revealed*, p. 269.

Page 139 Ibid., p. 267.

Page 140 Fahrenthold, D. A. (2016, October 7). Trump recorded having extremely lewd conversation about women in 2005. *Washington Post*.

Page 140 Hillary Clinton campaign responds to Trump's lewd 2005 comments about women. (2016, October 9). *Business Insider*.

Page 140 Kaine: Trump tape "makes me sick to my stomach." (2016, October 9). *Politico*.

Page 140 Harrington, R. (2016, October 8). RNC chair Reince Priebus condemns Trump for obscene comments about women in 2005 video. *Business Insider*.

Page 141 "I never said I was a perfect person," Trump says about lewd comments. (2016, October 8). *CBSNews.com*.

Page 141 Kranish and Fisher, *Trump Revealed*, pp. 166–167.

Page 141–142 Reiman, E. (2018, September 26). The 22 women who have accused Trump of sexual misconduct. *Business Insider*. For additional information on the case regarding Jill Harth, see Kranish and Fisher, *Trump Revealed*, p. 163.

Page 143 Palazzolo, J., Rothfield, M., and Alpert, L. (2016, November 4). *National Enquirer* shielded Donald Trump from *Playboy* model's affair. *Wall Street Journal*. See also Rutenberg, J. (2018, April 18). Ex-Playboy model, freed from contract, can discuss alleged Trump affair. *New York Times*.

Page 143 Daniels, S. (2018). *Full disclosure*. New York: St. Martin's Press.

Page 143–144 Trump and Bohner, *The Art of the Comeback*, pp. 117–118.

Page 144 Ruckerd, P. (2015, August 18). Trump says Fox's Megyn Kelly had "blood coming out of her wherever." *Washington Post*.

Page 144 Daly, M. (2016, February 24). Trump's female tower boss talks about his half-billion dollar debt, womanizing, and how he learned to be shameless. *The Daily Beast*. See also Res, B. A. (2013). *All alone on the 68th floor: How one woman changed the face of construction*. Self-published; see Chapters 7–9.

Page 144 Kranish and Fisher, *Trump Revealed*, p. 168.

Page 144–145 O'Brien, *TrumpNation*, p. 205; from *ABC Prime Time Live*, March 10, 1994.

Me

Page 147 Alford, H. (2015, November 11). Is Donald Trump actually a narcissist? Therapists weigh in. *Vanity Fair*.

Page 147 Wright, D., Kogan, T., and Winchester, J. (2016, May 3). Cruz unloads with epic takedown of "pathological liar," "narcissist" Donald Trump. *CNN Politics*.

Page 148 O'Brien, *TrumpNation*, p. 194.

Page 148 There are at least nine books he has written with his name (Trump) in the title. The three mentioned here are Trump and Zanker, *Trump: Think Big*; Trump, D. J., with M. McIver. (2008). *Trump: Never Give Up*. New York: Wiley; and Trump and Bohner, *Trump: The Art of the Comeback*.

Page 148 The Broadway play was to be entitled, "Trump." See Paulson, M. (2016, March 6). For a young Donald J. Trump, Broadway held sway. *New York Times*.

Page 149   Adenyi, L., Cao, R., Hogan, M., Juang, M., and Wojcik, N. (2017, February 16). Read the full transcript of Trump's first solo press conference. *CNBC.com*.

Page 149   Repeating an expression he had used at least once before, Trump characterized himself as a "stable genius" in an interview with *The Sun*: Chung, P. Q. W., and Cattenacci, T. (2018, July 13). Ranked: Trump's quotes on NATO, Germany, and being a "stable genius." *CNBC.com*.

Page 150   Cruz, L., and Buser, S. (2016). The Goldwater rule: Cross the border of assessing public figures. In L. Cruz and S. Buser (Eds.), *A clear and present danger: Narcissism in the era of Donald Trump* (pp. xv–xxi). Asheville, NC: Chiron. Original sources for the quotes themselves are these:

"The greatest builder . . .": Donald Trump campaign speech in South Carolina, May 2015.

"If I were a liberal . . .": Donald Trump interview with "Meet the Press," August 2015.

"I think apologizing . . .": Donald Trump on "The Tonight Show," September 2015.

"I get along with everybody . . .": Donald Trump, interview with Anderson Cooper, CNN, July 2016.

"All of the women . . .": Trump, D. (2004). *Trump: How to get rich*. New York: Random House.

Page 149–150   Blair, *The Trumps*, p. 455.

Page 150   Landler, M., and Alcindor, Y. (2017, October 18). Trump's condolence call to soldier's widow ignites imbroglio. *New York Times*.

Page 150   On Trump's response to the Puerto Rico hurricane, see: Cummings, W. (2017, September 12). Trump gives himself "A pluses" on "hurricane work," blames Maria on San Juan mayor. *USA Today*.

Page 150   Houston: Bruni, F. (2017, August 29). The waters swell. So does Trump's ego. *New York Times*.

Page 150   O'Brien, *TrumpNation*, p. 214.

Page 150   Singer, T. (2016). Trump and the American selfie: Archetypal defenses of the group spirit. In L. Cruz and S. Buser (Eds.), *A clear and present danger: Narcissism in the era of Donald Trump* (pp. 25–55). Asheville, NC: Chiron, p. 49.

Page 151   Cruz, L. (2016). Trumplestilskin: Narcissism and the will to power. In L. Cruz and S. Buser (Eds.), A clear and present danger: Narcissism in the era of Donald Trump (pp. 57–73). Asheville, NC: Chiron, p. 72.

Page 151   Lunbeck, E. (2014). *The Americanization of narcissism*. Cambridge, MA: Harvard University Press, p. 83. For emphasis, I have italicized *me*.

Page 151   Freud's views on narcissism appear in these two sources: Freud, S. (1914/1955). On narcissism: An introduction. In J. Strachey (Ed.), *The standard edition*. London: Hogarth. and Freud, S. (1931/1955). *Libidinal types*. In J. Strachey (Ed.), *The standard edition*. London: Hogarth.

Page 151   Lasch, C. (1978). *The culture of narcissism*. New York: Warner Books, p. 71.

Page 151   Ibid., p. 96.

Page 152   Kernberg, O. F. (1975). *Borderline conditions and pathological narcissism*. New York: Jason Aronson.

Page 152 Lunbeck, *The Americanization*, pp. 61–62.

Page 153 On Kohut's theory of narcissism, see Kohut, H. (1977). *The restoration of the self*. New York: International Universities Press. See also Kohut, H. (1971). *The analysis of the self*. New York: International Universities Press. For a related psychoanalytic perspective on healthy narcissism, see Alford, C. F. (1988). *Narcissism: Socrates, the Frankfurt school, and psychoanalytic theory*. New Haven, CT: Yale University Press.

Page 153–154 Regarding narcissism as a continuous dimension, one of the best-known measures of narcissism is the Narcissistic Personality Inventory (NPI), a 54-item self-report questionnaire that taps into four dimensions of narcissism: exploitiveness/entitlement, superiority, leadership, and self-absorption. The original citation for the NPI is Raskin, R. N., and Hall, C. J. (1981). The Narcissistic Personality Inventory: Alternative form reliability and further evidence for construct validity. *Journal of Personality Assessment, 45*, 159–162.

Page 153 An integrative theory of narcissism is in Krizan, Z., and Herlache, A. D. (2018). The narcissism spectrum model: A synthetic view of narcissistic personality. *Personality and Social Psychology Review, 22*, 3–31.

Page 154–155 The distinction between narcissistic admiration and narcissistic rivalry is described in Wurst, S. N., Gerlach, T. M., Dufner, M., Rauthmann, J. F., Grosz, M. P., Kufner, A. C. P., Denissen, J. J. A., and Back, M. D. (2017). Narcissism and romantic relationships: The differential impact of narcissistic admiration and rivalry. *Journal of Personality and Social Psychology, 112*, 280–306.

Page 155–156 For evidence that narcissism often leads to short-term attraction followed by subsequent rejection, see Back, M. D., Schmukle, S. C., and Egloff, B. (2010). Why are narcissists so charming at first sight? Decoding the narcissism-popularity link at zero acquaintance. *Journal of Personality and Social Psychology, 98*, 132–145.

Page 155 For evidence that people high in narcissism tend to show more hostility and anger when challenged, see Rhodewalt, F., and Morf, C C. (1998). On self-aggrandizement and anger: A temporal analysis of narcissism and reactions to success and failure. *Journal of Personality and Social Psychology, 74*, 672–685.

Page 155 On the link between narcissism and mood swings, see Emmons, R. A. (1987). Narcissism: Theory and measurement. *Journal of Personality and Social Psychology, 52*, 11–17.

Page 155 On the link between physical attractiveness and narcissism, see Holtzman, N. S., and Strube, M. J. (2010). Narcissism and attractiveness. *Journal of Research in Personality, 44*, 133–136.

Page 156 On flashy dressing and cleavage, see Vazire, S., Naumann, L. P., Rentfrow, P. J., and Gosling, S. D. (2008). Portrait of a narcissist: Manifestations of narcissism in physical appearance. *Journal of Research in Personality, 42*, 1439–1447.

Page 156 On the relationship between narcissism and leadership, see Grijalva, E., Harms, P. D., Newman, D. A., Gaddis, B. H., and Fraley, R. C. (2015). Narcissism and leadership: A meta-analytic review of linear and nonlinear relationships. *Personnel Psychology, 68*, 1–47.

Page 156 Watts, A. L., Lilienfeld, S. O., Smith, S. F., Miller, J. D., Campbell, W. K., Waldman, I. D., Rubenzer, S. J., and Faschingbauer, T. J. (2013). The double-edged sword of grandiose narcissism: Implications for successful and unsuccessful leadership among U.S. presidents. *Psychological Science, 24,* 2379–2389.

Page 156 Isaacson, W. (2011). *Steve Jobs.* New York: Simon and Schuster. On Steve Jobs and narcissism, see McAdams, *The Art and Science,* pp. 161–167.

Page 160 The story of little Dennis Burnham is told first in my chapter, "Venom." The original source is Kranish and Fisher, *Trump Revealed,* p. 33.

Page 160 Lasch's speculation regarding the developmental origins of narcissism comes from Lasch, *The Culture.* Lasch writes: "The combination of emotional detachment with attempts to convince the child of his favored position in the family is a good prescription for a narcissistic personality structure" (p. 102).

Page 160 On theory of mind, see Wellman, H. M. (1993). Early understanding of mind: The normal case. In S. Baron-Cohen, H. Tager-Flusberg, and D. J. Cohen (Eds.), *Understanding other minds: Perspectives from autism* (pp. 10–39). New York: Oxford University Press. See also Apperly, L. A. (2012). What is "theory of mind"? concepts, cognitive processes, and individual differences. *Quarterly Journal of Experimental Psychology, 65,* 825–839.

Page 160 On the age 5 to 7 shift, see McAdams, *The art and science of personality,* pp. 139–169. See also Sameroff, A. J., and Haith, M. M. (Eds.). (1996). *The five to seven year shift: The age of reason and responsibility.* Chicago: University of Chicago Press.

Page 161 On "concrete operations," see Piaget, J. (1970). Piaget's theory. In P. H. Mussen (Ed.), *Carmichael's manual of child psychology* (2nd ed., vol. 1, pp. 703–732). New York: Wiley.

Page 162 On the development of self-esteem, see Harter, S. (2006). The self. In N. Eisenberg (Ed.) and W. Damon and R. M. Lerner (Series Eds.), *Handbook of child psychology.* Vol. 3, *Social, emotional, and personality development* (pp. 505–570). New York: Wiley.

Page 162 On the agency theory of narcissism, see Campbell, W. K. (1999). Narcissism and romantic attraction. *Journal of Personality and Social Psychology, 77,* 1254–1270.

Page 162 Research showing that narcissism is positively correlated with fantasies of power is described in Raskin, R. N., and Novacek, J. (1991). Narcissism and the use of fantasy. *Journal of Clinical Psychology, 47,* 490–499.

Page 163 On the sharp decline in self-esteem in adolescence, see Robins, R. W., and Trzesniewski, K. (2005). Self-esteem development across the lifespan. *Current Directions in Psychological Science, 14,* 158–162.

Page 163 D'Antonio, *Never Enough,* p. 43.

Page 163 Ibid., p. 44.

Page 163 Ibid., p. 43.

Page 163–164 O'Brien, *TrumpNation,* p. 50.

Page 164 D'Antonio, *Never Enough,* p. 46.

Page 164 Ibid., p. 46.

Page 164 Arnett, J. J. (2000). Emerging adulthood: A theory of development from the late teens through the 20s. *American Psychologist, 55,* 469–480.

Page 164 On recovery of self-esteem in 20s, see Robins and Trzesniewski, "Self Esteem."

Page 165 Blair, *The Trumps*, p. 238.

Page 165 Ibid., p. 240.

Page 166 Influential books on identity written by Erik Erikson in the 1960s are Erikson, *Childhood and society*; Erikson, E. H. (1964). *Insight and responsibility*. New York: Norton; and Erikson, E. H. (1968). *Identity: Youth and crisis*. New York: Norton. On identity pathways and the concepts of moratorium, identity achievement, and foreclosure, see also Marcia, J. E. (1966). Development and validation of ego identity status. *Journal of Personality and Social Psychology, 3*, 551–558. See also Kroger, J., and Marcia, J. E. (2011). The identity statuses: Origins, meanings, and interpretations. In S. J. Schwartz, K. Luyckx, and V. L. Vignoles (Eds.), *Handbook of identity theory and research* (Vol. 1, pp. 31–53). New York: Springer.

Page 168 Hurt, *Lost Tycoon*. 258.

Page 168 Ibid., p. 162.

Page 169 Grynbaum, M. M. (2017, February 17). Trump calls the news media "the enemy of the American people." *New York Times*.

Page 169 Haberman, M., Thrush, G., and Baker, P. (2017, December 9). Inside Trump's hour-by-hour battle for self-preservation. *New York Times*.

Page 170–171 Ibid.

Page 171 Ibid.

Page 171 Kakutani, *The Death of Truth*, pp. 28–29.

Page 171 Haberman et al., "Inside Trump's."

Page 173 Forgey, Q. (2018, November 25). Trump thanks 'President T' in Thanksgiving weekend tweet. *Politico*.

Goldwater

Page 174 McAdams, "The Mind of Donald."

Page 175 American Psychiatric Association. (2013). *Diagnostic and statistical manual of mental disorders* (5th ed.). Washington, DC: American Psychiatric Association.

Page 174 American Psychiatric Association. (2000). *Diagnostic and statistical manual of the mental disorders* (4th ed.). Washington, DC: American Psychiatric Association. For NPD, see also Konnikova, M. (2011, May 3). Less than artful choices: Narcissistic personality disorder according to Donald Trump. *Bigthink.com*.

Page 174 Loudon, G. (2018). *Mad politics: Keeping your sanity in a world gone crazy*. Washington, DC: Regenery.

Page 174–175 Regarding the requirement that mental distress be experienced by the patient if a diagnosis of a personality disorder is to be made, the psychiatrist Allen Frances wrote this in a letter to the *New York Times*, published on February 15, 2017: "Most amateur diagnosticians have mislabeled President Trump with the diagnosis of narcissistic personality disorder.

I wrote the criteria that define this disorder, and Mr. Trump doesn't meet them. He may be a world-class narcissist, but this doesn't make him mentally ill, because he does not suffer from the distress and impairment required to diagnose a mental disorder."

Page 177 Mann, R. (2016, April 13). How the "Daisy" ad changed everything about political advertising. *Smithsonian.*

Page 177 From Barry Goldwater's acceptance speech at the 1964 Republican National Convention.

Page 177 Vote tallies and comments from the survey conducted by *Fact* magazine regarding the mental fitness of Barry Goldwater come from Lilienfeld, S. O., Miller, J. D., and Lynam D. R. (2018). The Goldwater Rule: Perspectives from, and implications for, psychological science. *Perspectives on Psychological Science, 13,* 3–27. See also Levin, A. (2016, August 25). Goldwater Rule's origins based on long-ago controversy. *Psychiatric News.*

Page 178 Black, H. (1969). United States Supreme Court. 396. U. S. 1049. *Ginzburg v. Goldwater.* Dissent.

Page 178 On the relationship between the American Medical Association and the American Psychiatric Association regarding the Goldwater case, see Gersen, J. S. (2017, August 23). Will Trump be the death of the Goldwater Rule? *The New Yorker.*

Page 177–178 Quotes from the text of the Goldwater Rule come from Lilienfeld et al. *The Goldwater Rule,* p. 8.

Page 179 On President Lincoln's depression, see Shenk, J. W. (2005). *Lincoln's melancholy: How depression challenged a president and fueled his greatness.* New York: Houghton Mifflin.

Page 179 Lilienfeld et al., *The Goldwater Rule,* p. 4.

Page 177 Ibid., p. 5. See also Kuntzman, G. (2017, January 29). President Trump exhibits classic signs of mental illness: shrinks. *New York Daily News.*

Page 179 Gersen, "Will Trump Be."

Page 180 Ibid.

Page 180 Lilienfeld, *The Goldwater Rule,* makes a strong scientific case for abandoning the Goldwater Rule. They raise and refute five traditional arguments for the acceptance of the rule. These pertain to (i) the alleged need for direct personal examination in making psychiatric diagnoses; (ii) the desire to protect the reputation of the mental health profession; (iii) the alleged irrelevance of mental health issues for performance in office; (iv) the fear of politicization of psychiatry and psychology; and (v) the alleged lack of incremental validity for diagnostic information. In what is probably the paper's strongest section, the authors critique common assumptions regarding the need for direct clinical interviews in making psychiatric diagnoses and in assessing and attributing psychological dimensions more generally. This is important because defenders of the Goldwater Rule have typically held up direct clinical interviewing as the gold standard for psychiatric diagnosis. The authors' authoritative review of studies documenting (i) the shortcomings of unstructured psychiatric interviews and (ii) the relative validity of other forms of assessment (such as those employing observational data, life-history data, and the like) strikes at the heart of the justification for the Goldwater Rule.

Page 181 Lilienfeld et al., *The Goldwater Rule,* p. 20.

Page 182 Quoted in Isaacson, *Steve Jobs*, p. 266.

Page 184 Editorial Board. (2018, January 10). Is President Trump nuts? *New York Times.* See also Friedman, R. A. (2017, February 17). Is it time to call Trump mentally ill? *New York Times;* Klitzman, R. (2016; March 7). Should therapists analyze presidential candidates? *New York Times.* For other perspectives, see also McNally, R. J. (2018). Diagnosing at a distance: Is the Goldwater Rule relevant today? *Perspectives on Psychological Science, 13,* 28–30.; Davis, N. J. (2018). Questioning the Goldwater Rule: Commentary on Lilienfeld, Miller, and Lynam. (2018). *Perspectives on Psychological Science, 13,* 31–32.

Us

Page 185 On the life and career of Andrew Jackson, see Meacham, J. (2008). *American lion: Andrew Jackson in the White House.* New York: Random House. See also Rank, M. (2016). *American history and Donald Trump.* Kansas City, MO: Five Minute Books.

Page 185 Rank, *American History,* p. 29.

Page 187 Donald Trump announced his candidacy for the Republican nomination for president on June 16, 2015, at Trump Tower, in New York City. See DelReal, T. A. (2015, June 16). Donald Trump announces presidential bid. *Washington Post.* Quotes from the speech come from *Time* staff. (2015, June 16). Here's Donald Trump's presidential announcement speech. *Time.com.*

Page 188 Fisher, M. (2017, June 12). "Tear down this wall": How Reagan's forgotten line became a defining moment. *Washington Post.* Reagan's speech urging the Soviet Union to tear down the Berlin Wall was given at the Brandenburg Gate in Berlin, Germany, on June 12, 1987.

Page 188 The words from the inscription on the Statue of Liberty are contextualized in Hunter, W. (2018, January 16). The story behind the poem on the Statue of Liberty. *The Atlantic.*

Page 188 Quoted in Wang, A. B. (2017, February 4). Trump lashes out at "so-called judge" who temporarily blocked travel ban. *Washington Post.*

Page 188 Quoted in Shane, S., Rosenberg, M., and Lipton, E. (2017, February 1). Trump pushes dark view of Islam to center of U. S. policy-making. *New York Times.*

Page 188 Ibid.

Page 189 Rogers, K., and Stolberg, S. G. (June 24, 2018). Trump calls for depriving immigrants who illegally cross border of due process rights. *New York Times.*

Page 189 Quote from Michael Savage, in Peters, J. W. (October 29, 2018). How Trump-fed conspiracy theories about migrant caravan intersect with deadly hatred. *New York Times.*

Page 189 A tweet from President Trump, October 29, 2018.

Page 189–190 Quote from Alicia Hooten, in Peters, "How Trump-Fed Conspiracy."

Page 190 The original book on the authoritarian personality is a classic in psychology and the social sciences: Adorno, T. W., Frenkel-Brunswik, E., Levinson, D. J., and Sanford, R. N. (1950). *The authoritarian personality.* New York: Harper and Brothers. See also Wolin, R. (2016, November 4). Our "prophet of deceit": WWII-era social scientists explained Trump's appeal. *Chronicle of Higher Education,* B9–B13.

Page 190 Evidence for a link between authoritarianism and avoidant attachment is reviewed in Pettigrew, T. (2016). In pursuit of three theories: Authoritarianism, relative deprivation, and intergroup contact. *Annual Review of Psychology, 67,* 1–21. See also Weber, C., and Federico C. M. (2007). Interpersonal attachment and patterns of ideological belief. *Political Psychology, 28,* 389–416.

Page 190–191 Items from the RWA taken from Altemeyer, B. (1996). *The authoritarian specter.* Cambridge, MA: Harvard University Press.

Page 191–192 The research literature on the correlates of authoritarianism is huge. Selected sources of special relevance include Altemeyer; *The Authoritarian Specter;* Jost, J. T., Glaser, J., Kruglanski, A. W., and Sulloway, F J. (2003). Political conservatism as motivated social cognition. *Psychological Bulletin, 129,* 339–375.; MacFarland, S. (2010). Personality and support for universal human rights: A review and test of a structural model. *Journal of Personality, 78,* 1735–1763.; Peterson, B. E., Pratt, M. W., Olsen, J. R., and Alisat, S. (2016). The authoritarian personality in emerging adulthood: Longitudinal analysis using standardized scales, observer ratings, and content coding of the life story. *Journal of Personality, 84,* 225–236; Peterson, B. E., and Zurbriggen, E. L. (2010). Gender, sexuality, and the authoritarian personality. *Journal of Personality, 78,* 1801–1826.; Sibley, C. G., and Duckitt, J. (2008). Personality and prejudice: A meta-analysis and theoretical review. *Personality and Social Psychology Review, 12,* 248–279.; Stenner, K. (2005). *The authoritarian dynamic.* New York: Cambridge University Press.;VanHiel, A., Onracet, E., and DePauw, S. (2010). The relationship between social-cultural attitudes and behavioral measures of cognitive style: A meta-analytic integration of studies. *Journal of Personality, 78,* 1765–1799.

Page 191 MacWilliams, M. (2016, January 17). The one weird trait that predicts whether you're a Trump supporter. *Politico.* See also Jacobs, T. (2016; January 21). Donald Trump's appeal to the authoritarian personality. *Pacific Standard.*

Page 191–192 The argument that authoritarianism is part of human nature is made in a very interesting way in this article: Hastings, B. M., and Shaffer, B. (2008). Authoritarianism: The role of threat, evolutionary psychology, and the will to power. *Theory and Psychology, 18,* 423–440.

Page 192 On the role of the emotions of fear, anger, contempt, and disgust in political conflict, see Matsumoto, D., Frank, M. G., and Hwang, H. C. (2015). The role of intergroup emotions in political violence. *Current Directions in Psychological Science, 24,* 369–373. For more on anger, see Lambert, A. J., Scherer, L. D., Schott, J. P., Olson, K. R., Andrews, R. K., O'Brien, T. C., and Zisser, A. R. (2010). Rally effects, threat, and attitude change: An integrative approach to understanding the role of emotion. *Journal of Personality and Social Psychology, 98,* 886–903.

Page 192 Quoted in Edsall, T. B. (January 6, 2016). Purity, disgust and Donald Trump. *New York Times.*

Page 193 On links between authoritarianism and dehumanization, see Haslam, N., and Stratemeyer, M. (2016). Recent research on dehumanization. *Current Opinion in Psychology, 11,* 25–29.

Page 193 Trump, *Crippled America,* p. 38.

Page 193 Kteily, N., and Bruneau, E. (2017). Backlash: The politics and real-world consequences of minority group dehumanization. *Personality and Social Psychology Bulletin,* 43, 87–104.

Page 193 Healy and Haberman, "95,000 Words."

Page 194 Main sources for the August 11–13, 2017 "Unite the Right" rally in Charlottesville, Virginia: Heim, J. (2017, August 14). Recounting a day of rage, hate, violence and death. *Washington Post;* Heim, J., Silverman, E., Shapiro, T. R., and Brown, E. (2017; August 12). One dead as car strikes crowd amidst protests of white nationalist gathering in Charlottesville; two police die in helicopter crash. *Washington Post;* Pearce, M. (2017, August 11). Chanting "blood and soil" white nationalists with torches march on University of Virginia. *Los Angeles Times;* Stanglin, D., and Cavallaro, G. (2017, August 12). 1 dead, 19 injured as car hits crowd after a "Unite the Right" rally in Charlottesville; driver in custody. *USA Today;* Stolberg, S. G., and Rosenthal, B. M. (2017, August 13). White nationalist protest leads to deadly violence. *New York Times;* Suarez, C. (2017; August 11). Faith leaders gather on eve of hate-driven Unite the Right rally. *The Daily Progress.*

Page 194 Thrush, G., and Haberman, M. (2017, August 13). Critics slam Trump's tepid condemnation of violence on "many sides" in Virginia. *New York Times.*

Page 194–195 Ibid.

Page 194 Ibid.

Page 195 Stolberg and Rosenthal, "White Nationalist."

Page 195 Thrush, G. (2017, August 15). Trump condemns racists but creates fresh uproar. *New York Times.*

Page 195 Gray, R. (2017, August 15). Trump defends white-nationalist protestors: "Some very fine people on both sides." *The Atlantic.*

Page 195 Quoted in Shear, M.D., and Haberman, M. (2017, August 16). Combative Trump again says 2 sides at fault at rally: Shifting stance and criticizing the left. *New York Times.*

Page 195 Ibid.

Page 195 Donald Trump denies he is a racist after "shithole" row. (2018, January). BBC News.

Page 195 Osnos, E. (2015, August 31). The fearful and the frustrated. *New Yorker.*

Page 195 Mahler, J. (2016, February 29). Donald Trump's message resonates with white supremacists. *New York Times.*

Page 195–196 Ibid.

Page 196 Ibid.

Page 196 Roose, K., and Winston, A. (2018, November 4). Far-right internet groups listen for Trump's approval, and often hear it. *New York Times.*

Page 196 Mahler, "Donald Trump's Message."

Page 196 On the history of the white power movement, see Belew, K. (2018). *Bring the war home: The white power movement and paramilitary America.* Cambridge, MA: Harvard University Press.

Page 197 Statistics regarding the changing racial makeup of American society come from Klein, E. (2018, July 30). White threat in a browning America. *Vox.*

Page 197 A nuanced explanation for Trump's support among working-class whites, blending economics and culture, can be found at Williams, J, C. (November 10, 2016). What so many people don't get about the U. S. working class. *Harvard Business Review.*

Page 197 Statistics on voting patterns in 2016 presidential election come from Huang, J., Jacoby, S., Strickland, M., and Lai, K. K. R. (2016, November 8). Election 2016: Exit polls. *New York Times.* See also Roper Center for Public Opinion Research. How groups voted 2016; Exit polls 2016. (2016, December 9). CNN.

Page 198 The studies by Craig and Richeson are described in Klein, "White Threat." See also Craig, M. A., and Richeson, J. A. (2014). On the precipice of a "majority-minority" America: Perceived status threat from the racial demographic shift affects white Americans' political ideology. *Psychological Science, 25,* 1189–1197; Craig, M. A., Rucker, J. M., and Richseon, J. A. (2018). Radical and political dynamics of an approaching "majority-minority" United States. *The Annals of the American Academy, 677*(1), 204–214.

Page 199 The study by Enos is described in Klein, "White Threat." See also Enos, R. D. (2014). Causal effect of intergroup contact on exclusionary attitudes. *PNAS: Proceedings of the National Academy of Sciences, 111*(10), 3699–3704;

Page 199 Norton, M. I., and Sommers, S. R. (2011). Whites see racism as a zero-sum game that they are losing. *Perspectives on Psychological Science, 6,* 215–218.

Page 199 Coates, T-N. (2017, September 14). The first white president. *The Atlantic.*

Page 200 Colvin, J., Lemire, J., and Woodward, C. (2019, July 16,). Trump digs in on racist tweets against "the squad." *Chicago Tribune.*

Page 201 Massing, M. (2018, April 19). How Martin Luther paved the way for Donald Trump. *The Nation*; Peters, J. W., and Dias, E. (2018, April 25). Brushing off Trump scandals, Christian right marshals forces for midterms. *New York Times.*

Page 202 Peters, J. W. (2017, February 14). For the religious right, success and access at the Trump White House. *New York Times.*

Page 202–203 D'Antonio, *Never Enough*, p. 154, based on an interview with *People* magazine.

Page 202 James, W. (1902/1958). *The varieties of religious experience.* New York: New American Library.

Page 203 On the link between evangelical Christianity and RWA, see Altemeyer, *The Authoritarian Specter.* Also see McAdams, D. P., Albaugh, M., Farber, E., Daniels, J., Logan, R. L., and Olson, B. (2008). Family metaphors and moral intuitions: How conservatives and liberals narrate their lives. *Journal of Personality and Social Psychology, 95,* 978–990.

Page 203–204 The study on RWA and the hypothetical scenario about there being no God is reported in McAdams, D. P., and Albaugh, M. (2008). What if there were no God? Politically conservative and liberal Christians imagine their lives without faith. *Journal of Research in Personality, 42,* 1668–1672. See also McAdams et al., "Family Metaphors."

Page 204 Quoted in Leibovich, M. (2010, September 13). The wish for a conservative dream duo. *New York Times.*

Page 205 Quoted in Peters, J. W., and Dias, E. (2018, April 25). Brushing off Trump scandals, Christian right marshals forces for mideterms. *New York Times.*

Page 205 "Onward Christian Soldiers." *The Lutheran Book of Worship*. Minneapolis, MN: Augsburg, 1978.

Page 205 Quoted in The Editorial Board. (2018, August 29). After Trump, the deluge? *New York Times*.

Page 206 Quoted in Landler, M. (2016, December 15). "It's so sad," Donald Trump says of Syria, promising "safe zones." *New York Times*.

Page 206 On Poland's Law and Justice Party, see Applebaum, A. (2018, October). A warning from Europe. *The Atlantic*. See also Poland's ruling Law and Justice party is doing lasting damage (2018, April 21). *The Economist*, .

Page 206 Santora, M., and Bienvenu, H. (2018, May 12). Having conquered Hungary, Orban turns his focus to Brussels. *New York Times*.

Page 206 Ibid.

Page 208 Wu, T. (2017, March 5). How Trump wins by losing. *New York Times*.

Page 208 Ibid.

Page 208–209 Cited in Wu, "How Trump Wins" and from the British film, *1984*, based on Orwell's novel.

Primate

Page 210 Portions of this chapter were originally published as McAdams, D. P. (2017). The appeal of the primal leader: Human evolution and Donald J. Trump. *Evolutionary Studies in Imaginative Culture*, 1(2), 1–13. See also McAdams, D. P. (2017, September 14). It's an alpha male thing: What dominant chimpanzees and Donald Trump have in common. *The Guardian*.

Page 210 The case of Yeroen appears in De Waal, F. (2007). *Chimpanzee politics: Power and sex among the apes* (25th anniversary ed.). Baltimore: Johns Hopkins University Press. (Originally published in 1982)

Page 210 Ibid., p. 4.

Page 210 Ibid., p. 4.

Page 210 Stevenson, *The Strange Case of Dr. Jekyll*, p. 77.

Page 210 The account of McGahn's calling Trump "King Kong" comes from Schmidt, M. S., and Haberman, M. (2018, August 18). White House counsel, Don McGahn, has cooperated extensively in Mueller inquiry. *New York Times*.

Page 211 The account of Bill Maher's joking challenge comes from Cohan, W. D. (2013, April). What exactly is Donald Trump's deal? *The Atlantic*.

Page 211 Woodward, *Fear*, p. xiii.

Page 211 On leadership by prestige and leadership by dominance, see Maner, J. K. (2017). Dominance and prestige: A tale of two hierarchies. *Current Directions in Psychological Science*, 26, 526–531. Maner, J. K., and Case, C. R. (2016). Dominance and prestige: Dual strategies for navigating social hierarchies. In M. P. Zanna and J. M. Olson (Eds.), *Advances in experimental social psychology* (Vol. 40, pp. 129–180). New York: Elsevier.

Page 212 Henrich's overall take on culture and his argument for culture-gene co-evolution are described in the excellent book: Henrich, J. (2016). *The secret of our success: How culture is driving human evolution, domesticating our species, and making us smarter*. Princeton, NJ: Princeton University Press. See also Henrich, J., and Gil-White, F. J. (2001). The evolution of prestige: Freely conferred deference as a mechanism for enhancing the benefits of cultural transmission. *Evolution and Human Behavior, 22*, 165–196.

Page 213–214 Boehm, C. (1999). *Hierarchy in the forest: The evolution of egalitarian behavior.* Cambridge, MA: Harvard University Press, p. 4.

Page 214 Henrich, *The Secret*, p. 118.

Page 214 Research on prestige leadership is reviewed in Maner, "Dominance and Prestige," and Maner and Case, "Dominance and Prestige." See also Case, C. R., Bae, K. K., and Maner, J. K. (2018). To lead or to be liked: When prestige-oriented leaders prioritize popularity over performance. *Journal of Personality and Social Psychology, 115*, 657–676.

Page 215 For a full exploration of *The Art of the Deal*, see Chapter 2 of this volume.

Page 215 Trump and Schwartz, *The Art of the Deal*, p. 47.

Page 215 Ibid., p. 58.

Page 215 Ibid., p. 53.

Page 215 Ibid., p. 53.

Page 215 Ibid., p. 108.

Page 215 de Waal, *Chimpanzee Politics*, p. 77.

Page 215 Cillizza, C. (2017, June 13). Donald Trump just held the weirdest cabinet meeting ever. *CNN.com*.

Page 217 Tackett, M., and Qiu, L. (2019, January 2). Trump's freewheeling and mostly fact-free cabinet meeting. *New York Times*.

Page 217 Moyar, M. (2016, December 9). The world fears Trump's America. That's a good thing. *New York Times*.

Page 218 Trump and Schwartz, *The art of the deal*, p. 5.

Page 218 Moyar, "The World Fears."

Page 218 Trump and Schwartz, *The Art of the Deal*, p. 6.

Page 218 Baker, P., and Erlanger, S. (2017, March 19). Britain furious as Trump pushes claim of spying. *New York Times*.

Page 219 Ibid.

Page 219 Research on dominance leadership is reviewed in Maner, "Dominance and Prestige," and Maner and Case, "Dominance and Prestige."

Page 219 Tracy, J., and Robins, R. W. (2007). Emerging insights into the nature and function of pride. *Current Directions in Psychological Science, 16*, 147–150. See also Tracy, J. (2016).

Take pride: Why the deadliest sin holds the secret to human success. Boston: Houghton Mifflin Harcourt.

Page 219 On fixed versus growth mindsets, see Molden, D. C., and Dweck, C. S. (2006). Finding "meaning" in psychology: A lay theories approach to self-regulation, social perception, and social development. *American Psychologist, 61*, 192–203.

Page 220 Shear, M. D. (January 20, 2017). Trump arrives, set to assume power. *The New York Times.*

Page 220 Tweet from Donald Trump on December 30, 2016. Quoted in Sanger, D. E., Schmitt, E., and Gordon, M. R. (December 30, 2016). Trump gets an opening from Russia, but the path is risky. *New York Times.*

Page 220 Trump, *Crippled America*, p. 99.

Page 220 Broomwich, J. E. (2017, January 27). Doomsday clock registers cold-war-type pessimism. *New York Times.*

Page 222 Kang, C., and Shear, M. D. (2017, March 30). Trump leaves science jobs vacant, troubling critics. *New York Times.*

Page 222 Research suggesting that people prefer prestige leadership in the worksplace: Locke, K. D., and Heller, S. (2017). Communal and agentic interpersonal and intergroup motives predict preferences for status versus power. *Journal of Personality and Social Psychology, 43*, 71–86.

Page 222 Research on social dominance orientation is reviewed in Duckitt, J., and Sibley, C. G. (2010). Personality, ideology, prejudice, and politics: A dual-process motivational model. *Journal of Personality, 78*, 1861–1894.

Page 223 Coppins, M. (November, 2018). Newt Gingrich says you're welcome. *The Atlantic*, p. 59.

Page 224 Bruni, F. (2017, December 5). Donald Trump could really use a friend. *New York Times.*

Page 225 Litt, D. (2017, September 17). Is nothing funny, Mr. President? *New York Times.* See also Comey, *A Higher Loyalty*, pp. 241–242.

Page 227 Kakkar, H., and Sivanathan, N. (2017). When the appeal of a dominant leader is greater than a prestige leader. *PNAS, 114*, 6734–6739; p. 6734.

Page 229 Healy and Haberman, "95,000 Words."

Redemption

Page 231 The three lines of personality development are described in full in McAdams, *The art and science.* See also McAdams, "The Psychological Self."

Page 236 Quoted in LaFraniere, S. (2018, December 2). Seeking truth, Mueller exposes a culture of lies around Trump. *New York Times.* (emphasis added)

Page 239 Gardner, H. (1995). *Leading minds: An anatomy of leadership.* New York: Basic Books, p. 9. See also McAdams, *Leaders.*

Page 239–240 On the psychological and cultural meaning of redemptive life stories in America, see McAdams, *The Redemptive Self.*

Page 240 For background on the concept of generativity, see Erikson, Childhood and Society, Chapter. 7. See also McAdams, D. P., and de St. Aubin, E. (Eds.). (1998). *Generativity and adult development: How and why we care for the next generation.* Washington, DC: APA Books. Also see McAdams, D.P. (2019). "I am what survives me": Generativity and the self. In J. A. Frey and C. Vogler (Eds.), *Self-transcendence and virtue: Perspectives from philosophy, psychology, and theology.* London: Routledge.

Page 240 For research findings on generativity and redemptive life stores, see especially Guo, J., Klevan, M., and McAdams, D P. (2016). Personality traits, ego development, and the redemptive self. *Personality and Social Psychology Bulletin, 42,* 1551–1563.; McAdams, D. P., Diamond, A., de St. Aubin, E., and Mansfield, E. D. (1997). Stories of commitment: The psychosocial construction of generative lives. *Journal of Personality and Social Psychology, 72,* 678–694.; McAdams, D. P., and Guo, J. (2015). Narrating the generative life. *Psychological Science, 26,* 475–483.

Page 240 On master narratives of culture, see Hammack, P. L. (2008). Narrative and the cultural psychology of identity. *Personality and Social Psychology Review, 12,* 222–247.; McLean, K. C., and Syed, M. (2015). Personal, master, and alternative narratives: An integrative framework for understanding identity development in context. *Human Development, 58,* 318–349.

Page 240 On four types of redemptive stories (atonement, upward social mobility, liberation, and recovery), see McAdams, *The redemptive self,* especially Chapters 1, 4, 5, and 7.

Page 241–242 For more on George W. Bush's life story, see McAdams, *George W. Bush.* See also Bush, *A Charge to Keep.*

Page 242 On Benjamin Franklin, see Franklin, B. (1961). *The autobiography and other writings.* New York: Signet. (Originally published in 1771)

Page 242 On Frederick Douglass, see Douglass, F. (1845/1987). *Narrative of the life of Frederick Douglass, an American slave, written by himself.* In H. L. Gates Jr. (Ed.), *The classic slave narratives* (pp. 243–331). New York: Penguin.

Page 242 For more on Barack Obama's life story, see McAdams, *The Redemptive Self.* See also Obama, *Dreams.*

Page 245 Landler, M. (2017, August 17). A presidential obligation to morality, set adrift by Trump. *New York Times.*

Page 245 Kakutani, M. (2015, July 4). A eulogy that found its place in history. *New York Times.*

Page 246 Bob Woodward's account of Robert Porter's urging President Trump to be a "redeemer" in the wake of Charlottesville: "'The country is counting on you rhetorically to help salve the wounds and point a direction forward,' Porter said. The president could inspire and uplift. He could make this about him, the redeemer." (Woodward, *Fear,* p. 241).

Page 246 Landler, M. (2018, November 20). In extraordinary statement, Trump stands with Saudis despite Khashoggi killing. *New York Times.*

Page 247 Stevenson, *The Strange Case of Dr. Jekyll,* p. 65.

Page 247 Cohen, R. (2018, February 23). John F. Kelly, secret sharer. *New York Times.*

Page 247 On the downsides of redemption stories, see Chapter 9 in McAdams, *The Redemptive Self.*

Page 247 Tuveson, E. L. (1968). *Redeemer nation: The idea of America's millennial role.* Chicago: University of Chicago Press, p. vii.

Page 248 Slotkin, R. (1973). *Regeneration through violence: The mythology of the American frontier, 1600–1860.* Middletown, CT: Wesleyan University Press.

Page 248 Robert Kagan, in Sanger, D. E. (2018, December 22). President is left to carry out his promise of "America First." *New York Times.*

Page 249 The argument regarding the contribution of Bush's redemptive narrative identity to his decision to invade Iraq is the central thesis of Chapter 4 in McAdams, *George W. Bush.*

Page 249 This quote is attributed to Representative Michael McCaul of Texas at the Republican National Convention in Cleveland in 2016. See Kranish and Fisher, *Trump Revealed,* p. 343.

Page 250 Baker, P. (2018, May 30). How Trump's election shook Obama: "What if we were wrong?" *New York Times.*

Page 250 Krastev, I. (2018, December 4). We will never be the same. *New York Times.*

Page 250 Fallows, J., and Fallows, D. (2018). *Our towns: A 100,000-mile journey into the heart of America.* New York: Pantheon.

Page 250 Brooks, D. (2018, May 16). The American renaissance is underway. *New York Times.* Brooks has also written about American redemption stories: Brooks, D. (2016, April 29). If not Trump, what? *New York Times.*

Index

Printed in the USA/Agawam, MA
August 9, 2024

870733.007